Globalisation Disrupted

Umair Hafeez Ghori • John Farrar
Editors

Globalisation Disrupted

Competing Futures in a Multipolar World

Springer

Editors
Umair Hafeez Ghori
Faculty of Law
Bond University
Gold Coast, QLD, Australia

John Farrar
Faculty of Law
Bond University
Robina, QLD, Australia

ISBN 978-981-95-3996-3 ISBN 978-981-95-3997-0 (eBook)
https://doi.org/10.1007/978-981-95-3997-0

This Springer imprint is published by the registered company Springer Nature Singapore Pte Ltd.
The registered company address is: 152 Beach Road, #21-01/04 Gateway East, Singapore 189721, Singapore

Acknowledgements

The editors acknowledge the expeditious work of the three research assistants Matin Pedram, Shaila Asha, and Lucinda Crouch. We also thank Minori Watanabe for her efficient administrative assistance and Professor Anthony Gray for his generous support of the project as the Associate Dean (Research) at the Faculty of Law, Bond University.

Contents

List of Abbreviations

AEC	ASEAN Economic Community
AI	Artificial Intelligence
AIIB	Asian Infrastructure Investment Bank
ASEAN	Association of Southeast Asian Nations
ASPI	Australian Strategic Policy Institute
BIMSTEC	Bengal Initiative for Multi-Sectoral Technical and Economic Cooperation
BRICS	Brazil, Russia, India, China, South Africa
CCD	Community of Common Destiny
CCP	Chinese Communist Party
CELAC	Community of Latin American and Caribbean States
CFSP	Common Foreign and Security Policy
CPEC	China–Pakistan Economic Corridor
CPTPP	Comprehensive and Progressive Transpacific Partnership
DSR	Digital Silk Road
EAA	Export Administration Act
EARs	Export Administration Regulations
EC	European Council
ECJ	European Court of Justice
EEA	European Economic Area
EU	European Union
EVs	Electric Vehicles
FDI	Foreign Direct Investment
FSB	Financial Stability Board
FTAs	Free Trade Agreements
GATT	General Agreement on Tariffs and Trade
GDP	Gross Domestic Product
GFC	Global Financial Crisis
GFCC	German Federal Constitutional Court
GSCL	Global Supply Chain and Logistics Network
GSI	Global Security Initiative

GVCs	Global Value Chains
IIMs	Indian Institutes of Management
IITs	Indian Institutes of Technology
IMEC	India-Middle East-Europe Economic Corridor
IMF	International Monetary Fund
IT	Information Technology
ITO	International Trade Organisation
JCPOA	Joint Comprehensive Plan of Action
JSI	Joint Statement Initiative
LAC	Latin America and the Caribbean
MFN	Most Favoured Nation
MIC2025	Made in China 2025
MIT	Massachusetts Institute of Technology
MNCs	Multinational Corporations
MPIA	Multi-Party Interim Appeal Arbitration Arrangement
NATO	North Atlantic Treaty Organization
NEV	New Energy Vehicles
NIEs	Newly Industrialised Economies
ODA	Official Development Assistance
ODI	Outward direct investment-
OECD	Organisation for Economic Cooperation and Development
PHEIC	Public Health Emergency of International Concern
PIF	Pacific Islands Forum
PPI	Producer Price Index
R&D	Research and Development
RCEP	Regional Comprehensive Economic Partnership
RDC	Rapid Deployment Capacity
SCO	Shanghai Cooperation Organization
SIFIs	Systemically Important Financial Institutions
SOEs	State-Owned Enterprises
SPV	Special Purpose Vehicle
SSBs	Standard Setting Bodies
STEM	Science, Technology, Engineering, and Mathematics
TRIPS	Trade-Related Aspects of Intellectual Property
TSMC	Taiwan Semiconductor Manufacturing Company
UEL	Unreliable Entity List
UK	United Kingdom
UN	United Nations
UNCTAD	UN Trade and Development
USA	United States of America
WHA	World Health Assembly
WHO	World Health Organization
WTO	World Trade Organization

Chapter 1
Introduction: Globalisation Disrupted

Umair Hafeez Ghori and John Farrar

Abstract We argue that the current upheaval in globalisation is best understood as a complex process of re-making rather than a straightforward collapse. The chapter refers to the geo-economic rivalry between the US and China, the exposed fragility of global supply chains, heightened technological rivalry, resource nationalism, and populist sentiments. We argue that these forces clash with enduring asymmetries and, resultantly, sustain interdependence between nations even where the strategic decoupling process is underway. We consider in our opening chapter institutional responses, mega-regional accords, plurilateral reform initiatives, BRICS expansion, the emergence of "friends clubs", tech blocs and explain why fragmentation and experimental governance arrangements will continue to coexist with commercial incentives that keep nations bound together. Rather than predicting a return to multilateralism, the chapter contends that the emergent order will be pluralistic and highly contested. It will be a patchwork of overlapping spheres of influence, continuously being shaped by economic complementarities and power politics.

1.1 Opening Thoughts

Globalisation and the world order that promoted it is undergoing a period of readjustment and transition. Globalisation has been a prominent theme in international discourse since the collapse of the USSR and has produced winners and losers alike. It led to trade growth, the expansion of economies within the developing world, the diversification of global supply chains and an overall increase in consumer welfare.

U. H. Ghori (✉)
Faculty of Law, Bond University, Gold Coast, QLD, Australia
e-mail: ughori@bond.edu.au

J. Farrar
Faculty of Law, Bond University, Robina, QLD, Australia
e-mail: jfarrar@bond.edu.au

U. H. Ghori, J. Farrar (eds.), *Globalisation Disrupted*,
https://doi.org/10.1007/978-981-95-3997-0_1

At the same time, it also led to the decline of industries in the West. The globalisation model operated originally under American hegemony and its so-called rules-based order. It has now been disrupted by a rising challenger in the form of China and by the US's declining interaction capacity.[1] And yet the US still celebrates its exceptionalism in the belief that the cycles of power will forever move favourably. It is now locked in a Thucydides Trap[2] with China and on course for a conflict that could usher in the next global order.

The US's self-induced disruption arose from populism and the desire to bring industries and manufacturing back into its socio-economic fabric. The US already dominates the technology and artificial-intelligence realms but made the mistake of outsourcing basic manufacturing a long time ago. Attempts to revive manufacturing by a populist leadership in Washington using tariffs as an instrument of coercion cannot resolve questions of improving quality, economies of scale, and vertical integration. The policies of the second Trump administration aimed at making the US "Great Again" may have the opposite result of precipitating the decline of the US's rules-based order.

These are challenging times and represent the rise of a multipolar world which may in fact ultimately represent a "multiplex" world in which there is no clear overall leader but competing models of leadership in different fields. While "multipolar" focuses on the distribution of power between different states, "multiplexity" emphasises the interconnectedness and complexity of interactions on many issues between states and non-state actors.[3]

Populism has spread to American allies as well. Most prominently, it led to anti-globalisation forces inducing Brexit (the UK's withdrawal from the European Union). This was an important event not only for the UK but also for Europe and the West. The remaining European Union (EU) members have banded together in a bid to resist the spread of Anti-Europe populism. Yet Trump's disdain for globalisation and fractures within the West have irreparably compromised the rules-based order. Conflicts in Ukraine and Palestine have further widened the fractures within the West and the United Nations, exposing systemic vulnerabilities, contrasting worldviews and a clash of competing standards of morals and ethics.

With the weakening of the US hold over the rules-based order, new alternatives are emerging to plug the gap, although it is noticeable that these emerging alternatives are only addressing limited aspects of the existing rules-based order. One notable initiative is the expansion of BRICS, and the proliferation of new regional trade agreements that reflect deeper shifts in the global economic order. China and, to a lesser extent, India have both emerged as dynamic engines of manufacturing and services that offer both opportunities and challenges to other developing economies.

Within the Asia-Pacific region, waning American influence is also clearly visible. The ill-fated American-led Trans-Pacific Partnership (TPP) of 2010 gave way to alternatives such as the Comprehensive and Progressive Agreement for

---

[1] Acharya et al. (2023, pp. 2343–2345).

[2] Allison (2017) and Inkster (2020, p. 11), and Oermann and Wolff (2022, pp. 153–158).

[3] Acharya, *supra*, n.1, pp. 2343–2345.

Trans-Pacific Partnership (CPTPP) and the Regional Comprehensive Economic Partnership (RCEP), which brought together the ten ASEAN members plus China, Australia, Japan, New Zealand and South Korea under a single framework in 2022.

Complementing recent developments in the treaty realm, China's Belt and Road Initiative (BRI), often compared to a modern Silk Road, has extended Chinese influence through infrastructure and investment projects across Eurasia and beyond. In addition to being the capstone project for China's grand ambitions, the BRI affords dark horses like Pakistan a second chance to recover from lost opportunities during the globalisation wave. Pakistan enjoys strong ties with China and a thawing relationship with Russia, yet its true potential as one of the world's largest consumer markets remains unrealised and it continues to be excluded from BRICS membership due to India's intransigence. Pakistan's unique, yet unrealised, geo-strategic potential illustrates the complex geopolitics that are now shaping new alliances while testing existing ones.

Established trends in globalisation have been dramatically upended by the policies of the second Trump administration, whose aggressive tariff regime seeks to rebuild American manufacturing and reclaim lost production. In its quest to become "Great Again", the US has undermined the very organisation it promoted a few decades ago, i.e., the World Trade Organization (WTO) and other multilateral bodies, replacing rules-based cooperation with neo-mercantilist tactics that threaten global economic stability. It has even jeopardised longstanding relationships with its European allies along with close security and trading partners such as Canada and Australia.

The US and the West are now wary of China's advantage in labour and manufacturing technology. Only a few decades ago, technology transfers helped spur China's rise in high-tech industries. It is now perceived as a direct threat to Western economic leadership, just as Japan was a few decades ago when it staged a remarkable comeback in the 1950s following the ravages of the Second World War.

The coronavirus pandemic compounded the complexities of globalisation and laid bare the fragility of global supply chains and the limits of international cooperation. Meanwhile, the ascendance of Big Tech has outpaced both domestic and transnational regulatory frameworks. Tech firms are now more powerful and influential than many developing countries and the Big Tech leaders made their triumphant presence felt during Trump's inauguration. In some contexts, tech platforms have overwhelmed state capacity; in others, they have enabled new forms of authoritarian control. As Ian Bremmer observes, advanced industrial economies may have little choice but to align with the American model, even as many countries of the Global South find China's state-capitalist alternative more attractive than neo-liberal morals.[4] The result is a world caught between competing economic paradigms: China's state-led capitalism and the faltering American "market-based model", each representing a distinct vision of globalisation's future.

[4] Bremmer (2025).

1.2 The Disruption: Is It Cyclical or Structural?

The alternating phases within globalisation may suggest a cyclical pattern where periods of interconnectedness give way to reactive protectionism before leading to another liberalising phase. The disruptions observable today in the form of tariff escalations, supply-chain readjustments, and technology competition should not be viewed as deviations but rather as repeating echoes of earlier eras when global trade networks collapsed and then reintegrated anew. For example, extensive seaborne trade during the height of global colonialism collapsed into the protectionism witnessed during the 1930s through to the post-Second World War recovery phase. The post-colonial, post-Second World War order exemplified through the Bretton Woods institutions led to an unprecedented reopening. With each cycle came macroeconomic shocks, political realignments, waves of human movements, resettlements, treaties and technological shifts that influenced the flow of goods and people, the liberalisation of economies, and the integration of global supply chains.

Yet the current disruption appears to be more than cyclical. The disruption is the harbinger of change within the post-Second World War structure that celebrated American leadership of a rules-based multilateral system and endorsed the US dollar-based trade. New technologies like AI, 5G networks and green tech and their purveyors have developed intense rivalries (exemplified by the Thucydides Trap between the US and China). The COVID-19 pandemic, pressing climate-change challenges, resurging far-right demagogues and their anti-immigration tropes have shaken the foundations upon which the post-Second World War order was built.

Hence, when states impose export controls on critical minerals and semiconductors, force global tech giants to switch to local hiring, or conclude regional pacts outside the multilateral order, they are reacting against the ideas of pre-existing paradigms within global interdependence. Originally, food and agriculture were areas where states drew the red line. Now, the red lines drawn are practically everywhere.

Reconciling the dichotomy of perspectives between structural and cyclical change requires accepting the uncomfortable truth that opposing forces can sometimes operate in tandem. To do so, a high degree of convergence is required between the competing actors, who may, more often than not, not be inclined to converge.

If the underlying forces (tech leadership, strategic competition and ethno-centric policies) and the actors that wield them persist in fragmenting, the post-Second World War framework may indeed result in a re-made form of globalisation. This form may see formation of "friends clubs", "tech blocs", and deeper regionalisation where the benefits of liberalised trade are reserved for the chosen few.

Conversely, should economic imperatives such as maximised consumer welfare, innovation, cost savings from integrated value chains, or the need to conserve a minimum baseline of domestic manufacturing present themselves as major themes, the current spate of global disruption might be temporary, and we may see a return to the "good old days".

If there is a reversion to the globalisation model, perhaps a more liberalised regime tempered by valuable lessons learned would become *en vogue*. It could revive stalled moves to reform the multilateral trading system, shock-proof supply-chain structures might emerge, and we may even see empowered multilateral institutions capable of maintaining a rules-based system in a multipolar world.

Globalisation, in summary, appears to be at a crossroads where the disruption question remains to be settled. The historical cycles of opening and closing may still be at play, but they are driven by rapid technology development, resource nationalism and realpolitik that complicate cyclical advancement or transition. Whether the current disruption phase is temporary or marks the end of an epoch depends on how soon the stakeholders, such as states, multinational corporations, Big Tech, and civil society, can recalibrate global frameworks to meet new challenges and questions of legitimacy. If the stakeholders succeed, the rejuvenated wave of globalisation may easily arrest the impact of recent shocks and resume its advancement. If not, a fragmented and hardened new order will emerge with new winners and losers.

1.3 Who Is Disrupting and What Replaces the Disruption?

The current wave of disruption is a direct result of the competing strategies by state and non-state actors that are struggling to steer the post-Second World War order. The US is fixated on selective decoupling and establishing "friends clubs" to maintain its dominance over global economic flows. To do so, it enacted several enabling legislations, introduced subsidies that incentivise reshoring of lost industries, and pursued frameworks with questionable utility like the Indo-Pacific Economic Framework (IPEF) that weave "friends club" allies into "trusted" and shock-proof supply chains. American measures are an effort to maintain a rules-based system that still works to its own advantage rather than to the advantage of adversaries or strategic competitors that may have dynamically adapted. In short, the US seeks to disrupt and revise the rules of the globalisation game while maintaining a veneer of legitimacy. Its European and Western partners are wary of the disruption because it has exposed the US's self-centred and unreliable tendencies.

China, by contrast, seeks to disrupt and revise the rules only selectively because it now knows that it is emerging as a winner and a de facto champion of the Global South. China's selective disruption of globalisation endorses a state-directed model which it is projecting through both hard and soft diplomacy, infrastructure development under the auspices of the BRI, and the rollout of 5G networks and the Digital Silk Road initiatives. China secured a high-profile triumph through the conclusion of the Regional Comprehensive Economic Partnership (RCEP). The RCEP represents a trade alternative that bypasses American control. China has also emerged as a voice of reform within the WTO after its paralysis by the US and its willingness to extend the membership of BRICS underscores efforts to develop feasible alternatives to Western-dominated financial systems.

On the other hand, China's disruption potential is best illustrated by its export-controls regime on rare earths and semiconductors, and its aggressive acquisition of strategic assets such as ports, industries and stakes in mining corporations. These efforts by China project its readiness to use, expand and maintain greater geopolitical advantage and regional influence, especially in the rare-earths sector where it has signalled an intent to crash worldwide prices in order to drive out emerging rare-earths suppliers. China intends to control the rare-earths supply chain for the long term and will act aggressively to preserve its dominance.

A major reason for the disruption is the reality of disparate factor endowments of nations.[5] Since nations are not endowed equally in all factors of production, they are compelled to engage in exchange even when there are historical hostilities at play. In fact, we may even attribute cycles of political, economic and social change to the uncertainties of factor endowments when painting the theme of Globalisation Disrupted. If we accept the reality that no empire, country or nation has owned, or will ever own, all factors of production in the right quantities, we will surely conclude that interdependence is not a choice. Rather, it is inevitable.

Even powerful, well-endowed nations like the US bow to pressure tactics such as export controls because they lack strategic minerals and rare earths. China, on the other hand, depends on large-scale imports of fuel and raw materials to run its factories and on imported food to sustain its population, while some developing countries may be constrained to export raw materials and intermediate goods in exchange for access to technology and value-added products.

In short, the asymmetry in factors of production reminds us that even where geopolitics, conflict, and technology reshape the dynamics of exchange, the structural reality of factor endowments continues to compel interaction. The challenge, following our acceptance of this inevitable reality, is the design of rules and institutions that utilise the complementarities of nations into something fair, resilient and enduring rather than the division inherent in zero-sum rivalry of policies such as "the US First".

The link between factor endowments and disruption is directly connected to nations acquiring new capabilities and developing improved processes, e.g., China's move from basic industries like textiles to large-scale manufacturing of electric vehicles, photovoltaics and semiconductors. Indeed, the disruption we allude to in this book is largely because of China's performance in international trade. In the early 2000s the US and the EU dominated global trade. However, by 2024, China overtook both to become the largest trading partner for Asia, Africa and the US. In the process, China's total trade went from USD 474 billion in 2000 to USD 6.2 trillion in 2024.[6] It is now an unstoppable force in international trade.

But the disruption is not just limited to China. India's efforts to become a hub of global services and digital trade, or the recent the US efforts to reshore industrial

[5] Highlighted by the work of Swedish economists Eli Heckscher and Bertil Ohlin [popularly referred to as the *Factor Proportions Theorem* (Ohlin 1998, pp. 12, 29–30)].

[6] Hinrich Foundation (2025).

activity that it outsourced a few decades ago in a bid to become a "knowledge economy" show that economic interests and strategic postures change over time. With this change, the relative endowments of nations may reshape the equation of cooperation, competition and exchange. Australia's emergence as the "safe" alternative for the supply of some rare earths to the US alters its bargaining position in trade and investment deals with the US, even where it continues to conclude mega-regionals involving China.

Therefore, even where globalisation is being disrupted, the natural programming of factor endowments and the inherent disparities will keep bringing nations back to the trade table. The only difference is that forms of engagement evolve and change: perhaps becoming less multilateral or more plurilateral, more or less inclusive, more or less regional or even mega-regional (as is the case with RCEP and CPTPP).

Because the compulsion to cooperate, negotiate and integrate remains structurally enduring (with only the venues and terms subject to shift) nations will continue to do business with each other despite the regular breakout of diplomatic hostilities or threats to use force or following periods of open war. This is why Taiwanese investors continue to flock to mainland China despite threats to annex Taiwan. the US–China trade in goods and Chinese investment in the US real estate also continue despite the extensive use of export controls on semiconductors and rare earths. Similarly, Türkiye and Russia continue defence cooperation, tourism, trade in goods, and investment in large-scale energy projects despite political friction over Syria, and Türkiye's uncomfortable NATO membership. Put simply, economic interdependence persists alongside strategic competition and political confrontation.

1.4 Adaptation, Collapse and a Re-made Post-Globalisation Order

The frameworks and treaties underpinning the rules-based trading system are causing decay and growing irrelevance. The WTO and its much-lauded dispute-settlement mechanism continue to be kneecapped owing to the non-functional Appellate Body crisis brought about by American intransigence. The WTO reform agenda is also bogged down, and several WTO members have turned to resolving the impasse plurilaterally. Prominent examples include the Multi-Party Interim Appeal Arbitration Arrangement (MPIA) and agreements such as the Joint Statement Initiative (JSI) on e-commerce.

Simultaneously, mega-regionals such as the RCEP and CPTPP signal that states are willing to coalesce around regional structures where global consensus fails to materialise. In addition to international trade, the investor–state dispute-settlement (ISDS) mechanism is also being challenged and revisited. There have been several alternatives such as the EU's Investment Court System (ICS) and the ISDS reform initiative by UNCITRAL.

Any adaptive legal experiments are an effort to contain and manage the fallout of disruption in globalisation. The US's efforts are of questionable utility largely because of internal divisions about the future direction. Under President Trump, even efforts like IPEF's supply-chain resilience pillar face displacement through overuse of tariffs, and some of the targeted export controls imposed on China under the CHIPS and Science Act have been lifted in exchange for resumed access to refined rare earths from China.

Similarly, China has leveraged its strength in rare earths and the gradual build-up of its export-controls regime to project negotiating strength. Even beyond China and the US, other states and middle powers have used a mix of tariffs, subsidies and FDI screening to safeguard national interests at the expense of predictability and non-discrimination. The resulting disruption, therefore, is a complex mosaic of overlapping commitments, layered standards, exceptions and competing norms that reflect a fragmenting rules-based system.

Yet the fragmentation also offers the opportunity to rebuild a more purposeful form of globalisation and a reincarnation of the decaying WTO model. Plurilateral agreements on data governance, e-commerce or carbon pricing provide a template for broader scaling into multilateral treaties.

The EU's Carbon Border Adjustment Mechanism (CBAM) is one such measure that demonstrates how environmental objectives can be integrated into international trade law and can influence how trading partners align their domestic regulations. Similarly, ESG-based screening of incoming FDI allows international investment laws to achieve sustainability-linked goals.

The future does not seem to promise a return to multilateralism, nor does it portend a collapse of global normative order. Rather, the emergence of "friends clubs" and regional security blocs will act as experimental laboratories for legal restructuring. Once successful norms emerge, outward diffusion creates greater adoption and the development of supporting structures that act as legitimising factors.

As traditional institutions decay, new partnerships and standards may fill the vacuum. Such departures may initially seem creative, but where they are guided by a clear public purpose embracing sustainability and fairness, they may evolve into pluralistic legal solutions appropriate for a fragmented yet still interdependent world.

1.5 A Bouquet of Diverse Thoughts

The contributors in *Globalisation Disrupted* offer a diverse analysis of the upheavals of the twenty-first century that define the interdependent and interconnected world. The chapters span law, policy, international relations, economics and public health. Together, the chapters highlight the fault lines in globalisation's disruption phase.

The book opens with Umair Ghori and John Farrar's Introduction and then John Farrar follows in "Globalisation, Brexit, and the Future of the UK," dissecting how sovereignty debates and democratic legitimacy drove the 2016 referendum and continue to shape the United Kingdom's trade and regulatory stance. Farrar's review of post-Brexit arrangements underscores the delicate balance between national autonomy and market access. Mirroring Farrar's chapter is the contribution by Jürgen Bröhmer that examines the EU's struggle to reconcile multilevel governance with public trust. By critiquing the "democratic deficit" and exploring subsidiarity debates, Bröhmer reveals the EU as both a prototype and a cautionary tale for supranational cooperation.

Louise Parsons and John Farrar, in "Financial Stability and Threats of World Disorder" extend the inquiry to global finance. They probe how nationalism, climate risk and digital-currency debates are straining the rules-based legacy and what regulatory innovations might safeguard financial stability in a deglobalising world.

Turning to the Global South, Laurence Boulle's "Building the Bloc, Brick by BRICS" assesses how an expanding BRICS coalition challenges Western-led institutions. His analysis of BRICS' secretariat-light governance, the New Development Bank, and climate-finance pledges spotlights the bloc's uneven progress and its potential to reshape multipolar governance.

Rosita Dellios and James Ferguson chart China's strategic outreach in "China and the Strategic Evolution of the Belt and Road Initiative." Blending historical context with scenarios on green and digital Silk Roads, they probe the BRI's sustainability reforms and resilience to geopolitical headwinds, offering a window into infrastructure diplomacy's future.

Australia's middle-power perspective comes next in Peter Draper and Nathan Gray's "Globalisation in a Destabilising World." Their analysis of weakened multilateral institutions and adaptive strategies (from friend-shoring to regional pacts) provides a model of how a middle power navigates fragmentation without forfeiting global engagement.

Umair Ghori's chapter explores how security-driven export controls (distinct from the traditional WTO-regulated concept of export restrictions) have emerged as a central element in the US–China decoupling, particularly in advanced technologies and critical minerals like rare earth elements. It details China's retaliatory measures on exports of gallium, germanium and other essential inputs, and examines the US' counterstrategies, including supply-chain diversification, reshoring initiatives and closer coordination with allies. Ultimately, the chapter argues that these developments are creating a "geoeconomic fulcrum" that will solidify parallel supply chains under competing regulatory regimes, with deep implications for the future of global trade governance and technological competition.

Darryl Lupton's "Globalisation in Flux: Implications for China and India" delivers a balanced comparative study. By juxtaposing China's manufacturing prowess with India's services-led growth, he evaluates whether India might emerge as a credible "China-plus-one" alternative within fractured value chains.

Mary Hiscock confronts the institutional underpinnings of trade in "The Future of the WTO." Her close reading of consensus-based decision-making, the Appellate Body paralysis, and plurilateral workstreams paints a candid portrait of an organisation on life support.

In closing, Wendy Bonython's "Global Health as the Canary in the Globalisation Coalmine" uses the COVID-19 pandemic to demonstrate globalisation's dual risks and rewards in health security. Her critique of WHO governance, the Pandemic Agreement and intellectual-property tensions shows that health cooperation both exemplifies and tests the resilience of global order.

Each contributor delves into legal, economic and policy dimensions to unravel the "disruption" of globalisation. We hope that these carefully curated perspectives will promote a greater understanding of how national agendas, institutional fractures and technopolitical rivalries are reshaping the world and how new hybrid orders are emerging from the remnants of the old.

References

Acharya, Amitav, Antoni Estevadeordal, and Louis W. Goodman. 2023. Multipolar or Multiplex? Interaction Capacity, Global Cooperation and World Order. *International Affairs* 99:2339–2365.

Allison, Graham T. 2017. *Destined for War: Can the US and China Escape Thucydides Trap?* New York: Houghton Mifflin Harcourt.

Bremmer, Ian. 2025. Technopolar Paradox: The Frightening Fusion of Tech Power and State Power. *Foreign Affairs*. https://www.foreignaffairs.com/united-states/technopolar-paradox-ian-bremmer-fusion-tech-state-power. Accessed 28 Aug 2025.

Hinrich Foundation. 2025. Trade and Geopolitics—Global Trade Dominance: US, EU, or China. https://www.hinrichfoundation.com/research/article/trade-and-geopolitics/global-trade-dominance-us-eu-or-china?utm_campaign=infographic-vc-how-global-trade-changed&utm_medium=email&_hsenc=p2ANqtz-8P_cbVItPDP3j8lf4bpVDH6YrzP-FESUiNRihrctDMOROAUon7nVzYl_c8B5W6J7A_hfjRWAI6Mi-X3AhWAbj1XndKy4A&_hsmi=375507549&utm_content=20250812-weekly-research-&utm_source=hinrich-thought-leadership. Accessed 14 Aug 2025.

Inkster, Nigel. 2020. *The Great Decoupling: China, America and the Struggle for Technological Supremacy*. London: C. Hurst & Co Publishers.

Oermann, Nils Ole, and Hans-Jurgen Wolff. 2022. *Trade Wars: Past and Present*. Oxford: Oxford University Press.

Ohlin, Bertil. 1998. *Interregional and International Trade*. New York: Routledge.

Chapter 2
Globalisation, Brexit and the Future of the United Kingdom

John Farrar

Abstract Brexit describes the United Kingdom's exit from the European Union after nearly 50 years membership. The campaign in respect of it was badly conducted but the result to some extent reflected complex social discontent with the results of globalisation. Brexit weakened the UK economy and its position in the world. The irony is that the EU is still the UK's largest trading partner.

2.1 Introduction

The term Brexit developed to describe the United Kingdom's exit from the European Union.[1] As a process it started with a referendum in 2016 and culminated with withdrawal in 2021. Brexit has an interesting relationship with globalisation, but its causes were various and more complex. The effects of globalisation feature in the analysis but are not conclusive. In this chapter we briefly discuss the history of globalisation and the UK's part in it. We then deal with the UK's membership of the European Union over nearly 50 years. After this we focus on the causes of dissension and then talk about the campaign for the referendum and its aftermath and consequences. In particular, we consider how this could lead to the breakup of the UK.

[1] See Oxford English Dictionary citing Peter Wilding in a blog post on the website Euroactiv. 15 May 2012. https://www.euractiv.com/section/politics/news/oxford-english-dictionary-the-man-who-coined-brexit/. Accessed 22 August 2025. See also MacShane (2015).

J. Farrar (✉)
Faculty of Law, Bond University, Robina, QLD, Australia
e-mail: jfarrar@bond.edu.au

U. H. Ghori, J. Farrar (eds.), *Globalisation Disrupted*,
https://doi.org/10.1007/978-981-95-3997-0_2

2.2 A Brief History of Globalisation

There have been different versions of globalisation over time.[2] To some extent the Roman Empire was an early form of globalisation which included at some time parts of the UK. The expansion of the British Empire can be seen as a form of colonial globalism. Four distinct periods of globalisation can be identified:

The first period	First industrial revolution 1780s to mid-nineteenth century.
The second period	The second industrial revolution 1870s to 1910s.
The third period	The third industrial revolution was marked by the growth of global supply chains 1960s to 1990s and dominated by the USA.
The fourth period	The fourth industrial revolution 2000 to 2008 marked by the growth of digital goods and services, e commerce and the rise of China.

To the above can be added a fifth period (from 2008 to 2020) which is the beginning of fragmentation. Although there is an element of dogma in this analysis it is convenient to adopt some division of history to understand the present.

The UK played a role in the first three stages. The fourth stage received some momentum on the collapse of the USSR in1990 and then the expansion of the WTO in 1995 and the inclusion of China on 11 December 2001.

The development of globalisation led to some benefits and some detriments. The benefits included the expansion of trade, migration and reduction in cost. The detriments were mainly the uneven spread of benefits. Also, the membership of China of the WTO had great effect. Western companies' pursuit of cheap labour led to a decline of industries in those countries and the rise of unemployment. This led to the rise of anti-globalisation forces in the West. It also led to growing dissatisfaction with the main international bodies such as the IMF, World Bank, WTO and in some respects the United Nations. This expressed itself eventually in the rise of populism of which Brexit and the rise of Donald Trump were manifestation. The UK like the USA benefited from globalisation but by the 1960s there was a feeling that it was starting to lose out if it did not join the EU. This led to membership in 1972 Later with the rise of China there has been a growing dissatisfaction with the EU and its economic and political roles.

The UK has always been ambivalent about EU membership for constitutional reasons and wary about its mercantilist nature. It was due to the tenacity of Edward Heath and Labour figures such as Roy Jenkins that led to membership. Later there was a referendum in 1975 which confirmed continued membership of the European Community by 67.2% of the electorate. It should be noted that the UK does not have compulsory voting. Overtime there have been numerous episodes of reluctance by the UK to join in an expansion of membership and the role of institutions of the EU.[3]

---

[2] Boulle (2009, Chap 1.3) and Farrar and Mayes (2013).

[3] See Neumann (2022, Chap. 14 Europe under Pressure).

2.3 Events in UK Membership of EU

The UK first applied to join in 1961 but was vetoed by De Gaulle. He also vetoed a second application in 1967. After De Gaulle retired as French President the UK made a third and successful application in 1972.[4] In June 1975 the Wilson government put continued membership to a referendum which was passed by 67.2%.[5]

In 1979 the UK opted out of the European Monetary System which was the precursor of the Euro system.[6] In the 1983 general election Labour campaigned on the commitment to withdraw without a referendum. This was heavily defeated. Labour changed its policy. The Thatcher government was elected but was ambivalent about the EU.[7] Nevertheless, it supported the Single European Act in 1985, and the UK joined the European Exchange Rate Mechanism in 1990. Thatcher became increasingly a Euro sceptic, and the UK was forced to withdraw from the ERM in 1992. The UK opted out of some EU measures. In particular, it opted out of the Schengen agreement about border controls. It resisted membership of the Euro system and secured a protocol on the Charter of Fundamental Rights. Later under Cameron there were further negotiations over EU measures.[8]

2.4 Causes of Dissension

The causes were various. Globalisation produced winners and losers. London and the Home Counties benefited. The Midlands and the North suffered decline in their industries and rising unemployment. There were similar but less pronounced features in Wales, Scotland and N Ireland.

Increasing immigration, cheap labour and the rise of multiculturalism led to growing anxieties amongst the indigenous population. This increased with Muslim immigration and the aftermath of September 11th and the increased terrorism. Overall, there was a nostalgia for earlier times when the UK performed a more heroic role.[9]

---

[4] O'Rourke (2018, Chap. 4).

[5] Ibid, 74.

[6] See generally, Jenkins (1989, p. 659).

[7] See Campbell (2009, p. 497 et seq) and Moore (2016, Chap. 12).

[8] Neumann, *supra*, n.3, at 169–70, 200.

[9] Oliver (2016, Chap. 34 What went wrong?).

2.5 The Brexit Campaign

The Cameron government made the fundamental mistake of calling a referendum on a complex issue. Referenda do not fit the Westminster system of government. As a result, the referendum became a proxy for many issues.[10] There were no effective public relations for the EU by the government which had stopped the EU mounting a campaign.[11]

The Remain campaign led by Britain Stronger in Europe, an across party lobbying group was both a strength and a weakness.[12] Jeremy Corbyn had always opposed the EU. Different parties had different agendas.

The Leave camp ran a dishonest campaign in a number of ways. Some key participants were unscrupulous in their speeches and writings. Nigel Farage, in particular, was a vigorous proponent with a history of dissent in the EU Parliament. Johnson and Gove were clever opportunists but in the end were startled by what they had achieved. The government's reading of polling that the economy would trump immigration turned out to be wrong. There was no compulsory voting.

The result was that 51.89% voted in favour of leaving and 48.11% voted to remain.[13] The table shows the breakdown of votes in the regions. Very significant is the percentages in Scotland, Northern Ireland, London and parts of the home counties which favoured Remain whereas the majority of the rest favoured Leave. This can in part be understood as a rejection of the government's austerity policy. There was a clear social divide between graduates and well-off workers who voted to remain and the working poor and unemployed. Lastly there was a generational divide or the 70% of 18- to 24-year-olds voted to remain and all the people who voted to leave 83% of over 65 voted whereas only one in three young people voted.[14]

2.6 The Aftermath and Its Consequences

Cameron resigned as Prime Minister and was replaced by Theresa May. On 29 March 2017 the Government, with permission from Parliament, began the withdrawal process by notifying its intention to withdraw under Article 50 of The Treaty on European Union. This was after messy debates and litigation. Theresa May bore the brunt of complex negotiations hardly assisted by her Foreign Secretary Boris Johnson who eventually resigned.[15] Johnson replaced May in 2019, and the

[10] Ibid 386.

[11] Ibid 386.

[12] Ibid 386.

[13] Results of the 2016 United Kingdom European Union Membership Referendum (2016).

[14] Barnier (2021, pp. 13–14).

[15] May (2023, Chap. 3 Case Studies of Power Misuse in Politics).

withdrawal agreement was ratified by the UK parliament.[16] This resulted in a transition period and what Denis MacShane has called *Brexiternity*. He argues that Brexit will unfold over the coming years, if not decades.

It would be tedious to discuss in depth the complex and protracted negotiations in which the EU had the stronger hand. The EU team led by Michel Barnier completely outclassed the fluctuating UK team.[17] The compromise consists of a financial settlement and a transition period of 5 1/2 years accompanied by a reduction of fishing quotas in British waters of around 25%. There is to be cooperation in research and innovation, nuclear safety and space and there is also to be non-discrimination between European citizens. Stress is put upon security of citizens and this has become very important in the light of common membership of NATO and the struggles in the Ukraine.

2.6.1 *Litigating Brexit*[18]

During the long-drawn-out process there was strategic litigation to influence the process. There was a variety of litigators-nstitutional actors, expats and EU nationals, politicians, lawyers, campaigners and campaign groups.[19]

Some cases were pro- remain, some pro-leave, some were to uphold Parliamentary authority or to subject executive action to law, some were concerned with quality of process and some with protecting the Northern Ireland peace process.[20]

This litigation has had constitutional impact. It has expanded the scope of justiciability in terms of substance and remedies. It has extended judicial control over prerogative powers and contributed to the development of common law constitutionalism.[21]

The constitutional change of Brexit was not initiated by Government against the wishes of the people. It was initiated by the people in the referendum but has strengthened government to use populist tactics to rely on the will of the people to push through constitutional change.[22] Paradoxically, the will of the people may not reflect the changing will of the majority of the electorate. This may explain the cautious way in which the courts have approached the matter.

[16] See Johnson (2024).

[17] See Stourton and Desmet (2019) and MacShane (2019).

[18] See McCorkindale and McHarg (2021) and Peers (2024).

[19] Ibid 270.

[20] Ibid 272.

[21] Ibid 290.

[22] See Young (2024). For populism see Young (2018).

2.6.2 *Economic Consequences*[23]

The majority of economists believe that Brexit has damaged the UK economy and reduced its real per capita income in the long term.[24] It has produced a decline in immigration from the European Economic Area (EEA) and prejudiced academic research. It has increased inflation. Brexit further led to increased offshoring to the EU by UK firms and reduced EU investments in the UK. Overall, there is general agreement that leaving the EU adversely affects the economy in the medium to long term.

In October 2021 the Office of Budget Responsibility calculated that Brexit would cost 4% of GDP per annum over the long term. London like the rest of the UK has lost a number of jobs and the financial services of the City of London have suffered from the resulting uncertainty. There was hope for new trade deals, but these proved difficult to negotiate and poor compensation for the loss of the EU markets. The process of negotiation takes time and needs expertise.

These economic consequences have exacerbated regional economic inequality in the UK.[25] Brexit did not solve any of the problems caused by deindustrialisation. If anything, it made them worse.

2.6.3 *Constitutional and Political Consequences*

The border with the Irish Republic has proved difficult.[26] Under the Windsor Framework negotiated after the Protocol to the withdrawal agreement Northern Ireland is still subject to EU single market rules for goods and maintains access to this market. The recent elections in Northern Ireland and the UK forces one to consider the reunification of Ireland. Sinn Fein is the majority party in Northern Ireland and the largest Northern Ireland party in the Westminster Parliament although its members do not attend due to unwillingness to swear the oath of allegiance to the Crown. Scotland generally supported the Remain campaign and there have been calls for independence and rejoining of the EU.[27] The UK's constitution makes this difficult. Labour is now the majority party representing Scotland in Westminster. Wales generally supported Brexit but has suffered as a consequence.

---

[23] UK Government (2018).

[24] See Summary of Media Coverage Wikipedia, Economic Effects of Brexit. Accessed 22August 2025.

[25] Carter and Swinney (2019).

[26] See Budd (2017, Chap. 8). See the Protocol on Ireland/Northern Ireland Jan 24, Official Journal of EU L29/72. 2020 This was a protocol to the Withdrawal Agreement and was amended by the Windsor Agreement.

For interesting criticism see Johnson, *supra*, n. 16, at 53–57.

[27] See Gallagher (2017, Chap.7).

There was increased political instability in the Westminster Parliament despite Conservative victories. A new election has led to a Labour victory. Labour chose not to play the Brexit card in the election but there are signs that a majority of Labour voters want Labour to drop its Brexit redlines. The new government has announced that work has begun on renegotiating the Conservative's Brexit deals, but the Prime Minister insisted that the UK will not rejoin the EU in his lifetime.

The paradox of the UK's membership of the EU was that it enabled the UK to be a hybrid between a European and a US socioeconomic model. The paradox of Brexit may well be, irrespective of any breakup of the UK, it forces the UK to be more European to survive.[28] This would reflect its economic reality if not its aspirations.

In 2024 the second Trump presidency of the USA has led to significant changes. The USA has pursued tariffs even against allies, weakened the WTO and its enforcement system and adopted a hostile approach to China and even in certain respects to the EU.

This is leading to the bifurcation of supply lines especially in semiconductors, rare minerals and technology.

2.7 Conclusion

Brexit now has to contend with an increasingly multipolar world. As a result, the UK has to renegotiate its relationship with the EU and the USA. At a late stage in the writing of this chapter the UK–US reached a trade deal on 8 May 2025. This is not a full trade deal but expands US market access in the UK. It secures the supply chain of US aerospace manufacturers through preferential access to UK aerospace components and also a secure supply chain for pharmaceutical products. It aims to create a new trading union for steel and aluminium and safeguards jobs in car and steel industries threatened by US tariffs. There was deep symbolism in that this was announced on the 80th anniversary of Victory Day for World War Two but the document does not constitute a legally binding agreement.[29]

Even later in May 2025, the UK struck a deal with the EU[30] that covers fishing, trade, defence, energy and strengthening ties in other policy areas still being negotiated. It has been realised both sides need each other in a time of geopolitical turbulence when they can no longer rely on US hegemony. The brute fact is that the EU is still the UK's largest trading partner.[31]

[28] See Sandbu (2019, pp. 187–198).

[29] US-UK Reach Historic Trade Deal (2025).

[30] See News Story Prime Minister's Office (2025).

[31] For a very interesting conclusion see Shipman (2024, p. 906).

References

Barnier, Michael. 2021. *My Secret BREXIT Diary: A Glorious Illusion*. Cambridge: Polity Press.

Boulle, Laurence. 2009. *The Law of Globalisation—An Introduction*. The Netherlands: Kluwer Law International.

Budd, Less. 2017. Stalling or Breaking? Northern Ireland's Economy in the Balance. In *The Political Economy of Brexit*, ed. David Bailey and Less Budd. Cheltenham: Edward Elgar Publishing.

Campbell, J. 2009. *The Iron Lady: Margaret Thatcher (One-Volume Abridgement)*. London: Jonathan Cape.

Carter, Andrew, and Paul Swinney. 2019. Brexit and the Future of the UK's Unbalanced Economic Geography. *Political Quarterly* 90:72–83.

Farrar, John H., and David G. Mayes. 2013. Globalisation, the Crisis and the State: Introduction. In *Globalisation the Global Financial Crisis and the State*, ed. John H. Farrar and David G. Mayes, 1–4. Cheltenham, UK: Edward Elgar Publishing.

Gallagher, J. 2017. A Scottish Perspective: Charting a Path Through the Rubble. In *The Political Economy of Brexit*, ed. David Bailey and Less Budd. Cheltenham: Edward Elgar Publishing.

Jenkins, Roy. 1989. *European Diary 1977–81*. London: Collins.

Johnson, Boris. 2024. *Unleashed*. New York: HarperCollins.

MacShane, Denis. 2015. *Brexit: How Britain Will Leave Europe*. London: I.B. Tauris.

MacShane, Denis. 2019. *Brexiternity: The Uncertain Fate of Britain*. London: Biteback Publishing.

May, Theresa. 2023. *The Abuse of Power—Confronting Injustice in Public*. London: Headline Publishing Group.

McCorkindale, Christopher, and Aileen McHarg. 2021. Litigating Brexit. In *The Brexit Challenge for Ireland and UK: Constitutions Under Pressure*, ed. Oan Doyle, Jo Eric Khushal Murkens, and Aileen McHarg. New York: Cambridge University Press.

Moore, Charles. 2016. *Margaret Thatcher, the Authorised Biography*. Vol. 2. Great Britain: Penguin Books.

Neumann, Peter R. 2022. *The New World Disorder—How the West Is Destroying Itself*. Brunswick: Scribe Publications.

News Story Prime Minister's Office. 2025. PM Secures New Agreement with EU to Benefit British People. https://www.gov.uk/government/news/pm-secures-new-agreement-with-eu-to-benefit-british-people. Accessed 19 May 2025.

Oliver, Craig. 2016. *Unleashing Demons—The Inside Story of Brexit*. London: Hachette, Hodder & Stoughton.

O'Rourke, K. H. 2018. *A Short History of Brexit: From Brentry to Backstop*. London: Pelican/Penguin.

Peers, Steve. 2024. Litigating Brexit: A Guide to the Case Law. http://eulawanalysis.blogspot.co.uk. Accessed 22 Aug 2025.

Results of the 2016 United Kingdom European Union Membership Referendum. 2016. Wikipedia. https://en.wikipedia.org/wiki/Results_of_the_2016_United_Kingdom_European_Union_membership_referendum. Accessed 23 Aug 2025.

Sandbu, Martin. 2019. Brexit and the Future of UK Capitalism. In *Britain Beyond Brexit*, ed. Gavin Kelly and Nick Pearce. Malden: Wiley-Blackwell.

Shipman, Tim. 2024. *Out: How Brexit Got Done and the Tories Were Undone*. London: William Collins.

Stourton, Edward, and Lode Desmet. 2019. *Blind Man's Brexit—How the EU Took Control of Brexit*. London: Simon & Schuster.

UK Government. 2018. EU Exit—Long-Term Economic Analysis. https://assets.publishing.service.gov.uk/media/5c00058b40f0b65af36c5d6c/28_November_EU_Exit_-_Long-term_economic_analysis__1_.pdf. Accessed 22 Aug 2025.

US–UK Reach Historic Trade Deal. 2025. The White House. https://www.whitehouse.gov/fact-sheets/2025/05/fact-sheet-u-s-uk-reach-historic-trade-deal/. Accessed 8 May 2025.

Young, Alison. 2018. Populism and the UK Constitution. *Current Legal Problems* 71:17–52.
Young, Alison. 2024. Dicey's Forgotten Constitution. In *Dicey + 100: Albert Venn Dicey: A Centennial Commemoration*, ed. Andrew Dickinson, Timothy Endicott, Wolfgang Ernst, and Sophie Ryan. Cambridge: Intersentia Uitgevers N.V.

Chapter 3
Globalisation and Sovereignty: The EU's Governance Dilemma

Jürgen Bröhmer

Abstract This chapter examines the European Union's governance dysfunction within the contemporary "Trumpian" political environment characterised by anti-establishment sentiment and institutional distrust. The analysis demonstrates how this context particularly disadvantages the EU's technocratic, multilevel governance structure. Drawing on Macron's Sorbonne speeches, the paper identifies core challenges: security, economic competitiveness, and defence capabilities. The institutional analysis reveals significant structural limitations. The Common Foreign and Security Policy (CFSP) remains constrained by unanimity requirements preventing rapid responses. Internal governance faces competing forces of "informal internationalisation" and "unilateral renationalisation." The German and Polish constitutional court's rejection of EU law primacy represent direct threats to foundational integration principles. The German Constitutional Court's "identity review" doctrine constrains EU development by reserving critical policy areas to national control. Contemporary crisis responses demonstrate both adaptive capacity and structural limitations. Ukraine-related cooperation advanced significantly, yet decision-making remains dependent on member state consensus rather than integrated institutional capacity. The paper concludes that the EU faces a fundamental governance dilemma: member states individually lack capacity to address global challenges, while collective action remains constrained by institutional frameworks designed for different circumstances. Drawing parallels to ancient Greece after Rome's rise, the analysis warns that without addressing these structural contradictions, the EU risks global relegation while member states face strategic marginalisation.

J. Bröhmer (✉)
School of Law, Murdoch University, Perth/Murdoch, WA, Australia
e-mail: j.brohmer@murdoch.edu.au

U. H. Ghori, J. Farrar (eds.), *Globalisation Disrupted*,
https://doi.org/10.1007/978-981-95-3997-0_3

3.1 Introduction

To write about globalisation from a legal perspective, be it in general or in the context of the EU, in this day and time is impossible without taking into view the political circumstances in which the world currently finds itself. The world has entered what is often referred to as a populist phase, notwithstanding the fact that the word populism generically may not be the best way to describe the phenomenon. Perhaps the word "Trumpian" is generically better suited to capture the content of this political basket. Core elements of this Trumpian approach to the world are a deep distrust of anything and anyone regarded as elitist or establishment, an equal distrust of institutions as representing the establishment and the status quo championed by it, and the extension of this distrust to science and scientific endeavour as part of the hegemony of the establishment. The latter is significant in itself as in modern times science remained largely outside the fray of profound controversy or complete disregard, notwithstanding notorious attempts to create fake science to bolster racist and other evil policies and beliefs, for example by the Nazis in Germany.

All of this is accompanied by or has already resulted in the disappearance or erosion of any resemblance to what one might call a common societal base of what is considered plausible and possible, and what can or must be deemed nonsense. The scope of what might appear plausible (to a number of people significant enough to impact the discourse) in a given situation has vastly expanded. The demarcation line between potentially plausible causes and effects and nonsensical obscurity has shifted significantly to the latter. It is in this context that politics takes place around the globe.

In Western democracies, under conditions of free speech, this shifting demarcation line is a centrepiece of the daily discourse. It complicates the role that this discourse plays in the governance process. If facts, opinions, evaluations, etc., become untethered from any process, one of the main tasks of the discourse, i.e., the reduction of complexity to a level digestible for decision-making, becomes increasingly impossible because the legitimacy and acceptability base for the outcome of any such process shrinks. In autocratic societies, this phenomenon is partially exploited by dispensing useful narratives and cracking down on threatening ones. In all societies, mis- and disinformation becomes a much more powerful tool.

This phenomenon cannot merely be described as post- or counter-factualism. Of course, the facts are readily negated if they do not fit the narratives, but the more significant problem manifests not so much in disputing the facts themselves (lying), bad enough as that is, but in foundational disputes over the evaluation of the facts. The loss of any common canon of possibilities and impossibilities, coupled with the ability of social media to assemble large numbers of people behind almost any narrative, however obscure it may sound, fuels tendencies to create or influence reality by changing perceptions.

The significance of the claim that some immigrants are eating the cats and dogs of locals is not captured by the factual assessment of whether this has happened at all, just a few times, even only once, or whether it is a common conflict when local and immigrant cultures meet. The significance lies in the transportation of the evaluation of a situation where immigrants are regarded as negatively different and a threat. The significance of the Brexit slogan "take back control" does not lie in a positive difference between the quantity and quality of domestic versus transnational decision-making by EU institutions. The narrative suggests that local decisions are "better", however one defines "better", and that EU decision-making is, *per se*, at least a problem, if not outright unacceptable.

A body politic such as the EU, which is part of a complex and complicated multilevel governance structure consisting of at least three (local, member state and EU) and, in the case of federal member states, even four levels of government and is inherently built on rational, highly abstract, bureaucracy-driven, technocratic and expert-led, governance is particularly ill-suited to cope with this new reality. Matters get even worse considering that the EU must rely on largely indirect means of creating tangible political accountability. Add to that the tendency of member states' political elites to claim positive outcomes for themselves and blame at least some negative outcomes "on Brussels" and/or conveniently hide behind the EU for measures that are unpopular but regarded as necessary.[1]

3.2 The Status Quo of the EU

Nobody has summed up the political state of the EU better than French President Emmanuel Macron in his two Europe speeches at the Sorbonne in 2017 and 2024 and it is worthwhile to recall the President's words.

In his first speech,[2] President Macron identified the archenemies of any fruitful transnational cooperation, both globally and regionally, as in the example of the EU, as "nationalism, identitarianism, protectionism, isolationist sovereignism".[3] Macron explained that transnational cooperation is necessary because "an inward-facing country can only hope to offer limited responses" to the present global challenges, ranging from climate change to digital transition, migration and terrorism.[4]

Looking at the EU in particular, he lamented a lack of political leadership and vision, hiding behind their own false allegation of the EU as a powerless bureaucracy. His alternative vision is the bold creation of a "European sovereignty" based on "six keys":

1. Security (both internal and external, including establishing a European defence fund);
2. Effective border control (solidarity among member states, reformed asylum procedures and migration policies);

[1] For a differentiated view on this, see the recent study of Hunter (2025).

[2] Macron (2017).

[3] Ibid.

[4] Ibid.

3. Foreign policy with an emphasis on the Mediterranean and partnership with Africa, including the creation of a financial transaction tax to finance all this;
4. The ecological transition as a basket of all kinds of measure and initiatives ranging from the transformation of the transport, housing and industry sectors, to the establishment of a carbon price, a European energy market, to the creation of a European industrial support and infrastructure program, the reform of the common agricultural policy with more allowance for national policies;
5. Digital technology and transformation, emphasising not only the need for innovation and the creation of digital champions, the creation of a European agency similar to DARPA in the US,[5] but also the need for tax reform and fair taxation wherever value is created;
6. Industrial and monetary economic power with the Euro as the common currency at its core, with competitive European industries on a global scale, including the harmonisation of corporate taxation within certain corridors and the creation of a new social compact with ambitious reforms for EU-wide social security reforms and common minimum social standards, not least to create competitive fairness.

The various topoi of the speech can easily be discarded as an outline of an undertaking so grand it is impossible to be achieved in the best of circumstances, reducing Macron's vision to all but a fanciful wish list of sorts. That said, Macron's (2017) vision contains an outline of challenges faced by all countries, not just the EU. It is striking, that much of what Macron presented in this speech can be found—hotly debated—in discussions in the US which culminated in the so-called "Inflation Reduction Act"[6] and "Chips Act"[7] of the US, which set out to provide massive support for climate change and energy measures and a massive program to reshore and expand the US capacity and leadership in leading edge chips manufacturing, including a USD 40 billion Chips for America fund.[8] China's "Made in China 2025" plan[9] goes back to 2015; whereas it is not a piece of legislation, it is and was a very concrete plan, aspects of which are now visible not only on Australian streets with the broad visibility of attractive Chinese EVs.

Apart from economic issues, Macron's emphasis on external, internal and border security is very much at the forefront of policy debates today in Europe, Australia, and very visibly and threateningly in the US, where the matter has become so divisive that a constitutional crisis might be looming. There and in the EU, the underlying question is whether and to what degree the respective governments are and will be able, if not to find solutions, then to at least achieve sufficient progress.

---

[5] DARPA (n.d.).

[6] Inflation Reduction Act of 2022 (2022).

[7] CHIPS and Science Act of 2022 (2022); See also the National Defense Authorization Act for Fiscal Year 2021 (2021).

[8] Ibid, sec 102 Chips Act: Creating helpful incentives to produce semiconductors (CHIPS).

[9] See, for example, McBride and Chatzky (2019); See also CSET (Center for Security and Emerging Technology) (2019); See also Center for Security and Emerging Technology (2021).

In 2024, French President Emmanuel Macron delivered a second Europe speech at the Sorbonne as a kind of stock-taking.[10] Macron recalled progress made, despite Brexit and amidst a pandemic and the aggression of Russia in Ukraine. The pandemic provided an avenue into mutualising debt at the EU level, something that Germany always bitterly resisted, by creating a roughly EUR 800 billion Covid recovery fund.[11] Macron explicitly referred to (then) German Chancellor Olaf Scholz calling this foundationally new development a Hamiltonian moment, referring to the US and the aftermath of the independence war, when then Finance Minister Alexander Hamilton assumed the debts of the states incurred because of that war.[12]

The Russian aggression created a sense of unity in the EU, leaving aside Hungary (in particular), and brought significant progress on EU energy independence and market coordination and on defence and joint defence projects, such as the Future Combat Air system, a sixth generation fighter jet initiative with Germany and France at the centre.[13] Just recently, a second EU debt instrument of EUR 150 billion was finalised in the military defence area.[14] It is to be expected that at least rejection of harmonised debt financing via the EU as a matter of principle will no longer be maintainable.

However, the centrepiece of Macron's second speech was the question of whether the achievements are sufficient. The question was a rhetorical one. Macron did not beat around the bush. "We must be clear on the fact that our Europe, today, is mortal", he said. "It can die", and it will die if it does not get its acts together on defence in the light of the reality in the US, Russia and Iran (Macron spoke in April 2024, after the Hamas massacres but before the Israeli military strikes against Iran and its nuclear arms program, which began on 13 June 2025), on economic growth and competitiveness and on the "cultural clash", which he describes as the "battle of imaginations, narratives and values" between liberal democracies and human rights on the one side and autocracies on the other. The catchword Macron uses to describe what is needed is sovereignty, understood in a political sense more than its legal sense: the notion that the entity claiming sovereignty is able "to make huge strategic decisions, to embrace paradigm shifts, and to address them with strength, prosperity and humanism." The decisions to be made are in areas central to both of Macron's speeches, i.e., internal and external security, both militarily and regarding border control, growth and competitiveness to secure and maintain prosperity and support for the European social model, and energy and food independence.

That is indeed the question the EU will have to answer, in the same way as other state entities will have to answer the same question. Will these entities be able to, i.e., will their respective governance frameworks and the political conditions on the

[10] Macron (2024).

[11] European Union (2020); See also European Commission (2025a).

[12] Issing (2020).

[13] Airbus. Future Combat Air System (n.d.); Müller (2025). See also Barrie (2022).

[14] European Union (2025, Arts. 6 and 9); See also European Council (2025a).

ground allow them to make the necessary decisions, of which most will have severe impacts on constituents at home, rather than merely being more or less tactical adjustments of this or that lever and all of which will be fundamentally controversial for many reasons, one invariably being that some of the policy goals are downright conflicting.

3.3 Governance in the EU: Current International Crisis Reaction

This paper is not the place to lay out the EU's institutional framework in detail. However, it is useful to highlight what was impressively illustrated—yet again—in the light of the ongoing crisis in the Middle East. On 17 June 2025, the EU Foreign Ministers conferred about the Israel-Iran conflict. The EU's High Representative for Foreign Affairs and Security Policy and Commission Vice-President, Kaja Kallas, was asked after the videoconference whether "the Ministers today agreed or discussed anything that would materially influence the calculus of either side in this conflict." Her answer (which is not what is criticised in this paper but indirectly illustrates the problem) was that "[F]or me, it is also important that when we have the meetings, there are clear outcomes. And today, the clear outcome was the coordination that we do for our own citizens to evacuate them from there."[15]

The answer translates as a "no"—the EU is, by and large, not a player of significance; it is a bystander, a spectator with little impact or influence. This assessment in regard to the Israel/Iran conflict around alleged nuclear proliferation is, if anything, exacerbated by the fact that the EU did have an important role at the table in this conflict. In 2015, the E3/EU+3 (China, France, Germany, the Russian Federation, the United Kingdom and the United States, with the High Representative of the European Union for Foreign Affairs and Security Policy) and the Islamic Republic of Iran created the Joint Comprehensive Plan of Action (JCPOA) to deal with Iran's nuclear ambitions.[16] After President Trump withdrew from the plan in 2018[17] despite Iran's verified compliance with the agreement by the IAEA,[18] the EU and its member states tried to salvage the JCPOA and find a way around secondary US sanctions. The result was the creation of INSTEX in early 2019,[19] a "special purpose vehicle" (SPV) created by France, Germany and the UK (as shareholders) and the EU to facilitate trade with Iran by avoiding dollar-denominated transactions or other exposure by market participants to secondary US sanctions targeting their

---

[15] EU External Action Service (2025).

[16] UN Security Council (2015); see also Arms Control Association (n.d.).

[17] See Trump White House (2018).

[18] Mills (2024).

[19] E3 Foreign Ministers (2019).

interests in US markets[20] and by doing so, "protect our economic sovereignty".[21] It is safe to conclude that INSTEX failed; apparently, it only scored one transaction and was rather unceremoniously liquidated in 2024.[22]

This impression of power political irrelevance of the EU is confirmed by the behaviour of Russia in the context of the aggression against Ukraine. It would appear that Russian President Putin and US President Trump largely regard this as a matter only they can resolve, despite the fact that the EU and its member states are the largest contributors to Ukrainian defence efforts, irrespective of the question of whether the assistance provided is sufficient or could and should be increased. There are structural reasons for the EU's difficulty in asserting the role it should play on the global stage.

3.3.1 The Common Foreign and Security Policy (CFSP)

Henry Kissinger's apocryphal yet famous rhetorical question about Europe's phone number can now be answered affirmatively: it is the EU High Representative for Foreign Affairs (Arts. 18 and 27 TEU) and Vice-President (Art. 18.4.1 TEU) of the European Commission, an office currently held by the former Prime Minister of Estonia, Kaja Kallas.[23]

In a questionnaire she had to answer as part of her confirmation as a member of the new European Commission,[24] the new HR/VP stated that she "personally believe[s] that the EU's success as a foreign policy actor is entirely dependent on our capacity to speak with one voice."[25] Indeed, herein lies the challenge.

The EU's CFSP has found its way into the current treaty (Treaty of Lisbon)[26] in a somewhat convoluted way as a result of the failed attempt to create a draft constitution in 2004. The failed draft constitution streamlined the old treaties into one integrated constitutional framework, which would have made the distinction between the intergovernmental collaboration on the one hand and the more integrated, supranational joint decision-making processes of the old European Community, hence the word "Community method", somewhat obsolete. The resulting Treaty of Lisbon kept a two-treaty structure, with the EUV[27] generally reflecting

[20] Thomas (2022).

[21] Borrell (2021).

[22] See Foreign, Commonwealth & Development Office (2023); see also Foreign, Commonwealth & Development Office (2020).

[23] See The Council of the Europe (2024).

[24] See European Parliament (2024a).

[25] European Parliament (2024b).

[26] The European Union (2007); See also Massay-Kosubek and Maciejewski (2025).

[27] The European Union (2025a).

more the intergovernmental side and the TFEU[28] the more supranational element. Against this background, it is therefore noteworthy that the TFEU creates a prima facie impression that the CFSP has now become part of the EU's supranational jurisdiction, when it stipulates in Art. 2.4 that:

> The Union shall have competence, in accordance with the provisions of the Treaty on European Union, to define and implement a common foreign and security policy, including the progressive framing of a common defence policy.

However, the actual conduct of the CFSP is dealt with in the TEU. There, the intergovernmental structure of the CFSP is immediately obvious. Art. 22 TEU states that the European Council (EC), i.e. the Heads of State and Government, the EC's President and the President of the Commission (Art. 15.2 TEU), is the core institution. The EC "identifies the strategic interests and objectives of the Union" (Art. 22.1 TEU). The Council, in this context as the Foreign Affairs Council, "elaborates" the EU's foreign policy subject to the strategic guidelines laid down by the EC (Art. 16.6.3 TEU). All of this happens in a rather complex procedure laid down in Art. 31 TEU. The principal procedure is decision by unanimity (Art. 31.1 TEU). Where, exceptionally, a majority decision is possible, there are safeguard clauses defending the interests of objecting member states.

Arts. 235.1.3 and 238.4 TFEU 47.7 are also noteworthy in this context. Both stipulate for the EC and the regular (here: Foreign Affairs) Council that "abstentions by Members present in person or represented shall not prevent the adoption by the Council of acts which require unanimity". It was on this basis that the Hungarian Prime Minister twice left the room so that voting could go ahead on crucially important questions concerning Ukraine and the opening of EU accession talks in December 2023.[29]

The example illustrates the institutional difficulties for the EU to make CFSP decisions. The double layer of strategic impetus by the heads of state and government in the European Council, coupled with unanimity requirements in the more operative Foreign Relations Council at the ministerial level, makes it very difficult for the EU to speak with one voice and almost impossible to speak with one voice quickly. The frustration at this state of affairs was tangible in a piece published by Gabrielius Landsbergis, a former minister of foreign affairs of Lithuania, where he claimed that Hungary "blocks more than half of the EU's foreign policy decisions" and asks whether the EU will "allow one state, acting against the interests of all, to repeatedly hold the union to ransom?". He then proceeds to suggest talking steps under Art. 7 TEU to invoke the imposition of sanctions such as the suspension of Hungary's voting rights.[30] Art. 7 TEU does indeed provide a procedure to sanction renegade member states, but it is tied to very important but also very general values espoused in Art. 2 TEU. Those values of "respect for human dignity, freedom, democracy, equality, the rule of law and respect for human rights, including the

[28] The European Union (2025b).

[29] See Von Der Burchard (2023).

[30] Landsbergis (2025).

rights of persons belonging to minorities" are hardly capable of capturing dissent on matters of foreign policy, absent perhaps the most extreme of scenarios where a lone position by a member state would manifestly be outside anything humanely conceivable as a serious political choice. As much frustration as Orbán might cause, his position regarding the Russian aggression or, for that matter, opinions voiced by other EU statesmen in regard to matters of the Israel/Gaza or Israel/Iran conflicts may draw well-founded and very strong responses but that is not nearly enough to invoke Art. 7 one way or another to overcome the institutional difficulties of the CFSP.

It is not surprising that matters are, from a one-voice perspective, even worse when it comes to military matters. The maintaining and use of military capabilities, most prominently, of course, the deployment of military forces in war scenarios with tangible risks of human casualties, is arguably the most central element of state sovereignty. To relinquish control over such foundational issues to a supranational body is politically incredibly difficult, even if there was a strong opinion that significant supranationalisation were needed even in this space. That is the prime difference between the US and the EU. The entering of the US into a potentially protracted ("never ending") war is, at the time of writing, hotly debated after the US attacked Iranian nuclear sites on 22 June 2025 in direct support of Israel's efforts to curtail Iran's nuclear arms ambitions. But that debate in the US is entirely a centralized foreign and security policy debate taking place on the national level and involving mainly the head of the executive branch, President Trump and a few top members of the US Congress. The debate will likely remain controversial and probably continue into future potential conflicts but it will not be a question where representatives from California, Texas, New York or some other state will contribute in that particular regional capacity to the discourse and even if they did, they would not hold any institutional sway over the decision being made. It is difficult to see the French President, the German Chancellor or any head of state or government of at least the larger EU member states playing a similar non-role as representatives of their countries in a EU context dealing with the EU going to war.

3.3.2 Common Security and Defence Policy (CSDP)

This reality is translated in Art. 42 TEU, which addresses the Common Security and Defence Policy[31] as a subset of the CFSP. Art. 42.2 TEU points to the evolutionary nature of this policy when it stipulates that "the common security and defence policy shall include the progressive framing of a common Union defence policy". The provision also makes it clear that EU common defence is not to interfere or compete with NATO obligations. Subsection 4 prescribes unanimity for policy decisions, including those initiating a mission. The linkage to NATO and the unanimity

[31] For a more detailed overview of CSPD evolution and initiatives, see Krentz (2025).

requirement demonstrates that the member states are in charge and that the EU is a subsidiary player, a kind of forum for the EU member states to conduct policy and juggle the need to strengthen the European pillar of NATO, maintain the "supremacy" of NATO given the weight of the US and at the same time integrate the EU member states which are not NATO members, Austria, Ireland, Malta and Cyprus.[32] One consequence of the Russian aggression was that in June 2022, Denmark by referendum abolished its opt-out from the CSDP which it had carved out in the negotiations leading to the Maastricht Treaty in 1992.[33]

Art. 42.7 TEU is noteworthy because it contains a mutual defence clause "if a Member State is the victim of armed aggression on its territory".[34] Curiously, the clause emphasises the point being made here of the dominant role of the states because the assistance for the attacked member state does not come from the EU; instead, "the other Member States shall have towards it an obligation of aid and assistance by all the means in their power". The reason is simple—military assets are exclusively in the hands of the states and not the EU. Collective defence requires structures and interoperability, which exist in the NATO context but not in the context of Art. 42.7 TEU.[35] The clause is therefore more of a theoretical or symbolic nature but could become legally relevant if a non-NATO member of the EU were subject to such an attack. Sweden and Finland clearly did not want to rely solely on Art. 42.7 TEU and recently joined NATO in the face of Russian aggression.[36]

Notwithstanding the dominance of the member states, steps have been undertaken to better enable foreign policy action, especially in reaction to the Russian aggression in Ukraine.[37] The European Council reacted swiftly with its Versailles Declaration of 11 March 2022,[38] roughly 2 weeks after the full-fledged Russian invasion in Ukraine on 24 February 2022. This declaration embodies the identification of the strategic interests and objectives of the Union, as intended by Art. 22.1 TEU. In the Versailles Declaration, the EC addressed three key dimensions, bolstering defence capabilities (especially by substantially increasing defence expenditure and industrial collaboration), reducing energy dependencies and building a more robust economic base.[39] It is safe to conclude that the similarities to the objectives expressed by French President Macron[40] are not merely coincidental. One major outcome of this process was the formal adoption of the Strategic Compass for

[32] See Lynes (2025).

[33] EU Information Centre (2025).

[34] See also the solidarity clause in Art. 222 TFEU in case of terrorist attacks or natural or man-made disasters.

[35] Virkunnen (2022).

[36] See Brooke-Holland (2024).

[37] For more detail see Genini (2025).

[38] Versailles Declaration (2022).

[39] Ibid, at 3.

[40] See Macron, *supra*, n. 2 and n. 10.

Security and Defence in March of 2022.[41] That included as one key deliverable objective the creation, by 2025, an EU Rapid Deployment Capacity (RDC) "that will allow us to swiftly deploy a modular force of up to 5000 troops, including land, air and maritime components."[42] That capacity has now become operational.[43] From today's perspective, one might be inclined to underrate this development. On the eve of the NATO summit in June 2025 where member states of the alliance intend to pledge an increase in their defence efforts to 5% of GDP when in 2022 hardly any NATO-member had even reached the earlier 2% threshold agreed on in 2014 and to be reached in 2024 a rather meagre RDC might not sound impressive.[44] But it is arguably the first major EU active military unit of sorts, notwithstanding the fact that its operational structure is still very much member state focussed and rests on member state contributions. Its somewhat opaque command structure—according to explanatory documents the "preferred command and control structure for the EU RDC" is the Military Planning and Conduct Capability[45] established in 2017 under the EEAS[46]—is another indication of the nascency of this new development of an EU fighting force under EU command.[47]

That said, it is nonetheless noticeable that the European Commission and especially the President of the Commission has gained significant visibility and stature, particularly in light of the Ukraine crisis. The Commission's role in developing the now 17 sanction packages[48] has been remarkable, notwithstanding the fact that trade as such is one of the areas of exclusive EU jurisdiction.[49] Trade sanctions are not only trade matters; Art. 215 TFEU deals with restrictive trade measures and explicitly links such restrictive measures to the CFSP provisions in the TEU (in particular the procedural regime of Art. 24 TEU), which, as stipulated above, safeguard the

---

[41] Council of the European Union (2022).

[42] Ibid, at 14.

[43] European Union External Action (2025).

[44] See, for example, the scathing critique by Witney (2022).

[45] See, for example, EEAS (2025).

[46] A concrete example of what this looks like is the Council Decision (EU) 2017/971 of 8 June 2017 determining the planning and conduct arrangements for EU non-executive military CSDP missions and amending Decisions 2010/96/CFSP on a European Union military mission to contribute to the training of Somali security forces, 2013/34/CFSP on a European Union military mission to contribute to the training of the Malian armed forces (EUTM Mali) and (CFSP) 2016/610 on a European Union CSDP military training mission in the Central African Republic (EUTM RCA), http://data.europa.eu/eli/dec/2017/971/oj. According to Art. 1 "the responsibility for the operational planning and conduct of EU non-executive military missions at the military strategic level shall be assigned to the Director of the Military Planning and Conduct Capability (MPCC)."

[47] For more info supporting a more sceptical view of the Strategic Compass and the RDC see Genini, *supra*, n. 37, at 3 et seq.

[48] European Council (2025b) with a list of the measures adopted at the end. The various measures can be found in the Official Journal L 2025 of 20/5/2025, https://eur-lex.europa.eu/oj/daily-view/L-series/default.html?&ojDate=20052025. Accessed 27 August 2025. See also the EU Sanctions Tracker (n.d.).

[49] Art. 3.1(e), 207 et seq. TFEU.

position of the member states. The steering and coordinating role of Commission President Ursula van der Leyen was probably as unprecedented in EU history as the extent of the ongoing crises stoked by the Russian aggression.[50]

3.3.3 Brief Excursion: The European Parliament and the Latest Developments Concerning Trade and Tariffs

The dictum above that trade sanctions are not only trade matters can easily be broadened to trade is not only a trade matter. Recent developments justify this brief excursion as it will shed at least a little light on the role of the EP and, perhaps, on the shrinking relevance of law as an instrument versus the rise of the executive political "deal".

CFSP decision-making is characterised by the European Parliament's rather marginalised role. Parliament's involvement is largely confined to consultation and information rights under Article 36 TEU rather than the co-decision procedures that characterise other EU policy areas, notwithstanding the Parliament's limited budgetary powers under Article 41 TEU and Article 314 TFEU. Whether that is a good or a bad idea is a question beyond the scope of this paper. However, it should be noted that the allocation of powers in this area is something that is generally in flux, in what appears to be an overall tendency to strengthen executive power. In the US, there is an argument whether the setting of tariffs is actually a congressional power and whether it can be abdicated to the executive branch, i.e., the President.[51] One could more generally ask whether foreign policy should be run executively or not. But unlike the US (and be it only because of congressional abdication under current majorities), in the EU the relatively weak role of the Parliament does not strengthen the Commission and its President; it strengthens the member states and thus often incentivises disunity. The treaties seek to combat that to some degree with the "Provisions on Enhanced Cooperation" in Article 20 TEU and Articles 326–334 TFEU. The Parliament is largely not involved when it comes to enhanced cooperation in the foreign policy arena, as Article 329.2 TFEU clearly stipulates. Not to mention that any enhanced cooperation by any group of at least nine member states (Article 20.2 TEU) lowers the political weight of what is happening because the disunity is inherently visible. That also explains why, in Article 20.2 TEU, enhanced cooperation in the CFSP area is regarded as "a last resort".

Trade, however, is legally a different matter altogether. Trade might also be foreign policy, but not all foreign policy is trade—at least until the reality on the ground no longer cares about such fine distinctions. Article 218 TFEU creates a much larger footprint for the European Parliament. Under Article 218.6(a)(v) all classical trade

[50] Cf. Håkansson (2024).

[51] For a good overview, see Silverberg (2021).

treaties (FTAs and the like, Article 207.3 TFEU) require the assent of the EP. In the US, the same would apply for the Senate under the advice and consent requirement of Article II.2(2) of the US Constitution. It follows that the "massive trade deal" recently "agreed" between the EU Commission President Ursula von der Leyen and US President Donald Trump, with its 15% tariff baseline for most goods, USD 750 billion in energy purchases by the EU[52] and "new investments" of USD 600 billion, both within 3 years,[53] is not a legal thing at all, as the EU Commission made abundantly clear in its press statement.[54] The qualification as a "political deal" and soft law instrument was confirmed by the subsequent development of that "deal" into a "framework of an agreement", which uses words like "intend to", or "commit to …" "… cooperate" or "… discuss" or which formulates certain expectations, for example, around investment levels of European companies in the US.[55] From a legal perspective, both the "deal" and the "framework for an agreement" might raise finer points around good faith in future negotiations towards achieving these goals, should a legal instrument (a trade treaty) ever be pursued. The EU has control only over the tariff component in procedures contingent on the member states and the EP. What is to be expected is that the matter will, for the time being, remain in the political sphere, rendering questions of institutional participation and power distribution largely irrelevant.

3.4 The Internal Status Quo of the EU: Renationalisation on the Rise?

It is perhaps not surprising that a look at the external challenges reveals the strong position of the member states vis-à-vis the EU, despite gains on the EU side, most noticeable perhaps in the significant rise in the perception and status of the President of the Commission.

In EU domestic politics, the two dominant challenges were the COVID pandemic and the migration and refugee crises. The global financial crisis is a bit further back, but still has pertinent repercussions today, especially because major courts—the European Court of Justice (ECJ) or the German Federal Constitutional Court (GFCC) had opportunities to speak to the constitutional relationship between the EU and its member states.

---

[52] In 2024, the EU imported 100 billion cubic meters of LNG, which roughly equates to 48 billion metric tonnes, and roughly 45 billion cubic meters (45%) of that came from the US, see European Council (2025c); The EU spent a total of EUR 215 on LNG imports from 2022 to 2024, with 2022 prices more than double those in 2024: Jaller-Makarewicz (2025).

[53] The White House (2025).

[54] "The political agreement of 27 July 2025 is not legally binding. Beyond taking the immediate actions committed, the EU and the US will further negotiate, in line with their relevant internal procedures, to fully implement the political agreement:" European Commission (2025b).

[55] European Commission (2025c).

3.4.1 Background

It is worthwhile to place the internal development of the EU into a broader framework. The foundation treaty of Rome was concluded in 1957. It took 30 years for matters to sufficiently settle for the first major amendments to come about in the 1986 amending treaty under the name of the Single European Act, which aimed to conclude the EEC's (as it was then known) internal market after the transitional period had expired in 1969 with the monumental but insufficient establishment of the customs union as the first major step. That amendment held through the oil crises in the 70s until 1992, when the Treaty of Maastricht expanded the integration project historically by creating the EU, adding the CFSP and creating the common currency. Four years later, in 2001, came the Treaty of Nice, and after the failed attempt to consolidate matters into a European Constitution, came, for the time being, finally, the Treaty of Luxembourg, adding further incremental institutional and structural reforms. Constitutionally speaking, the latest significant expansion of EU "constitutional", i.e., based on treaty amendments, power came with the Maastricht Treaty, now 35 years ago.[56]

The EU is not alone in this respect. Kreuder-Sonnen and Zangl found that there have not been any "treaty-based transfers of authority to IOs", be it by treaty amendment or by creating new IOs.[57] At the same time, Kreuder-Sonnen and Zangl observe that this "treaty-based stagnation" is accompanied by instances of "informal internationalisation" of authority on the one hand, and "unilateral renationalisation" on the other.[58] That can be shown for the EU as well, and the examples the two authors cite, the ECB's role in the European Debt crisis or the UK's "Brexit" from the EU, are potent examples indeed, but perhaps not the only ones. Brexit was, of course, the most tangible, significant and tragic renationalisation effort at least in EU history. On a constitutional level, however, the open revolt of the GFCC and the Polish Constitutional Court on the supremacy of EU law also fits the bill.

---

[56] A chronological overview of all the treaties is available at Eur-Lex: https://eur-lex.europa.eu/collection/eu-law/treaties/treaties-overview.html. Accessed 27 August 2025. Between the Treaties of Rome and the Single European Act 1986 were two smaller amendments, the Merger Treaty 1965 merging the institutions of the three communities, and the Treaty Amending Certain Budgetary Provisions in 1970 (sometimes also referred to as the Treaty of Luxembourg), putting the EEC's finances on a new footing and strengthening the role of Parliament in that regard.

[57] Kreuder-Sonnen and Zangl (2025).

[58] Ibid.

3.4.2 *"Informal Internationalisation" or Exercising Enumerated Powers?*

Whether the informal internationalisation moniker is a befitting descriptor depends on the point of view. From a legal perspective, it is well established that an IO as a collective of its member states can do whatever is covered by the purposes it is entitled to pursue under its foundation treaty. Even if that treaty is silent on specific powers allocated to this IO, under the implied powers doctrine, it is to be assumed, barring indications to the contrary, that the IO has been given the powers to do what it is supposed to do. In the EU, the implied powers doctrine in Art. 352 TFEU[59] (and especially the preceding provisions) played a substantial role and caused particular difficulties, especially in federally organised member states, because there were fears that the carefully calibrated allocation of power between the member states and the EU on the one hand and between the European Parliament and the Council (member states) in the EU legislative process could be somewhat undermined by reverting to the implied powers. These difficulties have now largely been overcome, mainly because what might have been qualified as implied powers have become explicit powers of the EU over the various treaty amendments. What remains is that the principle of enumerated powers, emphasis on enumeration as opposed to implication, is even stronger in the EU, consequently leaving less space for implied powers. At least in the EU context, internationalisation cannot be informal *stricto sensu*. The intra-EU internationalisation must, by definition, be based on authority based in the treaties. Whatever the ECB did, to pick up on Kreuder Sonnen's example mentioned above, it could only have done it if covered by the powers allocated to it in the treaties. If there were no such powers or if existing powers had been applied wrongly, the ECB's acts, or those of any other EU institution, would have been *ultra vires* and void. Rather than qualifying this as "informal internationalisation", in substance, what happened was making use of already internationalised powers in ways not seen or necessary before.

3.4.3 *The GFCC and "Quantitative Easing": An Attempt to Renationalise?*

The constitutional cornerstone of the EU is the supremacy of EU law. From its inception,[60] the ECJ was given the power to interpret the provisions of the founding treaties[61] and the Court inferred what is the only logical conclusion: if one creates a

---

[59] See Calliess and Ruffert (2022).

[60] See Silverberg, *supra*, n. 51.

[61] See Art. 19.1 of the Treaty on European Union (TEU): "The Court of Justice of the European Union shall include the Court of Justice, the General Court and specialised courts. It shall ensure that in the interpretation and application of the Treaties the law is observed." (text available at

treaty-based legal system and, as part of it, a Court with the power to interpret the law thus created then that law must be equally relevant in all member states as interpreted by the ECJ. For that to happen, that law must be hierarchically supreme and, in case of norm conflicts, prevail over all law of the member states.[62] The logic behind the supremacy doctrine is strikingly simple and very similar to the approach taken by the Australian Constitution in Section 109. That notwithstanding, the supremacy doctrine of EU law was never fully accepted by all member states but had always been upheld in practice. The point of contention always was the distribution of power between the EU and the member states and the question, who determines the extent of the transfer of power to the EU. The national (constitutional) court, when interpreting the legal acts by which that power was transferred, or the ECJ, when constructing the provisions into which the intended power transfer had been translated when the EU foundation treaties had been formulated. Or, to formulate differently, who is the final arbiter of disputes over power—the giver (the member states) or the receiver (the EU)?

In 2020, the GFCC, after a long history of threats, openly challenged the European Union's claim to the supremacy of EU law over national laws.[63] The GFCC used the controversy over a particular monetary policy issue known as "quantitative easing" (QE).[64] Critics claimed this policy was tantamount to "money printing" and hence was inherently inflationary. Critics also argued that QE's main goal, to lower interest rates and stimulate the economy, was harmful to pensioners and savers, thus pushing these groups towards riskier investments. On these grounds, the ECB interventions in the bond markets[65] were challenged as unlawful in Germany before the GFCC. As required by Art. 267.3 TFEU, the GFCC referred its reservations about the European Central Bank's (ECB) actions to the Court of Justice of the European Union (ECJ) via the preliminary ruling procedure.[66] In doing so, the GFCC made its views quite clear that the controversial ECB interventions could hardly be regarded as compatible with the EU treaties.[67] Nonetheless, the ECJ had the audacity to uphold the ECB's actions despite the GFCC's lecturing.[68] The GFCC took the gauntlet, rejected the ECJ's preliminary ruling and declared the ECJ's ruling *ultra vires*. The GFCC called the ECJ's decision "not

https://eur-lex.europa.eu/legal-content/EN/TXT/?uri=uriserv:OJ.C_.2016.202.01.0001.01.ENG#C_2016202EN.01001301. Accessed 27 August 2025).

[62] ECJ (1964).

[63] GFCC (BVerfG), Judgment of 5 May 2020—2 BvR 859/15, https://www.bverfg.de/e/rs20200505_2bvr085915en. Accessed 27 August 2025.

[64] For the following see also Bröhmer (2025).

[65] See European Central Bank (2025).

[66] GFCC (BVerfG), Order of 18 July 2017, 2 BvR 859/15, https://www.bverfg.de/e/rs20170718_2bvr085915en. Accessed 27 August 2025.

[67] Ibid, paras. 76 et seq., especially paras. 80, 114.

[68] ECJ, Case C-493/17, Heinrich Weiss and Others, https://eur-lex.europa.eu/legal-content/EN/TXT/?uri=CELEX:62017CN0493. Accessed 27 August 2025.

comprehensible" and argued it lacked grounding in the EU Treaties.[69] In the halls of higher justice, that was nothing short of a (judicial) affront of Trumpian proportions.

Practically, the GFCC's deviation and thus rejection of the EU law supremacy doctrine had no effect at all. In and by itself, what happened could be regarded as the quintessential storm in a teacup. Or, if one takes a more benign view, an attempt to "teach" the EU institutions, via the ECJ, that they need to stay grounded and heed the member states (and their constitutional courts). However, the stakes are much higher. The matter goes to the constitutional heart of the EU, the planet's only deeply integrated, highly complex, rule of law-based, and hitherto exceptionally successful, transnational political project.

The matter was effectively closed when, in June of 2020, the German Federal Parliament revisited the matter and, together with instruments provided by the ECB, resolved that the proportionality concerns expressed by the GFCC were now resolved, and the GFCC, in a different but related matter, endorsed this view expressly.[70] As a result, the EU Commission closed the treaty infringement procedure it had invoked against Germany, noting that Germany had issued formal commitments "clearly recognising the primacy of EU law and the authority of the Court of Justice of the European Union." The Commission underlined the seriousness of the transgression by further emphasizing that "the German government, explicitly referring to its duty of loyal cooperation enshrined in the Treaties, commits to use all the means at its disposal to avoid, in the future, a repetition of an *ultra vires* finding, and take an active role in that regard".[71]

Of course, the German government, as in the executive and legislative branches, can do literally nothing short of amending the Constitution (*Grundgesetz*) to keep the GFCC in bounds if the court decided to go on the warpath. And depending on how such a scenario might unfold, even such a constitutional amendment could be challenged under Art. 79.3 Grundgesetz. In the light of recent examples in the US, Israel, Poland, or Hungary, one cannot help but hope that all constitutional actors, in this case both on the EU and German side, exercise the restraint necessary to keep complex constitutional frameworks running smoothly.

What remains is that this marked the first time an important national court went into open rebellion and rendered a decision departing from the foundational principle of the supremacy doctrine of EU law. The supremacy of EU law had been openly rejected by one of the national judicial powerhouses of the EU. The nationalist dark forces were watching closely and with glee. A pillar of transnational decision-making is under threat again.

---

[69] GFCC (BVerfG), Judgment of 5 May 2020—2 BvR 859/15, para. 116. https://www.bverfg.de/e/rs20200505_2bvr085915en. Accessed 27 August 2025.

[70] See BVerfG, 29 April 2021—2 BvR 1651/15, paras. 89 et seq. http://www.bverfg.de/e/rs20210429_2bvr165115en.html. para. 116.

[71] European Commission (2021a).

3.4.4 *Poland: An Attempt to Renationalise?*

Poland's right-wing government has pursued policies undermining EU values, particularly the rule of law, as outlined in Art. 2 TEU. Since 2015, reforms affecting judicial independence, including the annulment of judicial nominations to the Polish Constitutional Tribunal, led to the EU initiating the Art. 7 TEU procedure,[72] which could suspend Poland's EU participation rights.[73] On 15 July 2021, the ECJ ruled that Poland violated TEU guarantees by allowing judicial decisions to be treated as disciplinary offences, threatening judicial impartiality (ECJ 2021).[74]

On 7 October 2021, Poland's Constitutional Tribunal declared Art. 1 and 19 TEU incompatible with the Polish Constitution,[75] asserting the supremacy of domestic law and challenging Poland's ability to function as a sovereign state (Petersen and Wasilczyk 2022).[76] This decision, a "judicial insurrection," inverts the EU legal order, undermines the rule of law and has the potential to create a constitutional crisis. Third-party powers, both still regarded as allies, like the US, and strategic competitors (China) or even adversaries (Russia), will feel empowered in their attempts to double down on *divide et impera*-style relationship management. After the change of government in Poland in 2023, the Commission closed the Art. 7 procedure with Poland.[77] This might yet prove to be premature because not all of the (necessary) counter-reforms thought necessary to undo the work of the previous regime in Poland have been put in place. The recent election of hardline nationalist President Karol Nawrocki on 1 June 2025,[78] who is affiliated with the previous nationalist PiS regime, has all but ensured that any progress in this area will be all but impossible. The treaty infringement procedure that had been brought against the country[79] after its challenge to the supremacy of EU law is still pending. The AG Spielmann delivered his opinion in March 2025 and—unsurprisingly—found, that Poland violated the primacy of EU law and did so via a Court, Poland's Constitutional Court no less, which "does not satisfy the requirements of an independent and impartial tribunal previously established by law as a result of irregularities in the procedures for the appointment of three judges to that court in December 2015 and for the appointment of its President in December 2016."[80]

---

[72] European Commission (2017).

[73] See, for example, Cameron (2021, 2022).

[74] ECJ (Grand Chamber) (2021).

[75] Constitutional Tribunal (2021). For the Polish original see https://trybunal.gov.pl/s/k-3-21. Accessed 27 August 2025.

[76] See also the extensive study by Petersen and Wasilczyk (2022).

[77] European Commission (2024a).

[78] See Ruy (2025).

[79] European Commission (2021b).

[80] CFEU (2025).

3.4.5 The GFCC's Identity Restraint

The GFCC's aberration on the supremacy of EU law is inherently tied to its decades-long struggle with the ECJ. It began with the principally laudable attempt of the GFCC to secure adequate fundamental rights and liberty standards in the light of intensifying European integration and transnational decision-making by EU (EEC/EC) organs. The flip side of that transnationalisation was the growing potential of EU acts, legislative and executive, to impact individuals. Unlike the member states' constitutions, the foundation treaties of the EU did not initially provide affected individuals or corporations with the substantial and procedural fundamental rights they enjoyed vis-à-vis member states' governmental acts. There was no "bill of rights" in the foundation treaties. The ECJ overcame this by resorting to the international law concept of general principles of (EU) common to all member states and adding to that concept the further important aspect that all member states are also part of the European Convention on Human Rights. It is a moot question whether the ECJ required the help of the GFCC to develop fundamental rights protection in this way or whether it would have done so anyway. Either way, the GFCC's approach was never compatible with the ECJ's supremacy approach. However, the rivalry remained but never turned virulent—the ECJ's supremacy doctrine stood in practice—until, as shown above, it no longer stood.[81]

Matters became more problematic after the Treaty of Maastricht when the noble cause of defending individual freedoms "as long as" the ECJ is unable to do so adequately turned into the potentially more disruptive cause of jealously ensuring that the EU operates tightly within the bounds set by transfer of powers afforded to it by the German Parliament, whose mandate to transfer powers elsewhere is regulated by the German Constitution (Grundgesetz) the ultimate guardian of which is the GFCC.

This guardianship, which in the GFCC's view has nothing to do with the guardianship of the ECJ over the EU treaties,[82] is different in nature. The "as long as" approach was always a bridge to cover a gap that was eventually closed, first by the ECJ's general principles approach and, since the Treaty of Lisbon entered into force in 2009, by the EU Charter of Fundamental Rights.[83]

[81] See the famous "as long as" ("Solange") decisions of the GFCC (BVerfG), BvL 52/71, 29/5/1974, BVerfGE 37, 271 (text available in German only) https://www.servat.unibe.ch/dfr/bv037271.html. Accessed 27 August 2025; (extensive) English excerpts headnote; BVerfG, 2 BvR 197/83, 22/10/1986, BVerfGE 73, 339 available at https://law.utexas.edu/transnational/foreign-law-translations/german/case.php?id=588. Accessed 27 August 2025; See further (text available in German only) https://www.servat.unibe.ch/dfr/bv073339.html. Accessed 27 August 2025; See also headnote 2 (extensive) English excerpts available at https://law.utexas.edu/transnational/foreign-law-translations/german/case.php?id=572. Accessed 27 August 2025.

[82] As stipulated by the GFCC in its Maastricht decision, see BVerfGE 89, 155 at 187–8 as translated in 33 I.L.M 388 at 422–3.

[83] European Union (2016).

The new *ultra vires* guardianship will always be there, because any exercise of power by EU organs can bring up the *ultra vires* question and when that question arises it will likely be around matters of foundational importance for the question here at issue: regionalisation by allowing for transnational, integrated decision-making or (re-)nationalisation by emphasising member state control. The tragedy lies in the fact that, on one level, this conflict is a classic conflict in multilevel governance. The conflict is important; the power distribution between the centre and the periphery must be continuously challenged. At the same time, this conflict has the potential to destroy the EU or at least significantly diminish its potential. And what is worse, there is no solution in sight.

The GFCC, in its decision on the constitutionality of the Lisbon Treaty, has created a test for this ongoing task—identity review.[84] The starting parameters for this identity review sound somewhat inconspicuous: to be integration-friendly and to safeguard principles of the Grundgesetz, which everybody will subscribe to, and which are very similar to the TEU's principles in Art. 2 TEU.[85] But the court does not leave it there. Identity review is much more than that and potentially stifling:

> cc) European unification on the basis of a treaty union of sovereign states may, however, not be achieved in such a way that not sufficient space is left to the Member States for the political formation of the economic, cultural and social living conditions. This applies in particular to areas which shape the citizens' living conditions, in particular the private sphere of their own responsibility and of political and social security, protected by fundamental rights, as well as to political decisions that rely especially on cultural, historical and linguistic perceptions and which develop in public discourse in the party political and parliamentary sphere of public politics. Essential areas of democratic formative action comprise, *inter alia, citizenship, the civil and the military monopoly on the use of force, revenue and expenditure including external financing and all elements of encroachment that are decisive for the realisation of fundamental rights, above all in major encroachments on fundamental rights such as deprivation of liberty in the administration of criminal law or placement in an institution.* These important areas also include cultural issues such as the disposition of language, the shaping of circumstances concerning the family and education, the ordering of the freedom of opinion, press and of association and the dealing with the profession of faith or ideology.[86]

The GFCC's sweeping definition of this identity review provokes the core question: how could, assuming the political will were there, the EU achieve the "sovereignty" goals formulated by President Macron? These goals did not include the abolishment of the French Republic into a European federal entity. They were about safeguarding European competitiveness, creating the ability to jointly deter foreign adversaries and keep the peace, develop the EU as a global player that is taken seriously on the world stage and not merely a stooge of US President Trump, as so vividly

---

[84] BVerfG, 2 BvE 2/08, 30/6/2009, http://www.bverfg.de/e/es20090630_2bve000208en.html. Accessed 27 August 2025.

[85] Ibid, at para. 240.

[86] BVerfG, 2 BvE 2/08, 30/6/2009, para. 249, italics added. http://www.bverfg.de/e/es20090630_2bve000208en.html. Accessed 27 August 2025.

displayed at the recent NATO summit[87] (not only by NATO General-Secretary Mark Rutte),[88] defend the European social model and find ways to raise the money to pay for it all. All of these objectives within the identity realm created by the GFCC, therefore, cannot be in the hands of the EU, and are not even at the disposal of the German executive or legislative branches of government, because the constitutional identity of Germany is ultimately under the control of the GFCC. If taken seriously and at face value, this kind of identity control is an act of self-castration; a legal counter-equivalent of what MAGA stands for in the US: Keep the EU small. The irony is that the flip side of the coin is not strong member states. Rather, the flipside is fragmentation, strategic emaciation and the relegation of Europe and its states as vassals of hegemonic powers. Small may be beautiful in the face of the US/China duopoly, enriched with considerable destructive force from Russia and other dubious players, is the very reason for Macron's call to arms to create a sovereign Europe, sovereign in substance, not necessarily sovereign in the legal sense. In a world of smaller and medium powers such as the EU member states, or, for example, Australia, Japan, South American, African and Asian states this approach may well have been necessary. In this new world, it creates potentially irresponsible constraints.

3.5 Ancient Greece: Europe's Future?

Many years ago, in the late 1980s, the late German intellectual and Social-Democrat Peter Glotz gave a presentation at my Alma Mater, the University of Mannheim, in which he warned that Europe is at risk of becoming what happened to ancient Greece after the rise of Rome. Ancient Greece became a cultural focus point, an intellectual playground for philosophies and philosophers, a tourist destination with pretty castles and landscapes.[89] In a recent interview with the New York Times, German-US billionaire investor and "contrarian" (to avoid attributes like hard-right, alt-right, reactionary, libertarianism or authoritarianism) intellectual Peter Thiel discussed his view of the world.[90] One of his central themes is the threat of stagnation. For Thiel, stagnation is economic stagnation (growth, productivity), cultural stagnation (risk averseness, overregulation, pessimism, lack of innovation) and limited ambition. In his view, stagnation is a danger generally, but he regards Europe as a stagnation leader, "declining and decaying". Regarding Europe, Thiel, controversial as he certainly is, has a point that latches on to Peter Glotz's "*Graecia Capta*"

---

[87] NATO (2025).

[88] See Addley (2025).

[89] See Alock (1993). The term "*Graecia Capta*" goes back to Horace's The Epistles, Book II, Epistle I, para 156–181—The Latin Drama, English translation at https://www.poetryintranslation.com/PITBR/Latin/HoraceEpistlesBkIIEpI.php?textLinkTarget=aG9yYWNl#anchor_Toc98154295. Accessed 27 August 2025.

[90] New York Times (2025).

thought. The stagnation risks are clear and present dangers in all European countries. President Macron's speeches are manifestos against a similarly perceived stagnation.

However, Thiel overlooks the important aspect of cultural/political stagnation. The major challenge for the West as a whole, including and perhaps even more for the EU, is the ability to formulate a governance system that manages to create unity where necessary and fruitful, and maintain diversity and decentralisation, at the same time. It cannot be overlooked that the US is at the brink of a major rupture; it is an open question whether it can pull itself together. But the US is not a conglomerate of self-aggrandising sovereign nations. Hence, the manifest extreme domestic polarisation in the US does not immediately translate into fragmented external relations and a geo-strategic void. On the contrary, the polarising "America First" moniker at home is, to some degree, drawing oxygen from a (more) unified "America First" position of ruthless transactionalism and isolationism. In the EU, by contrast, similar polarisation can be observed within the member states, reinforcing the risks of an already much more difficult geo-strategic positioning. Whether under these circumstances the external common interests can be bundled in a coherent CFSP of the EU is an open question.

In a way, stagnation is also the central theme of the 2024 Draghi Reports.[91] The reports, in essence, outline areas where significant changes or reforms are needed if the EU wants to successfully pursue its ambitions regarding social inclusion, climate change (carbon neutrality), and, more generally, geopolitical relevance. The gaps identified are enormous and stretch from an innovation and productivity gap to high energy costs, strategic dependencies from raw materials, to financing and capital markets shortcomings, to dramatic overregulation. Draghi illustrates the latter by pointing out that "around 3,500 pieces of legislation were enacted and around 2,000 resolutions were passed in the US at the federal level over the past three Congress mandates (2019–2024). During the same period, around 13,000 acts were passed by the EU."[92] One must not forget that member states are also active in the regulatory space. It is also quite impressive to see in both parts of the report and especially in Part B, how central the word "fragmentation" is. Market fragmentation (single market, capital markets), sector fragmentation (energy, defence, space) and regulatory fragmentation (in telecommunications, pharma, foreign direct investment (FDI) screening and in national policies (duplication, standards).

[91] European Commission (2024b). In-depth analysis and recommendations (Part B). https://commission.europa.eu/document/download/ec1409c1-d4b4-4882-8bdd-3519f86bbb92_en. Accessed 27 August 2025.

[92] Ibid, Part A at 69.

3.6 Conclusion

From a perspective of the challenges lying before it as the most successful transnational integration project in human history, the EU is currently dysfunctional. There are likely two core reasons for this dysfunction. The standard collective action dilemma is one reason. The EU appears to be unable to reform its governance systems, i.e., its own and that of its member states, in such a way as to effectively undertake the profound reform necessary to create a competitive and geostrategically relevant European Union envisaged by Draghi and others as the core of Europe. The second reason is perhaps even more consequential: As far as the challenges mentioned above go, the member states are also, in essence, dysfunctional. The propensity for foundational reforms within the EU's member states is not very high. The prevailing risk averseness and entrenched special interests favour the status quo and the rearranging of deckchairs but not foundational reform. Acute crises such as the war in Ukraine keep leadership and population preoccupied and portray a false sense of unity. The observable difficulties with any reform, even reforms smallish in scale, such as modest elevations of the retirement age in France or cutting diesel subsidies for farmers in Germany, become very hard or even too hard to implement. The governance and leadership crises of the EU and its member states might have to get worse before the strength for reform can prevail. It is an open question whether the EU and its member states will remain a credible player on the world stage or whether the EU and the member states will, in football terms, be relegated to the second league. One thing, though, is certain: going it alone is not an option for the member states.

References

Addley, Esther. 2025. 'Orchestrated Grovel': Critics React to Europe's Attempts to Tame Donald Trump. *The Guardian*. https://www.theguardian.com/us-news/2025/jun/27/critics-react-europe-donald-trump-nato-mark-rutte. Accessed 27 Aug 2025.

Airbus. n.d. Future Combat Air System. https://www.airbus.com/en/products-services/defence/future-combat-air-system-fcas. Accessed 27 Aug 2025.

Alock, Susan E. 1993. *Graecia Capta: The Landscapes of Roman Greece*. Cambridge: Cambridge University Press.

Arms Control Association. n.d. The Joint Comprehensive Plan of Action (JCPOA) at a Glance. https://www.armscontrol.org/factsheets/joint-comprehensive-plan-action-jcpoa-glance. Accessed 27 Aug 2025.

Barrie, Douglas, Bastian Giegerich, Fabian Hoffmann, Amanda Lapo, Charlotte Le Breton, and Ben Schreer. 2022. European Combat Air Power: A Snapshot. Institute for Strategic Studies (IISS). https://www.iiss.org/globalassets/media-library%2D%2D-content%2D%2Dmigration/files/research-papers/2022/03/european-combat-air-power-a-snapshot.pdf. Accessed 27 Aug 2025.

Borrell, Josep. 2021. Taking Action to Protect Our Economic Sovereignty. https://www.eeas.europa.eu/eeas/taking-action-protect-our-economic-sovereignty_en. Accessed 28 Aug 2025.

Bröhmer, Jürgen. 2025. Democracy Deficit or Governance Deficit—The Dilemma of Transnational Decision-Making. In *The Routledge Handbook of Global Sustainability Education and Thinking for the 21st Century*, ed. Michele John, 787–802. New York: Routledge.

Brooke-Holland, Louisa. 2024. NATO Enlargement: Sweden and Finland, House of Commons. https://commonslibrary.parliament.uk/research-briefings/cbp-9574/. Accessed 27 Aug 2025.

Calliess, Christian, and Matthias Ruffert. 2022. *EUV/AEUV*. München: Beck Juristischer Verlag.

Cameron, David R. 2021. *Dispute Between Poland and the EU Over the Courts Escalates with New Constitutional Tribunal Decision*. MacMillan Center. https://macmillan.yale.edu/news/eu-charges-polands-constitutional-tribunal-violating-eu-law. Accessed 27 Aug 2025.

Cameron, David R. 2022. *EU Charges Poland's Constitutional Tribunal with Violating EU Law*. MacMillan Center. https://macmillan.yale.edu/stories/eu-charges-polands-constitutional-tribunal-violating-eu-law. Accessed 27 Aug 2025.

Center for Security and Emerging Technology. 2021. Outline of the People's Republic of China 14th Five-Year Plan (2021–2015) for National Economic and Social Development and Long-Range Objectives for 2035. https://cset.georgetown.edu/publication/china-14th-five-year-plan/. Accessed 27 Aug 2025.

CFEU. 2025. Opinion of Advocate General in Case C-448/23, European Commission v Republic of Poland. https://eur-lex.europa.eu/legal-content/EN/TXT/?uri=CELEX:62023CC0448. Accessed 27 Aug 2025.

CHIPS and Science Act of 2022. 2022. Pub. L. No. 117–167, 136 Stat. 1366 (08/09/2022). https://www.congress.gov/117/plaws/publ167/PLAW-117publ167.pdf. Accessed 27 Aug 2025.

Constitutional Tribunal. 2021. Assessment of the Conformity to the Polish Constitution of Selected Provisions of the Treaty on European Union. https://trybunal.gov.pl/en/hearings/judgments/art/11662-ocena-zgodnosci-z-konstytucja-rp-wybranych-przepisow-traktatu-o-unii-europejskiej. Accessed 27 Aug 2025.

Council of Europe. 2024. EU High Representative for Foreign Affairs and Security Policy. https://www.consilium.europa.eu/en/council-eu/high-representative-foreign-affairs-security-policy/. Accessed 27 Aug 2025; See also The Diplomatic Service of the European Union. 2024. What Does the High Representative/Vice-President Do? https://www.eeas.europa.eu/eeas/high-representative-vice-president_en. Accessed 27 Aug 2025.

Council of the European Union. 2022. Strategic Compass for Security and Defence. https://data.consilium.europa.eu/doc/document/ST-7371-2022-INIT/en/pdf. Accessed 27 Aug 2025.

CSET (Center for Security and Emerging Technology). 2019. The National 13th Five-Year Plan (2016–2020) for the Development of Strategic Emerging Industries. https://cset.georgetown.edu/publication/national-13th-five-year-plan-for-the-development-of-strategic-emerging-industries. Accessed 27 Aug 2025.

DARPA. n.d. Defense Advanced Research Projects Agency (DARPA) Is an Independent Research and Development Agency Within the United States Department of Defense (DOD). https://www.darpa.mil/about. Accessed 27 Aug 2025.

E3 Foreign Ministers. 2019. Joint Statement on the Creation of INSTEX, the Special Purpose Vehicle Aimed at Facilitating Legitimate Trade with Iran in the Framework of the Efforts to Preserve the Joint Comprehensive Plan of Action (JCPOA). https://assets.publishing.service.gov.uk/media/5c542a92e5274a491448483e/19_01_31_Joint_Statement_E3.pdf. Accessed 28 Aug 2025.

ECJ. 1964. Flaminio Costa v E.N.E.L. https://eur-lex.europa.eu/legal-content/EN/TXT/?uri=CELEX:61964CJ0006. Accessed 27 Aug 2025.

ECJ (Grand Chamber). 2021. https://eur-lex.europa.eu/legal-content/EN/TXT/?uri=CELEX:62019CJ0791. Accessed 27 Aug 2025.

EEAS. 2025. European Union Rapid Deployment Capacity. https://www.eeas.europa.eu/eeas/european-union-rapid-deployment-capacity_en. Accessed 27 Aug 2025.

EU External Action Service. 2025. Foreign Affairs Council: Press Remarks by High Representative Kaja Kallas After the Informal Videoconference Meeting. https://www.eeas.europa.eu/

eeas/foreign-affairs-council-press-remarks-high-representative-kaja-kallas-after-informal-videoconference_en. Accessed 27 Aug 2025.

EU Information Centre. 2025. *The Danish Opt-Outs from EU Cooperation*. Danish Parliament. https://www.thedanishparliament.dk/en/eu-information-centre/the-danish-opt-outs-from-eu-cooperation. Accessed 27 Aug 2025.

EU Sanctions Tracker. n.d.. https://data.europa.eu/apps/eusanctionstracker/. Accessed 27 Aug 2025.

European Central Bank. 2025. How Does the ECB's Asset Purchase Programme Work? https://www.ecb.europa.eu/ecb/educational/explainers/tell-me-more/html/app.en.html. Accessed 27 Aug 2025.

European Commission. 2017. Reasoned Proposal in Accordance with Art. 7(1) of the TEU Regarding the Rule of Law in Poland for a Council Decision on the Determination of a Clear Risk of a Serious Breach by the Republic of Poland of the Rule of Law. https://eur-lex.europa.eu/legal-content/EN/TXT/?uri=CELEX:52017PC0835. Accessed 27 Aug 2025.

European Commission. 2021a. December Infringements Package: Key Decisions. https://ec.europa.eu/commission/presscorner/detail/en/inf_21_6201. Accessed 27 Aug 2025.

European Commission. 2021b. Commission Launches Infringement Procedure Against Poland for Violations of EU Law by Its Constitutional Tribunal. https://ec.europa.eu/commission/presscorner/detail/en/ip_21_7070. Accessed 27 Aug 2025.

European Commission. 2024a. Commission Decides to Close the Art. 7(1) TEU Procedure for Poland. https://ec.europa.eu/commission/presscorner/detail/en/mex_24_2986. Accessed 27 Aug 2025.

European Commission. 2024b. The Draghi Report: A Competitiveness Strategy for Europe (Part A). https://commission.europa.eu/document/download/97e481fd-2dc3-412d-be4c-f152a8232961_en. Accessed 27 Aug 2025.

European Commission. 2025a. The Recovery and Resilience Facility. https://commission.europa.eu/business-economy-euro/economic-recovery/recovery-and-resilience-facility_en. Accessed 27 Aug 2025.

European Commission. 2025b. EU-US Trade Deal Explained. https://ec.europa.eu/commission/presscorner/detail/en/qanda_25_1930. Accessed 27 Aug 2025.

European Commission. 2025c. Joint Statement on a United States-European Union Framework on an Agreement on Reciprocal, Fair and Balanced Trade. https://policy.trade.ec.europa.eu/news/joint-statement-united-states-european-union-framework-agreement-reciprocal-fair-and-balanced-trade-2025-08-21_en. Accessed 27 Aug 2025.

European Council. 2025a. SAFE: Council Adopts €150 Billion Boost for Joint Procurement on European Security and Defence. Press release. https://www.consilium.europa.eu/en/press/press-releases/2025/05/27/safe-council-adopts-150-billion-boost-for-joint-procurement-on-european-security-and-defence/. Accessed 27 Aug 2025.

European Council. 2025b. Russia's War of Aggression Against Ukraine: EU Agrees 17th Package of Sanctions. https://www.consilium.europa.eu/en/press/press-releases/2025/05/20/russia-s-war-of-aggression-against-ukraine-eu-agrees-17th-package-of-sanctions/. Accessed 27 Aug 2025.

European Council. 2025c. Where Does the EU's Gas Come From? https://www.consilium.europa.eu/en/infographics/where-does-the-eu-s-gas-come-from/. Accessed 27 Aug 2025.

European Parliament. 2024a. Confirmation Hearings for the European Commission. https://elections.europa.eu/european-commission/en/. Accessed 27 Aug 2025; See also European Parliament. 2024. Kaja Kallas. https://elections.europa.eu/european-commission/en/kallas/. Accessed 27 Aug 2025.

European Parliament. 2024b. Questionnaire to the Commissioner Designate Kaja KALLAS, High Representative for Foreign and Security Policy. https://hearings.elections.europa.eu/documents/kallas/kallas_writtenquestionsandanswers_en.pdf. Accessed 27 Aug 2025.

European Union. 2016. Charter of Fundamental Rights of the European Union. *OJ C 202, 7.6.2016, 389*. http://data.europa.eu/eli/treaty/char_2016/oj. Accessed 27 Aug 2025.

European Union. 2020. Council Regulation (EU) 2020/2094 of 14 December 2020 Establishing a European Union Recovery Instrument to Support the Recovery in the Aftermath of the COVID-19 Crisis. https://eur-lex.europa.eu/eli/reg/2020/2094/oj/eng. Accessed 27 Aug 2025.

European Union. 2025. Council Regulation (EU) 2025/1106 of 27 May 2025 Establishing the Security Action for Europe (SAFE) Through the Reinforcement of the European Defence Industry Instrument. http://data.europa.eu/eli/reg/2025/1106/oj. Accessed 27 Aug 2025.

European Union External Action. 2025. Common Security and Defence Policy: EU Rapid Deployment Capacity Becomes Operational. https://www.eeas.europa.eu/eeas/common-security-and-defence-policy-eu-rapid-deployment-capacity-becomes-operational_en. Accessed 27 Aug 2025.

Foreign, Commonwealth & Development Office. 2020. INSTEX Successfully Concludes First Transaction. https://www.gov.uk/government/news/instex-successfully-concludes-first-transaction. Accessed 27 Aug 2025

Foreign, Commonwealth & Development Office. 2023. The 10 INSTEX Shareholder States Have Decided to Liquidate INSTEX Due to Continued Obstruction from Iran: E3 Statement. https://www.gov.uk/government/news/the-10-instex-shareholder-states-have-decided-to-liquidate-instex-due-to-continued-obstruction-from-iran. Accessed 27 Aug 2025.

Genini, Davide. 2025. How the War in Ukraine Has Transformed the EU's Common Foreign and Security Policy. *Yearbook of European Law*. https://doi.org/10.1093/yel/yeaf003

Håkansson, Calle. 2024. The Ukraine War and the Emergence of the European Commission as a Geopolitical Actor. *Journal of European Integration* 46:25–45.

Hunter, Tom. 2025. Credit Claiming in the European Union. *The Journal of Politics* 87:889–904.

Inflation Reduction Act of 2022. 2022. Pub. L. No. 117–169, 136 Stat. 1818 (2022), https://www.congress.gov/117/plaws/publ169/PLAW-117publ169.pdf. Accessed 27 Aug 2025.

Issing, Otmar. 2020. The COVID-19 Crisis: A Hamilton Moment for the European Union? *International Finance* 23:340–347.

Jaller-Makarewicz, Ana Maria. 2025. *Déjà vu as EU risks Overreliance on One Gas Supplier*. Institute for Energy Economics and Financial Analysis. https://ieefa.org/resources/deja-vu-eu-risks-overreliance-one-gas-supplier. Accessed 27 Aug 2025. It Is Questionable Whether These Numbers Are Worth the Paper They Are Written On.

Krentz, Oliver. 2025. *Factsheet: Common Security and Defence Policy*. European Parliament. https://www.europarl.europa.eu/ftu/pdf/en/FTU_5.1.2.pdf. Accessed 27 Aug 2025.

Kreuder-Sonnen, Christian, and Bernhard Zangl. 2025. The Politics of IO Authority Transfers: Explaining Informal Internationalisation and Unilateral Renationalisation. *Journal of European Public Policy* 32:954–979.

Landsbergis, Gabrielius. 2025. *Suspend Hungary's Voting Rights to Save the EU's Credibility*. Carnegie Europe. https://carnegieendowment.org/europe/strategic-europe/2025/02/suspend-hungarys-voting-rights-to-save-the-eus-credibility. Accessed 27 Aug 2025

Lynes, Matt. 2025. *EU's Defence Push Puts Its Neutral Members in Tough Spot with an Emphasis on the Irish Case*. The Parliament. https://www.theparliamentmagazine.eu/news/article/eus-defence-push-puts-its-neutral-members-in-tough-spot. Accessed 27 Aug 2025.

Macron, Emmanuel. 2017. Speech on New Initiative for Europe. https://www.elysee.fr/front/pdf/elysee-module-795-en.pdf. Accessed 27 Aug 2025.

Macron, Emmanuel. 2024. Europe Speech, 25 April 2024. https://www.elysee.fr/front/pdf/elysee-module-22625-en.pdf (via https://www.elysee.fr/en/emmanuel-macron/2024/04/24/europe-speech). Accessed 27 Aug 2025.

Massay-Kosubek, Katharina, and Mariusz Maciejewski. 2025. *Fact Sheets on the European Union; The Treaty of Lisbon*. The Policy Department for Justice, Civil Liberties and Institutional Affairs. https://www.europarl.europa.eu/factsheets/en/sheet/5/the-treaty-of-lisbon. Accessed 27 Aug 2025.

McBride, James, and Andrew Chatzky. 2019. *Is 'Made in China 2025' a Threat to Global Trade?* Council on Foreign Relations. https://www.cfr.org/backgrounder/made-china-2025-threat-global-trade. Accessed 27 Aug 2025.

Mills, Claire. 2024. *What Is the Status of Iran's Nuclear Programme and the JCPOA?* House of Commons. https://researchbriefings.files.parliament.uk/documents/CBP-9870/CBP-9870.pdf. Accessed 27 Aug 2025.

Müller, Tobias. 2025. The Economic Costs and Benefits of the European Future Combat Air System. *Defence and Peace Economics*. https://doi.org/10.1080/10242694.2025.2452867

National Defense Authorization Act for Fiscal Year 2021. 2021. Public Law No. 116–283, 134 Stat. 3388 (01/01/2021). https://www.congress.gov/116/statute/STATUTE-134/STATUTE-134-Pg3388.pdf. Accessed 27 Aug 2025.

NATO. 2025. NATO Summit. https://www.nato.int/cps/en/natohq/235800.htm. Accessed 27 Aug 2025.

New York Times. 2025. Peter Thiel and the Antichrist. https://www.nytimes.com/video/opinion/100000010244372/peter-thiel-and-the-antichrist.html. Accessed 27 Aug 2025.

Petersen, Niels and Patrick Wasilczyk. 2022. *The Primacy of EU Law and the Polish Constitutional Law Judgment*. Policy Department for Citizens' Rights and Constitutional Affairs—Directorate-General for Internal Policies. https://www.europarl.europa.eu/RegData/etudes/STUD/2022/734568/IPOL_STU(2022)734568_EN.pdf. Accessed 27 Aug 2025.

Ruy, Donatienne. 2025. *The Implications of Poland's Presidential Elections*. Center for Strategic & International Studies. https://www.csis.org/analysis/implications-polands-presidential-election. Accessed 27 Aug 2025.

Silverberg, Daniel. 2021. Trading Power: Tariffs and the Nondelegation Doctrine. *Stanford Law Review* 73:1289–1335.

The European Union. 2007. Treaty of Lisbon Amending the Treaty on European Union and the Treaty Establishing the European Community. https://eur-lex.europa.eu/legal-content/EN/TXT/?uri=OJ:C:2007:306:TOC. Accessed 27 Aug 2025.

The European Union. 2025a. Consolidated Version of the Treaty on European Union. https://eur-lex.europa.eu/legal-content/EN/TXT/?uri=CELEX:12016M/TXT. Accessed 27 Aug 2025.

The European Union. 2025b. Consolidated Version of the Treaty on the Functioning of the European Union. https://eur-lex.europa.eu/legal-content/EN/TXT/?uri=CELEX:12016E/TXT. Accessed 27 Aug 2025.

The White House. 2025. Fact Sheet: The United States and European Union Reach Massive Trade Deal. https://www.whitehouse.gov/fact-sheets/2025/07/fact-sheet-the-united-states-and-european-union-reach-massive-trade-deal/. Accessed 27 Aug 2025.

Thomas, Clayton. 2022. Iran Sanctions. Congressional Research Service. https://www.congress.gov/crs_external_products/RS/PDF/RS20871/RS20871.318.pdf. Accessed 27 Aug 2025.

Trump White House. 2018. President Donald J. Trump Is Ending United States Participation in an Unacceptable Iran Deal. https://trumpwhitehouse.archives.gov/briefings-statements/president-donald-j-trump-ending-united-states-participation-unacceptable-iran-deal/. Accessed 27 Aug 2025.

UN Security Council. 2015. https://documents.un.org/doc/undoc/gen/n15/225/27/pdf/n1522527.pdf with text of the JCPOA in Annex A.

Versailles Declaration. 2022. Informal Meeting of the Heads of State and Government. https://www.consilium.europa.eu/media/54773/20220311-versailles-declaration-en.pdf. Accessed 27 Aug 2025.

Virkunnen, Henna. 2022. The EU's Mutual Defence Clause? Article 42(7) of the Treaty on European Union. *European View* 21:22–26.

Von Der Burchard, Hans. 2023. Scholz Gets Orbán Out the Room to Open Ukraine's Membership Talks. *Politico*. https://www.politico.eu/article/olaf-scholz-gets-viktor-orban-out-the-room-to-approve-ukraine-accession-talks/. Accessed 27 Aug 2025.

Witney, Nick. 2022. *The EU's Strategic Compass: Brand New, Already Obsolete*. European Council on Foreign Relations. https://ecfr.eu/article/the-eus-strategic-compass-brand-new-already-obsolete/. Accessed 27 Aug 2025.

Chapter 4
Financial Stability and the Threat of World Disorder

John Farrar and Louise Parsons

Abstract Financial stability has been an important concern for central banks in the era of globalisation. This chapter traces its relationship with the development of US hegemony and the rules-based order since 1945. Now the whole framework has been challenged by the second Trump presidency with its neo-mercantilist revision of the US position in the world. This may mark the end of the rules-based system and the beginning of power politics in an increasingly multipolar world. The possible impact on the governance structures of financial stability should not be underestimated.

4.1 Introduction

Globalisation in its earlier form of globalism has been talked about since the old Silk Road and the rise of nation states and colonialism. Globalism, however, led to mercantilism which prioritises the nation state and is inconsistent with modern globalisation. Modern globalisation probably dates back to 1990 around the collapse of the USSR. Globalisation has been closely associated with US hegemony evidenced in the rules-based order, which is a loose network of international rules.[1] It forms part of international governance without technically being part of international law. Globalisation has also resulted in a world that is more interconnected and prosperous, but also a world where risks can spread relatively easily through the system,[2] to

[1] "A rules-based international order is typically used to refer to the system of political, legal, and economic rules which have arguably governed international relations since the second world war" (sic): Tobin (2025).

[2] Donnery (2025).

J. Farrar (✉) · L. Parsons
Faculty of Law, Bond University, Robina, QLD, Australia
e-mail: jfarrar@bond.edu.au; lparsons@bond.edu.au

U. H. Ghori, J. Farrar (eds.), *Globalisation Disrupted*,
https://doi.org/10.1007/978-981-95-3997-0_4

the detriment of financial stability. Financial stability is a concept which has been discussed by central banks since around that time and a contrast is made between domestic financial stability and global financial stability.

The Global Financial Crisis challenged conceptions of global financial stability based on the rules-based financial order under USA leadership. It should be emphasised that the rules in question were soft law.[3] Regardless, globalisation, and financial stability, rely on "internationally agreed rules to provide stability".[4] We however now live at a time when this faces challenges from the rise of China and BRICS but also paradoxically by the new Trump-regime in the USA which favours neomercantilism. There is currently disconcerting pressure on these rules and the institutions that uphold them because of "rising geopolitical fragmentation"[5] and related threats.[6]

4.2 Financial Stability and International Governance

Trade and finance are closely linked but their organisation has gone down separate paths particularly since 1945. There has been closer cooperation on international trade than international finance at least until the Global Financial Crisis threatened the foundations of international finance. Even today the foundations of international finance remain shaky. One foundational concept is financial stability.

4.2.1 Defining Financial Stability

It is important to first consider what the term "financial stability" means. The concept lacks clear definition, but despite definitional variances, those using the term even in a regulatory sense do so pragmatically, confidently and without apparent difficulty. In 2018 we referred to it as an "intuitive common sense approach".[7] Often "financial stability" is described by its opposite, as it is easier to describe "stability" as the "absence of instability".[8]

---

[3] See generally Guzman and Meyer (2010).

[4] Donnery, *supra*, n. 2.

[5] Ibid.

[6] Andrew Bailey, recently appointed Chair of the Financial Stability Board, emphasized, "[i]t is vital that policy makers can act collectively in response to a global shock. We should not take this capability for granted, particularly against the backdrop of geopolitical tensions and rising fragmentation risk": Bailey (2025).

[7] See Farrar and Parsons (2019).

[8] See Laker (1999). Laker also highlights the problems of defining financial stability by the absence of its opposite.

There is no single definition of financial stability, but what many definitions have in common, is "that financial stability is about the absence of system-wide episodes in which the financial system fails to function (crises). It is also about resilience of financial systems to stress".[9] It refers to "a condition in which the financial system, which includes financial intermediaries, markets, and market infrastructures, is capable of withstanding shocks and the unravelling of financial imbalances. This resilience helps prevent disruptions in the financial intermediation process that could adversely impact real economic activity".[10]

The scope of the term "financial stability" however varies and is important for this chapter. A narrow conception of the term "financial stability" is limited to the stability of institutions within the financial system itself, i.e. the "institutional units and markets that interact, typically in a complex manner, for the purpose of mobilizing funds for investment and providing facilities, including payment systems, for the financing of commercial activity".[11] Referring to financial stability in that sense could therefore mean the absence of banking or financial crises. Sometimes the term is used more broadly and indiscriminately to mean "continued and predictable economic prosperity and growth",[12] inferring macroeconomic prosperity. Nevertheless, in most instances, the term financial stability focusses on "the conditions in the financial system when funds flow in such a manner that productive investment opportunities can be utilised without disruption for the benefit of society at large"[13] and that is the meaning and approach adopted in this chapter.

Although the term "financial stability" was used long before the Global Financial Crisis (GFC), it became a particularly important concept during the GFC when the banking and financial systems in the USA and further afield were overwhelmed by the subprime mortgage crisis and the subsequent credit crunch. The GFC ended the period sometimes referred to as the "Great Moderation".[14] Large-scale efforts to alleviate the crisis and devise and implement new regulations in multiple jurisdictions under the direction of international organisations, institutions and standard setting bodies (SSBs) eventually brought the crisis under control. Post-GFC initiatives to continue to secure financial stability have been largely successful.[15]

Although more than a decade has passed since the height of the GFC, financial stability remains an important concept. It is often considered to be one of the mandates of the typical central bank and has been included in the mandates of some central banks such as the Bank of England and the South African Reserve Bank. The

---

[9] World Bank Group (2016).

[10] European Central Bank (2025). Schinasi adopts a similar description: "Financial stability is defined as the ability of the financial system to facilitate and enhance economic processes, manage risks, and absorb shocks. Moreover, financial stability is considered a continuum, changeable over time and consistent with multiple combinations of finance's constituent elements": Schinasi (2006).

[11] International Monetary Fund (2006) as referenced in Allen (2014, p. 944).

[12] Parsons (2019, p. 59).

[13] Ibid, 49.

[14] See Bernanke (2004).

[15] Farrar and Parsons, *supra*, n. 7.

role of international regulators in financial stability, such as the Financial Stability Board remains important, and groups such as the G20 and G7 continue to monitor and emphasise the importance of financial stability. Both the IMF and the Financial Stability Forum, the predecessor of the Financial Stability Board (FSB, have published financial stability reports since 2002 and 2000 respectively. Although "financial stability" is much less of a "buzz word" and is no longer treated by the media as a prime "threat", it remains a critical consideration for regulators, governments and the financial institutions such as the IMF.[16] In April 2025, the IMF pointed out that global financial stability risks had increased significantly. These risks were fuelled by "tighter global financial conditions and heightened trade and geopolitical uncertainty".[17]

4.2.2 International Governance and Regulation of Financial Stability

The law has an important role to play in international, regional and national financial stability.[18] Since the GFC, national financial sector legal frameworks supporting financial stability have been strengthened, and importantly, new standards for resolution regimes have been introduced. For example, the so-called "Systemically Important Financial Institutions" (SIFIs') became a particular focus during and in the aftermath of the GFC because cross-border problems caused by SIFIs can threaten financial stability. The importance of adopting an international perspective on their regulation was also highlighted during and in the aftermath of the GFC.

A key component of the role of law in financial stability is the work of international financial institutions and SSBs, whose importance cannot be overstated. The FSB, the key international financial institution in international financial stability, recognises the importance of several key international SSBs,[19] including bodies

---

[16] See for example, International Monetary Fund, Fiscal Affairs Department (2025). Especially note the remarks by the Chair at the conclusion of the Executive Board's discussion of the Fiscal Monitor, Global Financial Stability Report, and World Economic Outlook on April 11, 2025. See International Monetary Fund (2025a, pp. xv–xvi).

[17] See International Monetary Fund (2025b).

[18] This has been acknowledged by the IMF. See International Monetary Fund (2020). This book contains a collection of essays from the IMF"s Legal Department's high-level flagship seminar in May 2016.

[19] "The FSB promotes international financial stability; it does so by coordinating national financial authorities and international standard-setting bodies as they work toward developing strong regulatory, supervisory and other financial sector policies". The FSB specifically mentions 15 key International Standards and Codes. See Financial Stability Board (2025b). See also Financial Stability Board (2025d). The FSB includes in their Compendium of Standards the following key standard setting bodies: Basel Committee on Banking Supervision (BCBS), Committee on the Global Financial System (CGFS), Committee on Payments and Market Infrastructures (CPMI), Financial Action Task Force on Money Laundering (FATF), International Association of Deposit

such as IOSCO, the FATF and the OECD. These make recommendations and/or agree on expectations that can be broadly referred to as "international financial standards". The FSB and the FSF have published and updated a "Compendium of Standards" in conjunction with various SSBs since 1999. The Compendium lists economic and financial standards that are "internationally accepted as important for sound, stable and well-functioning financial systems".[20] The FSB notes that "[t]he development and implementation of internationally accepted economic, financial and statistical standards can help promote sound domestic financial systems and international financial stability. While a broad range of political, social, legal and institutional factors affect financial stability, the focus of the FSB is on economic and financial standards which are generally accepted by the international community as important for sound financial systems".[21]

The international SSBs have a significant regulatory role. They are transnational networks and create multilayered governance.[22] International financial institutions and SSBs are sometimes intergovernmental organisations, non-governmental organizations, organizations with a transitional status, or para-organizations.[23] Some SSBs are international intergovernmental organisations and may be considered to be tools for coordinating the will of states; others (without state or government membership) are more industry-based.[24] The charters of these international rule-makers have an intentionally non-binding character, which is also reflected in international financial standards. However, broad adoption by and collaboration between states are vital for the functioning of financial systems. These distinctive characteristics, along with the measures ensuring international financial standards are implemented, help shape both global financial relations and the domestic legal systems of states.[25] The SSBs represent "the most crucial elements of the so-called global

---

Insurers (IADI), International Association of Insurance Supervisors (IAIS), International Accounting Standards Board (IASB), International Auditing and Assurance Standards Board (IAASB), International Organisation of Pension Supervisors (IOPS), International Organisation of Securities Commissions (IOSCO), International Sustainability Standards Board (ISSB), and Islamic Financial Services Board (IFSB). Financial Stability Board (2025a).

[20] Financial Stability Board (2025a).

[21] Ibid.

[22] See Gadinis (2013, p. 169).

SSBs include classic intergovernmental organisations, being informal international groups or institutions including heads of state and governments, for example the influential G20 forum: SSBs include classic intergovernmental organisations, being informal international groups or institutions including heads of state and governments, for example the influential G20 forum. See also Held and Young (2013, p. 177). They note that "the innovative and highly informal system that has evolved over the last few decades [can be described] as a resilient form of "network" governance", at 177.

[23] See for example De Vido (2019, p. 20180030). Like other SSBs, the FATF and FSB are "soft organizations". They can nevertheless exert significant influence over state compliance with international financial standards despite that, despite their informal structures.

[24] The members of the IASB, for example, are national accounting experts. See IFRS Foundation (2025).

[25] See Brummer (2015).

financial architecture, i.e. the international economic legal order",[26] and national legal systems (and the legal systems of integration associations like the EU) implement international financial standards in their legal systems.[27] Whilst central banks are not typical SSBs, the collaboration and agreements reached between central banks in forums such as the Basel Committee on Banking Supervision (BCBS) similarly create frameworks of conduct and rules.[28]

The power of the standards set by SSBs is cemented by the agreed monitoring of implementation of agreed practices and rules that takes place, for example, through peer reviews under the FSB.[29] Through the observance and/or formal adoption of international standards and/or approaches, national governments naturally play an important role in the governance of financial stability. Although formal intergovernmental bodies like the World Trade Organisation (WTO) and World Bank and IMF have lost importance in recent years in favour of more informal institutions like the G20 and FSB, the role of governments and international cooperation remains vitally important. Non-compliance even with non-binding international standards can be felt at national level, for example through an impact on a nation's credit rating, its access to finance and the cost of borrowing.[30] Compliance with standards can also be a condition for obtaining loans from the IMF and International Bank for Reconstruction and Development (IBRD).

It should also be noted that national legislation often reflects principles and standards adopted by international bodies, institutions and quasi-regulators. Much of domestic regulation in relation to financial stability has its origin in the work of international bodies and SSBs, highlighting that "international financial law is [effectively] promulgated by inter-agency forums with (at best) ambiguous legal status".[31] Even if standards and principles are not legislated, broad voluntary adoption give these principles and standards binding status.

It is in the development, adoption and observance of soft law developed through SSBs that the relevance and importance of globalisation and the rules-based order associated with globalisation become apparent. The importance of and respect given to international financial standards are reflected in the preambles and texts of the acts that implement them.[32] These standards are highly respected and are the result of the consensus of the regulators of the leading countries of the world.[33] Soft law is

---

[26] See Giovanoli and Devos (2010).

[27] See generally Brummer (2010).

[28] Hernández de Cos (2024). It should be noted that central banks are public bodies that are traditionally independent from governments, but within the broader political sphere.

[29] Financial Stability Board (2025e). See also Jordan (2012).

[30] For examples of how financial risk is no longer localised or treated as localised, see, Brummer, *supra*, n. 25, at 16.

[31] Brummer, *supra*, n. 27, at 623.

[32] Ibid.

[33] See generally Brummer, *supra*, n. 25. See also Lifshits and Ponamorenko (2020, p. 6).

therefore critical in financial stability and its regulation.[34] Soft law provides a lingua franca and normative backdrop against which regulators can evaluate foreign conduct and justify their own, and that forms the framework for the international financial system.[35] Although soft law has no formal binding force, it is vital in the international legal order. International norms developed as soft law are models for regulation and are also used as "guidelines for consideration in international legal disputes".[36] International economic cooperation and coordination are important in the international economic architecture.[37]

It is a key point in this chapter and our analysis of the state of globalisation that the effectiveness of law in the regulation of financial stability depends largely on voluntary adoption of soft law principles by national regulators and a general adherence to agreements reached in international fora. The success of the development of effective soft law principles depends on collaboration and cooperation, and a recognition of shared objectives/priorities. An overemphasis of nationalism and protectionism would work against effective soft law in financial stability, whereas respect for the principles of a rules-based order creates certainty and predictability. This is particularly important because although post-GFC regulation has (mostly) addressed the problems evident from the GFC, it cannot be assumed that financial regulation is now perfect. It is a fallacy to think that once one crisis has been resolved that there will not be another.[38]

The tightening of regulation since the GFC and the European credit crisis have contributed to stabilization of the global banking and financial system and the recent bank failures, such as Silicon Valley Bank, did not result in the same "systemic" issues experienced in the GFC and the European debt crisis. Much of the successful harmonised international regulation implemented since the GFC has its origin in the work of the SSBs and resulted from collaborative international effort not just in the creation of solutions to the crisis, but also in the implementation of regulatory changes. Much of the success of the post GFC regulatory changes relied on the work of bodies such as the Basel committee and "groups" not formal institutions (the G20 for example). Finance and financial systems therefore have also benefited from the advantages created by globalisation, not just because financial institutions and finance are linked to trade (through trade finance, payment systems, etc) but also because banks and financial services institutions have themselves also become increasingly internationalized. The interconnectedness of finance across borders through international finance and international banking that became particularly apparent through the GFC when almost all countries suffered from what was often described as a "made in America" crisis, was also reflected in the post-GFC

[34] Soft law is regarded as the optimal legal framework for global financial regulation. See Aleem (2022, p. 1).

[35] Brummer, *supra*, n. 25.

[36] Ibid, Chap. 5. See generally Slaughter (2000), cited in Brummer, *supra*, n. 27, at 634. See also Raustiala (2002), cited in Brummer, *supra*, n. 27, at 634.

[37] Buckley and Arner (2011, pp. 294–296).

[38] See Gorton and Zhang (2025). See also Bailey (2024).

recovery phase. The "demise of globalisation", and the accompanying demise of the rules-based order may lead to increased risks when "regulatory bodies" such as the SSBs and specifically "soft law" is disregarded or not given appropriate weight.

The elaborate network of institutions and their cooperation represent soft law in the sense that they are not part of international law. Some parts are in fact hard law in particular jurisdictions but the system rests on this network of cooperation.[39] In fact, both financial stability and globalisation rest on a system of soft law which is based on networks of cooperation in which the USA has had a leading role.[40]

4.3 Financial Stability, US Hegemony, Globalisation and Neo-Mercantilism

We now provide a brief historical perspective on globalisation and the threats posed by developing neo-mercantilism to financial stability.

Although globalism has been around for centuries since the old Silk Road and early colonialism, the connection between globalisation and financial stability has however developed more recently, as referred to above. It is now being affected by developing neo-mercantilism. Mercantilism[41] in essence represents economic nationalism. A mercantilist approach seeks to enrich a country by restraining imports and encouraging exports. As an approach it arose because of the consolidation of large competitive nation states and the expansion through colonialism. Mercantilism also led to increased warfare.[42] Britain stood at the forefront of globalism from the industrial revolution. It developed free market economics but after the First World War and world economic downturn there was a change to protectionist policies.

The historical events since 1945 which show the interface of economics and war under US leadership provide important context to current times and the state of globalisation. The Second World War led to destruction of much of Europe, and the negotiations between the allies led to the Bretton Woods Agreement[43] that included important international financial arrangements that contributed to post-war financial stability. It also paved the way for the importance of the US dollar in the

[39] "Like any social system, [the global financial system] has developed around a common set of rules, principles and norms, both explicit and implicit, that functionally underpin the system's architecture and establish trust between its actors, allowing firms to conduct business across borders. These elements include respect for property ownership rights, the fundamental rule of law and the independence of fiscal and monetary policy": Blake and Moynihan (2025, p. 3).

[40] De Vido, *supra*, n. 23, at 9. She argues that "[t]he FATF and the FSB can be considered the leading examples of "networks" that operate in the financial system, and that, thanks to their flexible structure and mandate, have been capable of effectively respond to the 2008 crisis".

[41] See Brezis (2003). However, see Backhouse (2023, pp. 11–12).

[42] Brezis, Ibid.

[43] See Ghizoni (2013).

international financial system, including in global trade and international economic stability as the world's reserve currency. Under the Bretton Woods arrangements each currency was pegged to a band around a fixed parity with the US dollar and the US dollar to a fixed price against gold. This together with the Marshall Plan reflected US leadership at the time,[44] encompassing both a moral and the military aspect.[45]

After the Second World War, global integration increased and the General Agreement on Tariffs and Trade in 1947 set the scene for economic integration. In 1995 the World Trade Organisation (WTO) was created as GATT's successor, reflecting a prolonged period of rules-based cooperation between an increasing number of nations.[46] In the Post-war period, fear of the expansion of Communism led to the Cold War, the Korean War and the war in Vietnam. These were a drain on the US dollar as well as other international currencies, but broad US global leadership prevailed. The US dollar remained strong as the global reserve currency and the main vehicle for international trade[47] despite its changed position when floating currencies were introduced and the gold standard was abandoned in 1971 under the Nixon presidency.

The period from 1970 onwards can be divided into five broad periods reflecting the state of the global financial system:[48]

- 1970s the foundation of the modern global system
- 1980s global deregulation and integration
- 1990s financial globalisation and new technologies
- 2000s continued integration
- 2010–2020s fragmentation processes.

Throughout all of these periods the important role of US hegemony and the US dollar was maintained. The time since 1947 was not without financial and economic disruption, and for example the oil crises of 1973 and 1979 created significant global economic turbulence.

The collapse of the USSR in 1991 coincided with the beginning of modern globalisation. This was strongly supported by the Clinton administration and coincided with the significant advance in information technology which was soon dominated by US companies. In 1997, the Asian financial crisis was the first modern financial crisis in a globalised world. It highlighted the consequences of the interconnectedness of global economies and revealed weaknesses in the financial systems of many

---

[44] Council on Foreign Relations (2023). See also Van Dormael (1978).

[45] The moral argument was used as a selling point with Congress.

[46] "The existing system of global financial governance is not the result of rational institutional design but rather is a consequence of a complex evolutionary process that has built up since the Second World War": Gadinis, *supra*, n. 22.

[47] See Farrell (2018, 446 et seq) and Kissinger (2022, pp. 147–149).

[48] The World Economic Forum (WEF) divided them into five in its timeline of events. See World Economic Forum (in collaboration with Oliver Wyman) (2025).

countries. However, globalisation has been marked by periods of openness and periods of retreat.[49]

The impact of the terrorist attack on the World Trade Centre on the world cannot be underestimated. It led to the War on Terror under the Bush administration.[50] This was a drag on US resources. Nevertheless, from a financial stability perspective, the years leading up to 2007 were overall stable and prosperous and often referred to as the "Great Moderation". This was however followed by the GFC and its aftermath. With the origins of the GFC firmly within financial practices within the US, US governance and policies especially financial and banking regulation and oversight, were cast into doubt. The GFC coincided with the rise of China after it joined the WTO, which increasingly led to Chinese scepticism about US leadership.

The responses of central banks to the GFC demonstrated a commitment to and inherent responsibility for the pursuit of financial stability although it had not been an express mandate for all central banks before the GFC.[51] The coordinated actions of the central banks in response to the GFC represented a broadening of their mandate. As Allen and Lastra point out, unlike monetary stability, financial stability is not national in nature:

> What is clear though is that financial stability complicates border problems because it transcends institutional mandates and geographical boundaries thus further challenging the traditional notion of sovereignty. Financial stability is indeed a national, regional and international goal: episodes of instability, like tsunamis and epidemics, do not respect territorial boundaries.[52]

Issues such as automation, technological change and public policies after the GFC have all created a backlash against globalisation.[53] Further, income losses by those who have lost out in globalisation and fear of immigrants particularly illegal immigrants contributed to criticism of globalisation. These influenced Brexit as we have seen.[54] Britain finally left the European Union on 31 January 2020.[55]

The coronavirus pandemic that commenced in 2020 created global turmoil across national boundaries. It proved costly and had a negative effect on supply chains, and was the first big test for the global financial system after the GFC.[56] It also highlighted "the importance of cross-border cooperation".[57] As we shall see in a later chapter it can be regarded as a failure of globalisation, and this has led to

[49] See The White House (n.d.). See also Holslag (2021, Chap. 9).

[50] See Bush (2022). See also Neumann (2022, Chaps. 5, 6, and 7).

[51] Even after the GFC, it is not a formal mandate for all central banks.

[52] See Allen and Lastra (2020, p. 525).

[53] Farrar and Parsons, *supra*, n. 7, at 99 et seq.

[54] See generally Farrar, John. 2025. Globalisation, Brexit and the Future of the United Kingdom. *Infra*, Chap. 2.

[55] See Walker (2021).

[56] Financial Stability Board (2021, p. 4).

[57] [53] Ibid.

increasing localism.[58] The coronavirus pandemic also led to rising inflation in many countries because of fiscal responses and changes in spending habits.[59] Central bank balance sheets also surged in size.[60] Increased digitalisation and outsourcing of digital services to third party providers led to increased cyber risk,[61] but cross-border crisis management groups established under the auspices of the FSB "provided the backbone for communication and coordination during the COVID-19 pandemic".[62]

Recent international events such as the Russian invasion of Ukraine and the Middle East conflict have all affected globalisation, as a world of growing divisions.[63] The presidencies of Donald Trump also reflect the growth of anti-globalisation forces in the form of nationalism, populism and neo-mercantilism in the USA. Classic mercantilism measures economic power in terms of bullion whereas contemporary neomercantilism is not primarily concerned with trade or balance of payments surplus. Trump has made economic prosperity the key feature of his national security policy but rejected globalisation. He took the view that the recent wars had little advantage for the USA and the USA did not gain enough from globalisation. He dropped the Transpacific Partnership Agreement and has cast doubt on ANZUS.[64] He has started a tariff war which disrupts international trade. As a result, he has made the world an unpredictable environment for friend and foe alike. As Oscar Wilde once said, "to be intelligible is to be found out".[65]

The USA thus struggles to come to terms with the aftermath of the GFC, to restore higher economic growth, meet the challenges of the labour market due to rapid changes[66] and to contend with the rise of China and its model of state capitalism. These events threaten the post war rules-based order and shift the emphasis to a more deal-based order. This is a disruptive force for domestic and global stability. It evidences an important shift in international political economy that is already substantially underway in a world where "geopolitics trump economics".[67] Whilst globalisation is characterised by "the embracement of free markets and the maintenance of a rules-based open global economy",[68] the neo-mercantilist view that "the loss in efficiency from redundancies and selective protectionism may be worth it if it reduces vulnerabilities and increases resilience"[69] is gaining ground, and has been

---

[58] See generally, Bonython, Wendy E. 2025. Global Health as the Canary in the Globalisation Coal Mine. *Infra*, Chap. 11.

[59] See Waller (2025).

[60] See Committee on the Global Financial System (2023).

[61] Financial Stability Board, *supra*, n. 56, at 9, 13.

[62] Ibid.

[63] World Economic Forum (2025, pp. 13–43).

[64] Farrar and Parsons, *supra*, n. 7, at 107.

[65] Wilde (n.d.).

[66] See Farrar and Parsons (2012, pp. 400–401).

[67] Steinberg (2023).

[68] Ibid.

[69] Ibid.

the strategy adopted by China for decades, resulting in an increase in its influence and power.[70]

There is a certain naivety in thinking that a tariff war will be successful and that it is possible to kickstart the US manufacturing sector. This approach pays little attention to America's Achilles' heel, the level of national public debt. The total US national public debt is $35.9 trillion. The US has the highest level of public debt of all OECD countries. Interest on debt is 14%; spending on defence is 17% and Medicare is 13%. There is a risk that the US dollar will be a source of increasing global financial instability and there will be a movement to diversify exposure.

4.4 Current Risks and Threats to Financial Stability in Light of the Changing World Order

In this part we consider key current risks[71] and threats[72] to financial stability in light of the decline of the rules-based order of soft law and the current state of changes in Washington and the changing role of the US in international cooperation.

The need to support global cooperation on financial stability has been noted as the first priority of work for the Financial Stability Board in 2025.[73] This is important given that "the deep architecture of the international economy [is] in flux for the first time in decades".[74] Paul Tucker identifies key "complexities and hazards" as being "economic globalization, discordant geopolitics, and strains in the legitimacy of domestic and international governance".[75]

Persistent inflation[76] in the aftermath of the coronavirus pandemic was one of the immediate risks for financial stability identified by the IMF in 2024. It had led to a cost-of-living crisis in many advanced economies.[77] Cost of living crises are detrimental on an individual and a societal level. However, at the time of writing, inflation appears to have been brought under control in many jurisdictions, but the IMF still warns of a lack of growth, noting that "the landscape has changed as governments around the world reorder policy priorities and uncertainties have climbed to new highs. Forecasts for global growth have been revised markedly down".[78] The

[70] Ibid.

[71] A risk is understood to be a "potential adverse outcome that could lead to harm". See Donnery, *supra*, n. 2.

[72] Threats are "risk drivers". Whereas "risks describe the "what" (the potential adverse outcome), risk drivers—the relevant threats and vulnerabilities—explain the "why" or "how"." Ibid.

[73] Financial Stability Board (2025c).

[74] Tucker (2022, p. 3). See also Harding et al. (2023).

[75] Tucker, Ibid, at 3–4. See also Lawrence (2024).

[76] See generally International Monetary Fund (2023). See continued concerns about persistent inflation: International Monetary Fund (2024).

[77] International Monetary Fund (2025d).

[78] Ibid.

IMF has emphasised the need for international collaboration: "[a]t this critical juncture, countries should work constructively to promote a stable and predictable trade environment and to facilitate international cooperation".[79] One of the key policy shifts is the change in the US position on tariffs. The IMF notes that "the global economy is now characterized by a high degree of economic and financial integration, with supply chains and financial flows crisscrossing the world, whose potential unwinding could constitute a major source of economic upheaval. For this reason, we expect that the sharp increase on April 2 [2025] in both tariffs and uncertainty will lead to a significant slowdown in global growth in the near term".[80]

A significant threat to financial stability comes from technological advancements. The digitalisation of finance and banking poses a key risk. The speed at which bank runs can take place in the digital age and lapses in bank and superannuation supervision raise questions about regulation. Added to this are dangers arising from emerging financial innovations including crypto assets. The widespread adoption of crypto assets could undermine the effectiveness of monetary policy, circumvent capital flow management measures, exacerbate fiscal risks, divert resources available for financing the real economy and threaten global financial stability.[81] These risks could reinforce each other as financial stability can make maintaining price stability more difficult,and vice versa, causing destabilising financial flows and strained fiscal resources.[82] The rapid evolution and international nature of crypto asset markets raises the problem of regulatory gaps and arbitrage between different systems. Managing the risks and maximising the profitability of crypto assets, which are typically cross-border financial instruments, rely on commensurable international approaches. The FSB for example published its FSB Global Regulatory Framework for Crypto-asset Activities in July 2023, setting out the FSB's attempt at creating a "global regulatory framework for crypto-asset activities to promote the comprehensiveness and international consistency of regulatory and supervisory approaches".[83] The FSB, together with SSBs, have developed a shared workplan.[84] This work demonstrates the importance of cooperation and respect for the development of soft law in areas that can reduce the risk of financial instability. In similar vein, the Bank for International Settlements published "BIS Crypto, tokens and DeFi: navigating the regulatory landscape", and in July 2024, finalised its disclosure framework for banks' crypto asset exposures. "The disclosure framework has been developed based on the disclosure requirements contained in the final prudential standard on banks' crypto asset exposures published in December 2022. It includes a standardised table and templates that cover the disclosure of both qualitative and

[79] International Monetary Fund (2025c).

[80] International Monetary Fund, *supra*, n. 77, at xii.

[81] International Monetary Fund and Financial Stability Board (2023).

[82] See Hudson et al. (2023).

[83] Financial Stability Board (2023, p. 1).

[84] Ibid.

quantitative information"[85] and are due to be implemented by 1 January 2026. This is a key global initiative but relies on adoption and implementation by domestic regulators.

While there are currently some national attempts at regulation and some broader regional initiatives surrounding different aspects of crypto assets, such as the European Union's Markets in Crypto-assets Regulation (the so-called MiCA, introduced in 2023), these are patchy. For example, MiCA primarily deals with stablecoins, responding to the collapse of the FTX Exchange in 2022.[86] Different approaches exist in different countries, and it is up to the SSBs, in this case the FSB and BIS, to assist with harmonisation, and for providing comparative oversight. Many jurisdictions, including the UK and now the US, are vying to be the "crypto capital of the world", using regulatory frameworks to facilitate such development. Whilst some regulatory frameworks such as MiCA are protective in nature, the current US policy is expansionist with an intentional loosening of regulatory restrictions. The risk exists however that multiple digital currency ecosystems could develop. This would lead to a more fragmented international monetary system with increased financial stability risks. In addition, different uses for cryptocurrency, including as reserve assets as envisaged by the Trump administration,[87] will introduce uncertainty. In fact, the "Trump administration appears to be moving swiftly to remove perceived obstacles to the widespread use of blockchain technology and development of the crypto asset markets".[88]

Technological risks exist more broadly, and by virtue of the nature of digital technology, requires international cooperation. Developments in artificial intelligence also impacts financial stability. It has the potential to improve productivity and to increase the prospects of economic productive growth.[89] However, the uncertainty associated with how artificial intelligence may be used in the decision-making processes of financial institutions and increased use of artificial intelligence in financial markets makes artificial intelligence a possible risk to financial stability.[90] Generative AI is used by financial institutions for code generation, document summarisation, and information retrieval, and financial supervisors use generative AI for operational efficiency and data analysis.[91] "GenAI could increase financial fraud and the ability of malicious actors to generate and spread disinformation in financial markets".[92]

---

[85] Basel Committee on Banking Supervision (2024).

[86] Hallak and Salén (2023, p. 2). Note that this piece of legislation aims to establish a harmonized regulatory framework for crypto assets, their issuers, and service providers, ensuring consumer protection and financial stability in the European Union. It deals with matters such as licensing for crypto-asset service providers (CASPs), requirements for stablecoin issuers, and trading platforms.

[87] See The White House (2025).

[88] Montgomery et al. (2025).

[89] Bank of England (2025).

[90] Ibid.

[91] Financial Stability Board (2024b, p. 1).

[92] Ibid.

Geopolitical tensions have been identified as a key current risk to financial stability. International strife raises constant problems particularly the Middle East and the Ukraine and at the time of writing, increased hostility between India and Pakistan. These are exacerbated by the US changing policies which leave its allies exposed. In April 2025, the IMF highlighted that "[s]hocks such as wars, diplomatic tensions, or terrorism can disrupt cross-border trade and investment. This can hurt asset prices, affect financial institutions, and curtail lending to the private sector, weighing on economic activity and posing a threat to financial stability".[93]

Other threats and risks to financial stability highlighted by the FSB as part of its 2025 priorities[94] include climate change risks, Increased frequency of natural disasters, rising sea levels and greater temperature volatility can create changes in employment, production and service provision. These can lead to changes in the value of financial assets, cost and availability of credit and losses. All these affects financial stability. Further, the growth of non-bank financial institutions raises new issues as they do not have access to the central bank and its role of lender of last resort. The FSB in 2025 is also focussing on the risks posed by non-bank financial intermediation. The SSBs will be involved with the FSB in enhancing Non-Bank Financial Institutions (NBFI) resilience because of risk associated with the use of leverage in the NBFI.[95]

There is a risk that the US dollar will be a source of global financial instability in the future with a resulting lack of confidence in US governance because of the mercantilist approach of the Trump administration. This could lead to wealthy nations pursuing domestic neoliberalism, ending the "international wave of globalization that began over thirty years ago", and moving towards "a new world of nation- and region-specific trade and foreign economic policies, moving away from universalism and internationalism and into neo-mercantilism".[96]

4.5 Decline of the Rules-Based Order

The first Trump administration challenged globalisation and cast doubts on the rules-based order. The second Trump administration has tackled the matter full on.[97] In a series of remarks and presidential edicts after the inauguration the seeds for significant change were sown. On 2 April 2025 President Trump invoked the International Emergency Economic Powers Act 1977 and declared foreign trade and economic practices have created a national emergency. He imposed a 10% tariff on all countries and increased tariffs on some. The rationale for these extreme

[93] Fendoglu et al. (2025). See International Monetary Fund (2025a).

[94] Financial Stability Board (2025f).

[95] Ibid, at 1.

[96] Milanović (2025).

[97] President Trump is not a supporter of globalisation. Ibid.

measures is that economic prosperity is the key feature of national security. These steps are graphic examples that in the US globalisation has been abandoned and Trump's version of Neo-mercantilism has been adopted.[98]

At the same time the US has also implemented measures to cut back regulation and reduce the number of public servants. Extreme measures have also been taken on immigration and sanctions lifted on illegal actions attacking Congress after the previous election. Attacks have been made on the judiciary and a changed approach to cryptocurrency raising issues of conflict of interest, has been adopted. These measures reflect populist nationalism and a grievance approach to governance and international affairs. They also reflect a paleo-conservatism combined with radicalism that plagued the USA in the 1930s and only ended in the Second World War and its aftermath when it was rejected. Its present resurrection throws the international system into extreme disorder. It will inevitably lead to great uncertainty and financial instability and to countermeasures. One view is that this is a deliberate deals-based technique of forcing other countries to negotiate on unfavourable terms as the tariffs are being imposed on friend and foe alike. They will undermine confidence in US leadership and inevitably lead to active consideration of another world order which does not reflect that leadership.

Meanwhile, China has been developing ambitions to rival the USA and to overtake it. This started after the GFC which cast doubt on US world leadership. Brexit and the first Trump administration together with the confused response to the coronavirus pandemic influenced this trend. It was described as "standing tall and seeing far".[99] China's strategy under Xi Jinping has been exercised through active membership of the United Nations and its committees. This has been supplemented by a hub and spokes approach to different regions. The most active initiative has been through the Belt and Road project, which is dealt with in Chapter 8. Vast amounts of money have been invested in technology as we have seen in Chapter 9 China is developing the first Central Bank Digital Currency (CBDC) and is attempting to build the digital infrastructure to service the trade of all CBDCs. These have been described as the rails for the future of money. They take the form of advanced semiconductor chips, cloud computing power, 5G networks and later AI and quantum computing. These need to be protected by guardrails in the form of cyber defences. China aims not only to develop the technology but also to set the international standards.

China's membership of BRICS provides another forum and BRICS expansion is a significant development although the financial aspects of this have been faltering to date. Europe benefitted from US hegemony but in the long run developed another elaborate soft mercantilist structure with US support. There was a grand bargain—guns versus butter. The NATO system allowed the defence of European countries to be subsidized by the USA. This worked reasonably well because of shared political

---

[98] Coggan (2025).

[99] Doshi (2021, Chap. 12, p. 277).

philosophy. Now all of this has been called into question by the second Trump presidency.[100]

In addition, the EU has yet to work out a satisfactory way of dealing with China which practices a state-run mercantilist system. Also, in its links with Russia it potentially is at odds with the EU over the Ukraine invasion. The EU has described China as a cooperation partner, economic competitor and a systemic rival. There are tensions in areas like trade imbalances, human rights and geopolitical dynamics. The EU is China's largest trading partner and China is the EU's second largest trading partner.

4.6 Conclusion

We live in a period of considerable disorder when globalisation has been fragmented, and financial stability seriously challenged. The USA threatened global financial stability in 2008–2009 and was bailed out by international cooperation in a system of sophisticated soft law and international networks of cooperation. The question is whether this system built on self-interest and goodwill can survive the challenges of the second Trump administration, which is predicated on Neo-Mercantilist policies of accentuated self-interest backing up a system of finance by very significant international debt.

These raise questions at the root of global financial stability. When the USA weakens its financial guardrails, others may follow suit, leading to brittle supply lines, slow growth and record levels of debt. Measured against increasing US instability, China presents more stable than Western democracies at the time of writing.

There is currently a trend to a more multipolar international financial system. This was fuelled by the coronavirus epidemic and supply chain disruptions; technological innovation has accelerated the process. Over 90% of central banks are exploring CBDCs. Important examples are China's CNY CBDCs and the mBridge multi-CBDC platform for cross-border payments. There are currently six entities jointly developing mBridge—the Hong Kong Monetary Authority, Bank of Thailand, Central Bank of United Arab Emirates, Peoples Bank of China and the BIS Innovation Hub Hong Kong Centre and Saudi Central Bank. At the same time, it is estimated that the USD share of global resources has declined from 71% in 1999 to 58% in 2024.[101]

We thus live in a period of great social and economic change which may lead to a multipolar world in which there is more than one hegemony. The global system is "becoming increasingly multipolar with many competing power centres; multidimensional with diverse, interconnected risks; and multilayered in terms of time

[100] Eichengreen (2023). See also Lagarde (2022).

[101] WEF, *supra*, n. 48, at 14.

horizons requiring simultaneous short-, medium-, and long-term planning".[102] Importantly, global financial governance is "multilayered, multidimensional and multi-actor".[103] Cooperation between regulators especially in some areas have however generally been well established,[104] but there is a sense of uncertainty.

In April 2025, the IMF implored countries to "work constructively to promote a stable and predictable trade environment, facilitate debt restructuring, and address shared challenges".[105] It noted that the path forward demanded "clarity and coordination".[106] Similarly, large projects that will benefit financial stability depend on international cooperation.[107] A case in point is the implementation of the G20's Roadmap for Enhancing Cross-border Payments. In the consolidated progress report for 2024, the FSB reported on progress on the 2022 targets of the G20 in relation to "quantitative global targets for addressing the four challenges in cross-border payments across three market segments: wholesale payments, retail payments and remittances".[108] The success of this and similar initiatives depends on "[a]t a high level,… two types of ongoing actions that operate across all three priority themes—stakeholder engagement and progress monitoring. Improvements in cross-border payments require commitment from a wide range of public sector authorities and private sector stakeholders, as well as global coordination. The FSB, CPMI and other partner organisations are bringing together strategic perspectives and subject matter expertise via fora such as joint working groups, taskforces, workshops, public consultation reports, and surveys".[109] Similarly, the May 2025 G7 Communiqué reiterated its members' shared commitment to the G7, emphasising the clear value of the G7 following 50 years of collaboration, "transcending national differences and promoting global prosperity".[110]

It has been suggested recently that there is in fact a multiplex world economic order emerging,[111] a concept that is preferable to that of hegemony or multipolarity.

---

[102] Donnery, *supra*, n. 2.

[103] Gadinis, *supra* n. 22, at 172.

[104] Ibid.

[105] International Monetary Fund, *supra*, n. 77.

[106] Ibid.

[107] See generally, Held and Young (2013, p. 5). The Editors note "while the demand for governance has been sharply rising as global interdependence has intensified, our ability to support it appears to be declining".

[108] Financial Stability Board (2024a).

[109] Ibid.

[110] Department of Finance Canada (2025, para. 2). The G7 also expressed the following concern (see paragraph 3 of the Statement): "In the face of multiple complex global challenges, we are committed to pursuing our shared policy objectives. We agree that the G7 can leverage our strong economic relationships to advance our common goals. International organizations signalled (sic) at our last meeting that trade and economic policy uncertainty was high and weighing on global growth. We acknowledge that economic policy uncertainty has declined from its peak, and we will work together to achieve further progress. We also shared our concerns over unsustainable global macro imbalances".

[111] Acharya et al. (2023). See also Acharya (2025, p. 366).

It is based on interaction capacity and interdependence and is broadly defined to include environment, sustainable development, security and connectivity. Leadership in this system is issue specific. Global cooperation is gradually becoming less hegemonic and US-centred. The result is that the post-American world is not so much defined by the decline of America but rather by the rise of everybody else.[112]

References

Acharya, Amitav. 2025. *The Once and Future World Order*. New York: Basic Books.

Acharya, Amitav, Antoni Estevadeordal, and Louis W. Goodman. 2023. Multipolar or Multiplex? Interaction Capacity, Global Cooperation and World Order. *International Affairs* 99 (6): 2339–2365. https://doi.org/10.1093/ia/iiad242.

Aleem, Yussuf A. 2022. Soft Law: The Optimal Legal Framework for Global Financial Regulation. *Emory Corporate Governance and Accountability Review* 9:1–27.

Allen, Hilary J. 2014. What Is "Financial Stability"? The Need for Some Common Language in International Financial Regulation. *Georgetown Journal of International Law* 45:929–953.

Allen, Jason Grant, and Rosa M. Lastra. 2020. Border Problems: Mapping the Third Border. *Modern Law Review* 83:505–538.

Backhouse, Roger E. 2023. *The Penguin History of Economics*. London: Penguin.

Bailey, Andrew. 2024. *Today's Challenges in Financial Stability—The New and the Not So New*. Speech at the Bloomberg Regulatory Forum. https://www.bankofengland.co.uk/speech/2024/october/andrew-bailey-keynote-address-at-the-bloomberg-global-regulatory-forum. Accessed 1 Aug 2025.

Bailey, Andrew. 2025. Letter to G20 Finance Ministers and Central Bank Governors. https://www.fsb.org/uploads/P140725.pdf. https://www.fsb.org/uploads/P140725.pdf. Accessed 4 Aug 2025.

Bank of England. 2025. Financial Stability in Focus: Artificial Intelligence in the Financial System. https://www.bankofengland.co.uk/financial-stability-in-focus/2025/april-2025. Accessed 4 Aug 2025.

Basel Committee on Banking Supervision. 2024. *Disclosure of Crypto asset Exposures*. Bank for International Settlements. https://www.bis.org/bcbs/publ/d580.htm. Accessed 4 Aug 2025.

Bernanke, Ben. 2004. *The Great Moderation*. Speech at the Meeting of the Eastern Economic Association, Washington, DC. https://www.federalreserve.gov/boarddocs/speeches/2004/20040220/. Accessed 1 Aug 2025.

Blake, Matthew, and Ted Moynihan. 2025. Forward, in *Navigating Global Financial System Fragmentation*. World Economic Forum in collaboration with Oliver Wyman. https://www.weforum.org/publications/navigating-global-financial-system-fragmentation/. Accessed 4 Aug 2025.

Brezis, Elise S. 2003. Mercantilism. In *The Oxford Encyclopedia of Economic History*. Oxford: Oxford University Press.

Brummer, Chris. 2010. Why Soft Law Dominates International Finance—And NOT TRADE. *Journal of International Economic Law* 13:623–643.

Brummer, Chris. 2015. *Soft Law and the Global Financial System: Rule Making in the 21st Century*. 2nd ed. Cambridge: Cambridge University Press.

Buckley, Ross P., and Douglas W. Arner. 2011. *From Crisis to Crisis: The Global Financial System and Regulatory Failure*. Alphen aan den Rijn: Wolters Kluwer.

[112] Zakaria (2008).

Bush, George W. 2022. *The Global War on Terror*. George W. Bush Presidential Library and Museum. National Archives. https://www.georgewbushlibrary.gov/sites/default/files/2022-07/ResearchGuide_GWOTJuly2022.pdf. Accessed 5 Aug 2025.

Coggan, Philip. 2025. *The Economic Consequences of Mr Trump: What the Trade War Means for the World*. London: Profile Books.

Committee on the Global Financial System. 2023. *Central Bank Asset Purchases in Response to the Covid-19 Crisis*. CGFS Papers No. 68. Report prepared by a CGFS Working Group co-chaired by Margarita Delgado (Banco de España) and Toni Gravelle (Bank of Canada). https://www.bis.org/publ/cgfs68.pdf. Accessed 4 Aug 2025.

Council on Foreign Relations. 2023. How Did the United States Become a Global Power? https://education.cfr.org/learn/reading/how-did-united-states-become-global-power. Accessed 4 Aug 2025.

De Vido, Sara. 2019. Soft Organizations, Hard Powers: The FATF and the FSB as Standard Setting Bodies. *Global Jurist* 19 (2): 1–13. https://doi.org/10.1515/gj-2018-0030.

Department of Finance Canada. 2025. *G7 Finance Ministers and Central Bank Governors' Communiqué*. Statement by G7 Finance Ministers and Central Bank Governors' Communiqué made at Banff, Canada. https://www.canada.ca/en/department-finance/news/2025/05/g7-finance-ministers-and-central-bank-governors-communique.html. Accessed 4 Aug 2025.

Donnery, Sharon. 2025. *Resilience, Risk and Regulation: Anchoring Stability in a Rules-Based International Order*. Speech presented at the Delphi Economic Forum. https://www.banking-supervision.europa.eu/press/speeches/date/2025/html/ssm.sp250410_1~053f19ec60.en.html. Accessed 18 Aug 2025.

Doshi, Rush. 2021. *The Long Game: China's Grand Strategy to Displace American Order*. Oxford: Oxford University Press.

Eichengreen, Barry. 2023. Is This How Globalisation Ends? Prospect. https://www.prospectmagazine.co.uk/world/globalisation/62824/is-this-how-globalisation-ends. Accessed 4 Aug 2025.

European Central Bank. 2025. Financial Stability. https://www.ecb.europa.eu/paym/financial%E2%80%91stability/html/index.en.html. Accessed 4 Aug 2025.

Farrar, John H., and Louise Parsons. 2012. Globalisation, the Global Financial Crisis and the Reinvention of the State. *Singapore Academy of Law Journal* 24:367–404.

Farrar, John H., and Louise Parsons. 2019. Financial Stability After the Global Financial Crisis: Globalisation, Nationalism and the Potential Demise of the Rules-Based Order. In *Scholarship, Practice and Education in Comparative Law: A Festschrift in Honour of Mary Hiscock*, ed. John H. Farrar, Vai Io Lo, and Bee Chen Goh, 81–111. Singapore: Springer.

Farrell, John A. 2018. *Richard Nixon: The Life*. New York: Doubleday.

Fendoglu, Salih, Mahvash S. Qureshi, and Felix Suntheim. 2025. *How Rising Geopolitical Risks Weigh on Asset Prices*. IMF Blog. https://www.imf.org/en/Blogs/Articles/2025/04/14/how-rising-geopolitical-risks-weigh-on-asset-prices#:~:text=Shocks%20such%20as%20wars%2C%20diplomatic,a%20threat%20to%20financial%20stability. Accessed 4 Aug 2025.

Financial Stability Board. 2021. Lessons Learnt from the COVID-19 Pandemic from a Financial Stability Perspective. https://www.fsb.org/uploads/P281021-2.pdf. Accessed 4 Aug 2025.

Financial Stability Board. 2023. Global Regulatory Framework for Crypto-Asset Activities: Umbrella Public Note to Accompany Final Framework. https://www.fsb.org/uploads/P170723-1.pdf. Accessed 4 Aug 2025.

Financial Stability Board. 2024a. G20 Roadmap for Enhancing Cross-border Payments: Consolidated Progress Report for 2024. https://www.fsb.org/uploads/P211024-1.pdf. Accessed 4 Aug 2025.

Financial Stability Board. 2024b. The Financial Stability Implications of Artificial Intelligence. https://www.fsb.org/uploads/P14112024.pdf. Accessed 4 Aug 2025.

Financial Stability Board. 2025a. About the Compendium of Standards. https://www.fsb.org/work-of-the-fsb/about-the-compendium-of-standards/key_standards/. Accessed 4 Aug 2025.

Financial Stability Board. 2025b. About the FSB. https://www.fsb.org/about/. Accessed 4 Aug 2025.

Financial Stability Board. 2025c. FSB Work Programme for 2025. https://www.fsb.org/2025/01/fsb-work-programme-for-2025/. Accessed 6 Aug 2025.

Financial Stability Board. 2025d. Key Standards for Sound Financial Systems. https://www.fsb.org/work-of-the-fsb/about-the-compendium-of-standards/key_standards/. Accessed 4 Aug 2025.

Financial Stability Board. 2025e. Peer Reviews. https://www.fsb.org/work-of-the-fsb/implementation-monitoring/peer_reviews/. Accessed 4 Aug 2025.

Financial Stability Board. 2025f. FSB Work Programme for 2025. https://www.fsb.org/uploads/P230125.pdf. Accessed 4 August 2025

Gadinis, Stavros. 2013. The Financial Stability Board: The New Politics of International Financial Regulation. *Texas International Law Journal* 48 (2): 157–176.

Ghizoni, Sandra Kollen. 2013. *Creation of the Bretton Woods System*. Federal Reserve History. https://www.federalreservehistory.org/essays/bretton-woods-created. Accessed 4 August 2025

Giovanoli, Mario, and Diego Devos. 2010. *International Monetary and Financial Law: The Global Crisis*. Oxford: Oxford University Press.

Gorton, Gary B., and Jeffery Y. Zhang. 2025. *Why Financial Crises Recur*. University of Michigan Law & Economics. https://papers.ssrn.com/sol3/papers.cfm?abstract_id=5317971. Accessed 4 Aug 2025.

Guzman, Andrew T., and Timothy L. Meyer. 2010. International Soft Law. *Journal of Legal Analysis* 2:171–225.

Hallak, Issam, and Rasmus Salén. 2023. *Non-EU Countries' Regulations on Crypto-Assets and Their Potential Implications for the EU*. European Parliamentary Research Service. https://www.europarl.europa.eu/RegData/etudes/BRIE/2023/753930/EPRS_BRI(2023)753930_EN.pdf. Accessed 4 Aug 2025.

Harding, Martin, Jesper Lindé, and Mathias Trabandt. 2023. *Understanding Post-COVID Inflation Dynamics*. IMF Working Paper. https://www.imf.org/en/Publications/WP/Issues/2023/01/20/Understanding-Post-COVID-Inflation-Dynamics-528404. Accessed 19 Aug 2025.

Held, David, and Kevin Young. 2013. From the Financial Crisis to the Crisis of Global Governance. In *Global Governance at Risk*, ed. David Held and Charles Roger. Cambridge: Polity Press.

Hernández de Cos, Pablo. 2024. *Global Cooperation as a Cornerstone for Financial Stability*. Speech at the 23rd International Conference of Banking Supervisors, Basel. https://www.bis.org/speeches/sp240424.htm. Accessed 1 Aug 2025.

Holslag, Jonathan. 2021. *World Politics Since 1989*. Cambridge: Polity Press.

Hudson, Callum, Samuel Kurian, and Michelle Lewis. 2023. Non-Bank Lending in Australia and the Implications for Financial Stability. *Reserve Bank of Australia Bulletin*, March 2023, p. 27. https://www.rba.gov.au/publications/bulletin/2023/mar/pdf/non-bank-lending-in-australia-and-the-implications-for-financial-stability.pdf. Accessed 4 Aug 2025.

IFRS Foundation. 2025. International Accounting Standards Board. https://www.ifrs.org/groups/international-accounting-standards-board/#members. Accessed 4 Aug 2025.

International Monetary Fund. 2006. *Financial Soundness Indicators: Compilation Guide*. Guide, March 2006. https://www.imf.org/external/pubs/ft/fsi/guide/2006/pdf/fsiFT.pdf. Accessed 4 Aug 2025.

International Monetary Fund. 2020. Law and Financial Stability. https://www.elibrary.imf.org/display/book/9781513523002/9781513523002.xml?code=imf.org. Accessed 15 July 2025.

International Monetary Fund. 2023. Global Financial Stability Report: Safeguarding Financial Stability amid High Inflation and Geopolitical Risks. https://www.imf.org/en/Publications/GFSR/Issues/2023/04/11/global-financial-stability-report-april-2023. Accessed 4 Aug 2025.

International Monetary Fund. 2024. Global Financial Stability Report 2024. https://www.imf.org/en/Publications/GFSR/Issues/2024/10/22/global-financial-stability-report-october-2024. Accessed 4 Aug 2025.

International Monetary Fund. 2025a. Global Financial Stability Report: Enhancing Resilience amid Uncertainty. https://www.imf.org/en/Publications/GFSR/Issues/2025/04/22/global-financial-stability-report-april-2025. Accessed 4 Aug 2025.

International Monetary Fund. 2025b. *Global Financial Stability Risks Have Increased Significantly, Driven by Tighter Global Financial Conditions and Heightened Trade and Geopolitical Uncertainty*. Global Financial Stability Report: Enhancing Resilience Amid Uncertainty. https://www.imf.org/en/Publications/GFSR/Issues/2025/04/22/global-financial-stability-report-april-2025. Accessed 4 Aug 2025.

International Monetary Fund. 2025c. Global Growth Is Expected to Decline and Downside Risks to Intensify as Major Policy Shifts Unfold. https://www.imf.org/en/Publications/WEO/Issues/2025/04/22/world-economic-outlook-april-2025. Accessed 4 Aug 2025.

International Monetary Fund. 2025d. World Economic Outlook: A Critical Juncture amid Policy Shifts. https://www.imf.org/en/Publications/WEO/Issues/2025/04/22/world-economic-outlook-april-2025. Accessed 4 Aug 2025.

International Monetary Fund and Financial Stability Board. 2023. IMF-FSB Synthesis Paper: Policies for Crypto-Assets. https://www.fsb.org/uploads/R070923-1.pdf. Accessed 4 Aug 2025.

International Monetary Fund, Fiscal Affairs Department. 2025. *Fiscal Monitor, April 2025: Fiscal Policy under Uncertainty*. IMF Executive Board discussion of the outlook, April 2025. https://www.elibrary.imf.org/display/book/9798229002516/9798229002516.xml. Accessed 4 Aug 2025.

Jordan, Cally. 2012. *International Financial Standards and the Explanatory Force of Lex Mercatoria*. Center for Transnational Legal Studies. https://scholarship.law.georgetown.edu/cgi/viewcontent.cgi?article=1002&context=ctls_papers. Accessed 4 Aug 2025.

Kissinger, Henry. 2022. *Leadership: Six Studies in World Strategy*. New York: Penguin Press.

Lagarde, Christine. 2022. *A New Global Map: European Resilience in a Changing World.* Speech at the Peterson Institute for International Economics, Washington, DC. https://www.ecb.europa.eu/press/key/date/2022/html/ecb.sp220422~c43af3db20.en.html. Accessed 19 Aug 2025.

Laker, John F. 1999. Monitoring Financial System Stability. *Reserve Bank of Australia Bulletin*. https://www.rba.gov.au/publications/bulletin/1999/oct/pdf/bu-1099-1.pdf. Accessed 10 July 2025.

Lawrence, Dana. 2024. *Bank Runs in the Age of Connectivity: Lessons for Internal Auditors*. Compliance, Wolters Kluwer. https://www.wolterskluwer.com/en/expert-insights/bank-runs-age-of-interconnectivity-lessons-for-internal-auditors. Accessed 4 Aug 2025.

Lifshits, Ilya, and Vladislav Ponamorenko. 2020. International Financial Standards in the Global Legal Order and in EU and EAEU Law. *Russian Law Journal* 8:4–31.

Milanović, Branko. 2025. *What Comes After Globalization*. JACOBIN. https://jacobin.com/2025/03/what-comes-after-globalization. Accessed 4 Aug 2025.

Montgomery, Brian H., David Oliwenstein, Tony Phillips, Daniel C. Wood, and Adam Goldberg. 2025. *Trump 2.0: A New Era for the Regulation of Cryptocurrency and Digital Assets*. Pillsbury Insights. https://www.pillsburylaw.com/en/news-and-insights/cryptocurrency-digital-assets-trump.html. Accessed 4 Aug 2025.

Neumann, Peter R. 2022. *The New World Disorder: How the West Is Destroying Itself.* Melbourne: Scribe Publications.

Parsons, Louise. 2019. *The Uneasy Mandate of the Reserve Bank of Australia for Financial Stability: Challenges for Governance and Accountability*. PhD Thesis, Bond University. https://pure.bond.edu.au/ws/portalfiles/portal/36066400/Louise_Parsons_Thesis.pdf. Accessed 15 Feb 2025.

Raustiala, Kal. 2002. The Architecture of International Cooperation: Transgovernmental Networks and the Future of International Law. *Virginia Journal of International Law* 43:1–92.

Schinasi, Garry J. 2006. *Safeguarding Financial Stability: Theory and Practice*. International Monetary Fund. https://www.imf.org/External/Pubs/NFT/2005/SFS/eng/sfs.pdf. Accessed 15 Feb 2025.

Slaughter, Anne-Marie. 2000. Governing the Global Economy Through Government Networks. In *The Role of Law in International Politics: Essays in International Relations and International Law*, ed. Michael Byers, 177–206. Oxford: Oxford University Press.

Steinberg, Federico. 2023. *The Neo-Mercantilist Moment*. Centre for Strategic and International Studies. https://www.csis.org/analysis/neo-mercantilist-moment. Accessed 4 Aug 2025.

The White House. 2025. *Fact Sheet: President Donald J. Trump Establishes the Strategic Bitcoin Reserve and U.S.* Digital Asset Stockpile. https://www.whitehouse.gov/fact-sheets/2025/03/fact-sheet-president-donald-j-trump-establishes-the-strategic-bitcoin-reserve-and-u-s-digital-asset-stockpile. Accessed 4 Aug 2025.

The White House. n.d. The Clinton Presidency: A Foreign Policy for the Global Age. https://clintonwhitehouse5.archives.gov/WH/EOP/NSC/html/global-age.html. Accessed 4 Aug 2025.

Tobin, James. 2025. *Challenges to a Rules-Based International Order*. UK Parliament House of Lords Library. In Focus Briefing. https://lordslibrary.parliament.uk/challenges-to-a-rules-based-international-order/. Accessed 14 Apr 2025.

Tucker, Paul. 2022. *Global Discord: Values and Power in a Fractured World Order*. Princeton: Princeton University Press.

Van Dormael, Armand. 1978. *Bretton Woods: Birth of a Monetary System*. London: Macmillan.

Walker, Nigel. 2021. *Brexit Timeline: Events Leading to the UK's Exit from the European Union*. House of Commons Library. https://researchbriefings.files.parliament.uk/documents/CBP-7960/CBP-7960.pdf. Accessed 4 Aug 2025.

Waller, Christopher J. 2025. *Challenges Facing Central Bankers. Speech at Lectures of the Governor*. Organization for Economic Cooperation and Development. https://www.federalreserve.gov/newsevents/speech/files/waller20250108a.pdf. Accessed 1 Aug 2025.

Wilde, Oscar. n.d. Lady Windermere's Fan, in Act 1, Line by Lord Darlington. *Standard EBOOKS*. https://standardebooks.org/ebooks/oscar-wilde/lady-windermeres-fan/text/act-1. Accessed 5 Aug 2025.

World Bank Group. 2016. Global Financial Development Report: Bank Regulation and Supervision a Decade after the Global Financial Crisis. https://www.worldbank.org/en/publication/gfdr/gfdr-2016. Accessed 4 Aug 2025.

World Economic Forum. 2025. Global Risks Report 2025. https://reports.weforum.org/docs/WEF_Global_Risks_Report_2025.pdf. Accessed 4 Aug 2025.

World Economic Forum (in collaboration with Oliver Wyman). 2025. *Navigating Global Financial System Fragmentation*. World Economic Forum Insight Report. https://www.weforum.org/publications/navigating-global-financial-system-fragmentation/. Accessed 4 Aug 2025.

Zakaria, Fareed. 2008. The Rise of the Rest. *Newsweek*, pp. 43–49. https://fareedzakaria.com/columns/2008/05/12/the-rise-of-the-rest. Accessed 5 Aug 2025.

Chapter 5
Building a Bloc, Brick by BRICs

Laurence Boulle

Abstract This contribution examines the place and roles of the BRICs+ group of nations operating as a transnational network in a context of shifting international norms and practices. It examines the evolutionary growth of the bloc, its current membership and governance, and it general policies and practices, and in some cases lack thereof. Its main focus is on the role of the bloc in the changing contours of international finance, with particular reference to the New Development Bank, its impetus for moving away from dollar denominated cross-border transactions and the starts and stops in developing a new reserve currency. A case study on planetary health highlights both the commonalities and differences among member states, and the chapter concludes with reflections on the extent to which the BRICs+ group acts collectively or its members, in particular China and India, operate individually.

5.1 Introduction

This chapter examines and evaluates the BRICs group of nations in terms of its status as a "transnational network".[1] The group operates in the interstitial zones between formal global institutions, such as the International Monetary Fund (IMF), World Bank and World Trade Organisation (WTO), and those which have occasional or sporadic interactions and interventions within looser organisational arrangements. While the group operates beyond the domestic level it is yet to attain the governance and policy functions of established international institutions. It does, however, exhibit "patterns of regular and purposive relations" across national

[1] Slaughter and Hale (2010, p. 4).

L. Boulle (✉)
Faculty of Law, Bond University, Robina, QLD, Australia
e-mail: lboulle@bond.edu.au

U. H. Ghori, J. Farrar (eds.), *Globalisation Disrupted*,
https://doi.org/10.1007/978-981-95-3997-0_5

borders and has "ties developed through frequent interaction rather than formal negotiation."[2]

The Chapter first identifies the international contexts within which the bloc[3] operates, its membership and governance, including comparisons between the BRICs and more established bodies. It then examines BRICs summit declarations and policies, or the absence thereof, in some of the contentious issues of the day. The chapter then turns to matters of international finance, including the New Development Bank, use of local currencies in trade transactions, and issues relating to the "de-dollarisation" of the global economy and promotion of a new global reserve currency. In light of the 2023 expansion of the World Bank's objectives, planetary health is used as a case study on the alignment, misalignment and actions of BRICs member states in relation to an important contemporary global issue. From this follows a discussion of the extent to which BRICs nations act together or apart, and in combinations thereof, on key global issues. Brief reference is made to Australia's stance towards the BRICs[4] before returning to some the thematic issues underlying the status and role of BRICs in the challenges to current trade, finance and security issues.[5]

Three themes twist and turn through different parts of the BRICs narrative:

- The first relates to the factors that unite an organisation despite the many and varied divergences among its members and its limited infrastructural support.
- The second relates to the discrepancies between the bloc's agendas, policies and summit declarations, on one hand, and actual progress in their implementation, on the other.
- The third relates to the scope for the BRICs, within the current inconsistencies and uncertainties in international affairs and the global economy, to become more influential in some of its goals and objectives.

The chapter suggests that many of the projections about the growth, influence and potential impacts of the BRICs have not been matched by what has actually occurred. Like the dog that did not bark in the Sherlock Holmes story, the BRICs is characterised as much by what it has not done as by what it has achieved. This is not, however, to foreclose the possibility of the bloc having significant future impacts in areas of trade, finance, currencies, the environment and the changing global order in an epoch of diminished multilateralism and economic deglobalisation.

---

[2] Ibid.

[3] Several collective terms are used in relation to the BRICs: partnership, grouping, bloc, alliance, forum. *Alliance* suggests a mutual defence pact but there is no military cooperation within the BRICs. *Bloc* suggests some ideological consistency among bloc members, which is also thin with the BRICs. The terms group and bloc are used here inter-changeably.

[4] Slaughter and Hale, *supra*, n. 1.

[5] The chapter includes some retrospective reflections on the contributions a decade ago in Lo and Hiscock (2014).

5.2 Global Contexts

There is no single context in which to consider the rise and expansion of the BRICs bloc, but rather numerous sub-contexts involving international and domestic powers, pressures and politics. There are currently many shifting allegiances and cross-cutting cleavages in the world order. While the shifts brought about by a new US administration in 2025 have significant impacts for the narrative, they also tend to be inconsistent and equivocal, and deeper level trends can sometimes be more significant than the immediate topical changes.

Recent decades have witnessed numerous challenges to the economics and politics of globalisation, partly driven by those who have not benefitted from the system. One of the central contentions is that the political economy of the world was created by developed western countries, the so-called Global North, at the expense of developing and emerging economies, the Global South. The challenges from the latter perspective revolve around their political insecurity, intractable social problems, long term debt problems and the perceived illegitimacy of international institutions and their programs. The challenges have been fuelled by the rise of economic nativism in Global North countries and uncertainties in governance and ideology not evident in the past. In practical terms the malaise has involved developed countries introducing subsidies, import tariffs, non-tariff barriers, economic sanctions and general trade and investment restrictions that undermine hallowed principles of the global order. The BRICs has been part of the current challenges to the status quo and the demands for a new global order.

The current pulses in globalisation involve, to lesser or greater extents, deviations from the economic orthodoxy that prevailed over the past 70 years[6] as countries and regions compete for influence and hegemony. The legitimating ideology of economic globalisation has lost its allure. Comparative advantage wears thin in situations of increasing subsidies, tariffs and protectionism. Shifts in public discourse have undermined the ideology of "small government" as nation states appreciate that state services are essential and resources have to be used, by the private sector or government, for the public good. Again, the BRICs nations have pushed, or at least bumped, against prevailing power relations in the international sphere.

An example of the disruption to orthodox thinking relates to semiconductor chips in which Taiwan has for some time been the largest global supplier. In 2024 its main manufacturer announced it would build a second plant in the US for development of its most advanced chips, with plans for a third. While this involves Taiwanese foreign investment in the host country, the second factory is being developed with a \$6.6 billion grant from the US government, and a further \$5 billion worth of loans under the host country's *Chips Act* 2022. Even larger grants and loans have been made to local chip manufacturers, and other countries have

[6] One of the local contributions to the trend is the *Future Made in Australia Bill* 2024 (Cth), introduced in the Commonwealth parliament and designed to unlock and encourage investment in local industry. See Parliament of Australia (2024).

replicated these policies.[7] While there are security and political reasons for the taxpayer contributions to private corporations, they have to be seen in the context of US competition with at least one BRICs country, namely China, and other current disruptions of global orthodoxy, referred to later.

In overall terms there is a new systemic fragility in the global economy and rules-based international order and challenges to hallowed institutions and precepts that have underlined globalisation in the past.[8] The question arises as to where and how the BRICs bloc sits and operates within the uncertainties over the changing rules of the game.

5.3 Membership

The broader context to the rise of BRICs is found in the many international and regional organisations to have emerged over the past 70 years. One was the non-aligned movement (NAM) that came together in the 1960s with the goal of allowing developing and emerging countries to avoid the competitive polarisation emerging between western countries, on one hand, and Russia, on the other.[9] While there is no institutional connection between the NAM and the BRICs, they both envisage a larger voice for middle- and small-power states otherwise, muted in international forums and diplomacy. Six BRICs countries are also NAM members, and two others are observers. The continuance of the NAM would suggest a middle path for the BRICs in international affairs as it is more representative of jurisdictions on the threshold of growth and influence.

The membership of the BRICs has grown since its inception, as reflected in the following Table 5.1, together with relevant dates:

In the early 2020s the original bloc began considering admission of additional countries to the established group. This led to periodic headlines speculating on the states apparently interested in seeking admission, though often without any follow through. However, the bloc was evidently open to new members that self-represented as "developing" and as representing the Global South. Elastic as those concepts can be they signify a large pool of potential members. In January 2025, for example, Indonesia became the 10th member state, after serving for a short time as an observer partner—its membership added further heft to the organisation and brought the bloc geographically closer to Australia.[10] The accession of new members signified a shift

[7] Protectionism has been particularly evident in the electric vehicle industry, with subsidies for local manufacturers and punitive tariffs on Chinese EV imports in the EU and North America. Tariffs invite retaliations from targeted jurisdictions.

[8] See generally Rasmus (2016).

[9] Among the 121 members of the NAM seven have BRICs connections: Egypt, UAE, Uganda, India, Indonesia, South Africa, Ethiopia.

[10] Indonesia had been invited to join the BRICs a decade earlier but there was internal political resistance at the time.

Table 5.1 Evolution of BRICs membership

Initial Members	Brazil, China, Russia, India	2009
'Original' Member (South Africa joined shortly after the bloc's founding, shifting nomenclature from BRIC to BRICs)	South Africa	2010
Additional Members	Ethiopia, UAE, Iran, Egypt	2023/4
Partner States	Belarus, Bolivia, Cuba, Indonesia, Kazakhstan, Malaysia, Thailand, Uganda, and Uzbekistan (There is some obscurity about the identity of the partner states and the countries that have sought membership. Neither category is clearly identified in BRICs sources)	2024
Recent Member	Indonesia	2025

from a "club" with closed membership, such as the G-7, towards a more open-ended institution.

There have also been equivocations in regard to membership. Saudi Arabia, for example, was invited to join in 2024 and its accession would have notionally enhanced the energy nucleus of the bloc. After appearing to accept the invitation the country deferred a decision and at the time of writing has neither accepted nor declined BRICs membership. There have been no public pronouncements about the equivocation. It could be a function of the country's close relations to the US, particularly in relation to arms and technology imports, though India has similar close connections.[11] More pragmatically it suggests that the cost-benefit equation is not at present sufficiently attractive to the Saudis. Another significant state mooted for membership, even before Saudi Arabia, is Türkiye. Its accession would be the first for a European state and a NATO member but has yet to materialise.[12]

The concept of observer states for prospective members was first introduced at the 2024 BRICs summit.[13] It provides for a kind of trial arrangement, on both sides of the equation. Nine states were invited to become partners and at the time of

[11] The US President has also threatened steep tariffs on BRICs members but in the malaise of conflicting tariff signals this threat may be too remote. However Saudi Arabia is a dialogue partner of the Shanghai Cooperation Organisation which is assertive vis-à-vis US interests.

[12] Ankara's dissatisfaction with the West derived partly from its support for Israel's activities in Gaza. There is also dissatisfaction over frustrated attempts to join the EU. Türkiye is a member of the US-led NATO but did not support NATO proposals for sanctions on Russia for the Ukraine invasion. Argentina applied for membership but withdrew after a change of government and recalibration of its foreign policy; Algeria also rejected a membership invitation.

[13] UN Secretary-General Antonio Guterres attended the expansion announcement, reflecting the bloc's growing influence. He echoed BRICs' longstanding calls for reforms of the UN Security Council, International Monetary Fund and World Bank. His presence was criticised in some quarters.

writing the nine referred to above have accepted.[14] While not formally part of the bloc, the partner states have observer status at summits and are potentially able to solicit support on crucial matters.[15] Indonesia, as noted, evolved from partner to full member at the beginning of 2025.

5.4 Common and Contrasting Attributes

From its inception commentators attempted to develop theories on what unites the originating members, and more recently the partner states. They evidence some overlaps and many divergences. Russia, the UAE and Iran are major suppliers of energy; Russia, South Africa and Brazil are exporters of minerals; India and China import raw materials; Russia, China and India possess nuclear weapons; China is a dominant global exporter of manufactured goods; Russia and China are permanent members of the UN Security Council; all states are members of the WTO, with Russia's position sometimes tenuous;[16]and India and China have long suffered border conflicts, including armed incursions. As shown shortly the members also display great divergences in their political, legal and social systems.

Among their shared attributes is the fact that no BRICs member belongs to the developed group of countries. They are all non-western "emerging nations" with interests in reforming international institutions and changing dominant power relations in the global economy—albeit not always in clearly defined ways. An incongruous common denominator is the ranking of individual members on the Wealth Inequality Table, measured in terms of the Gini coefficient.[17] South Africa sits at the head of the global inequality table with a coefficient of 82. It is followed closely by fellow BRICs nations, Brazil and the UAE, with India in seventh place and prospective member Saudi Arabia in the top 10. When tracked over the past decade wealth inequality has, broadly speaking, increased in developing economies and reduced slightly in developed states. While not too much can be made of these figures they are a recognisable common denominator in the BRICs countries.

It is a truism that there as many, if not more, differences among BRICs members as there are similarities. The new members and partners have created even greater diversity within the group. Iran, for example, is a major fossil fuel exporter, Ethiopia

[14] There is some obscurity about the identity of the partner states and the countries that have sought membership. Neither category is clearly identified in BRICs sources.

[15] The concept derives from the Shanghai Cooperation Organisation's system of staged accession—see The Shanghai Cooperation Organisation (2025).

BRICs members Russia and China are also part of this grouping.

[16] Russia only joined in 2012 after protracted trade and IP negotiations. It has threatened to withdraw, and been subject to expulsion proposals, but remains a member.

[17] Voronoi (2023). The Gini coefficient is based on index scores for each country, with a score of 100 indicating that one individual possesses all its wealth, and the lower the score the greater the distributive equality in the respective society.

experiences serious food shortages, the UAE is diminutive in territorial size and Indonesia has the largest Islamic population in the world. Among the many other differences among BRICs members are the population sizes of member states, their levels of political participation, the vigour, or otherwise, of the rule of law, and, not without significance, geographical locations. China, Brazil and Russia are major powers, while the others are in the middle- and lower-power ranks. China has the largest economy, at approximately $18 trillion annual GDP, and Ethiopia the smallest, though one of the fastest growing, at $0.3 trillion. Some member states are major energy producers and others are energy deprived.

BRICs members also have diverging foreign policy goals, a complicating factor for the group's consensus decision-making model. These diversities emphasise the fact that countries have different interests and priorities in their involvement in the bloc.[18] While China might see the primary advantages of the BRICs as an agent for extending its influence in the world, for Russia a priority is the imperative to overcome sanctions and preserve its economy, partly through new financial settlement systems referred to later. South Africa, Brazil and Indonesia have interests in retaining their influence as regional players in Africa, South America and south-east Asia respectively.

Accessing the BRICs is relatively simple, the application process comprising an expression of interest with no selection criteria or other formalities. Unless vetoed by one existing member the applicant is duly accepted.[19] Malaysia sought accession in 2024 through no more than an expression of interest submitted to Russia, the then coordinating country. It currently has partner status. This is unlike accession to the European Union with its requirements to bring political, legal and human rights regimes into alignment with the body's norms and policies; it is unlike the WTO which requires compliance with or commitments to multilateral trade rules; and it is unlike treaty-based organisations where there is scope for reservations, ratification formalities and protocols for treaty registration. However, unanimity among existing BRICs members is required for full membership and this has proved problematic for both Pakistan and Venezuela. The relative ease of access affords discretion to executive branches of sovereign states but there is no evidence of membership being a prominent issue in domestic politics.[20]

The 2024 expansions to the BRICs invited comparison with other non-contiguous international groupings, for example the G-7 and G-20 groups of nations.[21] In 2024

---

[18] Curtis (2024).

[19] In 2023 the BRICs established three sets of guidelines relating to new members: Guiding principles for BRICs membership expansion; Standards and criteria for membership expansion; Procedure for BRICs membership expansion. All the standards are generalised and relatively loose.

[20] Among many other countries both Thailand and Philippines in south-east Asia have expressed interest in BRICs membership.

[21] The contiguous European Union grouping is not a good comparator, but for the record the BRICs has a larger combined GDP than the EU.

the International Monetary Fund noted the dominance of the BRICs over the G-7 in four areas, reflected in the following Table 5.2:[22]

Trends are as important as static figures and since 2010 the BRICs percentage of global GDP has been steadily increasing while that of the G-7 has been declining. With India having joined China in 2024 in the top five global economies the momentum is with the BRICs, its current GDP growth rate nearly three times that of the G-7. The addition of new members can only increase discrepancies between the two. Needless to say there are other indicators in which the G-7 outranks the BRICs, such as per capita GDP and annual military expenditure. It also prevails in terms of access to the levers of the global political system and the soft power it can project.

Unlike the BRICs, the G-20 group of states, established in 1999, provides a forum for both developed and emerging nations to consider issues facing its members and the world as a whole. There are overlapping memberships between the two groups as the five original BRICs members, as well as Indonesia, are also part of the G-20, making comparisons less significant.[23] While the BRICs bloc constitutes a source of potential influence within G-20 deliberations, the different, and at times inconsistent, priorities among members have precluded the group acting as a cohesive force. This does not preclude the BRICs becoming more cohesive over time in attempting to influence G-20 decisions or having a brokerage role among dissenting voices.

A noteworthy factor in the current composition of the BRICs is the number of African countries represented in the bloc. There are currently three members and two partner states from west, east, north and southern Africa. The continent itself has a comprehensive trade and investment treaty embracing all 54 members of the African Union.[24] Moreover, several countries on the continent have the biggest economic growth figures in the world and have retained the demographic dividend, currently lost in countries in Europe, the Americas and Asia. The African presence

Table 5.2 BRICs vs. G7 countries

	BRICs (%)	G7 (%)
Share of total world population	45	19
Share of global GDP (in PPP terms)	36	30
Contribution to global economic growth	44	20
Share of global oil production	44	29

22 Statista (2024).

23 Further increases in BRICs membership would, paradoxically, cause it to become like the G-20 in several ways.

24 The African Continental Free Trade Area (AfCFTA) was finalised in 2018 by the African Continental Free Trade Agreement. After the WTO it establishes the largest trade area in terms of state members, including the largest in terms of territory and population.

in the BRICs epitomises the Global South credentials of the group, reinforced by the African Union's recent participation in BRICs meetings.[25]

5.5 Organisation and Governance

The BRICs has been slow to develop any central organisational infrastructure. It lacks a permanent secretariat and fixed headquarters and operates on a revolving presidency, the country of which serves as host for annual summits. To date the five original members have assumed the presidency and hosting rights on an annual rotational basis. The host country, in consultation with other members, has primary influence over the themes and agendas for summits, a wide discretion that can result in some discontinuity from one summit to the next. Convening countries also have discretion over the presence of observer countries or institutions such as the United Nations, European Union or African Union. The summits set priorities, develop policy and issue public communiques. There have been suggestions and proposals about institutionalising the BRICs to a greater extent to overcome the obstacle of operating without infrastructure, but there have been no concerted efforts in this direction.

At the 2024 summit in Russia 33 countries were represented, some by heads of state or government, and the UN by the Secretary-General. This summit, which confirmed the bloc's expansion, was noteworthy in that both the Prime Minister of India and the President of South Africa chose to attend the BRICs summit instead of the Commonwealth Heads of Government meeting taking place at the same time. This speaks to the bloc's increasing profile and influence, and possibly the greater gravitational pull provided by the Indian and Chinese presence. There is also ad hoc engagement with international bodies, for example with the World Health Organisation in relation to COVID-19.

Summit agendas have been wide-ranging, influenced by the agency available to the convening country. Its areas of focus shift from summit to summit. Over the past five years the following topics, inter alia, have appeared on the agenda papers: reform of international financial institutions, combating Covid-19, cooperation in food security, agricultural cooperation, transitioning to the digital economy, trade sanctions, grain negotiation arrangements and sustainable development goals. In 2024 a new focus area was the environment and climate change, referred to further below under the rubric of planetary health.

While annual summits are the main decision-making forums meetings of national ministers are also convened on matters within their portfolios, including finance, trade and energy. There are also BRICs working groups focused on technology, education, health and culture, and other topics as prioritised from time to time. The

[25] The African Union has also become a member of the G-20 group of nations, as has been the European Union.

bloc's Business Council, Think Tank Council and Academic Forum are specialised forums, supplemented more recently by the establishment of a BRICs Digital Ecosystem Cooperation Network. There are more than 50 intra-group councils, working groups and networks operating under BRICs auspices.

The array of summits, meetings and councils suggests substantial activity. Some of this is not, however, the subject of comment in western circles, partly because the bloc has not been an international body with a persistent presence in global affairs. Its interventions tend to be more eclectic and focused on nature. For example, the BRICs called for an immediate ceasefire between warring parties in Sudan and denounced the Israeli invasion and occupation of Gaza, but it has not presented as a major force in international crisis politics. This is a function of the diverse interests it reflects. For example, despite calls for reform of bodies such as the UN Security Council there are intra-group differences on its nature, with Russia and China already holding permanent positions.[26] India and China have had protracted disputes along their shared borders, with occasional encroachments and armed skirmishes, while Egypt and Ethiopia have ongoing conflicts over use of the waters of the river Nile. While there might be commonality of priorities and policies in various economic matters this is less the case in respect of other topical global issues.

In terms of broader policy issues the foundation BRICs members promoted reform to the international financial institutions and the UN Security Council to redress their historical exclusion from decision-making processes shaping the global economy and political world order. The proposals to reform the UN are about making it more representative of the emerging world and more effective in its operations. The BRICs also supports a new global monetary system, or systems, and a new reserve currency. The bloc's challenges to the legitimacy of financial institutions such as the IMF and World Bank, and its pursuit of multipolarity in the global order, have had it portrayed as having another common ingredient, namely in being anti-western and anti-American in nature. While there is some validity to the critique it could be reframed more benignly as promoting better treatment from the Global North to the Global South. In other words, as being not anti-west but non-west. In reality, the five original members have different concerns about how power is distributed and exercised globally.

Here brief comparison is provided with one of many parallel state groupings to the BRICs, namely the ASEAN Economic Community (AEC) founded in 1967. The AEC comprises ten countries in South and East Asia, with greater geographical contiguity than the BRICs members but with the same similarities and divergences of national interests among member states.[27] It has a more established infrastructure than the BRICs, with a rotating Secretary-General and permanent secretariat, and it convenes bi-annual summits. The bloc covers 600 million people with a combined

[26] BRICs members India and Brazil have claims to a permanent seat, and a case can also be made for permanent African representation on the Council, for example through the African Union.

[27] Brunei Darussalam, Cambodia, Indonesia, Lao PDR, Malaysia, Myanmar, Philippines, Singapore, Thailand, and Viet Nam.

market size of US $2.3 trillion, significantly smaller than the coverage of the BRICs, but with some fast-growing economies among its members.

In terms of policy and politics the AEC has been less a reflexive response to western-led institutions and more a push for greater and more effective inclusion in the global economy along neo-liberal lines. From its inception the bloc focused on key economic issues as it aimed at a "EU-style" organisation. It has maintained goads of achieving a single market through regional economic integration. Among other economic issues it has prioritised joint competition policies, consumer protections and intellectual property rights. It has supported both international trade agreements and closer economic partnerships, including agreements with BRICs countries Russia and China.[28] Unlike the BRICs it has not promoted an alternative reserve currency, but has attempted to develop its own common currency.

The AEC's latest Blueprint was produced in 2025. It promotes a focus on enhanced connectivity in energy, transport and tourism, less salient issues for the BRICs. The Blueprint also promotes ASEAN cooperation on the environment, guided by its Vision 2025, striving to promote and ensure balanced social development and sustainable environment. This reflects the inherent tension between policies of economic development and planetary health, with the former tending to prevail over the latter. The same conundrum faces the BRICs Laboratory on the environment, dealt with below.

5.6 Global Finance

There are several moving parts in global finance and its governance in the twenty-first century. They include, among others, the legitimacy of international institutions, the effectiveness of development banks, foreign direct investment trends, currency fluctuations, reductions in overseas development aid, remittances to home countries and high levels of national debt in sovereign states. Many BRICs states have debt narratives, involving risks of severe indebtedness and difficulties in raising capital. These factors have to lead calls, for most of the twenty-first century, for debt relief in respective countries. These are acknowledged in a 2024 UNCTAD report which suggests that debt weakness is not only the source of limited leverage for such countries, but also derives from weaknesses in governance systems, something not directly addressed by the BRICs.[29]

The liberalisation of global finance across national borders in past decades has been a significant feature of economic globalisation, providing for rapid cross-border movement of investment capital, royalties, profits and earnings, analogously to movements of manufactured goods and raw materials. This has created winners

[28] It has also negotiated partnership arrangements with Australia and New Zealand.

[29] UN Trade and Development (2024). The report also highlights the difficulties of developing countries in capturing tax revenues from cross-border activities.

and losers among nation states. As a consequence, many hallowed concepts and principles of financial liberalisation are currently under stress. Here three aspects relevant to the BRICs are considered.

5.7 New Development Bank

In 2014 the foundation BRICs members established the multilateral New Development Bank (NDB), a treaty-based institution supervised by a Board of Governors.[30] The NDB has the distinction of being the first multilateral bank established by, designed for and led by developing and emerging countries, with equality of power in its decisions. Members have equal shareholdings in the NDB, unlike arrangements at the World Bank where the US has the dominant role.

The NDB provides funding to its own members and other emerging nations.[31] The funds are geared mainly towards infrastructure, such as railways, water reticulation, bridges and electrification. Bank membership is not restricted to BRICs members and external states such as Algeria, Bangladesh and Uruguay have joined the institution since its inception. By 2024 the NDB had approved 96 projects in different jurisdictions and is regarded as one of the BRICs' main institutional achievements; the repeated desire to wean member states off the dollar, by contrast, has moved more slowly. Its most recent loan was made in mid-2025 when the NDB resolved to provide South Africa with a loan of US $400 million for revitalising road infrastructure and upgrading four major freeways, in response to the country's problems with aging transport systems.[32]

In some quarters the NDB has been seen to constitute a potential threat to the World Bank and International Monetary Fund. No real challenge to the Bretton Woods institutions has materialised and the NDB tends to act as a complement, and not a competitor, to the established financial institutions. The annual funding of the International Finance Corporation, part of the World Bank Group, remains well more than that provided by the NDB.

The BRICs Contingent Reserve Arrangement (CRA), with a currency pool of $100 billion, is designed to assist countries facing financial disruption, for example a run on the national currency too large to be managed by the respective central bank. This is also a treaty arrangement that came into legal force after ratification by BRICs members.[33] More than 50% of the currency pool was provided by China,

---

[30] New Development Bank (2014).

[31] The back story is that the BRICs pledged significant funds to the IMF, conditional on voting reforms in the institution. The IMF demurred. This led to the establishment of the NDB 3 years later, with the stated objective of cooperating with the western-dominated bodies.

[32] Ekanem (2025). An earlier application to the NDB by the country's road agency was unsuccessful and did not receive government backing because of problems in the toll road systems, since rectified.

[33] Treaty for the Establishment of a BRICs Contingent Reserve Arrangement (2014).

where the bank's headquarters are located, with the African HQ hosted by South Africa. The bank is authorised to contribute $30 billion annually to member states requiring urgent economic support. A BRICs CRA Governing Council supervises governance of the system.

While the CRA is a creative institutional development on the ground it has not been evenly accepted, even within the BRICs. Brazil was resistant to its development, although it did contribute to the currency pool. There is also concern that the CRA operates, ironically, through the US dollar and has not been as active in its lending services as had been anticipated.

5.8 Settling Trade Transactions

The second financial matter receiving BRICs attention relates to the settlement of international trade transactions. For over 70 years the US dollar has been the world's unofficial currency and upwards of 80% of annual global trade transactions have been denominated in USD. The historic status of the dollar as the "global reserve" currency was secured by a combination of factors. Central banks and other financial institutions were induced to hold dollars to facilitate payments in dollar denominated cross-border transactions and they required the currency as the only way of purchasing US Treasury bonds. Treasuries, in turn, were long regarded by other countries as one of the most secure assets and safest investments, particularly in times of political uncertainty and economic insecurity. They can be readily bought and sold but only in US dollars, adding to the currency's instrumental attraction. As yields on Treasuries increased during the early months of 2025 their stability and security declined. This led to reduced attraction for central banks and commercial financial institutions in holding US dollars. Many moved into alternative assets such as gold and other currencies. While the system had a self-sustaining logic for many decades it is currently being undermined, by political conduct from the US itself and by the policies and practices of the BRICs countries.[34]

Currency questions, and an alternative reserve currency, have been on BRICs' agendas for many years.[35] The common goal has been to circumvent the complications for member states arising from trade transactions denominated in USD which required contracting entities on both sides of the transaction to have holdings in a foreign currency, namely the dollar. Apart from being expensive, this exposed them to potential asset freezing and economic sanctions. BRICs members Russia and Iran have been impacted significantly by US trade sanctions and are strongly behind moves away from the dollar; China has long supported the move as part of its

[34] Central banks have responded by diversifying holdings to assets denominated in non-USD currencies.

[35] However, its salience has fluctuated—the BRICs declaration after the 2023 Summit included references to neither the dollar nor de-dollarisation. There is now a sense of urgency in respect of both.

aspiration for greater leverage in the global economy. Other bloc members have their own interests in the move, including future proofing their economies against sanctions. It also has attractions for other developing countries in terms of growth imperatives for their domestic economies. Whatever the range of motivations the BRICs has historically been the leading bloc attempting to challenge USD use in cross-border transactions.

In early 2025 China and Brazil announced that they would settle future trade transactions in the currencies of the two jurisdictions and not in USD. The stated intention is supported by the economic reality that in recent years business relations among major BRICs partners have become significant on both ends of the trades. For example, China now ranks as Brazil's largest trading partner and is a major foreign direct investor in energy, mining and manufacturing in the host country. Brazil ranks ninth among China's trading partners and is the country's most important source of agricultural and food supplies. The countries have bilateral treaties in trade, investment and finance, enhancing the initial economic relations between two foundation BRICs members. If the 2025 announcement is followed through in practice it will constitute a small, but significant, challenge to the dollar's pre-eminence.

Russia and China made a similar announcement soon after that of China and Brazil, again a significant repositioning of cross-border transactions with long-term consequences. In similar vein, former USSR republics, all members of the Commonwealth of Independent States, announced in April 2025 their intended transition away from the USD in pursuit of national economic sovereignty. Apart from Russia, the states include three BRICs partner countries: Belarus, Kazakhstan and Uzbekistan. These countries have small economies by global standards; no period is stipulated for completing the transition and it could take years for the countries to substitute their local currencies. Nonetheless the shift does reinforce the current challenges to US economic hegemony.

Since the 2022 imposition of sanctions on Russia the country has begun using alternatives to the USD, deploying the Chinese RMB for settlements with China, using its own currency the rouble (RUB) where it can, and sometimes even adopting the RMB in transactions with the non-Chinese states. In 2023–2024 Russia settled more international transactions in the RMB than in the USD for the first time. Other BRICs countries, such as Brazil, have also settled in RMB, particularly in the energy sector, sometimes in return for pricing discounts and delivery preferences. These arrangements include, ironically, a shift from the currency of one foreign country to that of another. However, the winds of change are blowing in every direction. Until a decade ago nearly 100% of oil trades were conducted in USD, but by 2023 nearly 20% of these trades were transacted in other currencies. Despite the various activities by BRICs members in relation to currency issues, it is noticeable that it is not the BRICs as a collective entity that has moved forward but individual states with the leverage to do so.

5.9 Payment Systems

Various options have been proposed in relation to alternative payment systems for transactions crossing national borders, although, as with some other BRICs business, there has been more speculation than activity on the ground. This is again an area where individual members have different interests and priorities—while China has long promoted the use of local currencies, India has at times indicated its preference for retention of the dollar. Other BRICs members have their own currency preferences, and these can fluctuate over time.

A first option involves denominating trades in non-dollar currencies, as reflected in the proposals referred to above. This is the easiest structural arrangement and sits wholly within the discretions of the contracting entities. There are also potential downsides to the arrangements in terms of fluctuations in the values of volatile local currencies. Fluctuations were once assumed not to apply to the existing reserve currency—but this is no longer a safe assumption. While the figures are hard to verify, it is estimated that by 2024 nearly 50% of intra-BRICs transactions were in non-dollar currencies, predominantly the RMB. Balance of payments issues are then managed by countries using their own currencies, or that of China. The BRICs does not stand alone in this regard. The ASEAN bloc has, over the course of a decade, raised local currency trade to nearly 30% in 2024, with RMB reserves also rising and with less reliance on the SWIFT payment system.[36] Similar trends are evident in the Gulf Cooperation Council, the African Union and the Eurasian Economic Union, all predictive of a plurality of payment systems in the future.

Another option is the promotion of an existing currency into the status of a new global reserve. Here the possibilities are the European Euro, the Japanese Yen and the Chinese RMB, regarded by the IMF as non-traditional reserve currencies.[37] Although the RMB is used increasingly in trade agreements it is unlikely, for political reasons, to find acceptance in many jurisdictions—there are concerns over the supervision of the Chinese central bank and over capital controls in the country. Moreover, the currency still constitutes only a small proportion of international reserves. It is a cause for surprise that the Euro has not been used more in a reserve capacity and with the current pressures on the dollar this might yet eventuate.[38] However the differences in BRICs member states' economies might have shifted the focus away from promoting a new reserve currency to other arrangements for escaping the US dollar. The dominance is also based on Visa, MasterCard and other major credit cards, all of which derive from the US—and involve financial, information and security implications for other countries and their citizens.[39]

[36] The Worldwide Interbank Financial Telecommunication System, known as SWIFT.

[37] Recent central bank diversification has also extended to gold serving as a reserve asset.

[38] While the Euro comprises 20% of foreign exchange reserves, significantly more than the YEN or RMB, it has not in recent years risen significantly from this percentage.

[39] There are continuous, almost ritualistic, media references to Chinese proposals to diversify their currency holdings and to advance alternative payment systems.

A further option involves the development of a crypto currency for the BRICs, serving as both a reserve and as a device for international transactions. This is currently a source of speculation in some individual jurisdictions, including those beyond the BRICs ambit. The advantage of financial transactions conducted in crypto is that they do not have to be denominated in any national currency. There is even speculation that the US will sell gold to stack Bitcoin, whereas China has for several years been stacking gold, a real asset which might protect its economy from sanctions and trade wars. BRICs' central banks could play key roles in the development of a Bitcoin or other crypto currency for the purposes referred to above.[40]

Finally, there is the option of a sui generis BRICs currency, backed by the NDB, by gold or by a basket of member currencies. An innovative BRICs currency could be supported by a currency union to reduce the costs of cross-border transactions. This was a topic at the 2024 Summit where the BRICs nations considered creating a gold-backed currency, known as the "Unit", as an alternative to the US dollar. If it eventuated the new currency would lead to a block chain-based payment system. The then Summit President flourished a prototype bank note, the R5 reflecting the first initials of foundation members' currencies. A BRICs currency such as this could assist members assert economic independence while competing with the existing international financial system.

The BRICs has raised expectations of a payment system being introduced in the second part of 2025 with no dependence on the USD or with the currently dominant SWIFT system, and other aspects of western financial institutions. Alternative systems of clearance and exchange that elude SWIFT dominance had first been considered in 2015, the fallow period suggestive of hurdles in the way of any new arrangement. There has been partial success, for example with China and Russia already able to exchange outside the SWIFT system. Each country has their own alternative: China has the Cross-Border Interbank Payment system, the CIPS, while the Bank of Russia has developed a financial messaging system, the SPFS, with the same effect. There is speculation that non-members of the bloc will also be able to use the former system, China being the main trading partner of many countries in South-East Asia, Africa and other regions of the world.

Resistance to currency and reserve moves by the BRICs has been inevitable, partly because of their implications for many US economic sectors, and for its national debt. In mid-2025 the US debt figure was over US $37 trillion and rising. Escalating debt figures were not historically problematic, given the reserve currency status of the USD. Any significant movement from that status will not only create more exposure for the national debt, but it could also affect America's credit rating and impact on the attraction of US Treasury bonds. There has been recent pressure on Treasuries—it was reported in April 2025 that China had off-loaded over $22 billion worth, its holdings declining to the same levels they were two decades ago. The country bought up gold instead. At the same time the US was reported to be

[40] The 'BRICs Bridge' allows member central banks to support cross-border transactions in their own digital currencies, the exchange rate for which they can control. The system is designed to be independent of the member states.

stacking crypto currencies, including those previously confiscated. Some commentators, however, consider that the off-loading of Treasuries might play into a US plan to devalue its dollar to retain it as the hegemonic currency. Nonetheless, shortly after it assumed office the current US administration threatened specific tariff sanctions against BRICs countries should the bloc progress its currency and payment proposals further.[41]

Despite several promising initiatives there is yet no comprehensive BRICs policy on currency settlements, payment systems and alternative reserves. As shown above, individual countries have shifted towards denominating alternative currencies in their trade agreements and business transactions. In bilateral situations the alternatives include a currency of one of the transacting parties. There have also been shifts towards denominating in the renminbi or euro by other transaction parties. Each arrangement has strengths and shortcomings, depending in part on perceived national perspectives and priorities. For Russia and Iran, they include reducing the consequences of sanctions, freezing of funds and other west-imposed threats and actions. These potential advantages are not shared by India or South Africa. In a well-worn platitude, BRICs policies on all aspects of international finance are still work in progress.

5.10 Case Study: Planetary Health

5.10.1 Dimensions

Planetary health has several dimensions, all focusing on the impacts of human activity on climate, biodiversity, air quality, deforestation, marine degradation and environmental refugees. They are linked to the United Nation's Sustainable Development Goals (SDG).[42]

The BRICs, as an entity, had a historically low profile on planetary health, partly because of most member states' resources in, or dependence on, fossil fuels: Brazil is well-endowed with oil, Russia earns extensive gas revenues, South Africa has large coal reserves and China is one of the main greenhouse gas emitters—though not on a per capita basis. On energy issues the bloc assumed the dominant neoliberal frame of economic discourse, within which environmental factors are subordinate to those of economic growth, trade, investment and employment. There seemed little likelihood of planetary health entering its dominant frame of discourse.

As early as 2015, however, the BRICs had established an Environmental Working Group with the objectives of discussing priority areas of cooperation in

[41] In January and February 2025, the US President threated BRICs countries with 150% tariffs if they pursued non-dollar alternatives. The US has also long accused China of mercantilist policies of artificially undervaluing its currency.

[42] Department of Economic and Social Affairs, United Nations (2025).

environmental and climate matters, the sharing of practices and the exchange of expertise. The priorities of the Russian Federation's BRICs chairmanship in 2024 fell under the following broad categories: Priorities in Policy and Security; Cooperation in Economy and Finance; Cooperation in Humanitarian Affairs; and Culture.[43] One of the items in the second category, though in the small print, was "Promoting a balanced and fair transition to a low-carbon economy".

As regards other initiatives BRICs environment ministers, noting UN policies on the topic[44] and the bloc's own policies on Clean Rivers, Urban Environmental Sustainability and Environmentally Sound Technology Platforms, set out a MOU on Environmental Cooperation. It encouraged member states to develop national policies and measures, for example in terms of the BRICs Clean Rivers programs, and to integrate biodiversity conservation in line with SDGs 14 and 15.[45] It expressed support for the 2030 Agenda for Sustainable Development and the UNFCCC Paris Agreement; it established a BRICs Contact Group on Climate Change and Sustainable Development and foreshadowed a BRICs Climate Research Platform.

Individual members, however, maintained mixed records in these areas: China and Brazil, and more recently India, moved relatively quickly into renewables, with much less progress in South Africa and Russia. However, the BRICs Policy Centre[46] indicated that climate and energy transitions would be among the priorities of the Brazilian Presidency and Summit in the second half of 2025. Brazil is a leader in this sphere as the third largest country in the world for renewable energy generation, 50% of which comes from hydro facilities. However, the winds of change soon began blowing across the BRICs.

5.10.2 Matters Arising

In early 2025 the Indian government encouraged fellow BRICs countries to unite together to mobilise $1.3 trillion annually over the next decade to assist members achieve domestic climate goals and international commitments.[47] This appeared to bring to prominence a new bloc priority, namely to promote and negotiate for climate goals, including in multilateral forums such as the IPCC.[48] The annual funding was justified in terms of the needs of developing countries that contribute little to emissions to be supported by emissions-producing developed states in meeting their international sustainability commitments and managing domestic prevention and

[43] TV BRICs (2024).

[44] Including the UN International Decade for Action on Water for Sustainable Development, the UN Decade of Ocean Science for Sustainable Developments and the UN Decade on Ecosystem Restoration.

[45] The Conservation of Big Cats has also featured on BRICs agendas.

[46] See BRICs Policy Center (2022).

[47] Mohan (2025).

[48] IPCC (2025).

adaptation programs.[49] In economic terms the policy can be seen as polluters paying for their accumulated negative externalities.

In making its BRICs-related announcement on the environment, the Indian government criticised the proposed $300 billion a year by 2035 committed under previous IPCC policy,[50] emphasising the need for collective action and shared responsibility for global environmental challenges.[51] India also urged BRICs members to join other sustainability programs such as the International Solar Alliance and the Global Biofuel Alliance. While environmentalism in all its forms had been on and off BRICs summit agendas for a decade, the Indian initiative suggested a higher profile for the subject. The following year another BRICs initiative emerged on the topic.

An anchor point for the 2025 BRICs initiative was the COP28 meeting of the IPCC in 2023, as well as its resolutions on fast-tracking the energy transition and reducing emissions before 2030. While not all decisions were unanimous at this meeting the Global Methane Pledge was agreed to by 155 member states. These initiatives developed momentum for the 2025 BRICs Laboratory project.

5.11 Laboratory for Climate

The BRICs Laboratory for Trade, Climate Change and Sustainable Development is based on terms of reference emanating from the BRICs Climate Leadership Agenda. The initiative promotes trade and climate objectives that are "mutually supportive", through "hybrid measures" compliant with the rules of both the WTO and the IPCC. Laboratory activities will include exchange of information, capacity-building for member states and evidence-based collaboration. All activities will occur on a voluntary basis, deferring to the sovereignty of member states.

Three aspects of the Laboratory project warrant comment. The first is that the deference to state sovereignty, while a standard principle in BRICs initiatives, leaves extensive discretion to member states with their differing priorities.[52] The second is that a balance between the economy and the environment is never easy to attain and the tone of the policy suggests that the former will be prioritised in the event of inconsistencies. The third concerns accountability for Laboratory activities, not something for which the BRICs is well-situated, despite the responsibility to

[49] Known as Nationally Determined Contributions in terms of IPCC agreements.

[50] This is the New Collective Quantified Goal on climate finance approved at the earlier COP 29 meeting but not followed through by developed world countries.

[51] In 2025 the Pacific Island states most impacted by climate changes called on developed countries to comply with UN policies to reduce emissions through domestic reductions and not offsets. A particular call was made to the G-20, which includes five BRICs members.

[52] Climate impacts different among different members as between, for example, the UAE, a desert state, South Africa, a coastal country, and Uganda, a landlocked state.

provide briefings to the BRICs High-level Meeting on Climate Change and Sustainable Development.

It is also not clear where the Laboratory's work will sit in relation to other transnational initiatives on climate. For example, apart from the IPCC, the UNDP's Climate Promise of 2025, in which India played a significant role in mobilising financial pledges, promises support to emerging countries in raising ambition on their national targets and helping accelerate implementation of these goals. There is also potential duplication with the Green Climate Fund, though most of the non-BRICs initiatives on climate are driven by western interests. In 2023, however, the new World Bank President introduced an additional dimension to the organisation's vision and mission statement by adding to the existing goal, "to create a world free of poverty", the phrase, "on a liveable planet".[53] While the new framing is symbolic in nature, frames of reference can change perceptions and provide a normative basis for evaluating policy and practice.

However, economic imperatives and security concerns rank highest in the priorities of both sovereign states and international institutions. There is no treaty-based body focusing exclusively on planetary health, nor is there an international court or tribunal with jurisdiction in these matters. While the BRICs is unlikely, in the short term, to elevate environmental policies on climate change and species biodiversity to a higher priority than the economy and security there may be a greater impetus from the bloc in this direction.

5.12 Enforcement challenges

There is no lack of international attempts to obligate countries to promote climate and other environmental policies and to expedite just energy transitions. The Sustainable Development Goals, the UN's IPCC, the OECD and even the International Energy Association have all promoted and supported movements away from the fossil fuels—that happen to be central to some BRICs country economies. In 2022 a UN General Assembly resolution referred a request to the International Court of Justice for an advisory opinion on the duties owed by sovereign states towards their citizens in relation to damages caused by polluters.[54] The UNGA's resolution was not the result of a BRICs initiative, but that of students in two Pacific countries. The ICJ decision was made in mid-2025 and made strong recommendations on countries' obligations to their citizens in respect of climate change. This effectively comprises soft law with no direct enforcement mechanism as state sovereignty is not easily trumped by international jurisprudence.

[53] World Bank Group (2023).

[54] The origins of the GA resolution lie in the pressure of students at different campuses of the University of South Pacific on their governments to get the proposal before the UN. It resulted in no fewer than 132 countries supporting it, thereby providing jurisdiction to the ICJ—see International Court of Justice (2022).

The international programs on climate face other difficulties. The first is that there is often wriggle room in relevant treaties, codes and declarations allowing for argument and contention in relation to compliance obligations. The second is the reality of national politics, and the recent ideology of shrinking government, which entails that governing parties are susceptible to the pressure and influence of energy lobby groups rather than to electoral and citizen demands. A third factor is the imperative for emerging nations in the BRICs and elsewhere to play economic catch up with the affluent states of the world. This does not, however, preclude the influence of soft political power, the so-called moral high ground, from sources in the BRICs.

There is another influential factor in an age of increased domestic nativism, competition and unilateral assertion of power internationally. Game theory indicates that it makes sense for individual states to prioritise short-term economic growth over long-term environmental safeguards, a factor acknowledged at the World Economic Forum.[55] There are concerns among individual jurisdictions about "going first" on their own, for example in moving away from polluting energy towards hydro, wind, solar and batteries—it allows other countries to take advantage of the situation and retain their polluting industries and negative externalities for short-term economic gain. However if all states act in terms of short-term advantage, it can mean disastrous consequences for all. These issues will arise again at the next COP meeting of the IPCC hosted by BRICs member Brazil in late 2025.

5.13 Operating Together Apart

The above analysis reveals the uneven nature of the BRICs in terms of proclaimed policies, operations and outcomes. While BRICs is a collective institution it has not been unusual for BRICs countries to act individually or in concert outside the bloc's umbrella. A prominent example occurred during the Covid-19 pandemic. South Africa and India made joint representations for modifications of intellectual property rules to allow generic drugs to be dispensed at reduced costs to their citizens, and to others in less privileged countries. While the process, like the virus response, was delayed by numerous obstacles it eventually had some impact. China, by contrast, was simultaneously pre-occupied with fending off allegations of having caused the pandemic. This is an example of where policies and priorities did not coincide among foundation BRICs members. It also reveals the potential drawback of the consensus principle in situations where time is of the essence for acting.

As with similar international bodies BRICs member states are motivated primarily by their own political and economic priorities and collective action is taken only when it coincides with these interests. While consensus is the norm it is inevitable

[55] See, for example, Zimmerman (2018). A practical application of game theory is known as the prisoners' dilemma exercise.

that dominant states such as India, China and Brazil will bend BRICs policies towards their own interests, with Kazakhstan, Ethiopia and the UAE having less gravitational pull towards their priorities. Nevertheless, group dynamics and complexity theory suggest that in some situations a dominant view can assume a life of its own and drag along individual members into a collective consensus. Support from the BRICs was a factor in supporting the Russian economy against sanctions and having its banks banned from SWIFT, and one can assume some long-term benefits for this support from countries other than Russia.[56]

In relation to conflict situations and humanitarian crises individual BRICs members have sometimes taken a stance but a united BRICs voice is seldom in evidence. The bloc has, however, held discussions on pressing situations in Afghanistan, Sudan and Syria. As regards joint public statements, the respective foreign affairs ministers in 2024 criticised Israel's persistent activities in Gaza in response to the earlier Hamas attacks. No statement was made in relation to Russia's war with Ukraine and interventions in these situations have been lessor-order priorities for the bloc.[57]

Indicators of BRICs members operating solo are found predominantly, but not exclusively, in the case of China. For example in 2025 it announced an "action plan" to promote its currency and international payment system, in conjunction with the People's Bank of China and its own financial regulators—without any reference to the BRICs.[58] Here it is able, unlike other members, to leverage Shanghai's role as a global financial hub to promote its currency, particularly in trade with the Global South. It can also enhance its Cross-Border Interbank Payment System as an alternative to SWIFT, something not availing the small BRICs members. Recent Chinese moves are understandable, given its sense of urgency in responding to the US trade war, which includes pressure on 70 trading nations to limit their economic ties with China in exchange for their own tariff exemptions. In short, the BRICs countries act together when they can and separately when they can't.

5.14 Australia and the BRICs

Australia appears to have no formal position on the BRICs. It has historically been supportive of, multilateral institutions, and has not been slow to join and be active in such bodies. It would be difficult, and futile, to oppose or attempt to block the expansion and growth of the BRICs, particularly as some of its efforts still linger in "talking shop" mode. If an expanded bloc were to assert itself politically and

[56] The World Bank reported that Russian GDP increased by 4.1% in 2024 despite headlines of imminent economic collapse.

[57] In the first half of 2025 the foreign ministers were unable to issue a joint communique, inter alia on Security Council reform, after a meeting in Brazil.

[58] Ghiselli (2025).

economically Australia's stance could change, in particular where the developments challenged the US and other western states.

Two members of the bloc: China and India are among Australia's major trading partners and sources of migrants, and the respective countries have significant bilateral relations. Important local neighbours, Indonesia and Malaysia, are member and partner states respectively. Australia rubs shoulders with Indonesia, Malaysia, Russia and China in the APEC, with India in the QUAD group of nations and with the five original BRICs states in the G-20. It connects with BRICs members and partners in multilateral organisations, from the United Nations to the World Trade Organisation, and from the World Bank to the World Health Organisation. In short, Australia has extensive relations with BRICs members and partners, but not with the entity as a whole.

Australian membership of the BRICs is unlikely for self-evident reasons. As a middle-strength state, Australia does not qualify as an emerging country, despite being in similar economic leagues as South Africa and Brazil. Apart from other considerations, the predominant position of China in the bloc renders it inconceivable that the US would join, and without this accession it is unlikely that Australia would seek admission, given its security and political alliances with America.

In strategic and defence terms Australia has chosen sides in relation to China-US rivalries with its military connections through ANZUS, AUKUS, the Pine Gap intelligence system and the Marine Rotational Force near Darwin. When it was reported in 2025 that Russia had requested use of Indonesian airports for military aircraft, not an unusual arrangement, there was consternation in local political and media circles, until the countries themselves indicated that there were no such plans. In fact, Indonesia and Russia, both BRICs members, have long-standing military ties but even if the reports had been accurate, it would not have been a BRICs-related project. Should the bloc develop military alliances and joint exercises the picture could change.

5.15 Themes Revisited

As noted earlier three themes run through this chapter and they are revisited here in the same sequence.

The first relates to the factors that unite the organisation despite the many and varied divergences among its members. Ironically as it has increased in the number of members and partner states it has also increased the divergences among them. There is, however, a counterfactual at play in this regard. The unilateral undermining of the multilateral trade regime and random imposition of tariffs by the US has provided a unifying factor among other multilateral bodies. There are suggestions, for example, that the 27 nations compromising the EU have for this reason become more cohesive and united on matters of security, trade and policy, although this has been precipitated by other factors as well. Despite the manifest differences among

BRICs entities some may well be overlooked in the pursuit of uniformity, particularly where the bloc is visited with targeted tariffs.

The second theme relates to the discrepancies between the bloc's agendas, policies and summit declarations, on one hand, and actual progress on the ground, on the other. This is a feature affecting all existing blocs of nations with good intentions tending to outstrip performance. Here the BRICs might become more operationally cohesive with a secretariat and Secretary-General, as in the ASEAN bloc. Progressing towards a treaty-based organisation would also provide a clearer sense of rights, duties and responsibilities. That this has not occurred could be a function of divided loyalties among the dominant members for whom the informal and the incidental avoid raising to the surface latent rivalries between them. The relative inertia might better suit domestic constituents in each member country.

The third theme relates to the potential scope for the BRICs, within the current inconsistencies and uncertainties in international relations and the global economy, to become more influential in some of its objectives. There are many moving parts in the global political economy, of which the BRICs is only one. It has succeeded in contributing to a greater degree of multi-polarity in the world. It is difficult to predict to which non-tariff restrictions and secondary sanctions by the US President will stir the BRICs into greater cohesion, possibly in relation to currency and climate. If this does occur it will involve greater engagement by the bloc in the dominant global order.

5.16 Conclusion

The current rapidly changing systems and discourse in international politics, economics and security have caught many by surprise. They have demanded equally rapid responses to tariffs, subsidies, export controls, secondary sanctions, breaches of trade agreements and new institutional alignments. The BRICs has not historically been structurally geared for rapid, let alone cohesive, changes in its policies and practices. How the bloc will contribute to multi-polarity trends in the emerging world orders, and manage western hegemony, is a matter for the intermediate-term future.

Critics have suggested that the BRICs has so far proved incapable of uniting as a meaningful force, and that it serves little purpose beyond symbolic gestures and lofty rhetoric.[59] While international politics and the global economy may have entered the era of multipolar groups the BRICs is yet to present as a cohesive and influential force. Though home to 45% of the world's inhabitants and a quarter of global GDP, internal differences have long frustrated BRICs ambitions of becoming a major operator on the world stage.[60] Even in the current "new normal" of a

[59] O'Neill (2024).

[60] Needless to say, internal divisions are not absent from bodies such as the G-7.

shrinking global economy the BRICs is promoting incremental change and not a full-bodied challenge to current systems of power. Small steps can only contribute incrementally to a long journey.

It is difficult not to see the BRICs and its emerging influence without reference to the rising challenges that China poses for US hegemony.[61] There are multiple signs: the four largest financial institutions in the world are Chinese; China is the biggest global creditor surpassing the IMF and World Bank,[62] the RMB has already surpassed the USD in China's trade transactions; the country enjoyed a $1 trillion budget surplus in 2024 while the US has not had a surplus in 50 years; it produces a third of global manufactured goods and owns half of the world's patents. Even life expectancy in China has surpassed that of the US. American tariffs and protectionism are unlikely to reverse the trends.

It may be that the "silver age" of the multilateral rules-based global economy is close to its demise and responsive to the change will come from small groupings. The BRICs is likely to be one of these, though not the only one, in a new age of plurilateral collaboration.[63] In this context economic security, market resilience, self-sufficiency and strategic interests will be higher priorities than comparative advantage, financial liberalisation and efficiency at all costs. With global trust in US unilateralism at a low ebb it may be that BRICs will be part of the recalibration of the world order currently underway. It is, however, too soon to talk about the global system fragmenting into mutually exclusive competing blocs. A larger BRICs might have greater potential influence but less cohesion.

The last word concerns the humanistic dimensions of blocs such as the BRICs. It is true that intricate trade practices, complex settlement systems, high frequency trading and artificial intelligence are responsible for many of the tectonic movements in the current world order. Within these factors of exchange, power and influence, there is at least some role for individuals. Here perceptions are paramount, and these can change. Joseph Stiglitz observes in his 2024 book, *Road to Freedom*,[64] that twenty-first century economics recognises the malleability of individuals in what he refers to as "endogenous preferences and beliefs". People see the world not as it is but as they are, through lenses shaped by peers, leaders, teachers, the media and individual experiences. Economists refer to these as social externalities which, when internalised, can be stubborn and difficult to change. In other words, beliefs

---

[61] Apart from its leadership in the BRICs China has many other forms of leverage, such the Shanghai Cooperation Organisation and the Belt and Road initiative.

[62] China is the biggest global creditor surpassing the IMF and World Bank.

[63] In a speech at Waseda University, Tokyo, on 11 March 2025, WTO Deputy Director-General Angela Ellard cited opportunities offered by plurilateral arrangements in highlighting the need to revitalize the multilateral trading system. She called for reforms in areas such as dispute settlement and agriculture. She also cited the importance of securing entry into force of the Agreement on Fisheries Subsidies and completing the 'second wave' of fisheries subsidies negotiations. See World Trade Organization (2025).

[64] Stiglitz (2024, pp.146–8).

and preferences are socially formed such that the way people think of the world does not necessarily correlate with its true picture.

There are many implications of this perspective in relation to the role of BRICs. Perceptions have a significant role in both the maintenance and adaptation of systems. The normalcy bias suggests that the intellectual and normative framework of western-led multilateralism is natural and inevitable. The BRICs and similar institutions may be changing these perceptions and prove this not to be the case. New cognitive thinking about how global affairs will come to operate can itself be a factor in shifting from the seeming irreversible to the new.

References

BRICS Policy Center. 2022. https://BRICspolicycenter.org/en/about/. Accessed 11 Apr 2025.

Curtis, John. 2024. The BRICS Group: Overview and Recent Expansion. https://researchbriefings.files.parliament.uk/documents/CBP-10136/CBP-10136.pdf. Accessed 15 Apr 2025.

Department of Economic and Social Affairs, United Nations. 2025. Sustainable Development: The 17 Goals. https://sdgs.un.org/goals. Accessed 12 June 2025.

Ekanem, Solomon. 2025. South Africa secures R7 billion lifeline from BRICS Bank for road infrastructure. *Business Insider Africa*, July 25. https://africa.businessinsider.com/local/markets/south-africa-secures-r7-billion-lifeline-from-BRICs-bank-for-road-infrastructure/rz05d2n. Accessed 30 July 2025.

Ghiselli, Andrea. 2025. *South China Morning Post- 22 April 2025*. Torino World Affairs Institute. https://www.twai.it/south-china-morning-post-22-april-2025/. Accessed 14 July 2025.

International Court of Justice. 2022. Obligations of States in Respect of Climate Change. https://www.icj-cij.org/case/187/request-advisory-opinion. Accessed 15 March 2025.

IPCC. 2025. The United Nations Intergovernmental Panel on Climate Change. https://www.ipcc.ch/. Accessed 17 Mar 2025.

Lo, Vai Io, and Mary Hiscock, eds. 2014. *The Rise of the BRICS in the Global Political Economy: Changing Paradigms?* Cheltenham: Edward Elgar Publishing.

Mohan, Vishaw. 2025. India Urges BRICS Nations to Unite on Mobilising $1.3 Trillion Annually to Achieve Climate Action Goals. *The Times of India*, April 3. https://timesofindia.indiatimes.com/india/india-urges-BRICS-nations-to-unite-on-mobilising-1-3-trillion-annually-to-achieve-climate-action-goals/articleshow/119952936.cms. Accessed 20 Apr 2025.

New Development Bank. 2014. About NDB. https://www.ndb.int/about-ndb/. Accessed 7 June 2025.

O'Neill, Jim. 2024. The BRICS Still Don't Matter. *Project Syndicate*. https://www.project-syndicate.org/commentary/moscow-BRICS-summit-expanded-bloc-still-rudderless-and-ineffective-by-jim-o-neill-2024-10. Accessed 12 Feb 2025.

Parliament of Australia. 2024. Future Made in Australia Bill 2024. https://www.aph.gov.au/Parliamentary_Business/Bills_LEGislation/Bills_Search_Results/Result?bId=r7219. Accessed 12 June 2025.

Rasmus, Jack. 2016. *Systemic Fragility in the Global Economy*. Atlanta: Clarity Press.

Shanghai Cooperation Organisation. 2025. https://eng.sectsco.org/

Slaughter, Anne-Marie, and Thomas Hale. 2010. Transgovernmental Networks and Emerging Powers. In *Rising States, Rising Institutions: Challenges for Global Governance*, ed. Alan S. Alexandroff and Andrew F. Cooper, 48–62. Washington: Brookings Institution Press.

Statista. 2024. Empowering People with Data. https://www.statista.com/. Accessed 10 May 2025.

Stiglitz, Joseph. 2024. *The Road to Freedom—Economics and the Good Society*. London: Allen Lane.

Treaty for the Establishment of a BRICS Contingent Reserve Arrangement. 2014. http://www.BRICs.utoronto.ca/docs/140715-treaty.html. Accessed 25 Apr 2025.

TV BRICs. 2024. Russia's BRICS Chairmanship: Priorities and Goals. https://tvBRICS.com/en/news/russia-s-BRICS-chairmanship-priorities-and-goals/. Accessed 10 May 2024.

UN Trade and Development. 2024. Rethinking Development in the Age of Discontent. https://unctad.org/publication/trade-and-development-report-2024#chapter2. Accessed 18 Jan 2025.

Voronoi. 2023. Where Data Tells the Story, Based on UBS Data. https://www.voronoiapp.com/explore. Accessed 11 May 2025.

World Bank Group. 2023. The World Bank's Bold New Vision: Ending Poverty on Liveable Planet—On the World Bank president Ajay Banga 2023 Annual Meeting Plenary. https://www.worldbank.org/en/news/immersive-story/2023/10/13/world-bank-president-on-ending-poverty-on-a-livable-planet. Accessed 15 May 2025.

World Trade Organization. 2025. DDG Ellard Cites Urgent Need to Boost Multilateral Trading System in University Speech. https://www.wto.org/english/news_e/news25_e/ddgae_11mar25_e.htm. Accessed 22 June 2025.

Zimmerman, Leda. 2018. *What the Prisoner's Dilemma Tell Us About the Climate Change*. World Economic Forum. https://www.weforum.org/stories/2018/06/the-moral-calculus-of-climate-change/. Accessed 18 June 2025.

Chapter 6
Globalisation in a Destabilising World: How Australia Will Need to Adapt in Times of Institutional Weakness

Peter Draper and Nathan Gray

Abstract In an era marked by increasing geopolitical tensions and institutional instability, the concept of globalisation faces unprecedented challenges. This paper explores the evolving dynamics of global integration amidst weakened institutions, rising protectionism, and how Australia, as a middle-power nation reliant on international trade and investment, must adapt to a destabilising global landscape. Through an analysis of current global trends, economic data, and policy shifts, we examine the impacts of institutional fragility on global trade, investment flows, and international cooperation. The analysis examines the multifaceted impacts of weakened global institutions on Australia's economic, political, and social spheres. The study highlights the necessity for adaptive strategies in globalisation, focusing on resilient supply chains, diversified trade partnerships, and enhanced global governance frameworks. By proposing a multi-faceted approach to sustain global interconnectedness, this paper underscores the need for robust, flexible, and inclusive globalisation practices that can withstand the pressures of a destabilised world. Key strategies are proposed to enhance Australia's resilience, including diversifying trade partnerships, investing in domestic industries, and strengthening regional alliances. The paper also highlights the role of innovative policy frameworks in navigating the complexities of global interdependence amidst institutional fragility. The findings aim to inform policymakers, business leaders, and scholars about the policy adjustments required to navigate an increasingly fragmented global landscape.

P. Draper (✉)
School of Economics and Public Policy, Adelaide, SA, Australia

Institute of International Trade, The University of Adelaide, Adelaide, SA, Australia
e-mail: peter.draper@adelaide.edu.au

N. Gray
Institute for International Trade, The University of Adelaide, Adelaide, SA, Australia
e-mail: nathan.gray@adelaide.edu.au

U. H. Ghori, J. Farrar (eds.), *Globalisation Disrupted*,
https://doi.org/10.1007/978-981-95-3997-0_6

6.1 Introduction

Globalisation pivots on the driving forces of economic and technological integration and advancement. It has always generated winners and losers in an historically anarchic international economic system.

Since the end of World War Two multinational corporations (MNCs) domiciled in developed country democracies conveyed trade and investment flows to developing countries and each other, governed by global trading rules anchored in the World Trade Organisation (WTO) which the same developed countries controlled. Other significant international economic organisations, notably the International Monetary Fund (IMF) and World Bank, again controlled by the same developed countries, set the rules by which global finance and exchange rates were managed, and international development capital allocations were determined.

These institutional arrangements ensured the rich west's dominance of globalisation, while delivering a long peace to Europe. This "Liberal International Order"[1] was anchored in democratic market capitalism and underpinned by the US global economic and military primacy, spawning the theory of hegemonic stability to explain,[2] or perhaps justify,[3] it.

Accelerating geopolitical contestation in the aftermath of the 2008 GFC, underpinned by the relative economic rise of the BRICS[4] countries, particularly China, and the corresponding sharp rise of populist politics in key Western developed countries, have significantly stressed the liberal international order. Most recently Donald Trump's second presidential term in the US marked a likely systemic break from the liberal international order with the US no longer prepared to underwrite the system.

For decades developing countries had chafed against these institutional arrangements, specifically the trade rules they embodied. Owing to this combination of the new economic power some developing countries wield and the West's desire to overhaul, if not abandon, the system, the institutional arrangements that channel economic globalisation are under sustained pressure.

To discern where economic globalisation and the liberal international order may be headed, and the implications for Australia, this chapter proceeds as follows. First, key economic trends and policy responses are briefly summarised through the lenses of "Slowbalisation", supply chain restructuring and technological change in a context of weakening institutions. Next, the increasing securitisation of international trade is analysed in relation to supply chain resilience and trade diversification

[1] It is not clear who first used this term.

[2] Kindleberger (1973).

[3] Strange (1987).

[4] Founded in 2009 by Brazil, Russia, India, and China, with South Africa joining in 2010. The Heads of State formally convened an informal BRICS grouping modelled on the G7, with an eye on reforming global economic governance institutions.

imperatives, and what these matters portend for global trade governance institutions. The final part concludes.

6.2 Evolving Dynamics of Global Integration and Their Implications for Australia

6.2.1 "Slowbalisation", Protectionism, Supply Chain Restructuring, and Technological Change

Since the Second World War MNCs, through their trade and investment activities, were central to global economic integration. Consequently, the post-World War Two decades prior to the GFC were characterised by rising trade openness, as measured in the global trade to gross domestic product (GDP) ratio. From 2008 that ratio plateaued below 60%, ushering in the commonly labelled "slowbalisation" era.[5] Whereas the era of rising trade openness, or modern economic globalisation encompassing investment and capital markets liberalisation too, was substantially shaped by the post-World War Two liberalising economic and trade policy institutional frameworks and reduced barriers to trade, the slowbalisation era has been marked by escalating trade protectionism.

Since the end of the Cold War and the formerly communist bloc's opening to market economics expanding MNC trade and investment footprints were mediated through what came to be termed "global value chains" (GVCs). These value chains globalised after the dominant advanced triad economies:[6] the EU, Japan, and the US, were joined by the newly industrialised east Asian "tiger" economies (NIEs): Hong Kong, Singapore, South Korea, Taiwan, in pouring FDI into Southeast Asia, then post-Mao China as the latter reformed, opened up, and joined the WTO. This "flying geese" pattern[7] with the lead MNCs geese periodically "flying" to new locations to access varying combinations of cheap, productive labour and host governments eager to attract export-oriented manufacturing.

Notwithstanding the term "global" value chains, the world economy was never truly "flat"[8] rather characterised by three "Factory complexes" in North America, Europe, and Northeast Asia centred on the dominant manufacturing powerhouses in each region.[9] For decades centred on the rich G7 economies, as the NIEs took off and industrialised so the G7's shares of global trade declined mirrored by the rise of Asian economies, especially China.[10]

[5] Gopinath et al. (2025).

[6] Ohmae (2002).

[7] Akamatsu (1961) and Akamatsu (1962).

[8] Friedman (2007).

[9] Baldwin (2006).

[10] Baldwin and Forslid (2013).

In all regions trade agreements, particularly free trade agreements (FTAs), facilitated the flow of capital, goods, and people across borders. The creation of the General Agreement on Tariffs and Trade (GATT 1947) kick-started post war trade liberalisation, that was boosted by the establishment of the European Coal and Steel Community (1951) and subsequent formation of the European Economic Community (1958) and ultimately the EU (1993). The North American Free Trade Agreement's entry into force (1994), as well as the conclusion of the Uruguay Round of GATT negotiations (1994) and 1995 establishment of the WTO provided major boosts. From then FTAs proliferated and spread with the triad economies, particularly the EU, being the most trade dependent, leading the charge to open markets for their MNCs. This left the major economies in varying positions of reliance on trade to support employment;[11] a key relationship in domestic political debates in which growing anti-globalisation discourse features ever-more prominently, notably in the US and, to a lesser extent, Europe.

However, this had been evident since the 1970s "Nixon shocks" and the consequent US move towards "aggressive unilateralism".[12] Thus, the US has increasingly sought to wriggle free of the institutional constraints imposed on its freedom of action to impose import protection. The first Trump Administration (2017–2021) accelerated an already extant US reluctance to play the primary role in supporting the liberal international order. The Biden Administration (2021–2024) consolidated and extended the protectionist policies it inherited from Trump 1 while rebuilding multilateral institutional ties. The Second Trump Administration took office in 2025 and sought to seriously disrupt those arrangements.

From the US's standpoint the liberal international order was not built to accommodate the rise of peer industrial competitors. While the main ruptures occurred in the early 1970s with the dismantling of the Bretton Woods system of fixed exchange rates, the major wave of developing countries unilateral trade liberalisation characterised by the "Washington consensus"[13] succeeded this. Nonetheless, the US's willingness to underwrite the system through continuing to offer mostly free access to its market became increasingly conditioned on reciprocal changes in trading partners' trade policies, notably Japan which, in the 1980s, was subjected to a series of sectoral managed trade arrangements, but also the EU through a variety of increasingly high stakes WTO disputes from taxation arrangements to Boeing-Airbus subsidies.

Since 2016 US trade protectionism has focused on China. Whereas the US supported China's accession to the WTO in 2001, from the advent of the Xi Jinping government the US sees China as a major strategic rival and non-market economy. Hence the US's trade policies have become increasingly focused on derisking their trade and investment from Chinese anchored GVCs. A less pronounced shift has

---

[11] Cernat (2025).

[12] Bhagwati and Patrick (1991).

[13] Williamson (2004).

taken place in the EU, with China being seen as at once a partner, economic competitor, and strategic rival.[14]

Alfaro and Chor[15] find that a "great reallocation" in supply chain activity has in fact been underway since 2017, featuring a combination of reduced sourcing from China in favour of low wage "connector" countries,[16] particularly Mexico, aligned to a broadly defined US trading bloc that benefitted from such investments. This was accompanied by a shift towards the US importing relatively more upstream products, indicating that more manufacturing was being reshored.[17] Alfaro and Chor[18] conclude that these trends confirm "nearshoring" and "friendshoring", or reducing reliance on China, was gathering pace. However, AT Kearney[19] while affirming the broad reshoring and nearshoring trend for the US, also sound the cautionary note that it is limited by several economic factors in the US and Mexico, principally labour and infrastructure bottlenecks, meaning the transition is limited by the slow evolution of prevailing comparative and competitive advantages.

While estimates of Chinese dominance vary according to the GVC in focus, there is little doubt over China being the manufacturing powerhouse of the world. Moreover, US dependence on Chinese suppliers is perhaps greater than previously thought, even though the US predominantly sources its industrial inputs domestically.[20] The extent of other countries' reliance on Chinese suppliers is almost certainly large for most, particularly those with less diversified economies, smaller domestic markets, higher trade to GDP ratios and weaker manufacturing sectors.

In a recent report the OECD noted that from a global standpoint production has become increasingly concentrated at the product level with China accounting for 15% of their members' strategic products import dependencies in 2020–2021 versus 4% in 1997–1999.[21] Jean et al. conclude that Chinese export products in world markets had dominant positions in nearly 600 lines out of 5000 in 2019.[22] At the same time, OECD countries accounted for 70% of China's strategic products import dependencies, which are dominated by the US and Japan at 15% and 12%, respectively.[23] Clearly dependencies cut both ways.

---

[14] European Commission (2016).

[15] Alfaro and Chor (2023).

[16] These countries, notably Mexico, Vietnam, and Malaysia, benefited from the first Trump Administration's China tariffs through FDI relocation away from China into their markets. Thus MNCs, including many Chinese companies, were able to avoid the bilateral China tariffs by exporting from their new connector country base while sourcing key inputs from China. See Gopinath et al., *supra,* n. 5.

[17] See generally Alfaro and Chor, *supra* n. 15.

[18] Ibid.

[19] Kearney (2025).

[20] Baldwin et al. (2023).

[21] Arriola et al. (2024).

[22] Jean et al. (2023).

[23] Ibid, at 19.

Despite years of trade policies intended to "derisk" US supply chains from Chinese suppliers, the main measured result was to lengthen those supply chains through relocation of Chinese and other suppliers into third markets rather than diversification of supplier relationships,[24] giving rise to select "connector countries."[25]

Nonetheless, the second Trump Administration, based on a disingenuous formula[26] on April 2, 2025, unleased "reciprocal tariffs" on the world, dramatically escalating import protection. As discussed in the next section this has placed great strain on the WTO as an institution, and members are grappling with how to respond without undermining the system themselves through retaliation, or cutting discriminatory bilateral deals with the US, or both. These reciprocal tariffs were also enacted almost without regard to the US's existing network of FTAs. Moreover, they explicitly targeted countries with structural goods trade surpluses with the US, notably the "connector countries", meaning that merely finding new connector countries for MNCs to base their US-targeting export-oriented investments in was probably not a sustainable strategy.

Consequently, the accelerating geoeconomic fragmentation characterising the slowbalisation era is now greatly challenging the GVC networks built up in the preceding decades, as well as the institutional arrangements in which they are embedded.

Against this it is important to briefly return to the underlying technological drivers of change in the global economy. Cernat[27] finds that across economies exports have become less labour-intensive in the last three decades substantially owing to the adoption of labour-saving technologies, particularly robotics and artificial intelligence (AI) mirrored by the rise of "globotics" enhanced by rapidly expanding digital trade.[28] These developments are propelling digitally enabled services to the forefront of global trade and altering long-established services industries production patterns while services continue to grow faster than global goods trade.[29] Schwab[30] labelled this technological drive, in combination with related developments such as advanced biotechnologies and additive manufacturing, the "Fourth Industrial Revolution".

The full implications of these changes are too widespread and profound to trace here, but these technological fusions are rapidly escalating and impacting not only how MNCs think about their optimal trade, investment, and supply chain footprints, but also challenging traditional notions of comparative advantage. They also enable a variety of adaptation strategies, since these technologies enable both

[24] Gopinth et al, *supra*, n. 16.

[25] Qiu (2023).

[26] Draper and Hing (2025).

[27] Cernat, *supra*, n.11.

[28] Baldwin (2019).

[29] World Trade Organization (2023).

[30] Schwab (2017).

concentration (digitalisation promoting 3D printing combined with robotics) and dispersion (services growth enabling localised manufacturing footprints).

It is also important to note that the pressing planetary crisis presaged by rapidly advancing global warming is challenging all countries to embrace and manage complex green transitions, challenging legacy energy systems and the myriad production, transportation, and logistics processes that depend on energy systems. It is also propelling rapid technological change to replace legacy fossil fuel-based energy systems with a variety of alternative technologies.

Moreover, access to key resources, notably a host of critical minerals, to enable the green transition has become highly contentious owing to geopolitical contestation. Given the dual-use nature of many processed critical minerals, geopolitical considerations will increasingly constrain and condition market access and channel investment flows, with governments beyond China becoming more involved in securing the trade. This manifests most obviously in export control regimes, particularly China's evolving export controls on processed critical minerals given its dominance of global processing capacity, but also in inward investment screening mechanisms.

This raises the prospect of major tensions emerging in the trading system as countries race to dominate these future-facing industries and avoid the economic security implications of energy dependence on foreign suppliers. The WTO, as the apex global trade governance body, is struggling to adapt to these developments, which are also placing further strains on multilateral governance in general.

6.2.2 *Weakened Multilateral Institutions*

The contemporary erosion of global institutions represents a fundamental reversal of the post-1945 multilateral framework that enabled unprecedented economic integration and development worldwide. For over seven decades, institutions such as the WTO, United Nations (UN), and World Health Organisation (WHO) served as the institutional architecture facilitating "hyperglobalisation" the deepening of economic, social, and political connections across national boundaries that lifted billions from poverty and created the most integrated global economy in human history.[31] The systematic weakening of these institutions by major powers now threatens to unravel the foundations of globalisation that have underpinned global economic development, representing an increasing shift toward "deglobalisation" with profound implications for economic security and development prospects worldwide.[32]

The post-World War Two multilateral system was designed to facilitate global economic integration through institutional mechanisms that reduced transaction

[31] Kozul-Wright (2020).

[32] Aiyar et al. (2023).

costs, provided predictable rules, and enabled developing countries to participate in GVCs. The WTO and its predecessor, the GATT, created the legal framework that enabled the expansion of global trade from US$124 billion in 1948 to over US$19 trillion by 2019, while the UN system provided the broader governance architecture supporting decolonisation, development assistance, and international cooperation.[33] These institutions were central to what Baldwin[34] characterises as the "great convergence" where developing economies increasingly integrated into global production networks, leading to unprecedented reductions in global poverty and improvements in living standards.[35]

The WHO exemplifies how multilateral institutions facilitated globalisation beyond purely economic dimensions. Through coordinated disease surveillance, standard-setting, and technical assistance programs, the WHO enabled the global mobility of people and goods by managing health risks that could otherwise fragment international connections. The organisation's success in eradicating smallpox and reducing the burden of communicable diseases created the health security foundations that made deeper economic integration possible across national boundaries.[36] Similarly, the various UN development institutions facilitated globalisation by building state capacity in developing countries, enabling their progressive integration into global markets. International cooperation to address economic, social, cultural and humanitarian problems was essential for creating the institutional infrastructure that allowed developing countries to participate effectively in global value chains.[37] This institutional support was particularly crucial to allow developing economies to "catch up" with the developed economies through leveraging global integration to accelerate their economic development.[38]

The Trump administration's assault on the WTO represents a direct attack on the institutional foundations that enabled global economic integration. The paralysis of the Appellate Body through the blocking of new appointments has fundamentally undermined the predictability and stability that enabled the expansion of global value chains.[39] This institutional vandalism reflects a broader rejection of the multilateral constraints that facilitated globalisation, with the US seeking to wriggle free of the institutional constraints imposed on its freedom of action that previously enabled global economic integration.

The implementation of the US's "reciprocal tariffs" in April 2025, targeting countries with structural goods trade surpluses with the United States, represents a

[33] UNCTAD (2021).

[34] Baldwin (2016).

[35] Caselli et al. (2021).

[36] Prato and Adams (2021).

[37] Montes (2021).

[38] Ocampo (2020).

[39] Draper and Hing, *supra* n. 26.

fundamental departure from the MFN[40] principle that underpinned seven decades of trade liberalisation.[41] Global merchandise trade was expected to decline substantially marking a potential reversal of the globalisation process that drove economic development worldwide.[42]

China's economic coercion campaigns further demonstrate how major powers are weaponising the interconnectedness that globalisation created. The systematic removal of Lithuania from China's customs database following diplomatic disagreements, and the imposition of a range of punitive trade blocks on Australian products owing to different diplomatic disputes illustrate how economic integration can become a vulnerability when institutional constraints on state behaviour weaken. These actions represent hybrid coercion exploiting the interdependencies created by globalisation while simultaneously undermining the institutional frameworks that managed these relationships.

Russia's military aggression since 2014, culminating in the full-scale invasion of Ukraine in 2022, represents perhaps the most direct assault on the institutional foundations of globalisation. The annexation of Crimea and ongoing violations of international humanitarian law demonstrate how the breakdown of institutional constraints enables the return of territorial conquest and military force as instruments of state policy—precisely the dynamics that the post-1945 multilateral system was designed to prevent. The deployment of Russian mercenary forces across Africa further illustrates how institutional weakening enables the return of predatory practices that globalisation and multilateral governance were designed to constrain. These actions directly contradict the UN's role in facilitating decolonisation and supporting developing country sovereignty which was central to enabling global economic integration.

The COVID-19 pandemic further exposed fundamental weaknesses in the multilateral institutions that underpin globalisation while accelerating institutional fragmentation across multiple domains. The WHO's challenged response to the pandemic highlighted how the failure of member states to comply with the International Health Regulations and other multilateral provisions for COVID-19 signifies not only an institutional weakness but also an enduring feature of the global system: the self-interested behaviour of sovereign states.[43] This institutional failure had cascading effects on global economic integration, with 90% of countries reporting disruptions to essential health services, while routine immunisation services were affected in 70% of countries.[44] The pandemic's impact on global institutions extended far beyond health governance to encompass systematic disruptions

[40] MFN is established in Article I:1 of the General Agreement on Tariffs and Trade. It requires WTO members to extend to another members "like" products the best access they accord to all members. By adopting "reciprocal tariffs" and imposing differential rates on different countries, almost entirely WTO members, the US acted outside of the MFN principle.

[41] Junio (2025).

[42] Ibid.

[43] Prato and Adams, *supra*, n. 28.

[44] UNCTAD, *supra*, n. 33.

to the trade and investment flows that define globalisation. Supply chain disruptions, border closures, and uncoordinated national responses demonstrated how quickly decades of institutional integration could unravel when multilateral cooperation fails. The combination of health restrictions and institutional failures led to deindustrialisation pressures in developing countries, threatening to reverse decades of economic development gains achieved through global integration.[45] China's economic coercion of Australia during the pandemic after the Australian government called for an independent investigation into the origins of COVID-19 illustrates how global health crises can be weaponised. This demonstrated how public health governance failures cascade into trade conflicts, undermining both the health cooperation and economic integration that define contemporary globalisation.

The Trump administration's systematic withdrawal from international institutional commitments represents a fundamental threat to the development gains that globalisation enabled. The decision to withdraw from the WHO, citing concerns over "national sovereignty," directly undermined the health governance systems that enable global mobility and economic integration. This withdrawal threatens to destabilise global health initiatives, particularly in Africa, where American institutional leadership has been central to building state capacity that enables participation in global markets. The Trump Administration's comprehensive freeze on foreign aid programs implemented in January 2025 demonstrates how institutional withdrawal translates directly into development reversals impacting not only bilateral relationships but multilateral institutions that depend on American contributions for operational capacity. This pattern reflects institutional abandonment, where hegemonic powers withdraw from the governance frameworks that enabled global economic integration and development progress. The convergence of American unilateralism, Chinese economic coercion, and Russian military aggression creates "institutional entropy,"[46] i.e., the gradual degradation of the governance mechanisms that enabled global economic integration and development progress.[47]

The UN system faces unprecedented challenges as major powers systematically undermine the multilateral frameworks that have facilitated economic development and global integration for seven decades. Russia's violations of the UN Charter's prohibition on the use of force, China's circumvention of multilateral trade rules through economic coercion, and American withdrawal from key UN agencies represent a "crisis of multilateralism" that threatens the institutional foundations of global economic development.[48] The humanitarian consequences of institutional weakening extend far beyond procedural dysfunction to encompass measurable reversals in development outcomes. Rising levels of inequality globally highlighted that the benefit of economic development has not been equitably enjoyed across and

[45] Gopinth et al., *supra*, n. 16.

[46] A concept describing the gradual decline or fragmentation of an institution's structure, norms, or effectiveness over time, often due to internal complexity, loss of coherence, or insufficient adaptation to change.

[47] Pessali (2023).

[48] Saad Jaldi (2023).

within countries, while institutional breakdown accelerates these disparities.[49] The fragmentation of multilateral cooperation mechanisms undermines the collective action capacity that enabled global responses to poverty, disease, and underdevelopment.

The systematic weakening of multilateral institutions is driving geoeconomic fragmentation that could reverse decades of global integration and development progress. Increased fragmentation in trade will reduce economic opportunities, especially for developing economies; impede global poverty reduction; and lower living standards.[50] The costs of this fragmentation are particularly severe for emerging market economies and low-income countries, which are most at risk from trade and technology fragmentation because they lose disproportionately when access to global knowledge networks and technology transfer mechanisms are reduced.[51]

Quantitative estimates suggest the deeper the fragmentation, the greater the costs, with potential output losses ranging from 0.2% to 12% of GDP depending on the severity of institutional breakdown.[52] These losses reflect not merely reduced trade flows but the dismantling of the institutional infrastructure that enabled developing countries to participate in GVCs and access the technology transfer that drove their economic development. The systematic weakening of multilateral institutions represents more than cyclical adjustment in international relations; it constitutes a fundamental challenge to the globalisation process that has driven unprecedented economic development worldwide.

This institutional crisis reflects deeper structural tensions between the global integration that has driven economic development and the nationalist political pressures that now challenge multilateral governance and are creating conditions that threaten to reverse the development gains achieved through seven decades of institutional cooperation.[53] The erosion of institutional constraints on major power behaviour reduces the predictability and stability that enabled smaller economies to benefit from globalisation. The fragmentation of global governance mechanisms forces states to navigate an increasingly uncertain environment where the institutional foundations of economic integration lose their effectiveness.

The implications extend beyond immediate policy challenges to encompass questions about the future viability of the globalisation process itself. The systematic undermining of multilateral institutions suggests that the post-1945 international order may be reaching what historical institutionalists describe as a "critical juncture"—a moment when the institutional arrangements that enabled global economic development and integration face potential irreversible change.[54]

---

[49] Li et al. (2022).

[50] Qiu, Shin, and Zhang, *supra*, n. 25.

[51] Ibid.

[52] Ibid.

[53] Junio, *supra*, n. 41.

[54] Capoccia and Daniel (2007).

Notwithstanding the negative developments set out in this section, there are some grounds for cautious optimism to be found in the embrace of treaty-based cooperation mechanisms by a growing range of countries. Proponents of this view[55] argue that rather than evolving from a stable unipolar system characterised by liberal hegemonic stability anchored on the US to a multipolar system characterised by a power vacuum and consequent disorder, instead a "multiplex" system is evolving. The multiplex system is anchored on regionally-systemically significant middle powers such as Brazil, India, Germany, and France, wherein these powers increasingly forge international treaties across a range of cooperative domains, thereby dispersing normative power in the global economy while the US's network centrality declines in relative significance.

To the extent that this ameliorates these countries' relative hard and economic power incapacities compared to the great powers, and especially the US and China, this offers a measure of reassurance that international cooperation still has a future.

Nonetheless, the developments charted in this section create fundamental challenges to economic security and development strategy for middle powers such as Australia. The challenge for Australia and other middle powers lies in navigating this transition while preserving the institutional foundations that enabled their economic development and global integration, a theme we briefly explore in Sect. 6.3.

6.3 Australia's Adaptation Options

6.3.1 The Economic Security Imperative

The concept "economic security" has deep intellectual roots. Following Draper and Namo[56] it can be traced back to at least as far as the thinkers that Adam Smith, the father of free trade, dubbed "mercantilist".[57] "Geoeconomics"[58] is the modern framing, although Hirschman[59] produced the classic text on mitigating or mobilising trade vulnerabilities.

For hundreds of years free traders and their supporters have intellectually jousted with those advocating a greater role for states to curtail trade and investment to promote economic security, and the policy pendulum has swung between these positions as times and circumstances changed. Gilpin[60] frames this as the "persistent clash" between the sovereignty sacrifices the liberal international order requires, and states' enduring demands for national autonomy.

[55] Acharya et al. (2023).

[56] Draper and Namo (2025).

[57] Smith (1776).

[58] Luttwak (1990).

[59] Hirschman (1945).

[60] Gilpin (2001).

Reflecting on this long running and intricate debate Draper and Namo proffer a set of propositions to guide thinking about economic security in a more structured way:

1. Free trade delivers the most prosperity and promotes harmonious relations amongst states but must sometimes be subordinated to economic security considerations, notably to build key domestic economic capacities to advance the country's relative position in the global economy.
2. In a nuclear-armed, mutually assured destruction world, geoeconomics, or the use of economic toolkits deployed as weapons in inter-state relations to improve the country's relative economic position, assumes paramount importance in major states' international relations, or "statecraft".
3. To minimise its exposure to coercion a state must diversify its strategic supply sources while maximising its own influence potential in key competitors' political economies, and at the same time mobilise non-belligerents to its cause. States should also be cognisant of their relative bargaining power to maximise economic security gains while minimising exposures and/or losses.
4. A rules-based international system, or international regimes.[61] constraining power of major states to act unilaterally to undermine others' economic security, is essential. This is likely to work best amongst a group of relatively like-minded states, or allies, if the "system sponsor" or hegemon[62] is perceived to act largely in the interests of all.
5. In the modern context a rules-based order is also required to manage transboundary challenges requiring global solutions, particularly the existential climate change threat.

These propositions can be applied to the intensifying focus on derisking supply chains through the lens of economic security. PM&C[63] identifies Australia's imperatives as follows:

> Australia now balances multiple interdependent economic security policy objectives, including the need to bolster the resilience of supply chains and trade, build capacity to deter or respond to economic coercion, support a clean-energy transition, ensure the effectiveness of sanctions, protect critical infrastructure and technologies, and manage sensitive foreign investment.

Next, we analyse these issues in relation to Australia, where the discussion over economic security settings, and their connections with trade policy, is relatively new.[64]

---

[61] Krasner (1983).

[62] Gilpin, *supra*, n. 60.

[63] Department of the Prime Minister and Cabinet (2024).

[64] Recent contributions include: Mitchell (2024). Asia-Pacific Development, Diplomacy and Defence Dialogue (AP4D) (2024).

6.3.2 Building Supply Chain Resilience Through Investing in Domestic Industries

The destabilisation of global supply chains, driven by geopolitical tensions, pandemic disruptions, and the weaponisation of interdependence by major powers, has prompted a significant re-evaluation of industrial policy settings worldwide. For Australia, as for many advanced economies, the imperative to build supply chain resilience through domestic industry investment marks a notable departure from the globalisation-driven orthodoxy that has dominated economic policy over the past four decades. This has led to a resurgence of industrial policy as governments seek to secure critical capabilities and reduce strategic dependencies.[65]

This new wave of industrial policy is not simply a return to old-style protectionism. Rather, it reflects a more nuanced approach to market intervention, with governments targeting sectors deemed essential for national security, economic resilience, or the green transition. In the Australian context, this has been exemplified by the "Future Made in Australia" policy, which aims to foster domestic manufacturing in areas such as critical minerals, clean energy, and advanced manufacturing.[66] The "Future Made in Australia" initiative represents a strategic response to the risks of over-reliance on global supply chains, particularly in sectors critical to economic and national security. The policy's objectives include building sovereign capability in key industries, supporting the energy transition, and creating high-value jobs. It seeks to leverage Australia's comparative advantages in resources and innovation while addressing gaps exposed by recent global shocks. A central pillar of this policy is investment in the processing and value-adding of critical minerals, such as lithium and rare earths, which are essential for batteries, renewable energy technologies, and advanced electronics. The government's approach is to support the entire supply chain, from extraction to processing and manufacturing, through targeted incentives, public-private partnerships, and regulatory reform.[67] The policy also recognises the need for collaboration between federal and state governments, industry, and research institutions to build the necessary skills and infrastructure.

A distinctive feature of the contemporary industrial policy revival is its integration of sustainability objectives with supply chain resilience. The transition to a net-zero economy is both a driver and beneficiary of domestic industry investment. By developing local supply chains for renewable technologies, Australia can reduce its exposure to external shocks while contributing to global emissions reduction goals.[68] Resilient and sustainable supply chains are mutually reinforcing investments in clean technology manufacturing not only create economic opportunities but also reduce the carbon footprint associated with long, complex global supply

[65] Aiginger and Rodrik (2020).

[66] Australian Government (2024).

[67] Ibid.

[68] Productivity Commission, Australian Government (2021).

chains.[69] However, achieving this dual objective requires careful policy design to avoid unintended consequences, such as inefficiencies or trade distortions.

The shift towards domestic industry investment and supply chain resilience is not without tension. It marks a clear departure from the globalisation paradigm that prioritised efficiency and specialisation through international trade. Critics, including Australia's Productivity Commission, caution that poorly designed interventions risk undermining the benefits of open markets and could provoke retaliatory measures from trading partners.[70] There is a risk that such policies, if not carefully targeted and time-limited, may devolve into protectionism, raising costs for consumers and businesses and reducing overall economic welfare.

Moreover, the renewed focus on national industrial policy sits uneasily alongside Australia's longstanding commitment to trade liberalisation and multilateralism. While the "Future Made in Australia" policy seeks to build resilience, it must also navigate Australia's obligations under the WTO and its network of free trade agreements. This creates a complex policy environment where the pursuit of resilience must be balanced against the risks of trade fragmentation and the erosion of global economic integration.[71]

Australia's embrace of supply chain resilience through investment in domestic industries reflects a broader global trend towards the strategic management of economic interdependence. The "Future Made in Australia" policy embodies this shift, aiming to secure critical capabilities and support the green transition. However, the revival of industrial policy also highlights the inherent tensions between resilience, sustainability, and the globalisation paradigm that has shaped economic policy for decades. As Australia moves forward, it will need to ensure that its pursuit of resilience does not undermine the openness and integration that have underpinned its economic success, and that its policies remain consistent with both domestic priorities and international commitments.

6.3.3 *Diversifying Trade Partnerships and Strengthening Regional Alliances*

The World Bank and IMF highlight that trade diversification is associated with greater resilience to external shocks and higher long-term growth.[72] For Australia, a more diversified trade portfolio will help mitigate the risks of overconcentration, enhance economic security, and support sustainable development in a more uncertain global environment.

[69] Yadav (2020).

[70] Australian Government, *supra*, n. 66.

[71] Qiu, Shin, and Zhang, *supra*, n. 25.

[72] The World Bank (2025). Alfaro and Chor, *supra*, n. 15.

Australia's approach to trade diversification and regional alliance-building is increasingly shaped by the realities of a more fragmented and geopolitically contested global economy. As the chapter's earlier discussion of globalisation and institutional weakening demonstrates, overreliance on a single market, particularly China, has heightened Australia's trade vulnerability, while the erosion of multilateral rules has made diversification both more urgent and more complex.[73] Australia's export profile remains highly concentrated, with China accounting for over 32% of total goods and services exports in 2023.[74] This concentration is especially pronounced in sectors such as iron ore, where China alone absorbs more than half of Australia's output. Such dependence exposes Australia to risks of economic coercion and market disruption, as seen during the 2020–2022 period. Recent global shocks underscore the importance of trade diversification as a buffer against external shocks and policy-driven disruptions.[75] Excessive trade concentration has been shown to increase vulnerability to both demand and supply shocks, while diversified trade baskets enhance economic resilience and adaptability.[76]

Australia's diversification strategy must contend with the dual challenge of security dependence on the US and Chinese trade dependence. The US remains a critical security ally and an important trading partner (the US accounted for 5.5% of Australia's goods exports in 2023), and this has seen Australia pursue enhanced security and defence cooperation through the AUKUS agreement. Australia's contemporary approach to trade, technology, and security adaptation is increasingly intertwined with new regional governance structures such as AUKUS and Indo-Pacific Economic Framework for Prosperity (IPEF). AUKUS, established as a trilateral security partnership between Australia, the United Kingdom, and the United States, primarily focused on advanced defence technology cooperation, including nuclear-powered submarines, but has since broadened to cover quantum computing, artificial intelligence, cyber, and undersea capabilities.[77] AUKUS is not solely about military capability, but additionally about sharing research, industrial innovation, sovereign technology skills development, and enhancing the security of critical industries.[78]

Australia's participation in IPEF enables engagement with like-minded partners, including the United States, Singapore, India, Japan, South Korea, and Southeast Asian economies on digital trade, supply chain resilience, decarbonisation, and anti-corruption measures.[79] Through shaping standards and cooperation frameworks in critical and emerging technologies (such as AI and quantum), IPEF offers new

---

[73] Department of Foreign Affairs and Trade (2024); The World Bank, *supra*, n. 72.

[74] Department of Foreign Affairs and Trade (n.d.b).

[75] Parteka (2020).

[76] Benedictis et al. (2009) and Department of Foreign Affairs and Trade, Australian Government (2023).

[77] Prime Minister of Australia (2023).

[78] UK Government (2023).

[79] Department of Foreign Affairs and Trade, Australian Government (2024).

avenues for Australia to diversify economic relationships, promote best regulatory practices, and secure access to vital supply chains, particularly as traditional WTO mechanisms weaken. This regional architecture adds strategic value by allowing Australia to contribute to and benefit from the co-design of regional rules and standards that can underpin economic integration and digital connectivity in the Indo-Pacific region.

Despite these strong links with US regional initiatives, the recent US trade policy has created uncertainty even for close allies.[80] This underscores the need for Australia to pursue a more autonomous and multi-pronged trade strategy, rather than relying solely on traditional partners. At the same time, China's role as Australia's largest trading partner is unlikely to diminish in the near term, however the risks of overdependence are now widely recognised in government and industry circles. The challenge lies in managing this relationship pragmatically, while actively seeking to expand Australia's trade footprint elsewhere in the Indo-Pacific and beyond.[81]

Japan and South Korea remain vital economic partners, collectively accounting for over 18% of Australia's goods exports in 2023.[82] Both countries have proven reliable markets for Australian resources, energy, and agricultural products, and are key collaborators in critical minerals, hydrogen, and clean energy supply chains. Southeast Asia is central to Australia's diversification ambitions. The ASEAN-Australia-New Zealand Free Trade Area (AANZFTA) and the Regional Comprehensive Economic Partnership (RCEP) provide institutional frameworks for regional economic integration, covering a market of over 2.3 billion people and a combined GDP of more than US$38 trillion.[83] These agreements facilitate preferential market access, harmonise standards, and support supply chain connectivity across the region.

Vietnam exemplifies the opportunities for deeper engagement. With trade representing 166% of GDP in 2023—one of the highest ratios globally—Vietnam is integrating into regional and global value chains.[84] Australia's two-way trade with Vietnam reached A$23.5 billion in 2023, and both countries have upgraded their Comprehensive Partnership to a Strategic Partnership, with a focus on digital trade, education, and agri-food sectors.[85] Vietnam's participation in AANZFTA, RCEP, and the Comprehensive and Progressive Agreement for Trans-Pacific Partnership (CPTPP) further strengthens the institutional basis for bilateral and regional cooperation.

Similarly, the Philippines, with a population of over 115 million and a rapidly growing middle class, represents another priority for Australian trade

[80] Department of Foreign Affairs and Trade (2025a).

[81] Department of Foreign Affairs and Trade (2025b).

[82] Department of Foreign Affairs and Trade (2023).

[83] ASEAN Secretariat (2023); The World Bank, *supra*, n. 72.

[84] Ibid.

[85] Yadav et al., *supra*, n. 69.

diversification. Australia's two-way trade with the Philippines stood at A$6.6 billion in 2023, with significant potential for growth in education, services, and agri-food exports.[86] Enhanced engagement through AANZFTA and RCEP, as well as targeted bilateral initiatives, can help unlock new opportunities in this emerging market.

Beyond Southeast Asia, South Asia presents emerging opportunities for Australian exporters. Bangladesh, now the world's second-largest ready -made garment exporter and among the fastest-growing economies, recorded GDP growth of 7.2% in FY2021–2022 and continues to attract international investment.[87] Bangladesh's export-oriented industrialisation and growing pharmaceutical and green manufacturing sectors align well with Australia's strengths in resources, education, and technology. Sri Lanka, despite recent economic challenges, remains an important regional trading partner. In 2021, Sri Lanka's total exports were valued at US$13.3 billion, with apparel, rubber, and agricultural products as leading sectors.[88] Australia's engagement with Sri Lanka, through both bilateral and regional frameworks, can support trade diversification and contribute to Sri Lanka's economic recovery and integration into regional value chains.

The EU represents far more than an additional diversification opportunity for Australia; it embodies a strategic partnership that could serve as a critical counterweight to the systematic assault on globalisation and multilateral institutions described throughout this chapter. With two-way trade valued at over A$106 billion in 2023, the EU stands as Australia's third-largest trading partner, yet the relationship's strategic importance extends well beyond these impressive figures. As both Australia and the EU confront similar challenges from major power economic coercion and institutional fragmentation, their partnership represents what could become a vital bulwark for preserving and revitalising the rules-based international order. The EU-Australia partnership is fundamentally grounded in shared democratic values, commitment to human rights, rule of law, and multilateral cooperation—principles that directly contrast with the unilateral approaches adopted by the United States, China, and Russia in their systematic undermining of global institutions. The 2017 EU-Australia Framework Agreement,[89] which entered into force in 2022, formalises this cooperation across foreign policy, security, trade, and sustainable development, demonstrating mutual commitment to addressing global challenges through institutional mechanisms rather than power politics.

This values-based partnership becomes particularly significant in the context of the institutional weakening outlined earlier in this chapter. Europe represents a reliable and predictable partner that respected the rule of law and knew how to keep a deal, drawing explicit contrast with the Trump administration's trampling over free-trade agreements and systematic violation of multilateral commitments. This reliability becomes crucial as Australia seeks partners committed to preserving rather than destroying the institutional foundations of global economic integration. The

[86] Philippines Import Data (2023).
[87] The World Bank (2024).
[88] UN Comtrade Database (2023).
[89] European Commission (2024).

EU's single market represents an opportunity to access a large integrated market of 450 million consumers which would represent not merely trade diversification but engagement with a successful model of institutional economic governance that directly counters the fragmenting forces unleashed by major power competition. The stalled EU-Australia Free Trade Agreement negotiations, which collapsed in late 2023 over agricultural market access, have gained renewed urgency as both sides recognise the strategic imperative of closer integration amid global institutional breakdown. EU Commission President Ursula von der Leyen and Prime Minister Albanese's agreement to resume negotiations at the November 2024 G20 meeting reflects growing recognition that an FTA represents given current geopolitical circumstances. The economic benefits of such an agreement extend beyond traditional trade gains to encompass supply chain security and secure export markets between like-minded partners. Their potential partnership offers mutual protection against hybrid warfare tactics while demonstrating that democratic partners can maintain prosperous economic relationships without sacrificing sovereignty or values.

6.3.4 *Reinvesting in Global Trade Governance Frameworks*

Finally, given the challenges the WTO confronts, and Australia's longstanding desire to boost the multilateral rules-based trading system, there is a clear imperative to find ways to put a floor under the system's erosion. For the Australian government this means a combination of finding ways to pioneer new rules to reflect changing global economic dynamics, on a multilateral basis if possible but recognising this is unlikely and therefore on a plurilateral basis.

This explains why the Australian government co-chaired the Joint Statement Initiative (JSI) on e-Commerce and is involved in other regional and bilateral initiatives to advance digital trade rules (DFAT Services and digital trade).[90] The e-commerce JSI was signed by 86 WTO members and aims to agree a minimum framework of rules to govern, as well as facilitate, electronic commerce to enable flows of goods and services enabled by electronic means (Geneva Trade Platform).[91] Involving so many countries inevitably leads to compromises, but the JSI nevertheless offers a minimum platform for constructing rules frameworks to govern digitally enabled services, and trade in goods. Still, to pioneer more far-reaching commitments the Australian government has negotiated a bilateral Digital Economy Agreement with Singapore and is a member of the Comprehensive and Progressive Transpacific Partnership (CPTPP), a high standards trade agreement that includes a chapter on e-commerce concluded in 2015, and hence in need of updating given the rapid pace of technological advance as briefly set out in Part 6.3.1.[92]

[90] Department of Foreign Affairs and Trade (n.d.a).

[91] Geneva Trade Platform (n.d.).

[92] Honey (2025).

From a variety of discussions, the authors have held with senior DFAT officials in recent years it is also clear that WTO reforms, to reposition the organisation to effectively confront the systemic changes described in this chapter, are a high priority notwithstanding the many challenges in that path.

6.4 Conclusion

Economic globalisation is undergoing significant changes, and placing great stress on the multilateral institutional fabric built up over decades after the Second World War. Consequently, many countries, notably middle powers such as Australia, are under significant stress. In this chapter we explored the broad contours of Australian government responses to those stresses, notably the elevation of modern forms of industrial policy to build supply chain resilience and adaptability, reposition trade relationships with emphasis on derisking supply chains while opening new markets and sources of supply, as well as working to bolster the WTO as the apex of the global trading system's rules-based order. The challenges are growing inexorably, but countries are not without options as this chapter hopefully demonstrates.

References

Acharya, Amitav, Antoni Estevadeordal, and Louis W. Goodman. 2023. Multipolar or Multiplex? Interaction Capacity, Global Cooperation and World Order. *International Affairs* 99 (6): 2339–2365.

Aiginger, Karl, and Dani Rodrik. 2020. Rebirth of Industrial Policy and an Agenda for the Twenty-First Century. *Journal of Industry, Competition and Trade* 20 (2): 189–207.

Aiyar, Shekhar, Jiaqian Chen, Christian H. Ebeke, Roberto Garcia-Saltos, Tryggvi Gudmundsson, Anna Ilyina, Alvar Kangur, et al. 2023. *Geo-Economic Fragmentation and the Future of Multilateralism.* International Monetary Fund. https://doi.org/10.5089/9798400229046.006. Accessed 2 Sept 2025.

Akamatsu, Kaname. 1961. A Theory of Unbalanced Growth in the World Economy. *Weltwirtschaftliches Archiv* 86:196–217.

Akamatsu, Kaname. 1962. A Historical Pattern of Economic Growth in Developing Countries. *Journal of Developing Economies* 1:3–25.

Alfaro, Laura, and Davin Chor. 2023. *Global Supply Chains: The Looming "Great Reallocation".* NBER. https://papers.ssrn.com/sol3/papers.cfm?abstract_id=4567667. Accessed 2 Sept 2025.

Arriola, Christine, Mattia Cai, Przemyslaw Kowalski, Sébastien Miroudot, and Frank van Tongeren. 2024. *Towards Demystifying Trade Dependencies: At What Point Do Trade Linkages Become a Concern?* OECD Trade Policy Papers. https://doi.org/10.1787/2a1a2bb9-en.

ASEAN Secretariat. 2023. ASEAN Key Figures 2023. https://asean.org/serial/asean-key-figures-2023/. Accessed 2 Sept 2025.

Asia-Pacific Development, Diplomacy and Defence Dialogue. 2024. What Does It Look Like for Australia to… Navigate a New Era of Economic Statecraft in the Indo-Pacific? https://apo.org.au/node/327659. Accessed 2 Sept 2025.

Australian Government. 2024. A Future Made in Australia: National Reconstruction Fund and Industry Policy. https://www.aph.gov.au/About_Parliament/Parliamentary_departments/

Parliamentary_Library/Research/Budget_Review/2024-25/NewIndustryPolicy. Accessed 2 Sept 2025.

Baldwin, Richard. 2006. Globalisation: The Great Unbundling (S). https://www.researchgate.net/publication/252858331_Globalisation_The_Great_UnbundlingS. Accessed 2 Sept 2025.

Baldwin, Richard. 2016. *The Great Convergence: Information Technology and the New Globalisation*. Cambridge: Harvard University Press.

Baldwin, Richard. 2019. *The Globotics Upheaval: Globalisation, Robotics, and the Future of Work*. Oxford: Oxford University Press.

Baldwin, Richard, and Rikard Forslid. 2013. The Development and Future of Factory Asia. https://www7.econ.hit-u.ac.jp/cces/trade_conference_2013/paper/Richard_Baldwin.pdf. Accessed 2 Sept 2025.

Baldwin, Richard, Rebecca Freeman, and Angelos Theodorakopoulos. 2023. *Hidden Exposure: Measuring US Supply Chain Reliance*. Brookings Papers on Economic Activity. https://www.brookings.edu/articles/hidden-exposure-measuring-us-supply-chain-reliance/. Accessed 2 Sept 2025.

Benedictis, De Luca, Marco Gallegati, and Massimo Tamberi. 2009. Overall Trade Specialisation and Economic Development: Countries Diversify. *Review of World Economics* 145:37–55.

Bhagwati, Jagdish, and Hugh Patrick. 1991. *Aggressive Unilateralism: America's 301 Trade Policy and the World Trading System*. Ann Arbor: University of Michigan Press.

Capoccia, Giovanni, and Kelemen R. Daniel. 2007. The Study of Critical Junctures: Theory, Narrative, and Counterfactuals in Historical Institutionalism. *World Politics* 59:341–369.

Caselli, Marco, Andrea Fracasso, and Silvia Schiavo. 2021. Trade Policy and Firm Performance: Introduction to the Special Section. *Economia Politica (Bologna)* 38:1–6.

Cernat, Lucian. 2025. *Trade, Jobs and Technological Change: What to Expect in the Next Five Years?* ECIPE Policy Brief. https://ecipe.org/wp-content/uploads/2025/01/ECI_25_PolicyBrief_01-2025_LY02.pdf. Accessed 2 Sept 2025.

Department of Foreign Affairs and Trade. 2023. Australia's Trade in Goods and Services by Top 15 Partners. https://www.dfat.gov.au/sites/default/files/australias-goods-and-services-by-top-15-partners-2023.pdf. Accessed 2 Sept 2025.

Department of Foreign Affairs and Trade. 2024. Trade and Investment at a Glance. https://www.dfat.gov.au/about-us/publications/trade-investment/trade-at-a-glance/Pages/trade-at-a-glance. Accessed 2 Sept 2025.

Department of Foreign Affairs and Trade. 2025a. Latest on US Tariffs. https://www.dfat.gov.au/trade/trade-and-investment/latest-us-tariffs. Accessed 2 Sept 2025.

Department of Foreign Affairs and Trade. 2025b. Australia in the World—2025 Snapshot. https://www.dfat.gov.au/publications/international-relations/australia-world-2025-snapshot. Accessed 2 Sept 2025.

Department of Foreign Affairs and Trade. n.d.a Digital Trade and the Digital Economy. https://www.dfat.gov.au/trade/services-and-digital-trade/e-commerce-and-digital-trade. Accessed 1 June 2025.

Department of Foreign Affairs and Trade. n.d.b Doing Business with China. https://www.dfat.gov.au/trade/agreements/in-force/chafta/doing-business-with-china/doing-business-with-china. Accessed 2 Sept 2025.

Department of Foreign Affairs and Trade, Australian Government. 2023. Joint Declaration Against Trade-Related Economic Coercion and Non-Market Policies and Practices. https://www.foreignminister.gov.au/minister/penny-wong/media-release/joint-declaration-against-trade-related-economic-coercion-and-non-market-policies-and-practices#:~:text=We%20are%20particularly%20concerned%20with,or%20action%20in%20order%20to. Accessed 2 Sept 2025.

Department of Foreign Affairs and Trade, Australian Government. 2024. Indo-Pacific Economic Framework. https://www.dfat.gov.au/trade/organisations/wto-g20-oecd-apec/indo-pacific-economic-framework. Accessed 2 Sept 2025.

Department of the Prime Minister and Cabinet. 2024. Independent Intelligence Review. https://www.pmc.gov.au/international-policy-and-national-security/national-security/2024-

independent-intelligence-review#:~:text=The%20review%20was%20announced%20in,in%20protecting%20Australia%20s%20national%20interest. Accessed 2 Sept 2025.

Draper, Peter, and Vutha Hing. 2025. No, That's Not What a Trade Deficit Means—and That's Not How You Calculate Other Nations' Tariffs. *The Conversation*. https://theconversation.com/no-thats-not-what-a-trade-deficit-means-and-thats-not-how-you-calculate-other-nations-tariffs-253830. Accessed 2 Sept 2025.

Draper, Peter, and Freddie Namo. 2025. How Do the IPEF's Supply Chain and Clean Economy Pillars' Regulations Impact the Economic Security of the Region? In *IPEF Regulations and Their Impact on the Economic Security of the Indo-Pacific Region*, ed. Amitendu Palit and Saeeduddin Faridi, 48–63. Tokyo: NUS and Konrad Adenauer Stiftung.

European Commission. 2016. Joint Communication to the European Parliament and the Council: Elements for a New EU Strategy on China. https://www.eeas.europa.eu/sites/default/files/joint_communication_to_the_european_parliament_and_the_council_-_elements_for_a_new_eu_strategy_on_china.pdf. Accessed 2 Sept 2025.

European Commission. 2024. EU-Australia Trade Relations. https://policy.trade.ec.europa.eu/eu-trade-relationships-country-and-region/countries-and-regions/australia_en. Accessed 2 Sept 2025.

Friedman, Thomas L. 2007. *The World Is Flat: The Globalised World in the Twenty-first Century*. London: Penguin Press.

Geneva Trade Platform. n.d. Joint Statement Initiative on Electronic Commerce. https://wtoplurilaterals.info/plural_initiative/e-commerce/. Accessed 26 July 2025.

Gilpin, Robert. 2001. *Global Political Economy: Understanding the International Economic Order*. Princeton, NJ: Princeton University Press.

Gopinath, Gita, Pierre-Oliver Gourinchas, Andrea Presbitero, and Petia Topalova. 2025. Changing Global Linkages: A New Cold War? *Journal of International Economics* 153. https://doi.org/10.1016/j.jinteco.2024.104042.

Hirschman, Albert O. 1945. *National Power and the Structure of Foreign Trade*. Berkeley: University of California Press.

Honey, Stephanie. 2025. *Modernising the CPTPP's E-Commerce Chapter.* Hinrich Foundation. https://www.hinrichfoundation.com/research/article/ftas/modernizing-the-cptpp-e-commerce-chapter/. Accessed 26 July 2025.

Jean, Sébastien, Ariell Reshef, Gianluca Santoni, and Vincent Vicard. 2023. *Dominance on World Markets: The China Conundrum.* CEPII Policy Brief. https://www.cepii.fr/PDF_PUB/pb/2023/pb2023-44.pdf. Accessed 2 Sept 2025.

Junio, Don Rodney. 2025. *WTO Sounds Alarm on Trade Risks as 2025 Outlook Weakens*. World Economic Forum. https://www.weforum.org/stories/2025/04/global-trade-decline-2025-international-trade-stories-this-month/. Accessed 2 Sept 2025.

Kearney. 2025. The Great Reality Check: 2025 Reshoring Index. https://www.kearney.com/service/operations-performance/us-reshoring-index. Accessed 2 Sept 2025.

Kindleberger, Charles P. 1973. *The World in Depression, 1929–1939*. London: Allen Lane.

Kozul-Wright, Richard. 2020. Recovering Better from COVID-19 Will Need a Rethink of Multilateralism. *Development (Rome)* 63:157–161.

Krasner, Stephen D. 1983. *International Regimes*. Ithaca, NY: Cornell University Press.

Li, Yuefen, Daniel Uribe, and Danish. 2022. Challenges and Potential to Revamp the Normative Framework on the Right to Development. *Development (Rome)* 65:136–144.

Luttwak, Edward N. 1990. From Geopolitics to Geo-Economics: Logic of Conflict, Grammar of Commerce. *The National Interest* 20:17–23.

Mitchell, Helen. 2024. *Unlocking Economic Security: A Strategic Playbook for Australia.* United States Studies Centre Report. https://www.ussc.edu.au/unlocking-economic-security-a-strategic-playbook-for-australia. Accessed 2 Sept 2025.

Montes, Manuel F. 2021. Slaying the New Dragons that Threaten Peace: Renewing the UN's 'Systemic Issues' Agenda. *Development (Rome)* 64:19–28.

Ocampo, José Antonio. 2020. The Weakness of Economic Multilateralism. https://www.un.org/development/desa/dpad/wp-content/uploads/sites/45/Ocampo-Multilateralism.pdf. Accessed 2 Sept 2025.
Ohmae, Kenichi. 2002. *Triad Power: The Coming Shape of Global Competition*. New York: Free Press.
Parteka, Anna. 2020. What Drives Cross-Country Differences in Export Variety? A Bilateral Panel Approach. *Economic Modelling* 92:48–56.
Pessali, Huáscar. 2023. Institutional Entropy. *Journal of Economic Issues* 57:397–406.
Philippines Import Data. 2023. Philippines Import Export Data 2022–23. https://www.philippinesimportdata.com/. Accessed 2 Sept 2025.
Prato, Stefano, and Barbara Adams. 2021. Reimagining Multilateralism: A Long but Urgently Necessary Journey. *Development (Rome)* 64:1–3.
Prime Minister of Australia. 2023. Joint Leaders Statement on AUKUS. https://www.pm.gov.au/media/joint-leaders-statement-aukus. Accessed 2 Sept 2025.
Productivity Commission, Australian Government. 2021. *Vulnerable Supply Chains: Productivity Commission Study Report*. Canberra: Productivity Commission. https://www.pc.gov.au/inquiries/completed/supply-chains/report/supply-chains-overview.pdf. Accessed 2 September 2025.
Qiu, Han, Hyun Song Shin, and Leanne Si Ying Zhang. 2023. Mapping the Realignment of Global Value Chains. *BIS Bulletin*. https://www.bis.org/publ/bisbull78.htm. Accessed 2 Sept 2025.
Saad Jaldi, Abdessalam. 2023. *The Crisis of Multilateralism Viewed from the Global South*. Policy Center for the New South. https://www.policycenter.ma/publications/crisis-multilateralism-viewed-global-south. Accessed 2 Sept 2025.
Schwab, Klaus. 2017. *The Fourth Industrial Revolution*. New York: Crown Publishing Group.
Smith, Adam. 1776. *An Inquiry into the Nature and Causes of the Wealth of Nations*, Electronic Classic Series Publication. Pennsylvania: Pennsylvania State University.
Strange, Susan. 1987. The Persistent Myth of Lost Hegemony. *International Organization* 41:551–574.
The World Bank. 2024. Bangladesh Development Update: Strengthening Domestic Resource Mobilisation. https://thedocs.worldbank.org/en/doc/f6dd176b982714b6e3b04d7ac672a0ab-0310012024/original/Bangladesh-Development-Update-April-2024-w-cover.pdf. Accessed 2 Sept 2025.
The World Bank. 2025. Vietnam Trade (% of GDP). https://data.worldbank.org/indicator/NE.TRD.GNFS.ZS?locations=VN. Accessed 2 Sept 2025.
UK Government. 2023. The AUKUS Partnership: Factsheet. https://www.gov.uk/government/publications/implementation-of-the-australia-united-kingdom-united-states-partnership-aukus-fact-sheet. Accessed 2 Sept 2025.
UN Comtrade Database. 2023. Sri Lanka Trade Statistics. https://comtradeplus.un.org/. Accessed 2 Sept 2025.
UNCTAD. 2021. A More Resilient Multilateralism for Trade and Development: Transforming Trade and Development in a Fractured, Post-Pandemic World. https://unctad.org/system/files/official-document/osg2020d2_ch4_en.pdf. Accessed 2 Sept 2025.
Williamson, John. 2004. *The Washington Consensus as Policy Prescription for Development*. PIIE. https://www.piie.com/commentary/speeches-papers/washington-consensus-policy-prescription-development. Accessed 2 Sept 2025.
World Trade Organization. 2023. World Trade Report 2023: Re-Globalisation for a Secure, Inclusive and Sustainable Future. https://www.wto.org/english/res_e/booksp_e/wtr23_e/wtr23_e.pdf. Accessed 2 Sept 2025.
Yadav, Gunjan, Anil Kumar, Sunil Luthra, Jose Arturo Garza-Reyes, Vikas Kumar, and Luciano Batista. 2020. A Framework to Achieve Sustainability in Supply Chain Operations of Manufacturing Industries Using Industry 4.0 Technologies. *Computers & Industrial Engineering* 150. https://doi.org/10.1016/j.compind.2020.103280.

Chapter 7
The Future of the WTO

Mary Hiscock

Abstract This chapter evaluates the WTOs survival prospects amid deep institutional strain. It argues that the WTO's core functions remain crucial but are undermined by consensus paralysis, the Appellate Body impasse, rising use of national-security rationales, and protectionist measures. The chapter traces its historical origins in GATT's diplomatic, non-legalist ethos and explains why that legacy complicates enforcement today. It assesses plurilateral responses (open and closed agreements), the Multi-Party Interim Appeal Arbitration (MPIA) as a voluntary appellate stopgap, and the limits of regional and bilateral alternatives. While the WTO faces real risks of marginalisation amid geo-strategic rivalry and resource nationalism, the chapter stresses its resilience and concludes that the institution's future depends on pragmatic reform: preserving predictability and fairness while accommodating plural governance, clearer dispute mechanisms, and renewed political commitment from major powers.

7.1 Introduction

This chapter title infers, perhaps optimistically, that there is a future for the global regulatory trading institution. Many scholars and practitioners consider that the WTO is on life-support.[1] They cite spectacular dangers: the impact of trading agreements; the legal, political, and economic consequences of the admission of China to membership; the failure of the dispute resolution system; and the abuse of the national security provisions by the United States (US).

[1] Lester, Simon. 2023. Major Threats to the WTO and the World Trading System. In *the Future of Trade*, eds. David Gantz and Tony Payan, 229–251. Edward Elgar Publishing.

M. Hiscock (✉)
Faculty of Law, Bond University, Robina, QLD, Australia
e-mail: mhiscock@bond.edu.au

U. H. Ghori, J. Farrar (eds.), *Globalisation Disrupted*,
https://doi.org/10.1007/978-981-95-3997-0_7

However, a more considered judgment might well result in a different conclusion.[2] Daniel Moulis of Moulis Legal, a leading Australian trade law firm, who regularly participates in WTO matters, stated that the importance of the WTO is that it is a safe place for disputes. "WTO Members gain an appreciation of each other's positions, needs, and interests through dispute settlement. That comes from what is said in their submissions however bruising, in the diplomatic discussions that take place in the hallways of the building, and in the published reports."

How then should this institution be judged? Is it as a token of a set of political and economic values upheld and enforced at various points in the twentieth and in the first part of the twenty-first centuries? If so, the question is how far have these survived? Or, and this is my preference, should we not analyse the performance of its functions, and the likelihood of their continuing in a significant way,[3] even possibly without the membership of the US?[4]

It is not possible to do this within the confines of a single chapter: it must be a continuing task for all the stakeholders of the WTO. For every institution, the "mission statement," however expressed does not reveal as much as evidence of the operation of the infrastructure, the context, the environment and the people caught up in it.

The overriding objective of the WTO is the creation and maintenance of the global system for trading in goods, services,[5] and intellectual property. This was envisaged to be done through the functions of monitoring[6] trade and promoting transparency of action, regulating through rule making, furnishing the venue for the conduct of trade negotiations, and dispute resolution. The result should be predictability and security, leading to growing prosperity for its members.

---

[2] Moulis, Daniel. 2016. Comment post. *Linked-In*. https://www.linkedin.com/feed/update/urn:li:activity:7331823361104244736/. Accessed 29 August 2025.

[3] For example, the delivered decisions of the Appellate Body continue to be observed; and the numbers of requests for dispute settlement consultations have steadily increased in 2025.

[4] US trade policy has demonstrated a willingness to withdraw from international organisations or institutions with which it disagrees, for example UNESCO, The Paris Agreement, CTPP. That has never been a fatal blow to the organisation.

[5] On 13 June 2025, the Services Council held a thematic discussion on matters of general concern. However the International Trade Statistics of the WTO of 31 July 2024 showed a reduction in growth of trade in services of approximately one half of the last two years. This is attributed to fluctuations in value of the dollar and euro amid continuing instability. It considered the experiences of participating Members and international organisations. It compared experience of the WTO Discipline on reforming domestic regulation. It stressed predictability, proportionality, interagency collaboration, and the focus on results.

[6] World Trade Organisation (2024). WTO Trade Monitoring: Latest Trends. 8 July 2024. https://www.wto.org/english/news_e/news24_e/tmwto_08jul24_e.pdf. Accessed 29 August 2025. WTO Trade Monitoring: Latest Trends 8 July 2024 indicates a greater introduction of trade facilitating measures by Members, but also an increase in subsidies. This precedes the recent churn of tariff disruptions and accompanying action by the US. The Report indicates a belief that this trend will continue.

7.2 Historical Origins and Core Functions of GATT/WTO

Looking back to the original core functions of the General Agreement on Tariffs and Trade (GATT) as envisaged in the 1940s (disregarding the failed Havana Charter), it is hard to be optimistic about their survival. The provision of a multilateral environment for negotiation of tariffs was hoped to prevent the re-emergence of the damaging trade conflicts of the 1930s, waged through retaliatory tariffs.[7] The 23 original signatories accepted the aims of promoting trade and the values of a modified theory of comparative advantage.[8] Its proponent, Adam Smith, in his treatise The Wealth of Nations, excluded actions taken by the State because of its national security interests. He gave as an example:

> When any particular manufacture is necessary, indeed, for the defence of the society, it might not always be prudent to depend on our neighbours for the supply; and if such manufacture could not otherwise be supported at home, it might not be unreasonable that all the other branches of industry be taxed to support it. The bounties on the exportation of British-made sail cloth and gunpowder may, perhaps, both be vindicated on this principle.

The resulting dilemma, as the US Dept of Commerce discovered in 2023, is that the imposition of tariffs under Section 232 of the *Trade Expansion Act of 1962* without exemptions, had greatly increased the costs of transformers and related components. This led to reliance on importers to supply these essential products. The supply chain protection policy had fundamentally failed. That itself was a danger to national security.

GATT Regulation was desirably minimal, leaving ample scope for the operation of domestic policies.[9] Many decisions were in the collective or individual hands of Members. Ironically, although there is a provision in GATT dealing with harm caused by a "non-violation",[10] as the Understanding on Dispute Settlement (DSU) reflects, there is no compulsion to take action to react to a violation. The logic of the GATT can be understood only through its origin in diplomatic protocols and

---

[7] Each day at the time of writing there appear changes in tariffs announced or forecast by the US Administration that are manifestly retaliatory; to be changed only by bilateral agreement with the US. The erratic and unprincipled nature of these is illustrated by the Australian "base tariff" of 10%. As a matter of law, through the US-Australia Free Trade Agreement, the tariff was agreed to be zero. So, not only is the WTO principle of most-favoured nation scrapped, but further a binding international agreement is ignored by the US acting on a policy of "me-first"!

[8] Smith, Adam, cited in Henderson. David R. 2024. Does National Security Justify Trade Restrictions?. Hoover Institution. https://www.hoover.org/research/does-national-security-justify-trade-restrictions. Accessed 29 August 2025.

[9] Howse, Robert and Joanna Langille. 2022. Continuity and Change in the World Trade Organisation: Pluralism Past, Present, and Future. *American Journal of Trade Law* 117: 1–47. These scholars see the future of the institution tied to this flexibility and autonomy. The flow on effect of the international regulatory flexibility is anchored in domestic regulation. This has been on the WTO agenda for some time. *Supra* note 5.

[10] General Agreement on Tariffs and Trade, Art XXIII (1)(c). ('GATT')

decorum. The GATT was resolutely opposed to a legalistic approach, especially in dispute resolution.[11]

This opposition flowed over to constitutional principles, such as those of the European Union, where there are general principles of freedom of movement of goods, services, capital and persons. The GATT, and then its successor, the WTO texts, deal with specific measures, specific subject matter, with limitations and exceptions; all are the result of agreement.[12] The same specificity is observed in dispute resolution. Disputes need to be broken down to issues and relevant arguments, ruled on by the panel and the Appellate Body.[13] Hence the complexity of WTO law.

Where non-economic values were expressed, mostly by way of exceptions or defences, they were those accepted in international law since the 1920s, and reactions to events and current concerns of significance. How else to explain prison labour but not slave or child labour? Even the prohibition of embargoes had loopholes for party necessity.[14] Authorised retaliation is the ultimate remedy for international trade breaches, but only after a process of consultation, arbitration and mediation, carefully elaborated in the DSU of the WTO.

Treaty was the tool, and agreement by way of consensus was the operating mechanism of the original GATT. This made the dispute resolution system readily available to parties but weak in enforcement. Manipulating consensus is not difficult and is an established diplomatic strategy.

As post-colonial developments continued in the twentieth century, the importance of engaging and absorbing the growing number of independent, developing countries was recognised by the introduction of special and differential provisions for them. It was seen as the extension of a benevolent discipline. But the established scope of trade in goods meant little room for the new Members' concerns about agriculture, textiles, and food security generally. The growing importance of the environment and climate change was recognised only obscurely. References in the Preambles justified the establishment of a Committee on Trade and Environment. To some extent, access to the system of dispute resolution against powerful opponents was a great benefit to these new Members. But its operation depended on the voluntary making and, under the unreformed GATT, the enforcement of claims was also dependent on consensus. It was possible to win the battle and then lose the war.

The insignificance of developing countries was further evidenced in the Uruguay Round, transforming GATT into the World Trade Organisation (WTO). Regulation

---

[11] Hudec, Robert E. 1999. The New WTO Dispute Resolution Procedure: An Overview of the First Three Years. *Minnesota Journal of International Law* 8: 1–53. Robert E Hudec, a pre-eminent scholar in the field, worked diligently during the pre-WTO negotiations, believing strengthening dispute resolution would be the mark of success of the new institution.

[12] Howse and Langille *supra* note 10, 99.

[13] Reich, Arie. 2018. The Effectiveness of the WTO Dispute Settlement System: A Statistical Analysis. In *Transnational Commercial and Consumer Law: Current Trends in International Business Law* eds. Toshiyuki Kono, Mary Hiscock, and Arie Reich, 1–43. Springer.

[14] GATT, *supra* n.11, Art XI.

of trade in services through the General Agreement on Trade in Services (GATS), often the tool or subject matter of trade and investment, was not greatly developed, even though the ratio of its greater value to the value of trade in goods was growing apace. The emerging e-economy was overlooked. The provisions regulating Intellectual and industrial property transactions were wholly designed for the protection of developed countries' rights, ignoring the importance of technology access and transfer for developing countries.

Consensus is harder to achieve when the number of Members has grown. This has led to the increasing number of Agreements that are plurilateral, where less than the totality of Members have agreed. These are of 2 kinds: closed Plurilateral Agreements, such as the Government Procurement Agreement in Annex IV to the Marrakesh Agreement, which bind only those Members who agree to them. How these relate to the single undertaking of the WTO and Most-Favoured Nation (MFN) treatment is still a matter of controversy, both in principle and execution; although some scholars see this as the future of the WTO, because an Agreement accepted by some may be accepted by all.[15] Open Plurilateral Agreements (OPA) allow non-participating Members to participate in their benefits, once a critical mass of members has signed on or a Joint Statement Initiative (JSI) has been developed. This is done by relying on the basic concept of Most Favoured Treatment (MFN). This has produced developments such as the Investment Facilitation for Development (IFD). Measuring the achievements of the WTO must take into account such as these. However, enforcing such agreements is more difficult.[16]

7.3 Dispute Settlement Under Strain: The Appellate Body and Interim Fixes

However, the dispute resolution system continues to have teeth—too many teeth as it happened. The United States (US), unhappy with its strike record and with what were seen as activist panels, put the system into limbo. Decisions on particular issues going back to the earliest days of the AB were seen as not respecting particular policy issues important to the US. These included overreach in environmental protection, the refusal to accept the US concept of "zeroing" in US anti-dumping procedures and, of more significance, the scope of the national security defence and its self-judging nature.

[15] Bacchus, James. 2023. The Future of the WTO: Multilateral or Plurilateral?. Cato Policy Analysis. https://www.cato.org/policy-analysis/future-wto. Accessed 29 August 2025. James Bacchus is a former Chair of the AB.

[16] India challenged Australia's implementation of the Services Domestic Regulation plurilateral in its modification of the GATS schedules on the basis of structural inconsistency with the principle of the single undertaking. It failed because the finding was insufficient evidence, not demonstrated loss of benefit to India. The simplified amendments came into force in February 2025.

The US refused to nominate further AB members under the first Trump Administration, and this policy continued after the election of a new President, although notice of an appeal was lodged in 2024. The second Trump Administration has affirmed its previous policy even more stridently.

The call for reform of the WTO was not a single voice. An agenda for reform was agreed at the Twelfth Ministerial Conference (MC) in 2022. It was to report to the next MC in 2024. Dispute settlement, especially the issue of the AB, was made a separate item of inquiry and continues to be so to the present. Despite consistently large numbers of Members calling for nominations to the AB (the 88th occasion Columbia pointed out), no action has been forthcoming.

But no practical and generally acceptable solution has been found. Part of the divide is philosophical—the role and attributes of an ultimate decision maker. They may differ in procedure from one legal system to another, but the nature of it as final and binding on the parties does not. Whether its authority goes beyond that is fundamental. Only the common law system recognises that a decision may have significance beyond the parties in shaping the relevant legal rules. A further difficulty is that there is an assumption that the AB is a judicial institution. If it is characterised as an arbitral institution, the fundamental source of authority is different. It is not the Single Undertaking but the will of the parties. On this point, views will differ sharply. In the 1990s, when the AB was established, international arbitration was less usual. In international commerce, it is now endemic and is extremely sophisticated and resilient. The space created by the non-functioning of the AB must be filled. But how?[17]

Within the framework of the WTO, a new institution was devised. The Multi-Party Interim Appeal Arbitration Agreement (MPIA) was established by agreement between some of the WTO Members as a venue for voluntary appeals. It now has 31 Members, including the European Union (EU). In July 2025, the Arbitrators released the award in the second proceeding. The parties were the EU and China. The Arbitrators reviewed the panel findings in *China—Enforcement of Intellectual Property Rights* (DS611). The review was limited to issues of law. On some issues, the panel was upheld: on others, it was not. Apart from the exclusion of fact findings, the process was similar to the AB. One striking difference was the shorter period of time to complete the process.

Its voluntary nature is its strength and its weakness. In 2024, Stratos Pahis reviewed the reaction by Members to dispute resolution since 2022, using five disputes as his examples.[18] He questions whether, even without the MPIA, a process of facilitated negotiations would be a workable alternative to the AB. The MPIA Awards are briefer than recent AB decisions. They were given within 90 days as the

[17] Bown, Chad, P. and Petros C. Mavroidis. 2024. Things Have Changed: Dispute Settlement Inside and Outside of the WTO in 2022. *World Trade Review* 23: 269–270.

[18] Pahis, Stratos. 2024. Appeals After the Appellate Body. *World Trade Review* 23: 296–323.

DSU requires. The arbitrators accepted the findings of fact from the panel decision. There was variation from AB reasoning, and that tended to favour the national authority. He assesses that the differences between the reasoning of the panel and that of the Arbitrators are so slight that the panel decision could simply have been accepted without further ado. He rhetorically concludes that these adjudicators "may be signalling a way out of the swamp".

The MPIA does not meet the basic issue of the tension between the US and China.[19] It is too simplistic to see this as a battle for economic and political dominance. There are similarities in structure and practice between the two States, both political and economic. China's trade practices and economic structure still sit uneasily within the WTO structure, founded on market-oriented policies, despite the confines placed on its accession to Membership and its adherence to all rulings made against it. So questions relating to trade remedies such as subsidies and countermeasures and safeguards, and anti-dumping continue to be major issues.[20]

The monitoring of domestic systems is a frequent task. There are complexities based around a fundamental supply chain insecurity in the non-acceptance of interdependence. This concentration on dependence is what has pushed the US to develop its unacceptable extension of Adam Smith's original statement, which was only directed to risks of military insecurity—the preservation of independence from invasion or war.

The WTO also seeks an independent ruling of the exceptions and defences that have been agreed. Any self-determination of emergency needs to be justified to a tribunal.

This is the structural heart of the issue—the clash between domestic policies and assumed international obligations. It is not seen by the US as a retreat from global engagements but as an attempt to strike an effective balance between domestic and international mechanisms.

[19] See the perceptive analysis of Jingshia Xi, considering the Chinese point of view as well as that of the West. Xi, Jingshia. 2025. The Quest for the Future of the WTO: From the Perspective of World Order. *Yale Journal of International Law*. https://yjil.yale.edu/posts/2024-06-01-the-quest-for-the-future-of-the-wto-from-the-perspective-of-world-order. Accessed 29 August 2025.

[20] Dispute Settlement Board (2025). Members consider request for panel to examine Chinese duties on agriculture, fish products. *World Trade Organisation*. https://www.wto.org/english/news_e/news25_e/dsb_05jun25_e.htm. Accessed 29 August 2025. At the June 2025 meeting of the Dispute Settlement Board (DSB) Canada requested and was granted a panel to consider import duties imposed by China, and China also requested a panel to consider import duties imposed by Canada.

7.4 Plurilateralism, Regional Alternatives and Institutional Adaptation

There are available external frameworks of rules, standards, and dispute resolution mechanisms relevant to many Members of the WTO. These include bilateral and regional trade agreements.[21] Some of the latter cover major areas of international trade by volume and value. They represent a choice available to Members. But there is the risk of clashes of jurisdiction, differing interpretations of key clauses, and a long-term diminution of the importance and power of the WTO. Substantial State based structures include the BRICS.[22] It is not designed to eliminate access to the WTO for its Members but to tackle the issue of incompatibility of economic assumptions. It is still at a primitive stage in dispute resolution, rather concentrating on tasks of replacing financial institutions seen as in the control of the global west, such as the International Monetary Fund.

The twenty-first century has seen major disruptions in the political economy and in the natural world. The prospering impetus of globalisation has waned and virtually disappeared. The volume of global trade in the first quarter grew only 1%. States are looking to their own national interests more and more in imposing tariffs and sanctions. The defence of national security, a sleeper for many years, is being raised as a self-judging justification for protectionist policies and ignoring existing international commitments, whether inbound tariffs or relevant Free Trade Agreements. Perhaps this is more so in the great global spaghetti bowl of parallel trade agreements, bilateral and multilateral. So we are back to the 1930s policy of "beggar-my-neighbour".

7.5 Conclusion

As the United Nations (UN) and its various agencies have identified broad issues of sustainability, climate change and equality in accessibility to trade, but have failed to do anything about them, the WTO moved into focus. WTO has made progress in the Quadrilateral Agreement on Fisheries Subsidies which has almost reached the numbers for completion. But the institution is not structured to address "public goods negotiations", where no State has a driving interest, but there is a general community good. There is a large agenda coming from Ministerial Meetings, but small progress.

---

[21] Such as the Comprehensive and Progressive Trading Bloc (CPTPP). It covers about 15% of the global trading volume. The UK is the first European member to join. Although it has applied for membership, China is not a member. The US withdrew from its predecessor, bringing about the CTPTPP.

[22] Boulle, Laurence.2025. Building a Block: Brick by BRICS, *infra*, Chap. 5.

The greatest basis for optimism for the future of the WTO is that it and its predecessor, GATT, have survived 80 years of planning and operation. That is a testimony to resilience, but it may not be enough.

References

Bacchus, James. 2023. *The Future of the WTO: Multilateral or Plurilateral?*. Cato Policy Analysis. https://www.cato.org/policy-analysis/future-wto. Accessed 29 August 2025.

Bown, Chad P., and Petros C. Mavroidis. 2024. Things Have Changed: Dispute Settlement Inside and Outside of the WTO in 2022. *World Trade Review* 23:269–270.

Dispute Settlement Board. 2025. *Members Consider Request for Panel to Examine Chinese Duties on Agriculture, Fish Products*. World Trade Organisation. https://www.wto.org/english/news_e/news25_e/dsb_05jun25_e.htm. Accessed 29 August 2025.

Howse, Robert, and Joanna Langille. 2022. Continuity and Change in the World Trade Organisation: Pluralism Past, Present, and Future. *American Journal of Trade Law* 117:1–47.

Hudec, Robert E. 1999. The New WTO Dispute Resolution Procedure: An Overview of the First Three Years. *Minnesota Journal of International Law* 8:1–53.

Lester, Simon. 2023. Major Threats to the WTO and the World Trading System. In *The Future of Trade*, ed. David Gantz and Tony Payan, 229–251. Edward Elgar Publishing.

Moulis, Daniel. 2016. Comment Post. *Linked-In*. https://www.linkedin.com/feed/update/urn:li:activity:7331823361104244736/. Accessed 29 August 2025.

Pahis, Stratos. 2024. Appeals After the Appellate Body. *World Trade Review* 23:296–323.

Reich, Arie. 2018. The Effectiveness of the WTO Dispute Settlement System: A Statistical Analysis. In *Transnational Commercial and Consumer Law: Current Trends in International Business Law*, ed. Toshiyuki Kono, Mary Hiscock, and Arie Reich, 1–43. Springer.

Smith, Adam, cited in Henderson, David R. 2024. *Does National Security Justify Trade Restrictions*?. Hoover Institution. https://www.hoover.org/research/does-national-security-justify-trade-restrictions. Accessed 29 August 2025.

World Trade Organisation. 2024. *WTO Trade Monitoring: Latest Trends 8 July 2024*. https://www.wto.org/english/news_e/news24_e/tmwto_08jul24_e.pdf. Accessed 29 August 2025.

Xi, Jingshia. 2025. The Quest for the Future of the WTO: From the Perspective of World Order. *Yale Journal of International Law*. https://yjil.yale.edu/posts/2024-06-01-the-quest-for-the-future-of-the-wto-from-the-perspective-of-world-order. Accessed 29 August 2025.

Chapter 8
China and the Strategic Evolution of the Belt and Road Initiative

Rosita Dellios and R. James Ferguson

Abstract The history of the old silk road dates from the second century BCE to the fifteenth century. Its modern manifestation dates from 2013 when China announced the 'Silk Road Economic Belt' and the '21st Century Maritime Silk Road'. These land and sea routes became known as the Belt and Road Initiative (BRI). Instead of silk, however, the prized 'commodity' from China became infrastructure, investment and its associated connectivity, with expected gains in trade flows and resource access. The BRI includes 150 countries and over 30 international organisations, is likely to draw in a total investment of circa $8 trillion in coming decades, may boost global GDP by over $7.1 trillion annually by 2040, and has numerous economic corridors crossing continents with maritime extensions into the Arctic and the Indo-Pacific. It has been touted by some as a major developmental driver of non-Western globalisation but also has been attacked as a strategic form of geopolitical aggression used to promote China's global leadership and influence. Beyond these simplistic assessments, the reality of the BRI is that it has been through a continuing strategic evolution since its first announcement in 2013. At first it was a generalised framework to ensure China's access to resources and markets as part of its 'going out' into the global economy, designed to soak up excess production and support domestic job creation. It was thereafter modified several times in its policy emphasis. It was linked to China's model 'community of common destiny' as shared development among partner states, and to the goal of creating an Ecological Civilisation (from 2007) that would embed economic, social and environmental sustainability into the BRI, making it compatible with the UN's Sustainable Development Goals. This was followed from 2015 onwards by an effort to channel green investment and circular economic models onto the BRI, rebranding it as a Green BRI (GBRI). Unfortunately, over the BRI's first decade to 2023 this transition was problematic, with only 28–34% of China's BRI energy engagement being in green or hydropower projects, and with China's ongoing inability to curtail coal usage despite its planned goal of 'carbon neutrality' before 2060. There has also

R. Dellios (✉) · R. J. Ferguson
Faculty of Society and Design, Bond University, Robina, QLD, Australia
e-mail: rdellios@bond.edu.au; jferguso@bond.edu.au

U. H. Ghori, J. Farrar (eds.), *Globalisation Disrupted*,
https://doi.org/10.1007/978-981-95-3997-0_8

been uneven monitoring of the long-term social and ecological outcomes of many BRI projects, leading to some controversial failures for its megaprojects. China has re-emphasised its commitment to green development, and to supporting high-quality development and cooperation. Whether the BRI will promote sustainable development through economic, technological and green paths of progress or fall short of its promise is explored through three scenarios for the future evolution of the BRI. The Positive Path of development scenario is found to be the most desirable even though it may not be the most probable.

8.1 Introduction: History, Geography and Chinese Strategy

8.1.1 History

Like the Great Wall that extended over northern China during successive dynasties, China is now engaged in another project that is evolving across dimensions of time, space and purpose. This is a vast network of infrastructure—physical and virtual—connecting Asia, Europe, the Middle East, Africa, and beyond. The Belt and Road Initiative (BRI) has become the primary foreign policy vehicle for the People's Republic of China (PRC), but its historical footprint may be found in the continental trade routes collectively known as the Silk Road. These date from the second century BCE to the fifteenth century, though the name 'Silk Road' to describe the transregional trading routes spanning Asia and Europe, and involving a civilisational interchange including Indian, Persian, and Central Asian influences, emerged later in the European geographic lexicon.

A maritime silk road was also plied in early trading systems. It depended on monsoonal winds, which reverse direction seasonally, in the shipping of cargo along trade routes encompassing China, the Middle East and East Africa. The Malacca Strait that connects the Indian Ocean and the South China Sea in Southeast Asia marked an important inter-monsoonal hub. It was no surprise, then, that Indonesia—a Southeast Asian archipelagic nation—served as the venue for China's announcement of a the '21st Century Maritime Silk Road'. This came in 2013, shortly after China's President Xi Jinping announced the overland 'Silk Road Economic Belt' in Kazakhstan. These land and sea routes were simplified under the title of 'One Belt, One Road' (abbreviated to OBOR), even though there was more than one of each. This remains its Chinese name. 'Belt and Road Initiative', or just 'Belt and Road' without the 'One', later became the official English versions. While 'silk' was retained in the full title of both the economic belt and maritime road, evoking the past with its lessons of cooperative regionalism (the 'Silk Road spirit'[1]), it now

[1] Jinping, Xi. 2023. Chairman's Statement of the Third Belt and Road Forum for International Cooperation. http://www.beltandroadforum.org/n101/2023/1018/c134-1207.html. Accessed 25 May 2025.

forfeited its role of prized 'commodity' to the building of infrastructure and its associated connectivity and trade.

8.1.2 Geography

Such has been the development of the BRI since 2013 that it has gone beyond China's immediate neighbourhood, crossing oceans and continents, rendering it global in scope. The BRI in 2025 included 150 countries across Asia, Africa, the Middle East, Europe, Latin America and the Pacific Islands region. China's National Development and Reform Commission enumerates land-based economic corridors that follow "international transport routes, relying on core cities along the Belt and Road and using key economic industrial parks as cooperation platforms".[2] The economic corridors are: (1) China–Mongolia–Russia; (2) New Eurasian Land Bridge; (3) China–Central Asia–West Asia; (4) China–Indochina Peninsula; (5) China–Pakistan Economic Corridor; and (6) Bangladesh–China–India–Myanmar. Meanwhile, maritime extensions into the Arctic and the Indo-Pacific have expanded the map of BRI across the northern and southern hemispheres, with "transport routes connecting major seaports along the Belt and Road".[3]

These beginnings addressed the strategic requirements of China as an emerging global power: accessing energy, improving connectivity to markets, and decreasing industrial overcapacity by building abroad. Domestic economic and security concerns over the wealth gap between eastern and western China also acted as a driver in the initial development of BRI. Western China was not only poorer but prone to political unrest in the northwest where separatists have called for an independent 'East Turkistan'. From these and other needs of a rising superpower—such as promoting the international use of the national currency, the renminbi (RMB)—the purposes of the BRI have evolved in tandem with its expansion. Indeed, the BRI's evolving strategy, reflecting PRC policy guidelines, is adaptive to the changing needs of the Chinese state. All the while, this is occurring in a strategically competitive international environment.

8.1.3 Chinese Strategy

The seriousness with which China holds the BRI is evident in its incorporation into the Constitution of the Communist Party of China in 2017. It shows the party's commitment to the Belt and Road as a driving force for the nation's economic growth

---

[2] National Development and Reform Commission of the People's Republic of China. 2017. Vision and Actions on Jointly Building Belt and Road. http://2017.beltandroadforum.org/english/n100/2017/0410/c22-45.html. Accessed 25 May 2025.

[3] Ibid.

and global influence. Just as China's Active Defence strategy[4] is a form of proactive defence in the realm of military power—which crucially includes the policy of civil-military integration that had been elevated to a national-level strategy in 2015[5]—so too the BRI can analogously be conceived as a form of Active Defence in the economic and geopolitical spheres. Irrespective of whether the BRI appears haphazard, and despite its "lack of a discrete institutional identity",[6] its service to the state is clear: to secure state survival in the first instance (the initial needs of a modernising China) and state capacity to prevail in the longer term. The BRI as "a flexible endeavour"[7] represents a greater service to China's security as a global actor by being a 'non-strategy'. Unlike the former name, OBOR, with its definitive oneness and its sense of strategic directionality (which was far from the case), the Belt and Road is now called an 'initiative'; its vision is deliberately expansive and inclusive. It promotes the 'Silk Road spirit' of "peace and cooperation, openness and inclusiveness, mutual learning and mutual benefit."[8] It not only includes countries but also international organisations, of which it has engaged over 30.[9] The government's online *Belt and Road Portal* describes the BRI as an "international public good" and "the world's largest platform for international cooperation, with the broadest coverage".[10]

This renders China, through the BRI, a huge global actor with an inclusive outlook. Such 'soft power' sentiments add to Beijing's strength in the contest for influence with the world's preeminent power, the United States. This has been expressed, first and foremost, at the economic level. China has often been described as "the world's leading practitioner of geoeconomics".[11] Its investment into BRI countries in 2023 was almost 80% percent higher than in 2022, with close to $50 billion invested in BRI economies.[12] BRI is likely to draw in a total investment of circa $8

[4] The State Council Information, PRC. 2019. China's National Defense in the New Era. http://eng.mod.gov.cn/news/2019-07/24/content_4846443.htm. Accessed 25 May 2025.

[5] The State Council Information Office, PRC. 2015. China's Military Strategy. http://english.www.gov.cn/archive/white_paper/2015/05/27/content_281475115610833.htm. Accessed 25 May 2025; Yang, Xiaoxin, and Han Zhang. 2024. China's Civil-Military Integration and Regional Defence Innovation: A Quasi-Natural Experiment Based on National Industrial Zone Policy. *Defence and Peace Economics* 36: 653–682.

[6] International Institute for Strategic Studies (IISS). 2022. China's Belt and Road Initiative: A Geopolitical and Geo-economic Assessment. https://www.iiss.org/publications/strategic-dossiers/chinas-belt-and-road-initiative/. Accessed 26 May 2025.

[7] Ibid, at 16.

[8] Belt and Road Portal. 2025. Connotation of BRI. https://eng.yidaiyilu.gov.cn/p/00FUU20U.html. Accessed 27 May 2025.

[9] Ibid.

[10] Ibid.

[11] Blackwill, Robert D., and Jennifer M. Harris, 2016. *War by other means: Geoeconomics and statecraft.* Cambridge, Massachusetts: Harvard University Press.

[12] Nedopil, Christoph. 2024. China Belt and Road Initiative (BRI) Investment Report 2023. Griffith Asia Institute, Griffith University, Australia and Green Finance & Development Center, FISF Fudan University, China. https://doi.org/10.25904/1912/5140. Accessed 25 July 2025.

trillion in coming decades and may boost global GDP by over $7.1 trillion annually by 2040.[13]

Beijing's inclusivity, however, has a flipside: the erosion of Washington's traditional sphere of influence in the Latin America and the Caribbean (LAC) region. China has become the second largest trading partner for the LAC region (after the US), while sustaining major dialogues via regional groupings such as Community of Latin American and Caribbean States (CELAC) and BRICS, as well as individual countries. Brazil and Colombia signed numerous trade and investment agreements with China through 2023–2025, and Colombia formally joining the BRI in May 2025.[14]

Though still behind US and EU flows, the PRC and Chinese firms are also major investors into the region. Outward direct investment (ODI) reached $600.8 billion in 2023, comprising 20.3% of total Chinese ODI, including investment into infrastructure, ports, mining and energy sectors.[15] These trends demonstrate that Latin America can no longer be taken for granted in US policy circles. China's institutionalised presence in the Western hemisphere bolsters an emerging polycentric world order where the US no longer predominates.[16]

8.2 Strategic Evolution of BRI

This juxtaposition of the BRI acting as a developmental driver of non-Western globalisation on the one hand, with its capacity to promote China's global leadership (widely seen as geopolitical aggression) on the other, has largely defined debates about the merits or otherwise of China's most ambitious project in the twenty-first century. Beyond essentialising narratives when assessing the BRI, the reality of the Belt and Road, for over a decade of its existence, is that it has strategically evolved. The BRI is a developmental 'story' unto itself as it builds infrastructure and advances connectivity across the globe. This 'story' unfolds in the following sections.

---

[13] Ferguson, R. James. 2023. Of Global Concern: Governance and Sustainability Along the Belt and Road. Australian Outlook. https://www.internationalaffairs.org.au/australianoutlook/of-global-concern-governance-and-sustainability-along-the-belt-and-road/. Accessed 9 June 2025; Cebr. 2019. Belt and Road Initiative to boost world GDP by over $7 trillion per annum by 2040. https://cebr.com/reports/belt-and-road-initiative-to-boost-world-gdp-by-over-7-trillion-per-annum-by-2040/. Accessed 25 May 2025.

[14] Holmes, Steven. 2025. China in Latin America: May 2025. Council on Foreign Relations. https://www.cfr.org/article/china-latin-america-may-2025. Accessed 9 June 2025.

[15] Interesse, Giulia. 2024. China's Outbound Investment Trends: Sources, Destinations, and Key Sectors. China Briefing. https://www.china-briefing.com/news/chinas-outbound-investment-trends-sources-destinations-and-key-sectors/. Accessed 9 June 2025.

[16] Lazarus, Leland. 2025. How China is Seeking Dominance in Latin America. *Americas Quarterly*. https://www.americasquarterly.org/article/how-china-is-seeking-dominance-in-latin-america/. Accessed 9 June 2025.

8.2.1 'Going Out' Strategy

The prelude to the BRI was China's 'going out' strategy of the 1990s so that China could become engaged in the global economy. It was the logical outcome from the momentous 'opening up and reform' strategy of the late 1970s. 'Going out' or 'going global' saw an influx of foreign direct investment (FDI), double-digit annual growth rates, and China becoming a foreign direct investor in its own right (outward FDI). The PRC's accession to the World Trade Organisation (WTO) in 2001 was a high point of this policy trend.

China's rapid economic rise had the adverse result, however, of a development gap between the prospering eastern coast and the poorer western regions of the interior. It did lift over 800 million people out of poverty, but there remained significant swathes of poverty—some 200 million people by World Bank estimates.[17] The internationally recognised measure of income inequality, the Gini coefficient, shows China to be a country which has experienced a wide gap between rich and poor.[18] This was recognised in China's 14th Five-year plan (2021–2025) which called for a reduction in the differences between urban and rural standards of living.[19] President Xi Jinping has sought to reduce income inequality through 'rejuvenating' the Chinese nation, with the BRI passing through the western regions in an effort to expand the arc of prosperity beyond the coastal fringe. This was expected to assist in dealing with the restive region of Xinjiang in the northwest of China and periodic unrest in the adjoining area of Tibet. Not only would BRI development help increase living standards, and hopefully win over popular sentiment, but would also provide easier access for China's security forces to control these regions.

Finally, development of China's western expanse would facilitate energy imports from the Middle East via the China–Pakistan Economic Corridor (CPEC), connecting Xinjiang with Pakistan's deep sea ports of Gwadar (a major BRI infrastructure project) and Karachi on the Indian Ocean. CPEC allows for an alternative to reliance on Southeast Asia's Malacca Strait, through which most of China's imported oil and gas traverse. This narrow strait is vulnerable to closure or disruption in the event of hostilities in the disputed South China Sea or over Taiwan.

The BRI's advantages to China of accessing resources and markets, absorbing industrial overcapacity, and supporting domestic job creation do not always translate to benefits for the receiving end in host nations. First, businesses in BRI countries have had to contend with the influx of cheaper Chinese products. The situation

---

[17] Development Research Center of the State Council, the People's Republic of China, The World Bank. 2022. Four Decades of Poverty Reduction in China: Drivers, Insights for the World, and the Way Ahead. P. 61. https://openknowledge.worldbank.org/server/api/core/bitstreams/e9a5bc3c-718d-57d8-9558-ce325407f737/content. Accessed 10 June 2025.

[18] World Population Review. 2025. Gini Coefficient by Country 2025. https://worldpopulationreview.com/country-rankings/gini-coefficient-by-country. Accessed 11 June 2025.

[19] Asian Development Bank (ADB). 2021. The 14th Five-Year Plan of the People's Republic of China—Fostering High-Quality Development. https://doi.org/10.22617/BRF210192-2. Accessed 9 June 2025.

has been exacerbated since the first Trump administration by the imposition of punishing tariffs on Chinese goods. With the US "no longer the primary market or buyer of last resort",[20] Chinese products have been even more focused on BRI markets. This adds a double burden on small and medium-sized enterprises within host countries: locally, Chinese goods outcompete them, while externally US tariffs are affecting their own exports too. China's domestic market, long considered the prize of exporters the world over, has not proved helpful in soaking up China's excess production. Domestic consumption expenditure has long remained weak, while the PRC government has continued to prioritise and provide subsidies to manufacturing.[21]

8.2.2 Digital Silk Road and Made in China 2025

Such subsidies need to be seen in the light of the Made in China 2025 (MIC2025) plan introduced in 2015,[22] the same year that an accompanying Digital Silk Road (DSR) was announced. Turning first to the DSR as carving a prime sphere of influence for MIC2025, DSR has gone beyond the connectivity of physical infrastructure—roads, railways and ports—to cross the "digital gulf and diffuse AI norms" through "Chinese digital giants like Huawei, Alibaba and Tencent". [23] This would be laudatory it were not for the fear that that Beijing could use these technology companies "to 'rewire' the global digital architecture", challenging global—or Western-dominated norms—"of a free cyber commons to competing systems of cyber sovereignty or cyber freedom".[24]

But first, what are the digital 'nuts and bolts' of the DSR? What does it look like? It includes the construction of optical fibre networks, ground stations, satellite links and expanded internet access across Eurasia. This has been augmented by new undersea cable links (across the Atlantic, coastal East and Southeast Asia, across the north Pacific, along coastal Africa, and from Pakistan via the Mediterranean to

[20] International Institute for Strategic Studies (IISS). 2025. A geo-economic conundrum for the member states of ASEAN. Strategic Comments, Volume 31, Comment 10. https://www.iiss.org/publications/strategic-comments/2025/05/a-geo-economic-conundrum-for-the-member-states-of-asean/. Accessed 9 June 2025.

[21] Ibid.

[22] The State Council of the People's Republic of China. 2015. Implementation Stressed for Manufacturing Vision. https://english.www.gov.cn/policies/latest_releases/2015/05/19/content_281475110703534.htm. Accessed 9 June 2025.

[23] Au, Adam, and Felicia Feiran Chen. 2025. China expands AI globally through the Digital Silk Road. *East Asia Forum*. https://doi.org/10.59425/eabc.1744365600

[24] Gordon, David, and Meia Nouwens. 2022. *The Digital Silk Road: China's Technological Rise and the Geopolitics of Cyberspace*. Oxford: Taylor & Francis Group.

Europe[25]), the construction of smart surveillance cities, and the use of Chinese-derived 5G and AI systems.[26] This has led to major concerns about increasing hi-tech competition from China and to its ability to shape global regulation 'on the ground' before norm-shapers such as the UN and EU can gain strong support for cyber, internet and AI norms or liberal self-regulation models.

Indeed, China has been promoting its own version of AI governance that includes a people-centred (*yi ren wei ben*) approach; a diplomatic and economic focus on bringing the DSR to the Global South. At the 2024 UN Conference on Trade and Development (UNCTAD), Xi Jinping called for "an open, inclusive and non-discriminatory environment for the digital economy" and spoke of following "the people-centred, AI-for-good" perspective.[27] The emphasis has been on multilateralism in AI governance via the UN. However, this also allows for a multipolar approach in which the PRC's influence is heightened via the export of new digital capacities, including smart-city design, digital surveillance, social engineering, and social-media monitoring that enhance public security and top-down decision-making.[28]

Beyond this, major security concerns have been expressed about PRC access via BRI networks to government and corporate information around the world. Chinese regulations from 2016 onwards stipulate that its citizens and firms must provide information access to PRC security services in the interest of national security.[29] This has resulted in many states, included Australia, the US and Canada, blocking Chinese software and preventing Chinese firms from tendering for sensitive areas of infrastructure. Ironically, in China supporting sovereign control of its internet and cyber domains (via its 'Great Firewall', the Data Security Law and expanded standards in its Cybersecurity Classified Protection 2.0) and improving control of data flows across international borders,[30] its security stance may very well undermine the

[25] See Herlevi, April A. 2024. China's Strategic Space in the Digital Undersea. The National Bureau of Asian Research. https://strategicspace.nbr.org/chinas-strategic-space-in-the-digital-undersea/. Accessed 7 July 2025.

[26] For the evolution of the Digital Silk Road, see Ferguson, R. James. 2021. *Greening China's New Silk Roads: The Sustainable Governance of Belt and Road.* Cheltenham, UK: Edward Elgar Publishing Limited. Pp. 102–125; Eder, Thomas S., Rebecca Arcesati, and Jacob Mardell. 2019. Networking the 'Belt and Road' – The Future is Digital. MERICS Analysis. https://merics.org/en/analysis/networking-belt-and-road-future-digital. Accessed 9 July 2025.

[27] Ministry of Foreign Affairs, PRC. 2024. President Xi Jinping Delivers a Video Address at the Opening Ceremony of UNCTAD's 60th Anniversary Celebrations. Para 5. https://www.fmprc.gov.cn/mfa_eng/xw/zyxw/202406/t20240612_11435039.html. Accessed 9 June 2025.

[28] Ferguson, *supra,* n. 26.

[29] China Law Translate. 2017. National Intelligence Law of the People's Republic of China. Adopted at the 28th Session of the Standing Committee of the Twelfth National People's Congress of the People's Republic of China. https://www.chinalawtranslate.com/en/national-intelligence-law-of-the-p-r-c-2017/. Accessed 13 August 2025.

[30] Gong, James. 2025. China Data Protection and Cyber security: Annual Review of 2024 and Outlook for 2025 (II). Bird & Bird. https://www.twobirds.com/en/insights/2025/china/china-data-protection-and-cybersecurity-annual-review-of-2024-and-outlook-for-2025-(ii). Accessed 9 June 2025.

security of its many BRI partners. The trade-off can be briefly demonstrated in the Latin America case, where new action plans run through the China-CELAC (Community of Latin American and Caribbean States) forum in which :

> The Peace pillar, framed under the [PRC's] Global Security Initiative, delves into cybersecurity, transnational crime, and public safety. The plan proposes the creation of a liaison mechanism between national Computer Emergency Response Teams (CERTs)—a seemingly technical measure that, in practice, could give Chinese cybersecurity authorities privileged access to digital threat-sharing networks in the Americas. …
>
> The Action Plan acknowledges—albeit obliquely—the rise of Chinese-linked criminal syndicates in Latin America. … the Chinese government is sending a message that it is willing to assist LAC countries in addressing this issue through increased law enforcement cooperation.[31]

Such enhanced digital surveillance and cooperation, while needed in the age of cyber and transnational crime, can be used for political and social control of other actors. For the United States, this has become a major concern, affecting its sphere of influence in the Americas. The wider challenge to US global security leadership has also emerged via the PRC's China's Global Security Initiative (GSI), announced by XI Jinping at the Boao Forum for Asia in 2022.[32] These trends are increased by China's growing technological sophistication, its proliferating number of copyright and patent inventions, its investment in cyber and AI technologies, supported not just by the government and the PLA, but by a growing number of Chinese transnational corporations.[33]

This returns discussion to the larger picture for BRI's evolution into digital space: the Made in China 2025 plan. MIC2025 sought to expand China's digital influence, offer alternative data systems to Western ones, and promote its own digital technology standards as in the DSR. Its wider goal, however, was to push China to the forefront of manufacturing using self-developed advanced technologies. The defensive aspect of MIC2025 was to reduce dependence on foreign technology while the offensive component in this economic form of Active Defence aimed to increase global market share. Complaints about MIC2025 from the US and the prospect of tariff retaliation led to a downplaying of the program—it received no mention in the 2019 National People's Congress[34]—though not its disappearance. Referred to by the vaguer political slogan of 'new productive forces', it called for

[31] Lazarus, *supra*, n. 16.

[32] Green, Erik, Meia Nouwens, and Veerle Nouwens. 2024. The Global Security Initiative: China's International Policing Activities. IISS. https://www.iiss.org/research-paper/2024/10/the-global-security-initiative-chinas-international-policing-activities/. Accessed 9 June 2025.

[33] Kahl, Colin and Jim Mitre. 2025. The Real AI Race: America Needs More Than Innovation to Complete with China. Foreign Affairs. https://www.foreignaffairs.com/united-states/china-real-artificial-intelligence-race-innovation. Accessed 9 June 2025.

[34] Harada, Issaku. 2019. Beijing Drops 'Made in China 2025' from Government Report. Nikkei Asia, March 6. https://asia.nikkei.com/Politics/China-People-s-Congress/Beijing-drops-Made-in-China-2025-from-government-report. Accessed 9 August 2025.

taking the next step in a strategy for technology-led growth.[35] By 2025, the target year of MIC2025, China had succeeded in becoming self-reliant in many sectors but not without resistance. The US under the second Trump administration had embarked on an offensive tariff 'war'. Meanwhile China faced a crossroads: follow the spirit of MIC2025-style industrial pre-eminence or, as an EU official expressed it, take a path that ensures such a pursuit "minimises negative externalities"?[36] In other words, a genuine 'win-win' calculus was needed, rather than its mere rhetoric in PRC discourse. Strategic wisdom and China's own vision of its global relations would counsel the latter. Here is where the BRI has both followed policy through its cooperative 'Silk Road spirit' and made it possible for its enactment on the map.

8.2.3 'Community of Common Destiny', Green BRI and Its Philosophical Roots in Ecological Civilisation

The Belt and Road has been described as a key instrument for realising China's vision of a 'community of common destiny' (CCD),[37] also called a 'human community with a shared future'. It is a concept which President Xi Jinping articulated at about the same time as the BRI but which can be traced back to 2007 during Hu Jintao's presidency (2003–2013). His emphasis was on a 'harmonious world',[38] just as Xi Jinping's became the 'Chinese dream'. Within both resided the idea of a 'community of common destiny'. This is logical in a globalised world: "As transnational movement of goods, services, capital, technology, information and personnel develops and intensifies, all countries are in the state of mutual interdependence."[39] This means that: "If a State wants to develop, it must help others to develop, and the same is true for national security and social life."[40]

This logic did not dispel suspicion of China's geopolitical and geo-economic ambition behind the deceptive cloak of a 'community of common destiny'. The BRI was used as evidence of this with China being accused of 'debt-trap diplomacy'[41] to

---

[35] Kroeber, Arthur R. 2024. Unleashing "New Quality Productive Forces": China's Strategy for Technology-Led Growth. Brookings. https://www.brookings.edu/articles/unleashing-new-quality-productive-forces-chinas-strategy-for-technology-led-growth/. Accessed 13 August 2025.

[36] The European Chamber, China. 2025. The Cost of Technological Leadership. https://www.europeanchamber.com.cn/en/press-releases/3707. Accessed 13 August 2025.

[37] Wang, Linggui and Jianglin Zhao. 2019. *China's Belt and Road Initiative and Building the Community of Common Destiny*. World Scientific.

[38] Dellios, Rosita and Ferguson, R. James. 2013. *China's Quest for Global Order: From Peaceful Rise to Harmonious World*. Lanham Md: Lexington Books.

[39] Lingliang, Zeng. 2016. Conceptual Analysis of China's Belt and Road Initiative: A Road towards a Regional Community of Common Destiny. *Chinese Journal of International Law* 15: 517–541.

[40] Ibid, section 49.

[41] Chellaney, Brahma. 2017. China's debt-trap diplomacy. The Strategist. https://web.archive.org/web/20220716172623/https://www.aspistrategist.org.au/chinas-debt-trap-diplomacy/. Accessed 13 August 2025.

acquire resources or strategic assets from impoverished nations that could not repay China's debt.

Though the idea that China has intentionally sought to trap BRI partner countries into increasing debt burdens to seize national assets or resources has largely been debunked,[42] PRC lenders have at times restructured or forgiven debt. In the case of African BRI projects, this has usually involved concessional loans and credit financing that have served to boost infrastructure capacities, industrialisation and enhanced employment prospects.[43] Likewise, even the infamous case of Sri Lanka's Hambantota Port project had less to do with Chinese debt trap deliberations than problems from the recipient's end. Domestic political and electoral factors combined with Sri Lanka's poor balance of payments and prior debt—including emergency funding from the IMF from 2016 onwards—represented the broader issue of a failure of responsible governance.[44]

"Nevertheless", as Calabrese cautions, "it remains true that many countries have over-borrowed, often due to overly optimistic projections of the return on the projects for which they borrowed … But others have been managing financial risks cleverly, either through a sound macroeconomic framework or through negotiations with Chinese financiers."[45]

Beyond the debate of 'debt-trap diplomacy', the perception that China had embarked on carving a sphere of influence, was practising a form of neo-colonialism, and was using the BRI as a strategy to challenge US leadership, was not easily dispelled. Both the vision of a 'community of common destiny' and its discernible manifestations through the BRI became issues of contention.

However, neither the idea of a PRC-articulated global community nor the BRI remained unchanged. Instead, an effort to channel green investment and circular economic models onto the BRI resulted in its rebranding as a Green BRI (GBRI).[46]

The preparatory path for the GBRI, however, needs to be seen in the context of an allied goal to a 'community of common destiny', that of turning China into an

---

[42] Calabrese, Linda. 2025. The Belt and Road Initiative: what impact on China and the global economy? Economics Observatory. https://www.economicsobservatory.com/the-belt-and-road-initiative-what-impact-on-china-and-the-global-economy#. Accessed 13 August 2025.

[43] Li, Weiping, and Saite Lu. 2024. Assessing Structural Transformation and the Potential Impacts of Belt and Road Initiative Projects in Africa. *The European Journal of Development Research* 36: 548–570.

[44] Moramudali, Umesh, and Thilina Panduwawala. 2024. The political economy of Hambantota port: unveiling the realities of debt trap diplomacy and BRI vision. *Asian Journal of Political Science*, 32: 380–399. https://doi.org/10.1080/02185377.2024.2424758; see further Hameiri, Shahar. 2020. Debunking the myth of China's "debt-trap diplomacy". The Interpreter. https://web.archive.org/web/20220809054530/https://www.lowyinstitute.org/the-interpreter/debunking-myth-chinas-debt-trap-diplomacy. Accessed 13 August 2025; Brautigam, Deborah. 2020. A Critical Look at Chinese 'debt-trap diplomacy': The Rise of a Meme. *Area Development and Policy* 5(1): 1–14.

[45] Calabrese, *supra*, n. 42.

[46] Ferguson, *supra*, n. 26.

Ecological Civilisation. Besides drawing on the latest developments in environmental science,[47] the concept and policy of creating an Ecological Civilisation reflects Chinese philosophical outlooks, particularly Daoism and Confucianism, in which humans form a harmonious whole with nature.[48] Like a 'community of common destiny', humans need the natural world to fulfil their 'destiny', that is, realise their potential. As contemporary Confucian philosopher, Tu Weiming, expressed it: "Realising one's wider interconnectedness, inclusive of the planet, is what it is to become fully human, bestowing an 'ethic of responsibility'."[49] From this it is apparent that a civilisation is indeed being envisaged when appending to it the term 'ecological', and not only a codification of rules and regulations.

The impetus for this project included a desire for an improved leadership role for the PRC globally, combined with the need to face serious environmental, pollution, energy and food supply challenges within China itself.[50] The greening of China's modern-day civilisation, economy and BRI credentials gained momentum from 2015. This was the year in which the UN Climate Change Conference adopted the Paris Agreement to tackle climate change by limiting global warming and working towards a net-zero emissions target. Also in 2015, the UN's Sustainable Development Goals (SDGs) were adopted to address social, economic, and environmental dimensions of sustainable development by 2030.

By 2018, China as an Ecological Civilisation was embedded in the constitution of the PRC. Its realisation has been supported by a circular economy of using resources throughout their life cycle to minimise waste. A comprehensive approach was being pursued, to "improve the basic systems for ecological conservation, environmental governance systems, and mechanisms for green and low-carbon development".[51]

Hence economic, social and environmental sustainability became part of the BRI's identity, making it compatible with the UN's Sustainable Development Goals,[52] and China's own grand strategies of unity with the environment and with the global community.

[47] Ibid, at 57–62.

[48] Dellios and Ferguson, *supra,* n. 38, Ch. 2.

[49] Weiming, Tu. 2001. The Ecological Turn in New Confucian Humanism: Implications for China and the World. *Daedalus* 130(4): 243–264.

[50] Ferguson, *supra,* n. 26.

[51] Xinhua. 2024. Full text: Communique of the Third Plenary Session of the 20th Central Committee of the Communist Party of China. China Daily. https://www.chinadaily.com.cn/a/202407/18/WS6698f75aa31095c51c50ec9d.html. Accessed 13 August 2025.

[52] Belt and Road Portal. 2017. The Belt and Road Ecological and Environmental Cooperation Plan. https://eng.yidaiyilu.gov.cn/p/13392.html. Accessed 13 August 2025.

8.3 Major Responses and Counterstrategies

Responses to the BRI have greatly varied, ranging from enthusiastic engagement to criticism on developmental and environment grounds through to fervent opposition via alternative strategies.[53] These tensions reflect a battle over the nature of global processes—in the context of the existing developmental agendas via the World Bank, IMF and G7—or as efforts to sustain a multipolar world order with greater freedom of action by powers such as India, China, the EU and Japan. The scope of these reactions can be seen through contrasting Indian, Japanese, and US policies.

India, though willing to engage in some Chinese-led initiatives such as the Asian Infrastructure Investment Bank (AIIB) and initially considered engaging in the BCIM-EC corridor, remained highly critical of the BRI. By 2017 India's Ministry of External Affairs expressed concerns about a lack of transparency, possible trends towards unsustainable debt, limited tech-transfer, and poor support for local populations.[54] From the start, the Indian government saw the CPEC corridor as solidifying investment into disputed border areas controlled by PRC, with wider BRI policies as a means of expanding influence across the north of the Indian subcontinent and across the Asia-Pacific into the Indian Ocean.[55] Indian viewpoints, too, saw the narrative linkage of the BRI onto the cultural claims of the ancient silk roads as a form of soft power propaganda that displaced India's civilisational influence and historic trade flows with Central Asia and across the Indian Ocean.[56]

India has engaged in a number of regional and trade initiatives seeking to counterbalance Chinese influence in the Indo-Pacific. These include the 'Cotton Road' and proactive Gulf-Diplomacy,[57] the 'Look East' policies from the 1990s onwards seeking to engage the Association of Southeast Asian Nations (ASEAN), the Bay of Bengal Initiative for Multi-Sectoral Technical and Economic Cooperation (BIMSTEC, engaging Bangladesh, Bhutan, India, Nepal, Sri Lanka, Myanmar, and Thailand), the proposed development of the India-Middle East-Europe Economic Corridor (IMEC), and Project Mausam across the Indian Ocean, engaging in investment projects into adjacent parts of Africa and the Middle East (from 2014), using the inclusive SAGAR approach as "Security and Growth for All in the Region" to boost 'blue economy' networks.[58]

---

[53] Ferguson, *supra*, n. 26; Ferguson, *supra*, n. 13.

[54] Ministry of External Affairs, Government of India. 2017. Official Spokesperson's Response to a Query on Participation of India in OBOR/BRI Forum. http://www.mea.gov.in/media-briefings.htm?dtl/28463/Official_Spokespersons_response_to_a_query_on_participation_of_India_in_OBORBRI_Forum. Accessed 16 August 2025.

[55] Ferguson, *supra*, n. 26.

[56] Dalrymple, William. 2024. *The Golden Road: How Ancient India Transformed the World.* London: Bloomsbury Publishing.

[57] Ibid.

[58] Nanwani, Suresh. 2019. Belt and Road Initiative: Responses from Japan and India—Bilateralism, Multilateralism and Collaborations. *Global Policy* 10: 284–289.

Overall, India's strategies have kept it as a major global player and maintained its significance as a soft power and strategic military force in the Indo-Pacific. However, its total level of outward capital flows, though rising in 2024–2025 to US$ 35.9.4 billion (GOV 2025),[59] does not let it compete overall with China's global engagement via the BRI agenda.

Japan, too, has been active in hard and soft balancing China and the BRI as a strategic agenda. Beyond its ongoing military modernisation, Japan's engagement in non-traditional security approaches, and its US alliance, Tokyo has developed its own 'peace through development' agenda. Extensive aid programs that have a global reach support this. Japan ranks about fourth in terms of global Official Development Assistance (ODA) donors ($16.8 billion in 2024),[60] along with strong engagement with the ADB, IMF and World Bank—while it is not a member of the AIIB.

Japan's Official Development Assistance Charter is wide-reaching, seeing balanced development as a path towards human security, sustainable economies, global health, and socially-based human rights. The Charter engages special development corridors across different sectors of Asia, Africa and the Middle East.[61] After policy revisions in 2023, Japan's major aid projects focused on Thailand, Egypt and Bangladesh, with 56% disbursement into Asia, 20.5% into Africa and the Middle East, 4.2% into Europe (including Ukraine), and lesser sums in other regions.[62]

The US, too, saw the BRI as entrenching Chinese power globally and as a tool challenging the existing financial order and US pre-eminence. However, the Make America Great Again (MAGA) policies of the second Trump administration and unilateral tariff regimes have rendered a truly multilateral global response to the BRI problematic. Even strategic allies such as Australia and Japan improved diplomatic dialogue with China. Indeed, China may accrue indirect gains across the Global South, with BRI trade serving to buffer some impacts of the tariff war between the US and the PRC.

[59] Government of India. 2025. GOV Economic Survey 2024-2025: Statistical Appendix. https://www.indiabudget.gov.in/economicsurvey/doc/Statistical-Appendix-in-English.pdf. Accessed 13 August 2025.

[60] OECD—Organisation for Economic Co-operation and Development. 2025. Official Development Assistance. https://www.oecd.org/en/topics/official-development-assistance-oda.html. Accessed 13 August 2025.

[61] Ministry of Defense, Japan. 2020. Defense of Japan 2020. https://www.mod.go.jp/en/publ/w_paper/wp2020/DOJ2020_EN_Full.pdf. Accessed 17 August 2025.

[62] Ministry of Foreign Affairs, Japan. 2024. White Paper on Development Cooperation 2023: Japan's International Cooperation. https://www.mofa.go.jp/mofaj/gaiko/oda/files/100783436.pdf. Accessed 13 August 2025. OECD—Organisation for Economic Co-operation and Development. 2024. FDI in Figures. https://www.oecd.org/content/dam/oecd/en/publications/reports/2024/10/fdi-in-figures-october-2024_faad0bae/fcdc2fb2-en.pdf. Accessed 13 August 2025.

8.4 Taking Stock of Developments to Date

China and its BRI partners have reacted to these trends and learnt from the failures and criticisms made of some of its BRI projects. A new focus on green finance emerged and consultative procedures were improved, helping transform the BRI into a Green BRI (GBRI), as noted by major policy speeches from 2019 onwards. Xi Jinping's keynote address for the Belt and Road 2019 Forum emphasised the need for extensive consultation, and "to encourage participating companies to follow general international rules and standards in project development, operation, procurement and tendering and bidding",[63] with these issues remaining prominent in the 2021 Boao Forum. Likewise, there has been some shift towards smaller, more targeted BRI loans which include positive economic, social and environment outcomes.[64] High quality and local cooperation was called upon repeatedly through 2022–2025, with the 2025 Advisory Council for the BRI adding a special focus on capacity building, including digital connectivity, for the Global South:

> … it is essential to vigorously advance the high-quality Belt and Road cooperation, focus on high-quality infrastructure and industrial cooperation, build a multi-dimensional interconnected network, and strengthen the development of a green Silk Road and a digital Silk Road.… Within the framework of the BRI, participating countries need to step up cooperation in the digital economy and artificial intelligence and support capacity building in the Global South.[65]

Overall, there has been uneven monitoring of the long-term social and ecological outcomes of many BRI projects, leading to some controversial failures for its mega-projects. However, the average scale of projects has fallen, with one study pointing out that "wind and solar power could flexibly be implemented on smaller scales to answer the BRI countries' need for distributed energy".[66]

Beyond taking stock of developments for the BRI's relatively short existence since its announcement in 2013, it should be noted that—much like the Great Wall which was an ongoing project across dynasties—the 'silk roads' of the BRI had come from a geo-historical idea and continue to develop. The world's most ambitious infrastructure project has evolved to become not only world-wide in scope, known as China's "project of the century", but also "open, green and clean" and "small but beautiful", to quote Xi Jinping at the Third Symposium on the Construction of the Belt and Road Initiative in 2021.[67] The prioritisation of

[63] Jinping, Xi. 2019. Work together to create a better future for the Belt and Road Initiative. Xinhua. http://www.xinhuanet.com/politics/2019-04/26/c_1124420187.htm. Accessed 18 August 2025.

[64] Calabrese, *supra*, n. 42.

[65] Ministry of Foreign Affairs, PRC. 2025. The 2025 Meeting of the Advisory Council of the Belt and Road Forum for international Cooperation Held. https://www.mfa.gov.cn/eng/xw/wjbxw/202505/t20250516_11627291.html. Accessed 13 August 2025.

[66] Bega, François, and Lin Boqiang. 2023. China's belt & road initiative energy cooperation: International assessment of the power projects. *Energy* 270:1–9.

[67] Jinping, *supra*, n. 63.

high-quality jointly undertaken projects includes technology transfers, vocational training, and scholarships to assist in capacity-building, for example in Pacific Island countries.[68]

In 2023, the Third Belt and Road Forum for International Cooperation captured the trends informing the BRI's future in deepening and expanding connectivity, promoting the digital economy, and enhancing green development underpinned by a harmonious coexistence between humans and nature.[69] This takes the BRI to a global scale that is technologically empowered but seeks to be environmentally sustainable under the auspices of an ecological civilisation. What will this future look like?

8.5 Future Scenarios

One way of understanding alternative future trajectories for the BRI is to develop comparative scenarios. Here this takes the form of three scenarios set in the medium-term future of 2035. Such a timeframe is chosen as it is not subject to the short-term fluctuation of events or the multiple imponderables of long-term forecasting. The medium-term can better reflect discernible trends. The scenarios are the Positive Path of development, the Negative Narrative of unintended outcomes, and the Combination of Positive and Negative Influences. The first is relatively straightforward if it follows the sustainable development path, which is more likely to remain an aspiration than a reality in 2035. The second is longer as 'reality' complicates the BRI's evolution. The third combines both aspiration and complication, extending the treatment of this scenario into a consideration of the BRI as China's vast defensive network, which is brought out in the conclusion of this chapter.

8.5.1 The Positive Path

The positive aspect of Belt and Road is one in which a vast number of countries and regions around the world benefit from the creation of infrastructure that includes roads, railways, ports, energy projects, telecommunications, technology transfer and health access. With falling costs for renewable energy, older coal projects are slowly phasing out, bringing both economic and environmental benefits.[70] The BRI has much to offer in terms of development as it operates within the context of the UN Sustainable Development Goals. Just as the SDGs are all inclusive—no one is

[68] Chen, Victor. 2024. China's strategic shift to 'small but beautiful' projects. The Strategist. https://www.aspistrategist.org.au/chinas-strategic-shift-to-small-but-beautiful-projects/. Accessed 13 August 2025.

[69] Jinping, *supra*, n. 1.

[70] Nedopil, *supra*, n. 12.

to be left behind—so too the BRI is premised on being 'open to all'. This contrasts with the 'America First' policy which, in the aftermath of tariff wars, has caused many to de-risk from the US.

8.5.2 The Negative Narrative

The unintended outcomes from BRI mismanagement have lost China friends and investors. Negative consequences include intensified pollution, increasing transnational crime networks, and economic and cultural dislocation. The Bangladesh-China-India-Myanmar Economic Corridor (BCIM-EC), for example, has become the new route for illicit drugs (methamphetamines and opiates), contributes to labour exploitation through undocumented workers, and increases unregulated urban expansion. Likewise, The China-Pakistan Economic Corridor (CPEC) suffers from the flair-up of political and developmental problems, with the activities of Baloch separatist insurgents gaining momentum. As CPEC passes through Gilgit-Baltistan and Azad Jammu and Kashmir, which are Pakistani-administered but claimed by India, CPEC projects have become "vulnerable to an accidental or calculated Indian attack, which could draw China into the India-Pakistan conflict".[71] China's People's Liberation Army is engaging in joint military exercises with the Pakistan Armed Forces. China provides Pakistan with advanced weaponry, such as fighter jets. These proved superior to India's Russian and French built fighter jets and their missiles in a clash concerning Kashmir in May 2025. China is prepared for conflict on many fronts and degrees—from grey to hybrid to hot war. These include over Taiwan, the South China Sea, the East China Sea, a disputed land border with India and contestation with the United States along Maritime Silk Road trade routes. These lie along what the US calls the Indo-Pacific region, which it claims to defend as 'free and open'.

8.5.3 Combination of Positive and Negative Influences

With the BRI premised on being 'open to all', it has no difficulty in claiming a 'free and open' Indo-Pacific within its own order. This scenario describes the combination of high levels of sustainable development in the BRI and hard power-based security. China's hard power is both economic and military. Now the world's leading economy, China has been able to reward friends through trade and investment opportunities and punish critics by withholding them. In the military, China has modernised in all domains of warfare: land, sea, air, space and cyber. With cyber

[71] Suryanarayana, Pisupati Sadasiva. 2025. India's Pakistani Challenge Betwixt Two Behemoths. RSIS Commentary. https://rsis.edu.sg/rsis-publication/rsis/indias-pakistani-challenge-betwixt-two-behemoths/. Accessed 20 August 2025.

security Beijing has not only maintained internal controls but has influenced international norms of internet governance; 'internet sovereignty' is protected from outside forces—including the traditional Western tech giants. Thanks to the advances made possible by the Made in China 2025 policy, China's space, cyber and AI capabilities are formidable. Indeed, in 2035, the PLA has the requisite capabilities to defend its interests within the vastness of the BRI.

A turning point had been the geopolitical dynamics in the Middle East in 2025–2027, coupled with an unrelenting US pushback on Chinese influence—to the point of almost provoking war with China by supporting Taiwan's independence. This period of upheaval seriously tested the resilience of BRI corridors and China's risk management strategies, resulting in a determination by the party-state to strengthen its capabilities in pursuit of strategic dominance.

These capabilities have been aided by the creation of Chinese military operational bases in a number of BRI countries. It is a development frowned upon by China's critics but quietly accepted by those hosting the bases. This is because they are the beneficiaries of China's economic power and the regional stability it has fostered, in concert with organisations dedicated to a multi-faceted security. The multilateral Shanghai Cooperation Organisation (SCO) continues to evolve in this role. A loose maritime version of SCO has emerged in the 2030s to maintain security, orderly commerce, and environmental protection standards in the South China Sea. Participants in this Maritime Silk Road security grouping, which complements the Regional Comprehensive Economic Partnership (RCEP), are not only those of the Association of Southeast Asian Nations (ASEAN), but also other interested members including the Pacific Islands Forum (PIF) nations which have already established sanctuaries (marine protected areas) in parts of the Pacific. No one sees any irony in a 'militarised' South China Sea becoming an environmental park. It is sufficiently policed to prevent unlawful behaviour of any form. Much like the Korean DMZ of yesteryear, nothing passes unnoticed in the maritime watchtowers of public-spirited surveillance.

This combination of mixed outcomes can be seen as developmentally aspirational but marred by competing security networks working at different levels—that is, trade/investment gains with the PRC versus traditional military alliances with the US.

8.6 Conclusion

This chapter has reviewed the strategic evolution of the BRI. It has found that the underlying strength of the BRI has been to help China strengthen and diversify its energy sources and trade routes. In turn, this has made China a world leader in infrastructure development, as well as digital and green technologies. Understandably, the BRI's reputation has fluctuated, with suspicion often outweighing trust, while the uncoordinated proliferation of projects impelled the need for more controls and standard setting. The BRI was thereafter modified several times in its policy emphasis. It became more sophisticated in its appeal, matching China's vision of its own global relations. Threat perceptions in the West, particularly the United States, arise from the scale of the BRI as a tool of state. It competes on interrelated economic, strategic and technological levels.

For China, its most strategic chapter remains to be written as the second Trump administration opened by placing China in a defensive position through economic and strategic measures. Thanks to the BRI, China has the wherewithal to engage in an effective counter-offensive. Indeed, the BRI could be applied as an operational arena for China's Active Defence strategy in which a defensive goal is pursued through offensive means. The BRI, like the ports China has built and its civil-military integration policy, can be readily flipped into an offensive modality if indeed a serious techno-trade war erupts between the world's two largest economies. Though by no means the probable outcome, this hypothetical dimension of the BRI does represent high-impact consequences for global stability. This calls for the BRI's future evolution to be consciously strategic in the direction of the positive path that is developmentally and environmentally inclusive.

References

Asian Development Bank (ADB). 2021. *The 14th Five-Year Plan of the People's Republic of China—Fostering High-Quality Development.* https://doi.org/10.22617/BRF210192-2. Accessed 9 June 2025.

Au, Adam, and Felicia Feiran Chen. 2025. China Expands AI Globally Through the Digital Silk Road. *East Asia Forum.* https://doi.org/10.59425/eabc.1744365600.

Bega, François, and Lin Boqiang. 2023. China's Belt & Road Initiative Energy Cooperation: International Assessment of the Power Projects. *Energy* 270:1–9.

Belt and Road Portal. 2017. *The Belt and Road Ecological and Environmental Cooperation Plan.* https://eng.yidaiyilu.gov.cn/p/13392.html. Accessed 13 August 2025.

Belt and Road Portal. 2025. *Connotation of BRI.* https://eng.yidaiyilu.gov.cn/p/00FUU20U.html. Accessed 27 May 2025.

Blackwill, Robert D., and Jennifer M. Harris. 2016. *War by Other Means: Geoeconomics and Statecraft.* Cambridge, Massachusetts: Harvard University Press.

Brautigam, Deborah. 2020. A Critical Look at Chinese 'Debt-Trap Diplomacy': The Rise of a Meme. *Area Development and Policy* 5 (1): 1–14.

Calabrese, Linda. 2025. *The Belt and Road Initiative: What Impact on China and the Global Economy?* Economics Observatory. https://www.economicsobservatory.com/the-belt-and-road-initiative-what-impact-on-china-and-the-global-economy#. Accessed 13 August 2025.

Cebr. 2019. *Belt and Road Initiative to boost world GDP by over $7 trillion per annum by 2040.* https://cebr.com/reports/belt-and-road-initiative-to-boost-world-gdp-by-over-7-trillion-per-annum-by-2040/. Accessed 25 May 2025.

Chellaney, Brahma. 2017. China's Debt-Trap Diplomacy. *The Strategist.* https://web.archive.org/web/20220716172623/https://www.aspistrategist.org.au/chinas-debt-trap-diplomacy/. Accessed 13 August 2025.

Chen, Victor. 2024. China's Strategic Shift to 'Small But Beautiful' Projects. *The Strategist.* https://www.aspistrategist.org.au/chinas-strategic-shift-to-small-but-beautiful-projects/. Accessed 13 August 2025.

China Law Translate. 2017. *National Intelligence Law of the People's Republic of China.* Adopted at the 28th Session of the Standing Committee of the Twelfth National People's Congress of the People's Republic of China. https://www.chinalawtranslate.com/en/national-intelligence-law-of-the-p-r-c-2017/. Accessed 13 August 2025.

Dalrymple, William. 2024. *The Golden Road: How Ancient India Transformed the World.* London: Bloomsbury Publishing.

Dellios, Rosita, and R. James Ferguson. 2013. *China's Quest for Global Order: From Peaceful Rise to Harmonious World.* Lanham Md: Lexington Books.

Development Research Centre of the State Council, the People's Republic of China, The World Bank. 2022. *Four Decades of Poverty Reduction in China: Drivers, Insights for the World, and the Way Ahead.* https://openknowledge.worldbank.org/server/api/core/bitstreams/e9a5bc3c-718d-57d8-9558-ce325407f737/content. Accessed 10 June 2025.

Eder, Thomas S., Rebecca Arcesati, and Jacob Mardell. 2019. Networking the 'Belt and Road'—The Future is Digital. *MERICS Analysis*. https://merics.org/en/analysis/networking-belt-and-road-future-digital. Accessed 9 July 2025.

Ferguson, R. James. 2021. *Greening China's New Silk Roads: The Sustainable Governance of Belt and Road.* Cheltenham, UK: Edward Elgar Publishing Limited.

Ferguson, R. James. 2023. Of Global Concern: Governance and Sustainability Along the Belt and Road. *Australian Outlook*. https://www.internationalaffairs.org.au/australianoutlook/of-global-concern-governance-and-sustainability-along-the-belt-and-road/. Accessed 9 June 2025.

Gong, James. 2025. *China Data Protection and Cybersecurity: Annual Review of 2024 and Outlook for 2025 (II).* Bird & Bird. https://www.twobirds.com/en/insights/2025/china/china-data-protection-and-cybersecurity-annual-review-of-2024-and-outlook-for-2025-(ii). Accessed 9 June 2025.

Gordon, David, and Meia Nouwens. 2022. *The Digital Silk Road: China's Technological Rise and the Geopolitics of Cyberspace.* Oxford: Taylor & Francis Group.

Government of India. 2025. *GOV Economic Survey 2024-2025: Statistical Appendix.* https://www.indiabudget.gov.in/economicsurvey/doc/Statistical-Appendix-in-English.pdf. Accessed 13 August 2025.

Green, Erik, Meia Nouwens, and Veerle Nouwens. 2024. *The Global Security Initiative: China's International Policing Activities.* IISS. https://www.iiss.org/research-paper/2024/10/the-global-security-initiative-chinas-international-policing-activities/. Accessed 9 June 2025.

Hameiri, Shahar. 2020. Debunking the myth of China's "debt-trap diplomacy". *The Interpreter*. https://web.archive.org/web/20220809054530/https://www.lowyinstitute.org/the-interpreter/debunking-myth-chinas-debt-trap-diplomacy. Accessed 13 August 2025.

Harada, Issaku. 2019. Beijing Drops 'Made in China 2025' from Government Report. *Nikkei Asia*, March 6. https://asia.nikkei.com/Politics/China-People-s-Congress/Beijing-drops-Made-in-China-2025-from-government-report. Accessed 9 August 2025.

Herlevi, April A. 2024. *China's Strategic Space in the Digital Undersea.* The National Bureau of Asian Research. https://strategicspace.nbr.org/chinas-strategic-space-in-the-digital-undersea/. Accessed 7 July 2025.

Holmes, Steven. 2025. *China in Latin America: May 2025.* Council on Foreign Relations. https://www.cfr.org/article/china-latin-america-may-2025. Accessed 9 June 2025.

Interesse, Giulia. 2024. *China's Outbound Investment Trends: Sources, Destinations, and Key Sectors.* China Briefing. https://www.china-briefing.com/news/chinas-outbound-investment-trends-sources-destinations-and-key-sectors/. Accessed 9 June 2025.

International Institute for Strategic Studies (IISS). 2022. *China's Belt and Road Initiative: A Geopolitical and Geo-economic Assessment.* https://www.iiss.org/publications/strategic-dossiers/chinas-belt-and-road-initiative/. Accessed 26 May 2025.

International Institute for Strategic Studies (IISS). 2025. A geo-economic conundrum for the member states of ASEAN. *Strategic Comments*, vol 31. Comment 10. https://www.iiss.org/publications/strategic-comments/2025/05/a-geo-economic-conundrum-for-the-member-states-of-asean/. Accessed 9 June 2025.

Jinping, Xi. 2019. Work Together to Create a Better Future for the Belt and Road Initiative. *Xinhua*, April 26. http://www.xinhuanet.com/politics/2019-04/26/c_1124420187.htm. Accessed 18 August 2025.

Jinping, Xi. 2023. *Chairman's Statement of the Third Belt and Road Forum for International Cooperation*. http://www.beltandroadforum.org/n101/2023/1018/c134-1207.html. Accessed 25 May 2025.

Kahl, Colin and Jim Mitre. 2025. *The Real AI Race: America Needs More Than Innovation to Complete with China*. Foreign Affairs. https://www.foreignaffairs.com/united-states/china-real-artificial-intelligence-race-innovation. Accessed 9 June 2025.

Kroeber, Arthur R. 2024. *Unleashing "New Quality Productive Forces": China's Strategy for Technology-Led Growth*. Brookings. https://www.brookings.edu/articles/unleashing-new-quality-productive-forces-chinas-strategy-for-technology-led-growth/. Accessed 13 August 2025.

Lazarus, Leland. 2025. How China is Seeking Dominance in Latin America. *Americas Quarterly*. https://www.americasquarterly.org/article/how-china-is-seeking-dominance-in-latin-america/. Accessed 9 June 2025

Li, Weiping, and Saite Lu. 2024. Assessing Structural Transformation and the Potential Impacts of Belt and Road Initiative Projects in Africa. *The European Journal of Development Research* 36:548–570.

Lingliang, Zeng. 2016. Conceptual Analysis of China's Belt and Road Initiative: A Road Towards a Regional Community of Common Destiny. *Chinese Journal of International Law* 15:517–541.

Ministry of Defense, Japan. 2020. *Defense of Japan 2020*. https://www.mod.go.jp/en/publ/w_paper/wp2020/DOJ2020_EN_Full.pdf. Accessed 17 August 2025.

Ministry of External Affairs, Government of India. 2017. *Official Spokesperson's Response to a Query on Participation of India in OBOR/BRI Forum*. http://www.mea.gov.in/media-briefings.htm?dtl/28463/Official_Spokespersons_response_to_a_query_on_participation_of_India_in_OBORBRI_Forum. Accessed 16 August 2025.

Ministry of Foreign Affairs, Japan. 2024. *White Paper on Development Cooperation 2023: Japan's International Cooperation*. https://www.mofa.go.jp/mofaj/gaiko/oda/files/100783436.pdf. Accessed 13 August 2025.

Ministry of Foreign Affairs, PRC. 2024. *President Xi Jinping Delivers a Video Address at the Opening Ceremony of UNCTAD's 60th Anniversary Celebrations*. https://www.fmprc.gov.cn/mfa_eng/xw/zyxw/202406/t20240612_11435039.html. Accessed 9 June 2025.

Ministry of Foreign Affairs, PRC. 2025. *The 2025 Meeting of the Advisory Council of the Belt and Road Forum for international Cooperation Held*. https://www.mfa.gov.cn/eng/xw/wjbxw/202505/t20250516_11627291.html. Accessed 13 August 2025.

Moramudali, Umesh, and Thilina Panduwawala. 2024. The Political Economy of Hambantota Port: Unveiling the Realities of Debt Trap Diplomacy and BRI Vision. *Asian Journal of Political Science* 32:380–399.

Nanwani, Suresh. 2019. Belt and Road Initiative: Responses from Japan and India—Bilateralism, Multilateralism and Collaborations. *Global Policy* 10:284–289.

National Development and Reform Commission of the People's Republic of China. 2017. *Vision and Actions on Jointly Building Belt and Road*. http://2017.beltandroadforum.org/english/n100/2017/0410/c22-45.html. Accessed 25 May 2025.

Nedopil, Christoph. 2024. *China Belt and Road Initiative (BRI) Investment Report 2023*. Griffith Asia Institute, Griffith University, Australia and Green Finance & Development Center, FISF Fudan University, China. https://doi.org/10.25904/1912/5140. Accessed 25 July 2025.

OECD—Organisation for Economic Co-operation and Development. 2024. *FDI in Figures*. https://www.oecd.org/content/dam/oecd/en/publications/reports/2024/10/fdi-in-figures-october-2024_faad0bae/fcdc2fb2-en.pdf. Accessed 13 August 2025.

OECD—Organisation for Economic Co-operation and Development. 2025. *Official Development Assistance*. https://www.oecd.org/en/topics/official-development-assistance-oda.html. Accessed 13 August 2025.

Suryanarayana, Pisupati Sadasiva. 2025. *India's Pakistani Challenge Betwixt Two Behemoths*. RSIS Commentary. https://rsis.edu.sg/rsis-publication/rsis/indias-pakistani-challenge-betwixt-two-behemoths/. Accessed 20 August 2025.

The European Chamber, China. 2025. *The Cost of Technological Leadership*. https://www.europeanchamber.com.cn/en/press-releases/3707. Accessed 13 August 2025.

The State Council Information Office, PRC. 2015. *China's Military Strategy*. http://english.www.gov.cn/archive/white_paper/2015/05/27/content_281475115610833.htm. Accessed 25 May 2025.

The State Council Information, PRC. 2019. *China's National Defense in the New Era*. http://eng.mod.gov.cn/news/2019-07/24/content_4846443.htm. Accessed 25 May 2025.

The State Council of the People's Republic of China. 2015. Implementation Stressed for Manufacturing Vision. https://english.www.gov.cn/policies/latest_releases/2015/05/19/content_281475110703534.htm.

Wang, Linggui, and Jianglin Zhao. 2019. *China's Belt and Road Initiative and Building the Community of Common Destiny*. World Scientific.

Weiming, Tu. 2001. The Ecological Turn in New Confucian Humanism: Implications for China and the World. *Daedalus* 130 (4): 243–264.

World Population Review. 2025. *Gini Coefficient by Country 2025*. https://worldpopulationreview.com/country-rankings/gini-coefficient-by-country. Accessed 11 June 2025.

Xinhua. 2024. Full Text: Communique of the Third Plenary Session of the 20th Central Committee of the Communist Party of China. *China Daily*. https://www.chinadaily.com.cn/a/202407/18/WS6698f75aa31095c51c50ec9d.html. Accessed 13 August 2025.

Yang, Xiaoxin, and Han Zhang. 2024. China's Civil-Military Integration and Regional Defence Innovation: A Quasi-Natural Experiment Based on National Industrial Zone Policy. *Defence and Peace Economics* 36:653–682.

Chapter 9
The Geo-Economic Fulcrum: US–China Decoupling and the Use of Export Controls on Semiconductors and Rare Earths

Umair Hafeez Ghori

Abstract This chapter explores the role of export controls in the ongoing US–China decoupling. Export controls are primarily security-driven trade measures that have significantly affected global supply chains in the advanced technologies sector. The chapter highlights the distinction between traditional export restrictions (governed under WTO law) and export controls that are usually based on national security imperatives. The chapter also examines China's export controls on rare earth elements (REEs) and traces its genesis in response to US semiconductors and technology export controls on China. The chapter unpacks the US diversification strategy in REEs. The chapter argues that US–China decoupling will act as the geo-economic fulcrum that will lead to parallel supply-chains emerging around diverse regulatory regimes. The decoupling and increasing use of export controls in a security-driven environment will have enduring consequences in international trade and future technological competition.

9.1 Introduction

Reversing the decades-long trends of trade liberalisation and offshore manufacturing will be an uphill challenge for the US. The global economy is deeply interconnected through complex supply chains that stretch across multiple countries.[1] Ironically, it was the US that once championed open markets and free trade that is now taking a turn towards protectionism. While the international media's attention has largely focused on President Trump's imposition of tariffs on China and several

[1] Bacchus, James. 2022. *Trade Links*. Cambridge, UK: Cambridge University Press; Ghori, Umair. 2023. *Export Restrictions and Export Controls—From WTO to the Realm of Global Security*. Cheltenham, UK: Edward Elgar Publishing.

U. H. Ghori (✉)
Faculty of Law, Bond University, Gold Coast, QLD, Australia
e-mail: ughori@bond.edu.au

U. H. Ghori, J. Farrar (eds.), *Globalisation Disrupted*,
https://doi.org/10.1007/978-981-95-3997-0_9

other countries, discontent with the current global economic order is neither new nor limited to the US.

Export restrictions and export controls have emerged as new instruments of influence in the advanced technology sectors such as AI, quantum computers, semiconductors and green tech.[2] Export restrictions were largely neglected in the successive rounds of multilateral trade negotiations that led to the GATT, and later the formation of WTO.[3] Resultantly, the GATT/WTO framework is largely import oriented with very few provisions dealing with export restrictions.

Export restrictions and export controls create complex trade and investment policy issues. For example, the US reshoring efforts in the semiconductor sector while safeguarding sensitive technologies from reaching China show that a combination of export controls and export restrictions can be used to shape domestic manufacturing and attract FDI.[4] Additionally, export restrictions can be used by developing countries to divert valuable resources inward. Such diversion policies enable developing countries to breakout of their "specialised prisons".[5] The expression "specialised prisons" denotes decades of post-colonial periods where several developing countries remained a producer of raw materials while being a consumer of value-added goods imported from the developed countries.[6]

Even though the US is now increasingly keen to reshore its industrial production, its policymakers are realising how difficult the process is in terms of costs of production and of decoupling with nations possessing distinct advantages in industrial specialisation.[7] Similarly, developing countries attempting to breakout of their "specialised prisons", find themselves being challenged under the existing international trade rules that were designed to preserve certain paradigms, e.g., Indonesia's policy of imposing export restrictions on Nickel, in an attempt to establish the EV battery sector, faced stiff challenge in the WTO by the EU and Japan.[8]

---

[2] Ghori, Ibid, at 239–245, 278–300.

[3] Ghori, Ibid, at 5–9.

[4] Gao, Dan, & Wang, Dong. 2024. New Trends of US Economic and Trade Policy Toward China and China's Responses from the Perspective of Friend-shoring. *Journal of WTO and China* 14 (4): 87, 91–94.

[5] Ghori, *supra,* n.1, at 2, 35, 90, 99 & 148.

[6] Ibid.

[7] Gur, Nurullah & Serif Dilek. 2023. US–China economic rivalry and the reshoring of global supply chains. *The Chinese Journal of International Politics* 16: 61–83. D'Ambrosio, Anna & Katiuscia Lavoratori. 2025. Reshoring to survive? The other side of de-globalization. *Journal of Industrial & Business Economics*. https://doi.org/10.1007/s40812-025-00342-7: 1–23.

[8] Ghori, *supra,* n.1, 108–113. See also Kowalski, Przemyslaw & Clarisse Legendre. 2023. *Raw materials critical for the green transition: Production, international trade, and export restrictions* https://www.oecd.org/en/publications/raw-materials-critical-for-the-green-transition_c6bb598b-en.html. Accessed 24 June 2025. On economic development see Chang, Ha-Joon. *Kicking away the ladder*. 2005. London, UK: Anthem Press. Reuters. 2022. WTO backs EU in nickel dispute, Indonesia plans appeal. https://www.reuters.com/markets/commodities/indonesia-plans-appeal-after-losing-wto-nickel-dispute-with-eu-2022-11-30/. Accessed 23 June 2025.

US–China decoupling was already underway during the Biden Administration with the passing of the *US Chips and Science Act*.[9] President Trump's punitive tariffs on Chinese goods signalled that process is speeding up. Under the Trump Administration, China's access to the US market is gradually becoming difficult due to levy of high tariffs and uncertainty in the global market.[10] China responded to the US tariffs by imposing retaliatory tariffs on US imports along with a combination of export restrictions and export controls on REEs which it held as a key bargaining chip with the US.[11] The tit-for-tat response sent shockwaves throughout the global economy but at the same time created opportunities for new raw materials suppliers and fresh supply chains to emerge.

Assuming the US stays the course on decoupling with China, two new parallel supply chains are likely to emerge: one feeding the US economy while one linked with China. In other words, the US–China decoupling will not only impact the two primary economies involved in a struggle for trade dominance, but it will also have far-reaching consequences for restructured international trade and investment paradigms.

This chapter offers a brief look into China's contemporary use of export controls (as opposed to export restrictions) in response to the US decoupling strategy during the Biden and Trump Administrations. Following the introduction, Sect. 9.2 of the chapter begins by outlining the conceptual differences between export restrictions and export controls. This comparison enables a better understanding of the new Chinese measures controlling the exports of critical metals and materials to the US. Section 9.3 discusses the broader decoupling efforts by the US to gradually reduce reliance and decouple its economy from China. Section 9.4 briefly synthesises the practical implications in the context of US–China trade decoupling, while Sect. 9.5 concludes by arguing that decoupling driven by increasing use of export controls represents the new geo-economic fulcrum around which new supply chains will emerge.

---

[9] *CHIPS and Science Act of* 2022, Pub. L. No. 117–167, 136 Stat.1366. *The American Presidency Project*. 2022. ICYMI: The CHIPS Act has already sparked $200 billion in private investments for U.S. semiconductor production. https://www.presidency.ucsb.edu/documents/icymi-the-chips-act-has-already-sparked-200-billion-private-investments-for-us. Accessed 23 June 2025. For an overview see The White House. 2022. FACT SHEET: CHIPS and Science Act will lower costs, create jobs, strengthen supply chains, and counter China. https://bidenwhitehouse.archives.gov/briefing-room/statements-releases/2022/08/09/fact-sheet-chips-and-science-act-will-lower-costs-create-jobs-strengthen-supply-chains-and-counter-china/. Accessed 23 June 2025.

[10] He, Kai. 2025. The global costs of the US-China tariff war are mounting. And the worst may be yet to come. The Conversation https://theconversation.com/the-global-costs-of-the-us-china-tariff-war-are-mounting-and-the-worst-may-be-yet-to-come-254583?utm_source=clipboard&utm_medium=bylinecopy_url_button. Accessed 23 June 2025. Jeyaratnam, Miranda. 2025. How Trump's tariff unpredictability hurts businesses and consumers—and could help China. Time https://time.com/7286933/trump-trade-war-us-china-tariff-pause-businesses-costs-uncertainty/. Accessed 23 June 2025.

[11] Liu, John & Phil Mattingly. 2025. China has a valuable card to play as it holds trade talks with the US. CNN. https://edition.cnn.com/2025/06/09/business/us-china-fresh-trade-talks-london-intl-hnk. Accessed 23 June 2025.

9.2 Export Restrictions VS Export Controls: Why the Difference Matters?

Both concepts are often used interchangeably but actually refer to a broad range of measures that regulate the outflow of goods from an economy. Their specialised uses achieve diverse policy objectives ranging from revenue generation, conservation of natural resources, overcoming food and materials shortages, generation of regulatory leverage or to achieve national security aims.[12]

Export restrictions is a concept based in international trade law. Export restrictions refer to policy measures that limit or prohibit the outflow of goods, components or technologies. Export restrictions are usually imposed through export bans, quantitative restrictions, export taxes, voluntary export restraints or trade embargoes under national security rationales.[13]

GATT/WTO framework contains some provisions that cover export restrictions:

- GATT Article XI affects both imports and exports. The provision prohibits quantitative restrictions except where a WTO Member adopts measure to address critical food shortages or where certain restrictions are necessary for applying standards.
- GATT Article XX provides a series of general exceptions that can legitimise any measures against GATT/WTO framework, including imposition of export restrictions. These general exceptions cover public health, the environment, measures relating to the conservation of exhaustible natural resources, or measures taken against products in general or local short supply.
- GATT Article XXI allows WTO Members to adopt measures that are considered necessary to protect a nation's essential security interests relating to fissionable materials or traffic in arms, ammunition, or material for supplying to the military or during times of war or other emergencies in international relations.

Additionally, export restrictions are covered under Article 12 of the WTO Agreement on Agriculture. This provision states in paragraph 1 (a) that WTO Members 'must give due consideration' to any effects of export bans or restrictions on food items. Paragraph 1 (b) further provides that any WTO Member imposing export ban or restriction must give advanced notice in writing to the WTO Committee on Agriculture and consult with other Members that have a substantial interest related to the measure in question. Paragraph 2 excludes developing country Members from the coverage of the provision unless the restricting Member is a net-food exporter of the food item subject to the restriction.[14]

The GATT/WTO framework refers to the term "restrictions" but not "controls". The term "restriction" along with the terms "prohibition" and "restraints" have been

[12] Ghori, *supra,* n.1, at 8–49.

[13] Ibid, at 8–14.

[14] Ibid, at 8.

discussed in WTO dispute settlement jurisprudence. In *US—Export Restraints,* the terms "export restrictions" were defined as:

> ...a border measure that takes the form of a government law or regulation which expressly limits the quantity of exports or places explicit conditions on the circumstances under which exports are permitted, or that takes the form of a government-imposed fee or tax on exports of the product calculated to limit the quantity of exports.[15]

The definition was further expanded in *China—Raw Materials* case where the word 'restriction' was defined by the panel as a 'thing which restricts someone or something, a limitation on the action, a limiting condition or regulation'.[16] The Appellate Body in *China—Raw Materials* also endorsed the same definition.[17] The essence of the definition emerging from *China—Raw Materials* is that any measure carrying limiting effects on exports amounts to export restrictions. Such limiting effects encompass broad ranging measures like prohibitively high government taxes, or measures that restrict market access or measures that incentivise or disincentivise foreign investment.[18]

In contrast to export restrictions, export controls refer to security and foreign policy measures designed to "control" sensitive technologies, technical data, components, military equipment, and most prominently, dual-use items.[19] The legal basis for export controls is a combination of national laws as well as international understandings between nations in a security alliance such as the Wassenaar Arrangement and the Coordinating Committee for Multilateral Export Controls (COCOM).[20] Within the domestic realm, export controls are administered through licensing and certification mechanisms on dual-use items or sensitive technologies.[21] In short, export controls are based on security rationales as opposed to export restrictions that are traditionally based on international trade and economic rationales.

Export controls in recent times have been maintained by nations under a linear "Scale of Intensity" to achieve wide-ranging aims from nuclear non-proliferation,

---

[15] WTO. 2001. *United States—Measures Treating Export Restraints as Subsidi*es ('US—Export Restraints'). https://docs.wto.org/dol2fe/Pages/SS/directdoc.aspx?filename=q:/WT/DS/194-4.pdf&Open=True. Accessed 27 August 2025.

[16] WTO. 2011. *China—Measures Related to the Exportation of Various Raw Materials* ('China—Raw Materials'). https://docs.wto.org/dol2fe/Pages/SS/directdoc.aspx?filename=Q:/WT/DS/398RA1.pdf&Open=True. Accessed 27 August 2025.

[17] WTO. 2012. *China—Raw Materials.* https://www.wto.org/english/tratop_e/dispu_e/394_395_398abr_e.pdf. Accessed 23 June 2025.

[18] Panel Report, *China—Raw Materials, supra,* n.16, para.7.1078.

[19] Mineiro, Michael, C. 2012. *Space Technology Export Controls and International Cooperation in Outer Space.* Springer: 14–16; Ghori, *supra,* n.1, 14–15; Kazeki, Jun. 2005. *Looking Beyond Tariffs: The Role of Non-Tariff Barriers in World Trade.* Paris: OECD Publishing. 220.

[20] See generally the Wassenaar Arrangement. https://www.wassenaar.org/about-us/. Accessed 22 May 2025; Mineiro, Ibid, 23–24; Ghori, *supra,* n.1, 16–17; Joyner, Daniel, H. 2004. 'Restructuring the Multilateral Export Control Regime System'. *Journal of Conflict Security Law:* 9. 181, 182–188.

[21] Ghori, *supra,* n.1, at 14–20.

generation of regulatory leverage, counterterrorism, and to maintain military supremacy over geo-political rivals or even during times of hostilities.[22]

Export controls are made effective through coordination among defence, intelligence and foreign policy departments within allied nations. For example, the US Export Control Reform Act (ECRA), Export Administration Act (EAA) and its underlying Export Administration Regulations (EARs) are made effective through a dual-layered model.[23] Firstly, the ECRA and EARs are implemented domestically within the US and then, secondly, the implementation is coordinated through its security partners and their relevant government agencies in order to achieve the underlying security objectives.[24]

The US export controls on semiconductor fabrication and lithography technology that are designed to counter China's provides a good illustration of security-related export controls in action.[25] Following the enactment of domestic export controls on cutting edge semiconductors and related components, the US coordinated with the fabrication design and lithography equipment manufacturers in Japan (Nikon and Canon) and in Netherlands (ASML) to effectively limit China's access.[26] Similarly, the US used a mix of export controls and subsidies to encourage the world's largest semiconductor fabricator Taiwan Semiconductor Manufacturing Company (TSMC) to invest in the US state of Arizona to reshore domestic semiconductor manufacturing base.[27]

---

[22] Ibid, *supra,* n.1, at 20–25, 37–49.

[23] Export Control Reform Act (ECRA) §1741(2), P.L. 115–232 (August 13, 2018), codified as amended at 50 U.S.C. §4801(2); *Export Administration Act (EAA) of 1979,* Pub. L. 96–72*; Export Administration Regulations (EAR),* 15 C.F.R. § 730. For an overview see Congressional Research Service (CRS). 2021. *The U.S. export control system and the Export Control Reform Act of 2018.* https://www.congress.gov/crs_external_products/R/PDF/R46814/R46814.6.pdf. Accessed 23 June 2025.

[24] Xu, Jiayan. & Eddie Lam. 2024. "A review of foreign sanctions and export control developments involving China. Alix Partners." https://www.alixpartners.com/media/ydzcm24t/2024-sanction-ye-review-china.pdf. Accessed 23 June 2025. See also Mann, Tobias. 2025. Chip designers' latest casualties in US-China trade war. *The Register.* https://www.theregister.com/2025/05/30/eda_us_china/. Accessed 23 June 2025.

[25] Tan, Catherine. 2024. "Breaking the circuit: US—China semiconductor controls". *Foreign Policy* Research Institute. https://www.fpri.org/article/2024/09/breaking-the-circuit-us-china-semiconductor-controls/. Accessed 23 June 2025.

[26] Edwards, John. 2023. Chips, subsidies, security, and great power competition. *Lowy Institute Analysis.* https://www.lowyinstitute.org/publications/chips-subsidies-security-great-power-competition. Accessed 24 June 2025. Allen, Gregory C. & Emily Benson. 2023. "Clues to the U.S.-Dutch-Japanese semiconductor export controls deal are hiding in plain sight". *Center for Strategic & International Studies* (CSIS). https://www.csis.org/analysis/clues-us-dutch-japanese-semiconductor-export-controls-deal-are-hiding-plain-sight. Accessed 23 June 2025.

[27] Islam, Faisal. 2025. "The secretive US factory that lays bare the contradiction in Trump's America First plan". *BBC.* https://www.bbc.com/news/articles/cwywj0zgzwxo. Accessed 23 June 2025. See also Wu, Jessie. 2024. TSMC secures $6.6 billion US government subsidy for Arizona semiconductors expansion. Technode. https://technode.com/2024/04/09/tsmc-secures-6-6-billion-us-government-subsidy-for-arizona-semiconductor-expansion/#:~:text=The%20US%20

Distinguishing between export controls and export restrictions is important because the distinction carries significant policy implications. Export restrictions must comply with WTO/GATT rules and may be susceptible to a challenge under WTO dispute settlement system. On the other hand, export controls are either a national security concept deriving their legitimacy under international relations or refer to broad-ranging measures that are designed to generate regulatory leverage.[28] Countries maintaining export control under either heading exercise wider discretion and are less prone to multilateral challenge or scrutiny. Therefore, a mischaracterisation or incorrect framing of export restrictions as export controls, or *vice versa*, can expose countries to legal challenges, especially where the perception is that the measures are discriminatory or protectionist in nature.

Both export restrictions and export controls can be potential tools within the decoupling process. However, export controls are more targeted in nature since they can be enacted under national security rationales to reduce or eliminate strategic dependency.

The US–China decoupling process is heavily concentrated in the advanced sectors such as semiconductors, AI, and quantum computing. The US political establishment views China as a strategic adversary who must be stopped from acquiring advanced technologies. The export controls announced by the Biden Administration in 2022, the passing of the *US Chips and Science Act* in the same year, the debates within the US Congress clearly indicate that the US export controls are a response by the US to deny and impede China's access to advanced technologies.[29]

Export controls should not be looked upon as another form of trade sanctions. Rather, these are control measures intended to preserve technological supremacy and hinder the progress of the adversary.[30] Export restrictions, on the other hand, impose sector wide limitations as opposed to specific firms or technologies which is the case with export controls.

US export controls have extraterritorial reach which allows it to leverage its proprietary controls and dominance over foundational technologies to block foreign firms from supplying China with critical inputs.[31] In doing so, the US is weaponising interdependence wherein the centrality of global trade links is used as strategic leverage.

Department%20of%20Commerce,advanced%20semiconductor%20manufacturing%20facilities%20in. Accessed 24 June 2025.

[28] Ghori, *supra,* n.1, at 20–24.

[29] Krach, Keith. 2022. The Bipartisan CHIPS Act—and a United U.S.—are China's biggest fear. Newsweek. https://www.newsweek.com/bipartisan-chips-act-united-us-are-chinas-biggest-fear-opinion-1728573. Accessed 23 June 2025. See also Mak, Aaron. 2025. The chip war under Trump. *Politico.* https://www.politico.com/newsletters/digital-future-daily/2025/06/10/the-chip-war-under-trump-00397048. Accessed 25 June 2025.

[30] See the "Scale of Intensity" model in Ghori, *supra,* n.1, at 37–46.

[31] Shang, Carrie Shu. 2024. Mapping export control extraterritoriality in the US—China technology decoupling. *Journal of World Trade* 58: 545–570.

Weaponisation by the US enables to coordinates with allies like Japan and Netherlands to widen the effects of export controls on fabrication and lithography equipment. The aim is to hinder China's acquisition of advanced chip-making technologies. The coordination between US, Japan, and Netherlands highlights the political character of export controls as opposed to a more rule-based, multilaterally oriented concept of export restrictions.[32]

The exertion of pressure by the US on Japan and the Netherlands along with other countries in the semiconductor industry has squeezed multinational corporations between two large actors, both representing significant market potential and risks. For multinational corporations, understanding the difference between export restrictions and export controls carry practical implications. Though broader in nature, export restrictions must comply with WTO rules and the limited exceptions allowed under the GATT. In that sense, export restrictions cannot form the basis of a trade and development strategy.[33] Although, countries like Indonesia and China have both used export restrictions on Nickel and rare earths (higher export taxes or export bans) to develop their intermediate and refinery sectors. In both cases, the measures were challenged as a violation of GATT/WTO norms and were lost upon complaint by importing countries.[34]

The expanding use of export controls blurs the boundaries between trade and security policy. The encroachment of export controls triggers questions of legitimacy of existing WTO rules and legal norms that assumes a distinction between trade and security, particularly from a dispute settlement perspective.

The WTO dispute settlement system is wedded rigidly to the WTO framework and cannot deal with export control measures that are motivated by strategic objectives. Once strategic rivals like China and US frequently resort to export controls under national security imperatives, it creates the risk of eroding the normative legitimacy of the rules-based international trade. Overuse of security exceptions under GATT Article XXI or, in the alternative, using export controls to solve issues of trade policy will weaken trade flows and the role of multilateral institutions.

---

[32] Freifeld, Karen & Toby Sterling. 2024. US wants Netherlands, Japan to further restrict chipmaking equipment to China. Reuters. https://www.reuters.com/world/us-pushing-netherlands-japan-restrict-more-chipmaking-equipment-china-source-2024-06-18/. Accessed 23 June 2025.

[33] Ghori, *supra,* n.1, 8–14; See also Ghori, Umair. 2020. Three lessons on the construction of export controls under WTO Law. *The University of Queensland Law Journal* 39: 85–115.

[34] Sugihartono, Sekarsari. 2024. Indonesia's trade dispute on nickel ore in the WTO: Current progress and developments. Modern Diplomacy. https://moderndiplomacy.eu/2024/10/28/indonesias-trade-dispute-on-nickel-ore-in-the-wto-current-progress-and-developments/. Accessed 23 June 2025. Ghori, Umair. 2015. An epic mess: 'Exhaustible natural resources' and the future of export restraints after the *China—rare Earths* decision. *Melbourne Journal of International Law* 16: 397–430, 408–414. Zadeh, John. 2025b. China tightens export permits for rare Earth shipments in 2025. *Discovery Alert.* https://discoveryalert.com.au/news/rare-earth-export-permits-2025-strategic-importance/#:~:text=In%202014%2C%20the%20WTO%20ruled%20against%20China%20%28case,that%20its%20export%20restrictions%20violated%20international%20trade%20agreements. Accessed 23 June 2025.

9.3 China's Messaging in Adopting Export Control Measures

China began responding to US export controls by selectively announcing export controls of its own. China imposed export controls on Gallium and Germanium in August 2023, followed by Graphite in December 2023.[35] After the first wave of Trump tariffs announced in 2025 and the expanding use of export controls by the US, China (in February 2025) adopted additional retaliatory export control measures, including but not limited to, REEs and several critical minerals.[36]

China's export controls should be differentiated from earlier export restrictions on raw materials and rare earths. China's defence under GATT Article XX (b) and (g) was ultimately unsuccessful in the WTO dispute settlement process.[37] Typically, exceptions under Article XX (b) and (g) enable WTO Members to adopt policies to safeguard human, animal, plant life or health or to adopt measures for the conservation of exhaustible natural resources respectively.[38]

In contrast to the export restrictions on raw materials and rare earths, the retaliatory action by China featured the adoption of export controls on Tungsten, Tellurium, Indium and Molybdenum. Having learned some valuable lessons regarding the efficacy of the General Exceptions under GATT Article XX (b) and (g), China justified these export controls under national security grounds (not under GATT Article XXI).[39] In parallel, China also announced a series of import tariffs on various US exports such as crude oil, LNG, farm equipment, agriculture, and trucks.[40]

Commentators term China's import tariff response in February 2025 to US tariffs as relatively mild and rightly noted that export controls on rare earths could potentially be a much more powerful response.[41] China's calculated response in February 2025 avoided outright export bans but allowed export licensing for selected REEs

---

[35] Shivaprasad, Ashtitha., Amy Lv. & Lewis Jackson. 2025. What are the five critical metal exports restricted by China?. *Reuters*. https://www.reuters.com/markets/commodities/what-are-five-new-critical-metal-exports-restricted-by-china-2025-02-04/. Accessed 23 June 2025.

[36] Shivaprasad et al. What are the five critical metal exports restricted by China?. Lv, Amy, Lewis Jackson, and Ashtitha Shivaprasad. 2025. China expands key mineral export controls after US imposes tariffs. Reuters. https://www.reuters.com/world/china/china-expands-critical-mineral-export-controls-after-us-imposes-tariffs-2025-02-04/. Accessed 26 June 2025.

[37] Ghori, *supra*, n. 34, 408–414.

[38] Bhala, Raj. 2015. *International Trade Law: An Interdisciplinary, Non-Western Textbook*. LexisNexis.4th Ed, Vol. 2: 1155–1194.

[39] Lv et al. *supra*, n. 36; Zadeh, *supra*, n. 34.

[40] Bao, Anniek. 2025. "Economy China retaliates with additional tariffs of up to 15% on select U.S. imports starting Feb. 10". *CNBC*. https://www.cnbc.com/2025/02/04/china-levies-tariffs-on-select-us-imports-starting-feb-10.html#:~:text=China%20retaliates%20with%20additional%20tariffs%20of%20up%20to,controls%20on%20certain%20products%20related%20to%20critical%20minerals.?msockid=3ca814d307f56ccd3098010d06406d2b. Accessed 23 June 2025.

[41] Lv et al. China expands key mineral export controls after US imposes tariffs (see video Mui, Janet. 2025. Head of Market Analysis RBC Brewin Dolphin, at 00:52-01:32).

and critical minerals.[42] In doing so, China fired a warning shot and signalled its dominance on the global supply chains for REEs and critical minerals. The strategy worked since the two sides reached a framework trade agreement in June 2025 at trade talks held in London and Geneva. Under the deal, the US eased export restrictions on Nvidia's H20AI Chips and certain semiconductor design tools in exchange for China's resumption of exports of seven controlled medium-to-heavy REEs (e.g., Samarium, Dysprosium, Terbium, Gadolinium, Lutetium, Scandium and Yttrium) and their related magnets.[43]

China's selection of critical metals shows that its response to comprehensive US technology export controls and China-centric policies under the *US Chips and Science Act* is targeted and controlled. China is signalling that it is willing to respond to the US in kind, but with restraint. China's policymakers likely realise that, as things stand today, China will suffer more from the US–China decoupling than the US itself because alternative suppliers of rare earths are gradually emerging and eventually the US may further restrict market access for Chinese goods.[44] Therefore, the US–China deal of June 2025 is only a reprieve. The larger decoupling process between the two strategic competitors is well under way.

Table 9.1 below presents an overview of China's targeted export controls on REEs and critical minerals. Since the state of US and China trade and security relationship is highly fluid and reactionary, the information presented in Table 9.1 represents the inherent unpredictability associated with the US–China decoupling. There are no guarantees that Beijing will not impose export controls on medium-to-heavy REEs in order to further generate negotiating leverage with Washington.

After the temporary cooling-off of US–China trade hostilities, the Joint Statement issued by China and the US trade representatives in May 2025 at Geneva declared that US would reduce import tariffs for Chinese goods, while China undertook to suspend or cancel "non-tariff countermeasures" (covering export controls) against the US for a period of 90 days initially which was later relaxed following the trade deal in June 2025.[45]

As shown in Table 9.1, Beijing imposed targeted export controls on a range of critical inputs of interest to the US such as Gallium, Germanium, and several heavy

[42] Ibid.

[43] Baskaran, Gracelin. & Meredith Schwartz. 2025a. Trump strikes a deal to restore rare Earths access. *Center for Strategic and International Studies*. https://www.csis.org/analysis/trump-strikes-deal-restore-rare-earths-access. Accessed 4 August 2025. See also Kennedy, Scott. 2025. Does Xi have Trump's number?. Foreign Policy. https://foreignpolicy.com/2025/06/16/china-rare-earths-trade-war-deal-trump. Accessed 3 August 2025.

[44] Yang, Zeyi. 2025. Bad news for China: Rare Earth element aren't that rare. Wired. https://www.wired.com/story/rare-earth-minerals-china-tariffs/. Accessed 23 June 2025. DiPippo, Gerard, and Benjamin Lenain. 2025. Testing self-reliance: What the trade war reveals about China's vulnerabilities and power. Rand Corporation. https://www.rand.org/pubs/commentary/2025/06/testing-self-reliance-what-the-trade-war-reveals-about.html. Accessed 23 June 2025.

[45] Walter, Neetika. 2025. China pauses rare Earth export restrictions on 28 US entities after trade truce. Interesting Engineering. https://interestingengineering.com/energy/china-lifts-export-bans-on-rare-earths. Accessed 23 June 2025.

Table 9.1 Consolidated table of Chinese export controls on critical minerals and rare earth elements (REEs)

Material	Nature of Export Control	Effective Date	Notes (military application shaded)	Primary Uses
Gallium	Export license required	1 Aug 2023	China dominates global production (over 90%)	LEDs, solar cells, radar, satellites, semiconductor fabrication
Germanium	Export license required	Effective 1 Aug 2023	Key input for fibre optics and military night vision	Fiber optics, military technologies, infrared optics, semiconductors, night vision, solar panels
Graphite	Export permit required	Effective 1 Dec 2023	China controls around 67% of Graphite supply; essential for EV batteries	Lithium-ion battery anodes, lubricants, refractories, nuclear reactor moderators
Tungsten	Export controls (not bans). License required to export.	In force since February 2025. Not relaxed under June 2025 semiconductor-rare earths deal between the US and China.	Strategic importance in defence and aerospace	Armor-piercing projectiles, aerospace alloys, cutting tools, filaments
Antimony	Export license / quotas; subject to stricter scrutiny	Tightened in 2023	Flame retardant; used in electronics and batteries	Flame retardants, lead-acid batteries, semiconductors
REEs (describes 7 key elements)	Export control regime with reporting / approval system	Expanded Dec 2023	See below	Electronics, magnets, EVs, defence, medical imaging
Samarium	Export restriction under rare earth compound controls	Introduced in Dec 2023 – relaxed in June 2025	China is the dominant supplier. Bayan Obo mine in Inner Mongolia is one of the largest sources of REE globally.	Samarium-cobalt magnets, nuclear reactors, sensors, guided weapons, 5th generation aircraft engine components
Gadolinium	Export restriction under rare earth compound controls	Introduced in Dec 2023 – relaxed in June 2025	Vital for nuclear shielding and medical uses	MRI contrast agents, nuclear shielding, magnetic refrigeration

(continued)

Table 9.1 (continued)

Terbium	Export restriction under rare earth compound controls	Introduced in Dec 2023 – relaxed in June 2025	Enhances magnets and used in green phosphors, targeting and weapon systems	Displays, solid-state devices, magneto - strictive materials, laser targeting in combat vehicles
Dysprosium	Export restriction under rare earth compound controls	Introduced in Dec 2023 – relaxed in June 2025	Raises thermal resistance in magnets; key to EV and wind turbines	EV motors, wind turbines, HDDs, control rods, production of high-performance permanent magnets in advanced weapons,
Lutetium	Export restriction under rare earth compound controls	Introduced in Dec 2023 – relaxed in June 2025	Highest magnetic ordering temperature among the Lanthanides (REEs). Ability to convert X-rays into visible light.	PET scans, petroleum refining, advanced optics, defence electronics, high-tech imaging and catalysts
Scandium	Export restriction under rare earth compound controls	Introduced in Dec 2023 – relaxed in June 2025	Strengthens alloys for aerospace	Scandium-aluminium alloys, solid oxide fuel cells, high-intensity lamps
Yttrium	Export restriction under rare earth compound controls	Introduced in Dec 2023 – relaxed in June 2025	Essential for phosphors and superconductors. Used in lasers for rangefinders, target designation tech and illuminators	LEDs, CRTs, microwave filters, lasers, ceramics
Tellurium	Export restriction as part of 2024 expansion	Announced Jan 2024	Used in advanced solar tech; added to control list with semiconductors	Solar panels, alloys, optical media
Bismuth	Export restriction as part of 2024 expansion	Announced Jan 2024	Eco-friendly lead substitute in solder	Lead-free solder, pharmaceuticals, cosmetics, reactor coolant
Indium	Export restriction as part of 2024 expansion	Announced Jan 2024	Used in touchscreen technology and some semiconductors	Coatings, flat panel displays, solar cells, solder alloys
Molybdenum	Export restriction as part of 2024 expansion	Announced Jan 2024	Enhances steel; vital to defence and heavy industry	Steel alloys, catalysts, lubricants, missile components

Sources: Author's analysis based on various sources (Scott, *supra*, n. 43. Baskaran and Schwartz, *supra*, n. 43. Home, Andy. 2025. A tungsten-tipped answer to the West's critical metals dilemma. Reuters. https://www.reuters.com/markets/commodities/tungsten-tipped-answer-wests-critical-metals-dilemma-andy-home-2025-02-19/. Accessed 23 June 2025. Zhen, Liu. 2025. China's critical minerals dominance threatens US military supply chain, report says. South China Morning Post. https://www.scmp.com/news/china/military/article/3308045/chinas-critical-minerals-dominance-threatens-us-military-supply-chain-report-says. Accessed 23 June 2025. US Department of Energy. 2025. What are critical materials and critical minerals. *Critical Minerals & Materials Program.* https://www.energy.gov/cmm/what-are-critical-materials-and-critical-minerals. Accessed 23 June 2025. Vicente, Agustin de. 2025. China imposes export restrictions on critical metals in response to US tariffs. Mining Reporters. https://www.miningreporters.com/noticia/news/2025/02/china-imposes-export-restrictions-on-critical-metals. Accessed 4 February 2025)

REEs citing national security. Interestingly, Molybdenum features as one of the commodities controlled by China which was previously the subject of dispute settlement proceedings in the much-debated *China—Rare Earths* case. China imposed licensing requirements to export Molybdenum in February 2025, and its exports was not relaxed following the semiconductors—rare earths trade deal between the US and China signed in June 2025 following talks in Geneva and London.[46]

Note that China's measures are not outright export bans or prohibitively high levels of export taxes. This shows that China is still interested in exporting raw materials alongside managing domestic consumption. Furthermore, on a closer look the measures do not appear to be designed for the long run. Rather, these export controls were intended to generate leverage for negotiations with President Trump.

In hindsight, adopting a security driven concept like export controls on REEs enabled China to avoid triggering WTO rules, since export controls are not directly covered under its framework. In doing so, China clearly signalled that it understood the nuances of the global trade and security system. China showed willingness to use its dominant position in the REE supply chains to draw favourable outcomes, just as President Trump was willing to violate the WTO rulebook to extract concessions from major trading partners.

The timing and scope of China's export controls suggest a reactive pattern to geo-economic sensitivities. China's export controls emerged immediately after US semiconductor export bans.[47] The targets were sectors where US and its allies were perceived as vulnerable, but not limited to, advanced electronics, green tech, and defence systems. For example, Gallium and Germanium, essential for semiconductors fabrication, lithography equipment and various military application, were among the first to be targeted. Later, China's export controls were extended to Graphite (a common, yet vital raw material used in green tech) and medium-to-heavy REEs listed in Table 9.1 above, along with a return to restricting Molybdenum (restricted earlier by China in 2012 along with Tungsten). The gradual expansion, and later relaxation, of export controls underscores the Chinese intent to throttle critical minerals bottlenecks and supply chains.

China's export controls reflect two aims: firstly, to deter or, at the least, resist further restrictions on Chinese access to global technology, and secondly, to accelerate self-sufficiency by selectively decoupling from supply chains feeding US and Western markets. China's export controls are signalling to the US that it will not passively absorb external economic pressure but will retaliate in a calibrated manner to exploit its structural advantages in refining raw REEs. For the US and the West, the urgency is clear: strategic resilience requires urgent diversification away from Chinese dominated links in the global supply chain.

In summary, four stages of China's reactive response to the US export control policies are visible from Table 9.1 which clearly highlight the gradual escalation by China. Firstly, the Gallium and Germanium export controls in 2023 were a direct

---

[46] Vicente, *supra*, n.46.

[47] Ghori, *supra*, n.1, at 289–300.

response to US and its allies imposing export controls on semiconductors, advanced semiconductor fabrication and lithography equipment. Secondly, in late 2023, the focus of the reactionary export controls spread to dual-use REEs and critical metals such as Yttrium, Terbium and Tungsten that have highly specialised defence-related uses as well as use in high-powered magnets. Thirdly, the more comprehensive 2024 expansion signalled a wide-ranging coverage over critical metals that were used in optical technology, renewable energy, EV motors, batteries and advanced chips. Fourthly, the de-escalation by China considering the tariff deal between the US and China in June 2025 following trade talks in Geneva and London that saw a 115% reduction in reciprocal tariffs.[48] During the 90-day pause following the May 2025 talks in Geneva, exporters of REEs and other critical minerals capable of dual-use could apply for license to resume shipment.[49]

The information presented in Table 9.1 must be understood within the context of the US efforts to decouple from dependency on China's control on the refining process of REEs and critical minerals. Table 9.2 below highlights the accelerated efforts by the US to decouple from China in the supply of REEs which are critical to defence, renewable energy, and technology sectors. China's strategic use of export controls, most notably on Gallium and Germanium in 2023, and on Graphite and REEs in 2024–2025, has exposed the temporary vulnerability of US and allied industries to supply disruptions.

The US government launched a multipronged diversification strategy to secure alternative sources (see Table 9.2 below). The diversification underscores the US weaning its economy away from reliance on China. It further shows a disruption in "globalisation" trends that is acceptable to the US in a world where other aspirants are rising to challenge US hegemony.

The US strategy includes efforts to develop recycling and recovery of critical metals as by-products from primary ore processing,[50] bilateral agreements such as the 2023 US–Japan Critical Minerals Agreement,[51] the 2024 US–Canada co-investments in Antimony and Scandium production by Canadian companies Fortune Minerals Limited and Lomiko Metals Inc,[52] domestic capacity building, with the US Department of Energy (DOE) announcing US $725 million to boost domestic

[48] Walter, *supra*, n. 45.

[49] Ibid.

[50] US Department of Commerce (DOC). 2019. A federal strategy to ensure secure and reliable supplies of critical minerals. https://www.federalregister.gov/documents/2017/12/26/2017-27899/a-federal-strategy-to-ensure-secure-and-reliable-supplies-of-critical-minerals. Accessed 23 June 2025.

[51] Executive Office of the President, Office of the US Trade Representative (USTR). 2023. United States and Japan sign critical minerals agreement. https://ustr.gov/about-us/policy-offices/press-office/press-releases/2023/march/united-states-and-japan-sign-critical-minerals-agreement. Accessed 23 June 2025.

[52] Government of Canada. 2024. Government of Canada and the United States co-invest to strengthen critical mineral value chain. https://www.canada.ca/en/natural-resources-canada/news/2024/05/government-of-canada-and-the-united-states-co-invest-to-strengthen-critical-mineral-value-chains.html. Accessed 23 June 2025.

Table 9.2 US strategic vulnerabilities & diversification efforts for critical minerals and REEs

Critical Mineral / REE	US Strategic Vulnerability	Recent US Diversification Efforts
Gallium	China controls approximately 90% of global production[1]; Essential for semiconductors and defence applications.	In July 2024, the US DOE announced nearly $10 million for two projects aimed at producing REEs, including Gallium, from coal, coal waste, and coal by-products.[2]
Germanium	High dependency on Chinese exports; Critical for fibre optics and infrared technologies.	Projects underway to extract Germanium from domestic sources, such as from Zinc residue produced for steel wastes.[3]
Graphite	China dominates approximately 67% of global supply[4]; Vital for EV batteries and renewable energy storage.	In March 2023, the US and Japan signed a critical minerals agreement to strengthen supply chains, including for Graphite.[5]
Tungsten	US reliant on imports and China dominates 80% of the tungsten supply chain[6]; Used in aerospace and military applications.	In August 2024, diversification from China to Canadian suppliers. Almonty Industries from Canada investment in South Korea to re-open the Sandong Tungsten mine.[7]
Antimony	Dependence on Chinese exports; Used in defence technologies, semiconductors, flame retardants and solar panels.	January 2025, Canadian company Canagold announced development of Antimony production at the New Polaris Gold Project mine as a by-product of Gold production.[8]
REEs	China processes over 90% of global REEs[9]; Crucial for defence, electronics, and green tech.	In April 2023, the DOE announced $16 million in funding for REE extraction and separation facilities in West Virginia and North Dakota.[10]
Samarium	Used in permanent magnets for military applications; Limited alternative suppliers.	In April 2025, Energy Fuels Inc. facility in White Mesa in Utah announced processing capabilities for Samarium, Gadolinium, Dysprosium, Terbium, Lutetium, and Yttrium oxides.[11]
Gadolinium	Essential for medical imaging and nuclear reactors; High reliance on Chinese supply.	In November 2023, the DOE announced $5 million for projects exploring extraction of REEs, including Gadolinium, from macroalgae.[12]
Terbium	Critical for green phosphors and solid-state devices; Limited global availability outside China.	In September 2024, US Department of Defense announced US $ 4.22 million award to Rare Earth Salts in Beatrice, Nebraska for development and expansion of Terbium Oxide from recycled fluorescent light bulbs.[13]
Dysprosium	Key for high-temperature magnets in EVs and wind turbines; China holds significant processing capacity.	In May 2025, MP Materials signed an MoU with Saudi Arabia's Maaden to develop rare earths supply chain, including Dysprosium.[14]
Lutetium	Used in advanced optics and PET scans, specialised alloys and chemical catalysts; China holds significant processing capacity.	In April 2025, Energy Fuels Inc facility in White Mesa in Utah announced processing capabilities for Samarium, Gadolinium, Dysprosium, Terbium, Lutetium, and Yttrium oxides.[15]
Scandium	Strengthens aerospace alloys; limited global supply; High dependency on imports.	In May 2024, the US and Canada co-invested in Lomiko Metals Inc. to develop Scandium resources in Quebec.[16]
Yttrium	Vital for LEDs and superconductors; China is the primary supplier.	In April 2025, Energy Fuels Inc facility in White Mesa in Utah announced processing capabilities for Samarium, Gadolinium, Dysprosium, Terbium, Lutetium, and Yttrium oxides.[17]
Tellurium	Used in solar panels and thermo-electrical applications; Limited availability outside China.	In December 2024, the DOE invested $17 million across 14 projects to accelerate critical materials innovation, including Tellurium.[18]
Bismuth	Eco-friendly lead substitute: China is a major supplier; used in pharmaceuticals and electronics.	In May 2024, Canada and US make co-investment of US $ 32.5 million into Fortune Minerals Ltd (on exploration and mining of Bismuth and Cobalt).[19]
Indium	Used in tin oxide films, alloys, semiconductors, flatscreens, solders, solar cells, thermal interface materials, batteries and LEDs; High reliance onChinese exports.	In November 2022, Utah Geological Survey issued an exploration grant in Juab County.[20] Indium is extracted as byproduct from Zinc refining.[21]
Molybdenum	Enhances steel; essential for defence and heavy industry; China is a significant exporter.	In October 2023, the US House approved the 2024 Critical Mineral Consistency Act, ensuring molybdenum projects are eligible for the FAST-41permitting process.[22]

(continued)

Table 9.2 (continued)

[a] Zadeh, *supra*, n. 34
[b] National Energy Technology Laboratory. 2024. Two additional projects selected to advance rare Earth element and critical mineral and material processing technologies using coal and coal byproducts as Feedstocks. https://www.netl.doe.gov/node/13953#:~:text=%E2%80%94%20The%20U.S.%20Department%20of%20Energy%20%28DOE%29%20today,materials%20from%20coal%2C%20coal%20wastes%2C%20and%20coal%20by-products. Accessed 23 June 2025
[c] Ames National Laboratory. 2024. CMI project 1.1.18: Gallium, indium and germanium extraction from zinc residue produced for steel wastes. https://www.ameslab.gov/cmi-project-1-1-18-gallium-indium-and-germanium-extraction-from-zinc-residue-produced-for-steel#:~:text=This%20project%20will%20examine%20novel%20pyrometallurgical%20and%20hydrometallurgical,a%20sustainable%20domestic%20supply%20of%20these%20critical%20materials. Accessed 23 June 2025
[d] Unglesbee, Ben. 2023. China moves to limit exports of Graphite. Supply Chain Dive. https://www.supplychaindive.com/news/china-bands-graphite-exports-EV/697528/. Accessed 23 June 2025
[e] Executive Office of the President, United States and Japan sign critical minerals agreement
[f] CNBC. 2024. The US needs more of this critical metal—and China owns 80% of its supply chain. https://www.cnbc.com/2024/07/03/us-needs-more-tungsten-china-is-a-major-supplier-of-the-critical-metal.html?msockid=3ca814d307f56ccd3098010d06406d2b. Accessed 23 June 2025
[g] Park, Hey-Jin. 2024. U.S. looks to South Korean mine to boost Tungsten supply. https://www.ctol.digital/news/us-seeks-tungsten-source-in-south-korea/. Accessed 23 June 2025
[h] Financial Post. 2025. Canagold identifies significant antimony production potential at New Polaris. https://financialpost.com/pmn/business-wire-news-releases-pmn/canagold-identifies-significant-antimony-production-potential-at-new-polaris. Accessed 23 June 2025. US Government Accountability Office (GAO). 2024a. Technology assessment—critical metals: Status, challenges, and policy options for recovery from nontraditional sources. https://www.gao.gov/assets/gao-24-106395.pdf. Accessed 23 June 2025
[i] CKGSB Knowledge. 2025. Rare Earth resources: China's domination of a key global market. https://english.ckgsb.edu.cn/knowledge/article/china-dominance-of-rare-earth-and-impact-on-global-market/#:~:text=Almost%2090%25%20of%20global%20rare%20earths%20processing%20is,to%20do%20this%20for%20two%20decades%2C%E2%80%9D%20says%20Andrews-Speed. Accessed 23 June 2025
[j] US DOE. 2023a. Bipartisan Infrastructure Law: Rare Earth element demonstration facility. https://www.energy.gov/fecm/funding-notice-bipartisan-infrastructure-law-rare-earth-element-demonstration-facility#:~:text=On%20April%204%2C%202023%2C%20the%20U.S.%20Department%20of,America%20and%20reduce%20reliance%20on%20competitors%20like%20China. Accessed 23 June 2025
[k] Energy Fuels (EF). 2025. US based energy fuels poised to produce six of the seven rare Earth Oxides now subject to Chinese export controls at scale. https://investors.energyfuels.com/2025-04-17-U-S-Based-Energy-Fuels-Poised-to-Produce-Six-of-the-Seven-Rare-Earth-Oxides-Now-Subject-to-Chinese-Export-Controls-at-Scale. Accessed 23 June 2025
[l] US DOE. 2023b. Department of Energy announces teams selected to explore critical mineral extraction from ocean macroalgae. https://www.energy.gov/arctic/articles/us-department-energy-announces-teams-selected-explore-critical-mineral-extraction. Accessed 26 June 2025
[m] North American Mining. 2024. DoD invests millions in Terbium production. https://northamericanmining.com/index.php/2024/09/16/dod-invests-millions-in-terbium-production/#:~:text=The%20U.S.%20Department%20of%20Defense%20has%20announced%20a,rare%20earth%20magnets%20in%20many%20key%20defense%20systems. Accessed 21 June 2025. Easley, Mikayla. 2023. U.S. begins forging rare Earth supply chain. https://www.nationaldefensemagazine.org/articles/2023/2/10/us-begins-forging-rare-earth-supply-chain. Accessed 23 June 2025

(continued)

Table 9.2 (continued)

[n] MP Materials, *supra,* n.54
[o] Energy Fuels, *supra,* n.65
[p] Government of Canada, *supra,* n.52
[q] Energy Fuels, *supra,* n.65
[r] US DOE. 2024. US Department of Energy invests $17 million to shore up America's energy security with robust supply chain for critical materials. https://www.energy.gov/articles/us-department-energy-invests-17-million-shore-americas-energy-security-robust-supply-chain. Accessed 25 June 2025
[s] CBS News. 2024. Canada and U.S. make first co-investment in critical minerals producers. https://www.cbc.ca/news/politics/canada-us-invest-critical-mineral-production-1.7206655. Accessed 25 June 2025
[t] Higgins, Sean. 2022. Utah's West Desert could hold a decade's worth of indium. KUER. https://www.kuer.org/business-economy/2022-11-14/utahs-west-desert-could-hold-a-decades-worth-of-indium. Accessed 25 June 2025
[u] Stockhead. 2023. American West Metals' West Desert now hosts the only indium resource in the US. https://stockhead.com.au/resources/american-west-metals-west-desert-now-hosts-the-only-indium-resource-in-the-us/. Accessed 25 June 2025
[v] Mining.com. 2024. US House of Representatives approves 2024 Critical Mineral Consistency Act. https://www.mining.com/us-house-of-representatives-approves-2024-critical-mineral-consistency-act/. Accessed 25 June 2025

production of battery critical materials, battery components and advanced batteries along with accompanying supply chain.[53] To further de-risk the battery supply chain from Chinese interference, projects such as the MoU for joint venture between MP Materials with Saudi Arabia's Maaden are of critical importance.[54] Table 9.2 sheds light on many similar efforts by the US on a domestic scale as well as international level to re-risk and diversify away from China.

The key takeaway from Table 9.2 is that the US is actively reducing reliance on the global REE market dominated by China and, further, through a combination of co-investments with Canada, domestic subsidies, and non-traditional mining of critical metals as a by-product of host-metal mining.[55] In doing so, the US is seeking to reshape global supply chains by reshoring domestic manufacturing. The aim of reshaping global supply chains is to preserve or even enhance its share in the global technology and goods trade ostensibly to protect its national interests.[56]

---

[53] US Department of Energy (DOE). 2025. DOE issues notice of intent for funding in strengthening domestic critical materials processing and manufacturing to enhance national security. https://www.energy.gov/mesc/articles/doe-issues-notice-intent-funding-strengthening-domestic-critical-materials-processing. Accessed 23 June 2025.

[54] MP Materials. 2025. Maaden and MP Materials collaborate to establish full value chain for rare Earth magnetics. https://investors.mpmaterials.com/investor-news/news-details/2025/Maaden-and-MP-Materials-Collaborate-to-Establish-Full-Value-Chain-for-Rare-Earth-Magnetics/default.aspx. Accessed 23 June 2025.

[55] US Department of Commerce (DOC), *supra*, n. 51.

[56] Suominen, Kati. 2025. How should Trump 2.0 secure global supply chains?. Hinrich Foundation. https://www.hinrichfoundation.com/research/wp/trade-and-geopolitics/how-should-trump-2-0-secure-global-supply-chains/. Accessed 25 June 2025.

The US aims to achieve its de-coupling goals through a multi-pronged strategy involving industrial policy, international alliances, and long-term strategic investment. This shift reflects a broader national security framing of resource independence, especially in the face of rising geopolitical competition with China.

The implications of this shift are significant. The creation of parallel, non-Chinese supply chains may reduce US exposure to coercive economic measures. However, the establishment of new, complex and capital-intensive supply chains and the accompanying industrial infrastructure will take time and significant investment. Additionally, the US policymakers will have to grapple with the serious environmental damage that is associated with REE mining and processing. There are also no guarantees that after all this effort, the final products manufactured within the US will be competitive within the domestic market or the international market.

The US will not only have to invest in and explore domestic REE resources, but it will also have to modify, or in some cases, even water down environmental standards in order to expedite the de-coupling process with China. Meanwhile, global markets in a period of uncertainty and transition may fragment, see higher costs, and intensifying competition for non-Chinese suppliers. Nonetheless, the diversification efforts by the US mark a decisive turn towards ensuring a secure REE and critical minerals ecosystem.

9.4 Semiconductor Export Controls, National Security, and Decoupling

The readjustment of economic links between the US and China have demolished the assumption that closer economic interdependence would lead to deeper cooperation, reduce the risks of broader military conflict and promote overall global prosperity.

The US decoupling from China seeks to disentangle the two economies, not for economic reasons, but to address perceived national security risks from a strategic competitor.[57] The decoupling seems to be more pronounced in advanced technology and the associated supply chains. However, it is highly likely that the policy coverage and the broader consequences of the decoupling process will eventually trickle down to basic and intermediate industrial sectors within the US economy.

The decoupling process is based on the geo-economic rationale that economic leverage can no longer be separated from geopolitical strategy. The larger US–China decoupling process has thrust the increasing use of export controls into the spotlight. Policymakers in US (including President Trump during the first presidency) and China have both openly acknowledged that the imposition of export controls,

[57] Gao, Dan, & Dong Wang. 2024. New trends of US economic and trade policy toward China and China's responses from the perspective of friend-shoring. *Journal of WTO and China* 14(4): 87, 91–94.

supply chain security and the overall decoupling process is based on national security narratives.[58]

China's expanding use of export controls on sensitive technologies, dual-use goods,[59] along with imposition of rare earth export restrictions[60] (outlined in Table 9.1 in Sect. 9.2 above) were not only intended to disrupt key US industries but also as a response to prohibitively high tariffs imposed by the President Trump.[61] These measures represent just one dimension of the Thucydides Trap which the US and China currently find themselves in.[62]

Since the introduction of the *Export Control Law* in 2020, China has built a centralised system featuring an Unreliable Entity List (UEL) to regulate the export process of military or dual-use items.[63] Like the US system, China's export controls feature a list of controlled items, monitoring, and end-user licensing requirements. China has further spelt out sanctions on local and third parties that either violate Chinese law or threaten its national interests.[64]

According to the 2025 IISS report, China's moves go beyond regulatory fine-tuning.[65] These moves represent an evolution in its strategic attitude and willingness to capitalise on its dominance in REE, electronics, and green technologies to manipulate the actions of other states in its favour.[66]

The establishment by China of the UEL for overseas actors along with discretionary power to deny licenses or impose sanctions, reinforce the idea that China's trade policy is becoming explicitly political. China's moves signal that it has observed the lessons of US export control policy and is adapting those tactics for its own advantage. A prime example is that of China's export restrictions on REEs and derivative products, such as high-powered magnets, critical inputs for US defence application, clean energy, and automobile sectors (see Table 9.1 above).

According to a 2025 report by CSIS, China's action was a calculated response to a spate of US tariffs targeting Chinese goods.[67] Refined REEs are not easily replaceable in the short run. The use of export controls sent a powerful signal to the US

---

[58] Kati, How should Trump 2.0 secure global supply chains? Nouwens, Meia, Maria Shagina, & Erik Green. 2025. "China's use of export controls". *International Institute of Strategic Studies* (IISS). https://www.iiss.org/online-analysis/charting-china/2025/02/chinas-use-of-export-controls/. Accessed 23 June 2025.

[59] Meia et al., ibid.

[60] Baskaran, Gracelin. & Meredith Schwartz. 2025b. The consequences of China's new rare Earths export restrictions. Center for Strategic and International Studies. https://www.csis.org/analysis/consequences-chinas-new-rare-earths-export-restrictions. Accessed 24 June 2025.

[61] Ibid.

[62] Latham, Andrew. 2025. Are US and China really in a Thucydides trap? Asia Times. https://asiatimes.com/2025/04/are-us-and-china-really-in-a-thucydides-trap/#. Accessed 24 June 2025.

[63] Meia et al., *supra*, n. 81.

[64] Ibid.

[65] Ibid.

[66] Ibid.

[67] Gracelin & Schwartz, The consequences of China's new rare Earths export restrictions

since China continues to exercise controls over the global refining capacity for REEs, and the US continues to be dependent on import from China at least for the foreseeable future. The outcome and the messaging from China were simple: if the US economically pressures China, it should expect a targeted response where it is most vulnerable.

Following China's export controls the prices for REEs saw some increase and prompted US importers and manufacturers to begin searching for alternative suppliers.[68] China had demonstrated that economic interdependency can be weaponised to achieve geo-economic gains. For the US policymakers, this episode strengthened the justification for quickening the decoupling process. The information summarised in Table 9.2 spotlights the initial US efforts to reduce, and eventually eliminate, reliance on a strategic competitor.

China's weaponisation of economic interdependency further set the stage for the Geneva and London trade talks between US and Chinese officials in May and June 2025.[69] The talks resulted in a partial relaxation of tariffs and export controls. However, in May 2025 further complications arose when the US Court of International Trade in New York deemed that powers exercised by President Trump in imposing sweeping tariffs were illegal under the US *International Emergency Economic Powers Act* (IEEPA) 1977, which a day later, were subject to a ruling by the US Court of Appeals for the Federal Circuit in Washington allowing a temporary pause.[70]

While the Geneva ruling signalled an intent to reduce trade tensions and bring much needed stability to economic ties between two major powers, the confusion within the US polity on tariffs projected a message of weakness and uncertainty to China. Following the agreement in Geneva in May 2025 and follow up discussions in June 2025, China lifted some restrictions on REEs exports and agreed to start flow of strategic minerals to the US, while the US committed to reducing tariffs imposed earlier in 2024 on Chinese goods.[71] Table 9.3 illumines the hidden side of the trade breakthrough in June 2025. The major Chinese gain was access to Nvidia H20 AI GPUs and selected EDA tools and older node chips greater than 16 nm.

---

[68] Gruzer, Marina. 2025. How do China's export restrictions on rare Earths impact global trade and major industries? Bloomsbury Intelligence and Security Institute. https://bisi.org.uk/reports/how-do-chinas-export-restrictions-on-rare-earths-impact-global-trade-and-major-industries#:~:text=China%27s%20tightening%20of%20rare%20earth%20element%20%28REE%29%20export,REE%20mining%20and%2090%25%20of%20global%20REE%20refining. Accessed 23 June 2025.

[69] Gan, Nectar & John Liu. 2025. US and China agree on plan to ease export controls after trade talks in London. CNN. https://edition.cnn.com/2025/06/10/business/us-china-trade-talks-london-agreement-intl-hnk. Accessed 23 June 2025.

[70] ABC News. 2025. Donald Trump's sweeping global tariffs blocked by US Court of International Trade. https://www.abc.net.au/news/2025-05-29/donald-trump-trade-tariffs-block-us-court/105351386. Accessed 22 June 2025.

[71] Gan, Nectar. 2025. Trump says Xi agreed to restart flow of crucial minerals, but analysts say China won't give up its 'rare earth card'. CNN. https://edition.cnn.com/2025/06/07/business/trump-xi-restart-rare-earths-flow-intl-hnk. Accessed 22 June 2025.

There are several critical advanced technologies that remain restricted to China (see Table 9.3 below).

The selective easing by the US in semiconductor export controls is limited in scope. The US has only resumed access to China for the H20 AI GPUs made by

Table 9.3 Overview of US export controls on semiconductors and related equipment (as of August 2025)

Control category	Status	Details
Nvidia H20 AI GPUs to China	Relaxed	Ban relaxed on H20 AI accelerators[a]
Electronic Design Automation Tools (EDA) & Older-Node Chips above 16 nm	Relaxed	License requirements lifted in exchange for resumption of heavy REE exports[b]
Pending "50% Rule" on Entity-List Subsidiaries	Pending review. Subject to future BIS rulemaking	Planned amendment to the US EARs that treats any entity subject to the Entity-list requirements if it is 50% or more owned (either directly or indirectly) by a party on the US Entity-List[c]
Advanced Logic Chips below 16 nm	Still enforced since Oct 2022	Exports of Advanced logic chips at 16 nm or finer remain prohibited to China[d]
High-end Memory (DRAM less than 18 nm and NAND above the 128 layers threshold	Still enforced since Nov 2023	Cutting-edge memory devices remain restricted to China unless a license is granted[e]
Semiconductor Manufacturing Equipment	Still enforced since Oct 2022	Exports of DUV/EUV lithography, deposition, etchers, inspection, and other fabrication tools remain banned under the EAR for China based end-users[f]
Supercomputing & AI System End-Use	Still enforced since Nov 2023	Any chips used for supercomputing facilities or military-civil fusion projects are blocked from export to China[g]
Quantum Computing & Related Technologies	Still enforced since Sep 2024	Restrictions on quantum-hardware, software, and deemed-export scenarios[h]

[a] Reuters. 2025. Nvidia says its chips have no 'backdoors' after China flags H20 security concerns. https://www.reuters.com/world/china/nvidia-says-its-chips-have-no-backdoors-after-china-flags-h20-security-concerns-2025-07-31/?. Accessed 18 August 2025

[b] Hale, Thomas & Christian Davies. 2025. Chip software makers say US restrictions on sales to China lifted. Financial Times. https://www.ft.com/content/36b12cb9-68d4-4e31-84e8-6d96d676b45d?. Accessed 17 August 2025

[c] Moody's. 2025. The BIS and the proposed 50% rule—what's in the pipeline for export controls? https://www.moodys.com/web/en/us/kyc/resources/insights/bis-and-the-proposed-50-rule-whats-in-the-pipeline-for-export-controls.html. Accessed 18 August 2025. See also Buckland. 2025. BIS drafting 50% rule to expand entity list restrictions. https://buckland.com/news/bis-drafting-50-rule-to-expand-entity-list-restrictions/?. Accessed 18 August 2025

[d] US Department of Commerce BIS. 2022. Commerce implements new export controls on advanced computing and semiconductor manufacturing items to the People's Republic of China (PRC). https://www.bis.doc.gov/index.php/documents/about-bis/newsroom/press-releases/3158-2022-10-07-bis-press-release-advanced-computing-and-semiconductor-manufacturing-controls-final/file. Accessed 18 August 2025

(continued)

Table 9.3 (continued)

[e] US Department of Commerce BIS. 2023. Export controls on semiconductor manufacturing items (SME IFR) and implementation of additional export controls: Certain advanced computing items; Supercomputer and semiconductor end use; Updates and corrections. https://www.bis.gov/media/documents/semiconductors-advanced-computing-2023-frequently-asked-questions.pdf. Accessed 18 August 2025

[f] US Department of Commerce BIS, *supra*, n.98

[g] US Department of Commerce BIS, *supra*, n.99

[h] US Department of Commerce BIS. 2024. Department of Commerce implements controls on quantum computing and other advanced technologies alongside international partners. https://www.bis.gov/media/documents/quantum-press-release-final.pdf. Accessed 18 August 2025

Nvidia along with some older-nodes and design tools (see Table 9.3). At best, the US relaxation is a short-term negotiation concession and does not represent a strategic shift in policy. The product categories relaxed (outlined in Table 9.3) should, at best, be viewed as a bargaining chip for trade US–China trade talks in Stockholm, London and Geneva. The product categories are narrow and of slightly older tech and represent a narrow piece of the larger semiconductor cake that China wishes to take.

It is also noteworthy that Biden-era export controls imposed alongside the introduction of the US CHIPS and Science Act are largely in force. Hence, the picture on the US side is clear: decouple from China in the tech-realm and deny advanced-tech access to China to delay its development.

Additionally, Table 9.3 also shows that there have been no blanket policy reversals. The measures taken by the US in relaxing export controls on some product categories were explicitly tied to China's willingness to resume exports of heavy REEs needed by the US. Advanced semiconductors categories, next-generation memory, lithography, fabrication equipment and components thereof remain blocked for China-based end-users and fabricators.[72] The US DOC continues to maintain a policy of "presume denial" for any licence applications by US corporations concerning the export of advanced semiconductors and fabrication categories outlined in Table 9.3 above.

On a more macro scale, export controls have emerged as a central pillar in the technology decoupling process between the US and China. Since the passage of the US Chips and Science Act, the US policy has systematically expanded the coverage of the controlled components and technology exports to China by including supercomputing systems and components, chips driving modern AI models and quantum technologies.[73] Simultaneously, the US expanded its enforcement coverage by

[72] Shivakumar, Sujai, Charles Wessner, & Thomas Howell. 2024. Balancing the ledger: Export controls on U.S. chip technology to China. Center for Strategic and International Studies. https://www.csis.org/analysis/balancing-ledger-export-controls-us-chip-technology-china. Accessed 18 August 2025.

[73] Ghori, *supra,* n.1, at 241.

including intermediaries in its BIS Entity-List.[74] The US measures are designed to impede China's ability to acquire advanced semiconductors and to slow its longer-term capacity to domestically produce the equipment at scale.[75] In doing so, export controls are being used to mould global supply chains by explicitly keeping the "decoupling" process in mind as opposed to purely market economics.

Since China is dynamically adapting to the decoupling process and the greater prospects of its strategic competition escalating into a military conflict with the US, it is very likely relying on espionage and the use of third-party intermediaries to access advanced technologies subject to US export controls. Some sources have estimated that significant volumes of controlled US-tech have reached China via intermediaries and smuggling networks thereby exposing serious gaps in US enforcement mechanisms.[76] To respond to this challenge, the US is considering the integration of "location verification" or "chip-tracking" technologies within AI processors to prevent unauthorised flow to China. This strategy indicates that the US views semiconductor and technological decoupling as an enduring strategic imperative.[77] The US is further mulling the international corporate networks to stem the outflow of controlled technologies to China. The proposed "50% rule" expected to come into force later in 2025 is intended to automatically refuse export licence for controlled technologies to any business majority-owned by a foreign business listed on the US Entity-List.[78]

To sum up, the US export controls are a central policy instrument deployed as a delaying mechanism against China's acquisition of advanced technology and related component. It is also designed to decelerate and eventually erode US FDI into China's technology sector, thereby depriving Chinese tech developers of capital as well as access to proprietary technology.[79] Simultaneously, the US is exploring alternative supply chains from Allied nations to meet its own needs and expanding policies that encourage reshoring of fabrication and development of alternative software licensing models to insulate from Chinese influence and hedge against a multipolar global tech market.[80]

---

[74] Wu, Zijang. & Eleanor Olcott. 2025. Nvidia AI chips worth $1bn smuggled to China after Trump export controls. Financial Times. https://www.ft.com/content/6f806f6e-61c1-4b8d-9694-90d7328a7b54. Accessed 18 August 2025.

[75] Ghori, Umair. 2025. "Semiconductor skirmish: Unpacking US export controls against China". Paper presented at ILA-ASIL Asia-Pacific Research Forum, Taipei, Taiwan: 7–8 July at 5.

[76] Zijang and Olcott, *supra*, n.105.

[77] Potkin, Fanny, Karen Freifeld, & Jun Yuan Yong. 2025. "Exclusive: US embeds trackers in AI chip shipments to catch diversions to China, sources say." *Reuters*. https://www.reuters.com/world/china/us-embeds-trackers-ai-chip-shipments-catch-diversions-china-sources-say-2025-08-13/. Accessed 18 August 2025.

[78] Moody's, *supra*, n. 97.

[79] Shivakumar et al, *supra*, n.103.

[80] Ibid. See also US Government Accountability Office (GAO). 2024b. Export controls: Commerce implemented advanced semiconductor rules and took steps to address compliance challenges. https://www.gao.gov/assets/gao-25-107386.pdf. Accessed 18 August 2025.

9.5 Conclusion: The Three Roads to Decoupling

Despite the successive rounds of bilateral trade negotiation, the US is still decades away from breaking free from reliance on China in REEs, advanced batteries, and key semiconductor inputs. The current US strategy of imposing high tariffs on a strategic competitor and then engaging in trade talks is based on buying time to re-shore domestic capacity, diversify suppliers of REEs (such as from Australia and Canada), and to further invest in research and development of processing base that will gradually eliminate reliance on Chinese REEs imports. Therefore, the outcome of mid-2025 trade talks in Stockholm, London and Geneva were in no way a reversal of the decoupling process.

Rather, it was strategic pause that enables the US to fine-tune its long-term China strategy and overcome domestic roadblocks. The spate of legal actions challenging the legitimacy of President Trump's aggressive use of tariffs are an indication that the decoupling process by the US faces significant resistance from key domestic stakeholders.[81]

The US policymakers will also have to grapple with difficult questions on how to set the tone and tenor of the decoupling. Even where we agree that the process of decoupling has now begun, its long-term trajectory and true extent is yet to be revealed until publicly disclosed through policy decisions, bilateral negotiations and, perhaps, some reversals. The decoupling process pursued by the US against China can be divided into three foreseeable courses of actions, each bringing their own sets of challenges and advantages:

(a) **The managed decoupling option**: The most likely and sane option is to selectively manage and disengage the US economy from long-term reliance in strategic sectors, combined with extensive export controls that are coordinated with US allies in the advanced technology realm, namely, the Netherlands, Japan, South Korea and Taiwan. This option acknowledges that complete disengagement from China is economically unrealistic. Therefore, dependencies on China should be identified and eliminated in areas critical to national security. The coverage of decoupling includes semiconductors, telecommunications, AI, quantum computing, critical minerals, pharmaceuticals, and green technologies. Adoption of the US *CHIPS and Science Act*, the *Inflation Reduction Act*, tightened outbound investment screening, and coordinated export controls on semiconductor fabrication and lithography equipment all indicate that this is the current decoupling option pursued by the US.

[81] Covington. 2025. The status of recent legal challenges to the Trump IEEPA tariffs and implications for importers. https://www.cov.com/en/news-and-insights/insights/2025/06/the-status-of-recent-legal-challenges-to-the-trump-ieepa-tariffs-and-implications-for-importers. Accessed 23 June 2025. Stohr, Greg. 2025. Supreme Court refuses to expedite challenge to Trump's tariffs. Bloomberg. https://www.msn.com/en-us/money/markets/supreme-court-refuses-to-expedite-challenge-to-trump-s-tariffs/ar-AA1H7dGv?ocid=BingNewsSerp. Accessed 23 June 2025.

(b) **The expanded decoupling option:** This option goes a step further than the managed decoupling option by expanding the coverage of the decoupling process to include Western allies and security partners such as Canada, Australia, the UK and perhaps, even Europe. Exercising this option means that the US will have to use its diplomatic and political clout to convince its Western allies that decoupling in all technology sectors is in the long-term security interest of not just the US but also the West in general. Following the US lead, under the strategic decoupling option, the allied Western nations will also divest from China and may begin efforts like the US. The expanded decoupling option will carry immense economic consequences for the West. Following this option may even prompt China closing off its market access to the US and all its Western security allies that it will come to see as adversaries.

(c) **The deeper decoupling option:** This option would see a full and complete decoupling from China in all sectors (down to the most basic and intermediate sectors of goods), and it will not just be limited to sectors of strategic value. Purely speaking from an economic standpoint, this decoupling option is not only irrational, but it will also send shockwaves through the global trade and finance systems. It is well worth noting that despite the US decoupling efforts, both economies are deeply intertwined, with US exporting US $143 billion worth of exports to China in 2024 and China exporting US $438.9 billion to the US.[82] Businesses in the US take advantage of Chinese industrial efficiencies and gain access to a gigantic consumer market, while the Chinese rely on US capital injection, access to technology and trade on the US financial markets. A deeper US–China severance will not bring any noticeable advantage but would rather exponentially increase costs, disrupt trade links, and reduce industrial efficiencies.

The decoupling process, and the expanding use of export controls as an instrument in the decoupling process, are not driven by economics. Decoupling is purely a national security project, but its economic fallout cannot be ignored. The risk mitigation logic driving the US policy thinking is that in the event China crosses the Formosa Straits or aggressively annexes territory in South China Sea, or attacks US cyber infrastructure, the US could become exposed to supply chain disruptions, industrial decay, and eventually loss of regional control. The US strategists are willing to sacrifice cost savings and industrial efficiencies to ameliorate such risks.

China recognises that the decoupling process with the US within the larger redesign of globalisation is now an overtly declared US project. Beijing is leveraging the sheer size of its domestic market to pursue technological self-reliance and encourage "dual circulation" as a strategy to transition from export-led growth model to a more inward-looking state-led growth model.[83] In doing so China seeks

[82] Office of the USTR. 2024. "China trade summary." https://ustr.gov/countries-regions/china-mongolia-taiwan/peoples-republic-china. Accessed 23 June 2025.

[83] Yifu, Lin Justin, & Xiaobing Wang. 2022. Dual circulation: A new structural economics view of development. *Journal of Chinese Economic and Business Studies* 20: 303–322. Tang, Frank. 2020.

to reduce dependence on imported technologies, Chinese-localised innovation along with autonomous supply chains that are less prone to interference by the US and its Western allies.

Both countries are now preparing for a world which harks back to the era of mercantilism where economic interdependence is gradually minimised and preferably replaced with self-sufficiency. Like in the era of mercantilism, imports would be looked upon as a necessary evil, something to be avoided as much as possible or, where necessary, sourced from an allied bloc, or trading eco-systems consisting exclusively of security allies.

The evolving US and China dynamics points toward a future of **managed decoupling** as the likely direction of the US–China strategic competition as opposed to the expanded or deeper decoupling options (as outlined above). Europe and major Western allies are not yet fully onboard and may need further convincing since they see the dangers of the Thucydides Trap where the US and China find themselves.

In the near term, managed decoupling will create parallel supply chain ecosystems—one centred around the US and its allies, and another feeding China. These parallel supply chains will be led by competing governance models based on distinct standards, increased indigenisation, self-sufficiency, and restricted data flows. Trade and investment may continue in essential sectors such as food and life-saving medicines, but the deeper integration and outward production processing that defined the past three decades will no longer drive the global economy. The emergence of new parallel supply chains feeding China offers many developing countries (trapped in a basic commodity-driven "specialised prison") a non-Western alternative path to economic development.

Although not necessarily a better course of action, maintaining access to the Chinese market at a time when the US is closing its door would make developing countries in the Chinese-led bloc, a stakeholder in China's advancement. China's extensive investment of US $65 billion over the last decade in Indonesia's Nickel refinery sector is a perfect example where an economy seeking to develop downstream sector used export restrictions to attract FDI into its economy, albeit with drastic consequences for the local inhabitants.[84]

The mechanics of the "new", de-coupled globalisation will come to be defined by the emergence of parallel supply chains, a "normalised" use of export restrictions on natural resources, China's reactionary export controls on REEs and strategic

Explainer: What is China's dual circulation economic strategy and why is it important? South China Morning Post (SCMP). https://www.scmp.com/economy/china-economy/article/3110184/what-chinas-dual-circulation-economic-strategy-and-why-it. Accessed 23 June 2025.

[84] Zadeh, John. 2025a. China's investment in Indonesia's nickel industry: Impact on local communities. Discovery Alert https://discoveryalert.com.au/news/chinas-investment-indonesia-nickel-industry-2025/#:~:text=Over%20the%20past%20decade%2C%20China%20has%20invested%20over,chains%2C%20as%20nickel%20is%20essential%20for%20lithium-ion%20batteries. Accessed 23 June 2025. See also Verrender, Ian. 2025. "Lucky country: The critical minerals war." *Australian Foreign Affairs* 2: June 2025, at 61–64.

minerals, and the US efforts to re-shore domestic manufacturing while limiting China's access to advanced technology.

Both China and the US now understand that economic instruments can be used to shape strategic outcomes. In the new environment, export controls have come out of obscurity and are now instruments of influence and security. The outcome of the successive trade talks in 2025 between the US and China underscore the new reality: temporary compromises may be made in the short-term, but the underlying trajectory of decoupling will continue. Driven by national security imperatives rather than economic logic, decoupling is the fulcrum around which future geo-economic interests will be based and globalisation, as we know it, disrupted.

References

Aaron. 2025. The chip war under Trump. *Politico*. https://www.politico.com/newsletters/digital-future-daily/2025/06/10/the-chip-war-under-trump-00397048. Accessed 25 June 2025.

ABC News. 2025. *Donald Trump's sweeping global tariffs blocked by US Court of International Trade*. https://www.abc.net.au/news/2025-05-29/donald-trump-trade-tariffs-block-us-court/105351386. Accessed 22 June 2025.

Allen, Gregory C., and Emily Benson. 2023. *Clues to the U.S.-Dutch-Japanese semiconductor export controls deal are hiding in plain sight*. Center for Strategic & International Studies. https://www.csis.org/analysis/clues-us-dutch-japanese-semiconductor-export-controls-deal-are-hiding-plain-sight. Accessed 23 June 2025.

Ames National Laboratory. 2024. *CMI project 1.1.18: Gallium, indium and germanium extraction from zinc residue produced for steel wastes*. https://www.ameslab.gov/cmi-project-1-1-18-gallium-indium-and-germanium-extraction-from-zinc-residue-produced-for-steel#:~:text=This%20project%20will%20examine%20novel%20pyrometallurgical%20and%20hydrometallurgical,a%20sustainable%20domestic%20supply%20of%20these%20critical%20materials. Accessed 23 June 2025.

Bacchus, James. 2022. *Trade Links*. Cambridge, UK: Cambridge University Press.

Bao, Anniek. 2025. Economy China retaliates with additional tariffs of up to 15% on select U.S. imports starting Feb. 10. *CNBC*. https://www.cnbc.com/2025/02/04/china-levies-tariffs-on-select-us-imports-starting-feb-10.html#:~:text=China%20retaliates%20with%20additional%20tariffs%20of%20up%20to,controls%20on%20certain%20products%20related%20to%20critical%20minerals.?msockid=3ca814d307f56ccd3098010d06406d2b. Accessed 23 June 2025.

Baskaran, Gracelin, and Meredith Schwartz. 2025a. *Trump strikes a deal to restore rare Earths access*. Center for Strategic and International Studies. https://www.csis.org/analysis/trump-strikes-deal-restore-rare-earths-access. Accessed 4 August 2025.

Baskaran, Gracelin, and Meredith Schwartz. 2025b. *The consequences of China's new rare Earths export restrictions*. Center for Strategic and International Studies. https://www.csis.org/analysis/consequences-chinas-new-rare-earths-export-restrictions. Accessed 24 June 2025.

Bhala, Raj. 2015. *International Trade Law: An interdisciplinary, non-western textbook*. Vol. 2. 4th ed. LexisNexis.

Buckland. 2025. *BIS drafting 50% rule to expand entity list restrictions*. https://buckland.com/news/bis-drafting-50-rule-to-expand-entity-list-restrictions/?. Accessed 18 August 2025.

CBS News. 2024. *Canada and U.S. make first co-investment in critical minerals producers*. https://www.cbc.ca/news/politics/canada-us-invest-critical-mineral-production-1.7206655. Accessed 25 June 2025.

Chang, Ha-Joon. 2005. *Kicking away the ladder*. London, UK: Anthem Press.

CHIPS and Science Act of 2022, Pub L No 117-167, 136 Stat.1366.

CKGSB Knowledge. 2025. *Rare Earth resources: China's domination of a key global market.* https://english.ckgsb.edu.cn/knowledge/article/china-dominance-of-rare-earth-and-impact-on-global-market/#:~:text=Almost%2090%25%20of%20global%20rare%20earths%20processing%20is,to%20do%20this%20for%20two%20decades%2C%E2%80%9D%20says%20Andrews-Speed. Accessed 23 June 2025.

CNBC. 2024. *The US needs more of this critical metal—and China owns 80% of its supply chain.* https://www.cnbc.com/2024/07/03/us-needs-more-tungsten-china-is-a-major-supplier-of-the-critical-metal.html?msockid=3ca814d307f56ccd3098010d06406d2b. Accessed 23 June 2025.

Congressional Research Service (CRS). 2021. *The U.S. export control system and the Export Control Reform Act of 2018.* https://www.congress.gov/crs_external_products/R/PDF/R46814/R46814.6.pdf. Accessed 23 June 2025.

Covington. 2025. *The status of recent legal challenges to the Trump IEEPA tariffs and implications for importers.* https://www.cov.com/en/news-and-insights/insights/2025/06/the-status-of-recent-legal-challenges-to-the-trump-ieepa-tariffs-and-implications-for-importers. Accessed 23 June 2025.

D'Ambrosio, Anna, and Katiuscia Lavoratori. 2025. Reshoring to survive? The other side of de-globalization. *Journal of Industrial & Business Economics.* https://doi.org/10.1007/s40812-025-00342.

DiPippo, Gerard, and Benjamin Lenain. 2025. *Testing self-reliance: What the trade war reveals about China's vulnerabilities and power.* Rand Corporation. https://www.rand.org/pubs/commentary/2025/06/testing-self-reliance-what-the-trade-war-reveals-about.html. Accessed 23 June 2025.

Easley, Mikayla. 2023. *U.S. begins forging rare Earth supply chain.* https://www.nationaldefensemagazine.org/articles/2023/2/10/us-begins-forging-rare-earth-supply-chain. Accessed 23 June 2025.

Edwards, John. 2023. *Chips, subsidies, security, and great power competition.* Lowy Institute Analysis. https://www.lowyinstitute.org/publications/chips-subsidies-security-great-power-competition. Accessed 23 June 2025.

Energy Fuels (EF). 2025. *US based energy fuels poised to produce six of the seven rare Earth Oxides now subject to Chinese export controls at scale.* https://investors.energyfuels.com/2025-04-17-U-S-Based-Energy-Fuels-Poised-to-Produce-Six-of-the-Seven-Rare-Earth-Oxides-Now-Subject-to-Chinese-Export-Controls-at-Scale. Accessed 23 June 2025.

Executive Office of the President, Office of the US Trade Representative (USTR). 2023. *United States and Japan sign critical minerals agreement.* https://ustr.gov/about-us/policy-offices/press-office/press-releases/2023/march/united-states-and-japan-sign-critical-minerals-agreement. Accessed 23 June 2025.

Export Control Reform Act (ECRA) §1741(2), P.L. 115–232 (August 13, 2018), codified as amended at 50 U.S.C. §4801(2); *Export Administration Act (EAA) of 1979, Pub. L. 96-72; Export Administration Regulations (EAR),* 15 C.F.R. § 730.

Financial Post. 2025. *Canagold identifies significant antimony production potential at New Polaris.* https://financialpost.com/pmn/business-wire-news-releases-pmn/canagold-identifies-significant-antimony-production-potential-at-new-polaris. Accessed 23 June 2025.

Freifeld, Karen, and Toby Sterling. 2024. US wants Netherlands, Japan to further restrict chip-making equipment to China. *Reuters.* https://www.reuters.com/world/us-pushing-netherlands-japan-restrict-more-chipmaking-equipment-china-source-2024-06-18/. Accessed 23 June 2025.

Gan, Nectar. 2025. Trump says Xi agreed to restart flow of crucial minerals, but analysts say China won't give up its 'rare earth card'. *CNN.* https://edition.cnn.com/2025/06/07/business/trump-xi-restart-rare-earths-flow-intl-hnk. Accessed 22 June 2025.

Gan, Nectar, and John Liu. 2025. US and China agree on plan to ease export controls after trade talks in London. *CNN.* https://edition.cnn.com/2025/06/10/business/us-china-trade-talks-london-agreement-intl-hnk. Accessed 23 June 2025.

Gao, Dan, and Dong Wang. 2024. New trends of US economic and trade policy toward China and China's responses from the perspective of friend-shoring. *Journal of WTO and China* 14 (4): 87. 91–94.

Ghori, Umair. 2015. An epic mess: 'Exhaustible natural resources' and the future of export restraints after the *China—rare Earths* decision. *Melbourne Journal of International Law* 16:397–430. 408–414.

Ghori, Umair. 2020. Three lessons on the construction of export controls under WTO law. *The University of Queensland Law Journal* 39:85–115.

Ghori, Umair. 2023. *Export restrictions and export controls—From WTO to the realm of global security*. Cheltenham, UK: Edward Elgar Publishing.

Ghori, Umair. 2025. *Semiconductor skirmish: Unpacking US export controls against China*. Paper presented at ILA-ASIL Asia-Pacific Research Forum, Taipei, Taiwan: 7–8 July

Government of Canada. 2024. *Government of Canada and the United States co-invest to strengthen critical mineral value chain*. https://www.canada.ca/en/natural-resources-canada/news/2024/05/government-of-canada-and-the-united-states-co-invest-to-strengthen-critical-mineral-value-chains.html. Accessed 23 June 2025.

Gruzer, Marina. 2025. *How do China's export restrictions on rare Earths impact global trade and major industries*? Bloomsbury Intelligence and Security Institute. https://bisi.org.uk/reports/how-do-chinas-export-restrictions-on-rare-earths-impact-global-trade-and-major-industries#:~:text=China%27s%20tightening%20of%20rare%20earth%20element%20%28REE%29%20export,REE%20mining%20and%2090%25%20of%20global%20REE%20refining. Accessed 23 June 2025.

Gur, Nurullah, and Serif Dilek. 2023. US–China economic rivalry and the reshoring of global supply chains. *The Chinese Journal of International Politics* 16:61–83.

Hale, Thomas, and Christian Davies. 2025. Chip software makers say US restrictions on sales to China lifted. *Financial Times*. https://www.ft.com/content/36b12cb9-68d4-4e31-84e8-6d96d676b45d?. Accessed 17 August 2025.

He, Kai. 2025. The global costs of the US-China tariff war are mounting. And the worst may be yet to come. *The Conversation*. https://theconversation.com/the-global-costs-of-the-us-china-tariff-war-are-mounting-and-the-worst-may-be-yet-to-come-254583?utm_source=clipboard&utm_medium=bylinecopy_url_button. Accessed 23 June 2025.

Higgins, Sean. 2022. Utah's West Desert could hold a decade's worth of indium. *KUER*. https://www.kuer.org/business-economy/2022-11-14/utahs-west-desert-could-hold-a-decades-worth-of-indium. Accessed 25 June 2025.

Home, Andy. 2025. A tungsten-tipped answer to the West's critical metals dilemma. *Reuters*.. https://www.reuters.com/markets/commodities/tungsten-tipped-answer-wests-critical-metals-dilemma-andy-home-2025-02-19/. Accessed 23 June 2025.

Islam, Faisal. 2025. The secretive US factory that lays bare the contradiction in Trump's America First plan. *BBC*. https://www.bbc.com/news/articles/cwywj0zgzwxo. Accessed 23 June 2025.

Jeyaratnam, Miranda. 2025. How Trump's tariff unpredictability hurts businesses and consumers—and could help China. *Time*. https://time.com/7286933/trump-trade-war-us-china-tariff-pause-businesses-costs-uncertainty/. Accessed 23 June 2025.

Joyner, Daniel H. 2004. Restructuring the multilateral export control regime system. *Journal of Conflict Security Law* 9:181–211.

Kazeki. 2005. *Looking beyond tariffs: The role of non-tariff barriers in world trade*. Paris: OECD Publishing.

Kennedy, Scott. 2025. Does Xi have Trump's number? *Foreign Polic*.. https://foreignpolicy.com/2025/06/16/china-rare-earths-trade-war-deal-trump. Accessed 3 August 2025.

Kowalski, Przemyslaw, and Clarisse Legendre. 2023. *Raw materials critical for the green transition: Production, international trade, and export restrictions* https://www.oecd.org/en/publications/raw-materials-critical-for-the-green-transition_c6bb598b-en.html. Accessed 23 June 2025.

Krach, Keith. 2022. The Bipartisan CHIPS Act—and a United U.S.—are China's biggest fear. *Newsweek*. https://www.newsweek.com/bipartisan-chips-act-united-us-are-chinas-biggest-fear-opinion-1728573. Accessed 23 June 2025.

Latham, Andrew. 2025. Are US and China really in a Thucydides trap? *Asia Times*. https://asiatimes.com/2025/04/are-us-and-china-really-in-a-thucydides-trap/#. Accessed 24 June 2025.

Liu, John, and Phil Mattingly. 2025. China has a valuable card to play as it holds trade talks with the US. *CNN*. https://edition.cnn.com/2025/06/09/business/us-china-fresh-trade-talks-london-intl-hnk. Accessed 23 June 2025.

Lv, Amy, Lewis Jackson, and Ashtitha Shivaprasad. 2025. China expands key mineral export controls after US imposes tariffs. *Reuters*. https://www.reuters.com/world/china/china-expands-critical-mineral-export-controls-after-us-imposes-tariffs-2025-02-04/. Accessed 26 June 2025.

Mann, Tobias. 2025. Chip designers' latest casualties in US-China trade war. *The Register*. https://www.theregister.com/2025/05/30/eda_us_china/. Accessed 23 June 2025.

Mineiro, Michael C. 2012. *Space technology export controls and international cooperation in outer space*. Montreal: Springer.

Mining.com. 2024. *US House of Representatives approves 2024 Critical Mineral Consistency Act*. https://www.mining.com/us-house-of-representatives-approves-2024-critical-mineral-consistency-act/. Accessed 25 June 2025

Moody's. 2025. *The BIS and the proposed 50% rule—what's in the pipeline for export controls?* https://www.moodys.com/web/en/us/kyc/resources/insights/bis-and-the-proposed-50-rule-whats-in-the-pipeline-for-export-controls.html. Accessed 18 August 2025.

MP Materials. 2025. *Maaden and MP Materials collaborate to establish full value chain for rare Earth magnetics*. https://investors.mpmaterials.com/investor-news/news-details/2025/Maaden-and-MP-Materials-Collaborate-to-Establish-Full-Value-Chain-for-Rare-Earth-Magnetics/default.aspx. Accessed 23 June 2025.

National Energy Technology Laboratory. 2024. *Two additional projects selected to advance rare Earth element and critical mineral and material processing technologies using coal and coal byproducts as Feedstocks*. https://www.netl.doe.gov/node/13953#:~:text=%E2%80%94%20The%20U.S.%20Department%20of%20Energy%20%28DOE%29%20today,materials%20from%20coal%2C%20coal%20wastes%2C%20and%20coal%20by-products. Accessed 23 June 2025.

North American Mining. 2024. *DoD invests millions in Terbium production*. https://northamericanmining.com/index.php/2024/09/16/dod-invests-millions-in-terbium-production/#:~:text=The%20U.S.%20Department%20of%20Defense%20has%20announced%20a,rare%20earth%20magnets%20in%20many%20key%20defense%20systems. Accessed 21 June 2025.

Nouwens, Meia, Maria Shagina, and Erik Green. 2025. *China's use of export controls*. International Institute of Strategic Studies. https://www.iiss.org/online-analysis/charting-china/2025/02/chinas-use-of-export-controls/. Accessed 23 June 2025.

Office of the USTR. 2024. *China trade summary*. https://ustr.gov/countries-regions/china-mongolia-taiwan/peoples-republic-china. Accessed 23 June 2025.

Park, Hey-Jin. 2024. *U.S. looks to South Korean mine to boost Tungsten supply*. https://www.ctol.digital/news/us-seeks-tungsten-source-in-south-korea/. Accessed 23 June 2025.

Potkin, Fanny, Karen Freifeld, and Jun Yuan Yong. 2025. Exclusive: US embeds trackers in AI chip shipments to catch diversions to China, sources say. *Reuters*. https://www.reuters.com/world/china/us-embeds-trackers-ai-chip-shipments-catch-diversions-china-sources-say-2025-08-13/. Accessed 18 August 2025.

Reuters. 2022. *WTO backs EU in nickel dispute, Indonesia plans appeal*. https://www.reuters.com/markets/commodities/indonesia-plans-appeal-after-losing-wto-nickel-dispute-with-eu-2022-11-30/. Accessed 23 June 2025.

Reuters. 2025. *Nvidia says its chips have no 'backdoors' after China flags H20 security concerns*. https://www.reuters.com/world/china/nvidia-says-its-chips-have-no-backdoors-after-china-flags-h20-security-concerns-2025-07-31/?. Accessed 18 August 2025.

Shang, Carrie Shu. 2024. Mapping export control extraterritoriality in the US—China technology decoupling. *Journal of World Trade* 58:545–570.

Shivakumar, Sujai, Charles Wessner, and Thomas Howell. 2024. *Balancing the ledger: Export controls on U.S. chip technology to China*. Center for Strategic and International Studies. https://www.csis.org/analysis/balancing-ledger-export-controls-us-chip-technology-china. Accessed 18 August 2025.

Shivaprasad, Ashtitha, Amy Lv, and Lewis Jackson. 2025. What are the five critical metal exports restricted by China? *Reuters*. https://www.reuters.com/markets/commodities/what-are-five-new-critical-metal-exports-restricted-by-china-2025-02-04/. Accessed 23 June 2025.

Stockhead. 2023. *American West Metals' West Desert now hosts the only indium resource in the US*. https://stockhead.com.au/resources/american-west-metals-west-desert-now-hosts-the-only-indium-resource-in-the-us/. Accessed 25 June 2025.

Stohr, Greg. 2025. Supreme Court refuses to expedite challenge to Trump's tariffs. *Bloomberg*. https://www.msn.com/en-us/money/markets/supreme-court-refuses-to-expedite-challenge-to-trump-s-tariffs/ar-AA1H7dGv?ocid=BingNewsSerp. Accessed 23 June 2025.

Sugihartono, Sekarsari. 2024. Indonesia's trade dispute on nickel ore in the WTO: Current progress and developments. *Modern Diplomacy*. https://moderndiplomacy.eu/2024/10/28/indonesias-trade-dispute-on-nickel-ore-in-the-wto-current-progress-and-developments/. Accessed 23 June 2025.

Suominen, Kati. 2025. *How should Trump 2.0 secure global supply chains?* Hinrich Foundation. https://www.hinrichfoundation.com/research/wp/trade-and-geopolitics/how-should-trump-2-0-secure-global-supply-chains/. Accessed 25 June 2025.

Tan, Catherine. 2024. *Breaking the circuit: US–China semiconductor controls*. Foreign Policy Research Institute. https://www.fpri.org/article/2024/09/breaking-the-circuit-us-china-semiconductor-controls/. Accessed 23 June 2025.

Tang, Frank. 2020. *Explainer: What is China's dual circulation economic strategy and why is it important?* South China Morning Post (SCMP). https://www.scmp.com/economy/china-economy/article/3110184/what-chinas-dual-circulation-economic-strategy-and-why-it. Accessed 23 June 2025.

The American Presidency Project. 2022. ICYMI: The CHIPS Act has already sparked $200 billion in private investments for U.S. semiconductor production. https://www.presidency.ucsb.edu/documents/icymi-the-chips-act-has-already-sparked-200-billion-private-investments-for-us. Accessed 23 June 2025.

The Wassenaar Arrangement. https://www.wassenaar.org/about-us/. Accessed 22 May 2025.

The White House. 2022. *FACT SHEET: CHIPS and Science Act will lower costs, create jobs, strengthen supply chains, and counter China*. https://bidenwhitehouse.archives.gov/briefing-room/statements-releases/2022/08/09/fact-sheet-chips-and-science-act-will-lower-costs-create-jobs-strengthen-supply-chains-and-counter-china/. Accessed 23 June 2025.

Unglesbee, Ben. 2023. *China moves to limit exports of Graphite*. Supply Chain Dive. https://www.supplychaindive.com/news/china-bands-graphite-exports-EV/697528/. Accessed 23 June 2025.

US Department of Commerce (DOC). 2019. *A federal strategy to ensure secure and reliable supplies of critical minerals*. https://www.federalregister.gov/documents/2017/12/26/2017-27899/a-federal-strategy-to-ensure-secure-and-reliable-supplies-of-critical-minerals

US Department of Commerce BIS. 2022. *Commerce implements new export controls on advanced computing and semiconductor manufacturing items to the People's Republic of China (PRC)*. https://www.bis.doc.gov/index.php/documents/about-bis/newsroom/press-releases/3158-2022-10-07-bis-press-release-advanced-computing-and-semiconductor-manufacturing-controls-final/file. Accessed 18 August 2025.

US Department of Commerce BIS. 2023. *Export controls on semiconductor manufacturing items (SME IFR) and implementation of additional export controls: Certain advanced computing items; Supercomputer and semiconductor end use; Updates and corrections*. https://www.bis.gov/media/documents/semiconductors-advanced-computing-2023-frequently-asked-questions.pdf. Accessed 18 August 2025.

US Department of Commerce BIS. 2024. *Department of Commerce implements controls on quantum computing and other advanced technologies alongside international partners*. https://www.bis.gov/media/documents/quantum-press-release-final.pdf. Accessed 18 August 2025.

US Department of Energy. 2025. *What are critical materials and critical minerals*. Critical Minerals & Materials Program. https://www.energy.gov/cmm/what-are-critical-materials-and-critical-minerals. Accessed 23 June 2025.

US Department of Energy (DOE). 2025. *DOE issues notice of intent for funding in strengthening domestic critical materials processing and manufacturing to enhance national security*. https://www.energy.gov/mesc/articles/doe-issues-notice-intent-funding-strengthening-domestic-critical-materials-processing. Accessed 23 June 2025.

US DOE. 2023a. *Bipartisan Infrastructure Law: Rare Earth element demonstration facility*. https://www.energy.gov/fecm/funding-notice-bipartisan-infrastructure-law-rare-earth-element-demonstration-facility#:~:text=On%20April%204%2C%202023%2C%20the%20U.S.%20Department%20of,America%20and%20reduce%20reliance%20on%20competitors%20like%20China. Accessed 23 June 2025.

US DOE. 2023b. *Department of Energy announces teams selected to explore critical mineral extraction from ocean macroalgae*. https://www.energy.gov/arctic/articles/us-department-energy-announces-teams-selected-explore-critical-mineral-extraction. Accessed 26 June 2025.

US DOE. 2024. *US Department of Energy invests $17 million to shore up America's energy security with robust supply chain for critical materials*. https://www.energy.gov/articles/us-department-energy-invests-17-million-shore-americas-energy-security-robust-supply-chain. Accessed 25 June 2025.

US Government Accountability Office (GAO). 2024a. *Technology assessment—critical metals: Status, challenges, and policy options for recovery from nontraditional sources*. https://www.gao.gov/assets/gao-24-106395.pdf. Accessed 23 June 2025.

US Government Accountability Office (GAO). 2024b. *Export controls: Commerce implemented advanced semiconductor rules and took steps to address compliance challenges*. https://www.gao.gov/assets/gao-25-107386.pdf. Accessed 18 August 2025.

Verrender, Ian. 2025. Lucky country: The critical minerals war. *Australian Foreign Affairs* 2:61–64.

Vicente, Agustin de. 2025. China imposes export restrictions on critical metals in response to US tariffs. *Mining Reporters*. https://www.miningreporters.com/noticia/news/2025/02/china-imposes-export-restrictions-on-critical-metals. Accessed 4 February 2025.

Walter, Neetika. 2025. China pauses rare Earth export restrictions on 28 US entities after trade truce. *Interesting Engineering*. https://interestingengineering.com/energy/china-lifts-export-bans-on-rare-earths. Accessed 23 June 2025.

WTO. 2001. *United States—Measures treating export restraints as subsidies* ('US—Export Restraints'). https://docs.wto.org/dol2fe/Pages/SS/directdoc.aspx?filename=q:/WT/DS/194-4.pdf&Open=True. Accessed 24 June 2025.

WTO. 2011. *China—Measures related to the exportation of various raw materials* ('China—Raw Materials'). https://docs.wto.org/dol2fe/Pages/SS/directdoc.aspx?filename=Q:/WT/DS/398RA1.pdf&Open=True. Accessed 24 June 2025.

WTO. 2012. *China—Raw materials*. https://www.wto.org/english/tratop_e/dispu_e/394_395_398abr_e.pdf. Accessed 24 June 2025.

Wu, Jessie. 2024. *TSMC secures $6.6 billion US government subsidy for Arizona semiconductors expansion*. Technode. https://technode.com/2024/04/09/tsmc-secures-6-6-billion-us-government-subsidy-for-arizona-semiconductor-expansion/#:~:text=The%20US%20Department%20of%20Commerce,advanced%20semiconductor%20manufacturing%20facilities%20in. Accessed 24 June 2025.

Wu, Zijang, and Eleanor Olcott. 2025. Nvidia AI chips worth $1bn smuggled to China after Trump export controls. *Financial Times*. https://www.ft.com/content/6f806f6e-61c1-4b8d-9694-90d7328a7b54. Accessed 18 August 2025.

Xu, Jiayan, and Eddie Lam. 2024. *A review of foreign sanctions and export control developments involving China*. Alix Partners. https://www.alixpartners.com/media/ydzcm24t/2024-sanction-ye-review-china.pdf. Accessed 23 June 2025.

Yang, Zeyi. 2025. Bad news for China: Rare Earth element aren't that rare. *Wired*. https://www.wired.com/story/rare-earth-minerals-china-tariffs/. Accessed 23 June 2025.

Yifu, Lin Justin, and Xiaobing Wang. 2022. Dual circulation: A new structural economics view of development. *Journal of Chinese Economic and Business Studies* 20:303–322.

Zadeh, John. 2025a. *China's investment in Indonesia's nickel industry: Impact on local communities*. Discovery Alert. https://discoveryalert.com.au/news/chinas-investment-indonesia-nickel-industry-2025/#:~:text=Over%20the%20past%20decade%2C%20China%20has%20invested%20over,chains%2C%20as%20nickel%20is%20essential%20for%20lithium-ion%20batteries. Accessed 23 June 2025.

Zadeh, John. 2025b. *China tightens export permits for rare Earth shipments in 2025*. Discovery Alert. https://discoveryalert.com.au/news/rare-earth-export-permits-2025-strategic-importance/#:~:text=In%202014%2C%20the%20WTO%20ruled%20against%20China%20%28case,that%20its%20export%20restrictions%20violated%20international%20trade%20agreements. Accessed 23 June 2025.

Zhen, Liu. 2025. China's critical minerals dominance threatens US military supply chain, report says. *South China Morning Post*. https://www.scmp.com/news/china/military/article/3308045/chinas-critical-minerals-dominance-threatens-us-military-supply-chain-report-says. Accessed 24 June 2025.

Chapter 10
The Clash of Economic Models and the Remaking of World Economics: China and India

Darryl M. Lupton

Abstract Globalisation stands at a critical juncture, its future increasingly shaped by the divergent economic trajectories of China and India. This chapter provides a comparative analysis of these two economic giants, examining how their distinct development models impact both their domestic stability and the international trading system. First, we analyse China's pivotal role, arguing that its state-driven, export-oriented growth has created profound structural imbalances. While this model lifted millions from poverty, it also produced the "China shock" in Western economies and generated vast industrial overcapacity, fuelled by policies that suppress household consumption. We contend that these internal issues are the root cause of escalating global trade tensions. The chapter posits that for its own sustainable growth and the health of the global economy, China must enact deep domestic reforms. These include strengthening the social safety net, reforming the *Hukou* (household registration) and pension systems, and rebalancing the economy towards domestic demand. Second, we present India as a crucial counterpoint. Despite its success in the global services industry, India has failed to develop a comparable manufacturing export base. The analysis identifies key structural impediments hindering its industrial potential: persistent infrastructure deficits, restrictive labour laws, bureaucratic hurdles, and gaps in human capital development. A roadmap for reform is proposed to unlock India's manufacturing capabilities. Ultimately, this chapter argues that the future of a sustainable global economic order depends less on international trade negotiations and more on the willingness of these Asian powers to undertake the fundamental domestic reforms necessary to create more balanced and equitable growth.

D. M. Lupton (✉)
Taipei, Taiwan

U. H. Ghori, J. Farrar (eds.), *Globalisation Disrupted*,
https://doi.org/10.1007/978-981-95-3997-0_10

10.1 Introduction

Globalisation, long seen as a key engine of economic growth and international cooperation, now stands at a crossroads. Especially since 2018, its perceived benefits and vulnerabilities have come under renewed scrutiny, prompting serious debate about its future path. Global trade is shifting away from the previously seamless flow of goods, capital, and information toward more regionalised and politically influenced patterns.[1] Experts now argue that globalisation is not ending—it is evolving as countries derisk their supply chains. This transition marks a critical turning point. Trade flows, supply chains, and investment patterns are adapting to new geopolitical and economic pressures.[2]

What we are witnessing is a recalibration. Firms and governments alike are reconsidering long-held assumptions in light of rising costs, strategic vulnerabilities, and shifting alliances. The new reality is a more fragmented, cautious, and strategically driven global economy. China, as the world's factory and prime exporter, is at the centre of these changes and could decide the future of globalisation. This chapter will primarily focus on the effect that globalisation has had on China and in turn its impact on the global economic system. India's role in global trade will also be examined and evaluated as a rival to the China trade juggernaut.

The functionality of the international trading framework is fundamentally challenged by the existence of pronounced trade disparities, such as the substantial deficit experienced by the United States (the US) and the extensive surplus maintained by China. This chapter will propose a strategic framework for China to contribute to the development of a more equitable and sustainable global trading system, thereby enhancing its long-term viability. The urgency of implementing such reforms will be increasingly evident, as a failure by key international actors like China to address current challenges could precipitate the significant destabilisation, or potentially the collapse, of the multilateral trading framework.

10.2 China's Global Entry

Economists can debate how long modern globalisation has been in effect, but for the People's Republic of China (the PRC) it began with Chinese leader Deng Xiaoping's "reform and opening up" in 1978. From a poor agrarian economy that was closed to the Western world, China's economy faced a period of massive adjustment, yet already by the mid-1980s its gross domestic product (GDP) growth rate was above 14%. By the decade's end, the country's economic growth decelerated considerably.

[1] Jin, Keyu. 2023. *The new China playbook: Beyond socialism and capitalism*. New York: Viking.

[2] Setser, Brad. 2024. The dangerous myth of deglobalization: Misperceptions of the global economy are driving bad policies. Foreign Affairs. https://www.foreignaffairs.com/china/globalization-dangerous-myth-economy-brad-setser. Accessed 20 May 2025.

This slowdown was primarily attributed to the adverse impacts of elevated levels of inflation and pervasive government corruption that led to country-wide protests, the most visible being on Tiananmen square. The harsh crackdown resulted in economic sanctions that would temporarily halt economic progress, but that Western admonishment was short lived, and China's economy soon recovered. However, China's real integration into the global economy started with admission into the World Trade Organisation (the WTO) in 2001. What followed was sustained economic growth never before seen on such a scale. The transformation to Chinese society was immense. Economists also argue over the benefits of globalisation across the world and within societies. For China, it was unequivocally a life-changing opportunity for hundreds of millions, if not a billion people, that previously had lived rural existences not far removed from their ancient ancestors.

10.3 The Mechanisms of China's Manufacturing Growth

The awakening of this "sleeping economic giant" has had Newtonian consequences for manufacturing in other countries, especially in the US. A momentous year for both America and China was 2001. For the US, it was the beginning of the end of its "unipolar decade"—in effect since the collapse of the Soviet Union in 1991—as it began its disastrous "War on Terror" in Afghanistan and Iraq. Instead of spending trillions of dollars on an ill-throughout war, China was in the process of doing the opposite: absorbing and investing trillions of dollars into its domestic economy from its burgeoning exports. Companies in the US moved their factories abroad, in fact, if one factory in a manufacturing sector in the US moved to China, then all the others would have to follow or be outcompeted on prices. What began with low level manufacturing, steadily moved up the value chain to medium-value products as Chinese technology improved.

Chinese economic regulators were astute enough to protect their nascent industries from international competition, allowing them time to first become competitive through domestic competition. In addition, foreign companies wanting to access the Chinese market would often have to open factories in China with a local partner and be obliged to transfer technology to this Chinese partner. This helped accelerate local manufacturers' knowledge of management techniques, best practices and importantly how to manufacture products using cutting edge technology. After serving an "apprentice period", local Chinese manufacturers would have the business nous, technical expertise and market knowledge to now outcompete their former tutors.[3]

China's economic planners had also studiously observed how the four "Asian Tiger" economies (South Korea, Taiwan, Hong Kong, Singapore and preceded by

[3] Leahy, Joe, Nian Liu, and Ryan McMorrow. 2025. The lessons from China's dominance in manufacturing. Financial Times. https://on.ft.com/43ADe7w. Accessed 29 May 2025.

Japan) succeeded in lifting their economies from poor to high income status. This entailed the state choosing a "champion" in a favoured industry and heavily supporting it with cheap loans, tax breaks, subsidies in land purchase, research and development and development of infrastructure to support manufacturing and exports. In South Korea, this chaebol system propelled companies like Samsung, LG, Hyundai and others to dominate the local economy, before relinquishing state support and achieving success abroad. This "developmental state" model differed significantly from pure free-market approaches by using strategic government intervention to build internationally competitive industries.

With the considerable scale of its population and the financial capabilities of local administrations (facilitated by readily available credit), China's central economic planners advanced their development paradigm, integrating unique "Chinese characteristics" to optimise their hybrid economic system. There are many ways to describe China's economic model: a socialist market economy (the official title), state capitalism, developmental state model and mixed economy with Chinese characteristics, among others. The model combines state ownership of commanding heights (banking, energy, telecommunications, and heavy industry) with private enterprise in competitive sectors. The government uses industrial policy, state-owned banks, and Five-Year Plans to direct investment and developmental priorities. It is this economic model that has both elevated China to the world's second largest economy after the US but also produced massive challenges for other national economies and its own internal economy.

10.4 China Shock

China's state capitalism has overwhelmed the global economy. Initially it was a boon as foreign companies could capitalise on China's demographic dividend that ensured a vast and cheap labour pool and a government that did not allow independent labour unions. From exporting less than $10 billion in 1978, China reached $250 billion by the new millennium. Export growth truly accelerated after joining the WTO and reached almost $1.5 trillion in 2008, the worst year of the global financial crisis (the GFC). By 2010, China's economy had overtaken Japan's to take second place after the US.[4] Exports that translated into jobs in China were correspondingly lost in the US. Discontent in the rustbelt of America became more vehement with the GFC exacerbating the financial straits of these blue-collar workers. Industries like steel, automobiles, coal, machinery, furniture, among others, were hard hit by cheaper Chinese exports; moreover, skills transfer to other employment sectors in the US was difficult with underfunded retraining programs. This became known as the "China shock."

[4] World Bank. 2025a. Exports of goods and services (current US$)—China. https://data.worldbank.org/indicator/NE.EXP.GNFS.CD?locations=CN. Accessed 29 May 2025.

This phenomenon was formalised through a 2013 paper by Massachusetts Institute of Technology (MIT) economist David Autor and his colleagues David Dorn and Gordon Hanson. By 2011, almost 2.5 million jobs had been lost overall to this "shock" and the areas affected had not recovered more than a decade later.[5] This sowed the seeds for the rise of populist politicians like Donald Trump that would promise to tackle this problem and bring back manufacturing to the US. During President Trump's first term in office, his administration pushed back on China's trade imbalance with the US and used tariffs as a means to narrow down the trade deficit and attempt to boost American manufacturing.

Despite its inception in 2018 and subsequent interruption by the COVID-19 pandemic, the initiative demonstrated an insufficient impact on job creation and failed to induce a significant resurgence of domestic production. Furthermore, the US overall trade deficit actually worsened by 2020.[6] In his second term, the administration of President Donald Trump has articulated a strategic intensification of tariff implementation. This policy stance is ostensibly predicated on the dual objectives of reducing the prevailing trade deficit and fostering the expansion of domestic manufacturing sectors within the US. Tensions in all facets of the China-US relationship have been deteriorating since the Obama administration, though have reached their nadir with Trump's rhetoric, policies and tariffs against China in 2025. To fully understand how China rose to be the dominant manufacturing power that hollowed out US manufacturing in America's rust belt, together with dominating key strategic industries, a history and analysis of these circumstances is required.

10.5 Drivers of Chinese Industrial Policy and Resulting Trade Disputes

After 1978, the "latent entrepreneurial energies" of the Chinese workers were released by the previously economically repressive Marxist government.[7] With mass urbanisation that provided a cheap and proficient workforce without bothersome independent labour unions, China was set to shake the foundations of economic trade and commerce. This new economic model also underpaid workers relative to their productivity, which has persisted to present times and means that wage earners or "householders" are unable to consume at the rate of workers in

[5] Dizikes, Peter. 2021. Q&A: David Autor on the long afterlife of the 'China Shock.' MIT News. https://news.mit.edu/2021/david-autor-china-shock-persists-1206. Accessed 31 May 2025.

[6] U.S. Bureau of Economic Analysis. 2020. U.S. international trade in goods and services. https://www.bea.gov/index.php/news/2021/us-international-trade-goods-and-services-december-2020. Accessed 22 May 2025.

[7] Pettis, Michael, and Matthew C. Klein. 2020. *Trade wars are class wars: How rising inequality distorts the global economy and threatens international peace*. New Haven: Yale University Press.

other countries.[8] In addition, banks offer a very low interest rate for depositors meaning that households need to save more as their money does not appreciate by much. Due to constrained investment avenues, notably a domestic stock market characterised by significant volatility and perceived unreliability, coupled with stringent regulations on foreign investments, Chinese investors frequently opt to deposit surplus earnings in banking institutions. This provides state banks with significant funds to allocate at low interest rates to "state champions" like Huawei, state owned enterprises (SOEs) or projects considered to be of national strategic importance, like new energy vehicles (NEV), green energy, metallurgy or microchips. These industrial policies by Beijing have led to overinvestment in production facilities, the supply side of the market, housing and infrastructure, that has led to vast structural overcapacity.[9]

Marxist economics tends to focus on production rather than supply and demand pricing mechanics as neoclassical economics might or consumer demand as in Keynesian economics. Because of this alternative theory of viewing economic forces, China is producing far more goods than its domestic economy, or foreign markets, can sustainably absorb.[10] Local workers cannot afford to buy what they produced, and foreign manufacturers are being undercut by unfair (subsidised) competition. Currently, there is a belligerent American administration challenging this trade relationship with China. It is not alone. The European Union (the EU) through the European Commission has used its primary body, the Directorate-General for Trade (the DG TRADE) to investigate dumping and subsidy claims to ensure China is not causing material injury to EU industry. This has resulted in import duties on Chinese electric vehicles (EVs). Canada has also placed duties on Chinese steel, aluminium and vehicles. Reinforcing this Western solidarity, the latest Group of Seven (G7) meeting of finance officials in May 2025 stated in its communique that G7 members would continue to monitor "nonmarket policies and practices".[11]

Moreover, it is not just a Western alliance that has levied tariffs on China but also Global South countries like India, Brazil, Türkiye, Vietnam, and South Africa.[12] Countries' local industries cannot survive China's subsidised exports that threaten to put them out of business. This has been clearly stated by the European Commission

---

[8] National Bureau of Statistics of China. 2025. Households' income and consumption expenditure in 2024. https://www.stats.gov.cn/english/PressRelease/202501/t20250124_1958443.html. Accessed 29 May 2025.

[9] Liu, Zongyuan Zoe. 2024. China's real economic crisis: why Beijing won't give up on a failing model. Foreign Affairs. https://www.foreignaffairs.com/china/chinas-real-economic-crisis-zongyuan-liu. Accessed 29 May 2025.

[10] Harvey, David. 2010. *A companion to Marx's capital*. London: Verso.

[11] McCormick, Myles. 2025. G7 ministers threaten more sanctions against Russia over Ukraine war. Financial Times. https://on.ft.com/4dAMGg6. Accessed 29 May 2025.

[12] Douglas, Jason, Jon Emont, and Samantha Pearson. 2024. China's flood of cheap goods is angering its allies, too. The Wall Street Journal. https://www.wsj.com/world/china/chinas-flood-of-cheap-goods-is-angering-its-allies-too-51284954. Accessed 23 May 2025.

President Ursula von der Leyen who mentioned the "unsustainable" trade imbalances with China and by the former US Treasury Secretary Janet Yellen when she visited China in 2024. Yellen highlighted that such overcapacity, driven by extensive government support, results in artificially low-priced exports that threaten the viability of American and other foreign firms. She warned of "economic dislocation" and that "China is now simply too large for the rest of the world to absorb this enormous capacity."[13]

10.6 China's Investment Model: Overproduction and the Pivot to High-Tech

China's investment model has been highly successful in providing infrastructure to facilitate business and exports. In addition, this model helped to support government targeted industries such as EVs, green technology and telecommunications (particularly in 5G and 6G development) to invest billions in research and development (R&D). To accelerate market leadership and achieve international market dominance via large-scale manufacturing, another method employed by Chinese firms was the acquisition of Western companies for their technological assets and patents. This success, however, presented a challenge for the Chinese economy: production began to exceed both local and international demand.[14] Yet this cycle of overproduction and continued allocation of funds to industries that ought to be shuttered or restructured, is ideological and directed from the central government to local governments, despite awareness that the economy is unbalanced. In fact, this was admitted in 2007 by China's Premier Wen Jiabao, who described the Chinese economy as "unstable, unbalanced, uncoordinated, and unsustainable."[15] The central government sets GDP targets for the national economy and expects local governments to stimulate their economies to achieve these goals and also keep employment steady.

With the unfolding of the GFC in 2007, diminished international demand for Chinese goods prompted economic planners in China to foster growth by stimulating the local housing market. Investment flows were channelled into the real estate industry, initiating a period of significant expansion in the housing market with consistently escalating prices. For most Chinese citizens who could afford to buy an apartment—or even two or three—this represented an investment opportunity with

[13]Yellen, Janet L. 2024. Remarks by Secretary of the Treasury Janet L. Yellen at a press conference. U.S. Department of the Treasury. https://home.treasury.gov/news/press-releases/jy2241. Accessed 23 May 2025.

[14]Pettis, Michael. 2014. *The great rebalancing: Trade, conflict, and the perilous road ahead for the world economy*. Updated Edition. Princeton, NJ: Princeton University Press.

[15]Wen, J. 2011. Report on the work of the government. In: Delivered at the fourth session of the eleventh national people's congress. http://www.npc.gov.cn/npc/index.html. Accessed 20 May 2025.

far better gains than low interest rates in a state bank. Accordingly, a housing bubble developed and the central government elected to enforce the "Three Red Lines" policy in 2020 that would reign in profligate property developers who were overly indebted and similarly discourage people from speculating on the housing market instead of buying homes for living in.[16] However, with the property market now depressed, and previously representing a large share of the economy (between 25–30% with downstream industries included), the economy required impetus from an alternative growth driver. The options were to stimulate consumption or increase exports—the demand and supply sides of the economy.

The supply side was chosen, and investment was channelled towards production forces like new factories, industrial robots, and more subsidies for EVs and other strategic sectors. This was in fact an extension of the government's "Made in China 2025" program that began in 2015. This recognised the need for China to elevate its manufacturing from low and medium value levels that were more labour-intensive, to more technology-intensive areas that would make it more independent of foreign inputs. These areas included robotics, aerospace, advanced rail, biopharma, AI, and quantum computing. It is worth noting that an endorsement of the success of this initiative, that included previous decades of investment in Science, Technology, Engineering, and Mathematics (STEM) subjects, was published in an Australian Strategic Policy Institute (ASPI) report in 2024. Chinese R&D innovation ranked first in 57 of the 64 technologies evaluated, with the US leading in seven.[17]

If these technologies mature and can be commercialised at scale, then a boost will be provided to the Chinese economy. Until then, China is still relying on its regular manufacturing plus its strengths in EVs, battery production, solar panels, and wind turbines. Post-pandemic expansion of Chinese exports has led to heightened pressure on global markets to absorb surplus industrial capacity. Simultaneously, established mechanisms of financial repression, discussed previously, curtail the potential for increased domestic consumption by Chinese households.[18] This represents the core dilemma impacting both the economic trajectory of China and that of the international community. Beijing is aware of the need to stimulate the demand side of the economy, but so far, the measures taken to achieve this are not consequential enough. Despite the provision of consumer subsidies for automobiles, home appliances, and green products, in addition to temporary alleviations in

[16] Asia Society Policy Institute's Center for China Analysis and Stanford Center on China's Economy and Institutions. 2023. China's property sector: A roundtable summary report. https://asiasociety.org/new-report-chinas-property-sector-roundtable-summary-report. Accessed 25 May 2025.

[17] Australian Strategic Policy Institute. 2024. ASPI's two-decade critical technology tracker: The rewards of long-term research investment. https://www.aspi.org.au/report/aspis-two-decade-critical-technology-tracker-the-rewards-of-long-term-research-investment/. Accessed 26 May 2025.

[18] Claudio-Quiroga, Gloria, Luis Alberiko Gil-Alana, and Andoni Maiza Larrarte. 2025. Persistence in China's household consumption level: implications for the new growth model. *Journal of Economic and Finance* 49: 283–298. https://doi.org/10.1007/s12197-025-09709-x.

individual income tax, these interventions are generally considered to be of limited strategic impact due to their short-term focus and piecemeal implementation.

10.7 Addressing China's Economic Imbalances

President Xi is against "welfarism" and handouts; in addition, he favours SOEs over the private sector that mostly produces the innovation and employment but often lacks in the cheap and available finance reserved for SOEs. Persistently declining housing prices, coupled with a deflationary trend in the producer price index (PPI), signal underlying weakness in industrial demand. This PPI deflation, which can be self-reinforcing, has led economists to express concern regarding the potential onset of a deflationary spiral like that experienced by Japan. The resolution of China's deep-seated structural economic issues is heavily reliant on political will to enact difficult and far-reaching policy reforms. Such reforms demand more than broad endorsement from the current leadership; they necessitate the decisive, unambiguous, and proactive support of the figure considered China's most powerful leader of the post-Mao period, Xi Jinping, to ensure effective implementation and overcome potential resistance.

Lee Kuan Yew, Singapore's founder, guided the fledgling country from being poor and undeveloped to a high-income economy. He championed globalisation and welcomed Deng Xiaoping in 1978, who admired Singapore's economy and learned from its development model. It may be time for another lesson, more advice and some inspiration for China's current leader and his economic advisors. If China wishes to further its success as a trading nation, it needs to be, as Lee mentioned, a stakeholder. This means ensuring an equitable global trading system that benefits all. If there is no reciprocity, that is balanced trade, then the other trader will eventually lack the financial capacity to purchase goods and services. It is also important that the population at all levels benefits from the country's success and not just an elite number.[19] Lee Kuan Yew was a social reformer who lifted all classes of people in Singapore to ensure they had an equal opportunity to thrive.[20] China can still learn from Singapore.

[19] Pei, Minxin. 2016. *China's crony capitalism: The dynamics of regime decay.* Cambridge, MA: Harvard University Press.

[20] Allison, Graham, et al. 2013. *Lee Kuan Yew: The Grand Master's Insights on China, the United States, and the World.* Cambridge, MA: The MIT Press.

10.8 Rebalancing China's Economy Through Domestic Reform

To achieve these seemingly straightforward goals, China will need to embark on ambitious reforms that are challenging but might be more palatable than the possibility of a Japan-like economic torpor lasting decades. Some prescriptions are contained in the previously referenced book, *Trade Wars Are Class Wars*.[21] Specifically, the central thesis of this book is that global trade imbalances are not merely the result of international economic competition but are rooted in domestic income inequality within countries. These imbalances emerge when elites suppress wages and consumption to maximise savings and production, leading to excess savings that must be exported abroad, creating trade surpluses.

Trade wars, therefore, are manifestations of domestic class conflicts, where policies benefiting wealthy elites and producers are imposed at the expense of workers and consumers. Therefore, to benefit the householder, or average salaried employee, interest rates need to be raised to increase returns on savings. This will give the saver confidence to spend more. Likewise, a stronger social net is needed to assure the worker that housing, healthcare and education are affordable and can free up discretionary spending. This necessitates that excess housing that is plaguing the Chinese housing market is bought by the state and fashioned into social housing.

Unless the housing slide is arrested, new home seekers will be reluctant to buy if prices keep falling. With about 70% of a Chinese citizen's wealth invested in property, spending confidence will not return unless there is a stable housing market. According to Peking University economist, Yang Yao, Beijing needs to tackle the twin economic threats of the housing crisis and local government debt as priorities. Local government spending accounts for 30% of China's domestic demand and fiscally distressed councils are not paying wages consistently and are in arrears to business owners. Arbitrary fines to bolster revenues are also degrading business confidence. The central government has set aside some funds to settle their debts, but this is only temporary relief. Without more help from the central government, domestic demand and market confidence will not easily return.[22]

10.9 Migrant Workers

A forgotten sector of the Chinese population are the migrant workers. Internal migration in China is one of the largest and most significant demographic movements in the world. It refers primarily to the movement of rural Chinese citizens

[21] Pettis and Klein, *supra*, n.7.

[22] Yao, Yang. 2024. Top economist Yang Yao: Can Beijing save China's economy from real estate and debt? ThinkChina. https://www.thinkchina.sg/economy/top-economist-yang-yao-can-beijing-save-chinas-economy-real-estate-and-debt. Accessed 22 May 2025.

from poorer inland provinces to wealthier urban centres along the eastern coast, for example, Shanghai, Shenzhen, Guangzhou, and Beijing. Since the 1980s, China's economic liberalisation under Deng Xiaoping led to rapid industrialisation and urbanisation, which created a demand for labour in urban areas. However, a key facet of this system that heavily influences the lives of these migrants is the household registration system or *Hukou* system. Introduced in the 1950s, it is a registration policy that ties citizens to a specific location—urban or rural—and determines access to public services like education, healthcare, and housing. Migrant workers retain their rural *Hukou* even if they work in a city for decades. This can mean great difficulty for these workers trying to access city services and usually necessitates them having to leave their children in distant countryside homes being raised by their grandparents.

Yet migrants have formed the backbone of China's low-cost manufacturing, construction, and service sectors. Their labour powered China's economic boom but at a significant social cost. They are vulnerable to poor working conditions, delayed wages and limited legal protections. Additionally, they often live in segregated neighbourhoods and are prevented from buying property in cities. Nevertheless, it has been their remittances that have supported both their children and elderly parents in rural areas. By 2020, over two-thirds of China's working-age population were either migrants or dependent on migrant income. Currently, with 250–300 million migrant labourers, China still has a large labour pool to draw from, though they are rapidly aging and their inequality within China's social system makes them "second-class" citizens in their own country. Field researcher Scott Rozelle has long campaigned on behalf of China's rural community and emphasises the urgent need to invest more in this vast reservoir of human capital through education, healthcare, and *Hukou* reform. The upliftment of this cohort would significantly boost their participation in the national economy and help China to achieve high-income level status. If not, China may fall into the "middle-income trap."[23]

Chinese authorities have made incremental reforms in recent years to expand social services in some cities, including *Hukou* reforms in smaller and mid-sized cities, to allow them to settle permanently. However, major cities are reluctant to do so to manage the strain on infrastructure and local services.[24] However, this is an area that needs faster and more meaningful change. One solution could be converting surplus housing units into social housing for migrants, thereby giving them some domicile stability and financial confidence. If China wants to bolster its consumption and have a wider range of its society meaningfully participating in the economy, then it needs to provide a safety net—socially, legally and economically—to these migrant workers and their families.

[23] Rozelle, Scott, and Natalie Hell. 2020. *Invisible China: How the urban-rural divide threatens China's rise*. Chicago: University of Chicago Press.

[24] Wang, Zheng, Liyue Lin, Shuangshuang Tang, and Yang Xiao. 2023. Migration and migrants in Chinese cities: New trends, challenges and opportunities to theorise with urban China. *Transactions in Planning and Urban Research* 2(4): 317–331. https://doi.org/10.1177/27541223231217431.

10.10 Pension Reform

Pension systems constitute an intersecting concern relative to the urban-rural divide. China has a multi-pillar pension system, but in practice, it is dominated by the first pillar, that is public, pay-as-you-go pensions. For formally employed urban workers, the pension scheme is predominantly funded by employers, with comparatively minor contributions from employees. A separate, state-subsidised program exists for urban and rural individuals engaged in informal employment who are not covered by the plan; this scheme is characterised by low contribution levels. The result is that urban pensions are relatively robust, particularly if one has worked for an SOE. In contrast, rural and informal urban residents receive modest benefits, barely enough for subsistence. As China's demographic ages, the increasing number of retirees is expected to lead to disparate economic outcomes among pensioners. Those with a history of formal urban employment possess the financial capacity for consumption, whereas individuals previously engaged in informal employment or residing in rural areas face considerable economic hardship. The existence of separate schemes reinforces rural-urban inequality, contrary to China's goal of "common prosperity".

Although efforts are being pursued in China to unify pension fund management nationally—with the goals of standardising benefits and effecting inter-regional fiscal redistribution—the path to reform is challenging. The amalgamation of numerous, varied pension schemes into a cohesive system for enhanced equity and efficiency is advancing at a notably slow pace. This limited progress is largely attributable to significant political hurdles, including resistance from entrenched interests, and formidable fiscal challenges that complicate the implementation of a fully centralised and equitable pension structure.[25] With large pension payouts to retirees from SOEs, there is room to narrow the gap between the 100–200 yuan (14–28 USD) per month that rural pensioners might receive. China's pension system reflects the broader economic and social divisions that define much of its post-reform development: relatively strong provisions for the urban core, and meagre protections for the rural and informal periphery. Bridging this divide—through integration, redistribution, and reform—will be crucial to achieving a sustainable and equitable aging society that is able to consume on a more consequential level and help to balance China's overall economy.

[25] Zhang, Xiao, and Chand, Satish. 2024. An analysis of the Chinese pension system pointing to the urgent need for reform. *The Chinese Economy* 58 (2): 174–88. https://doi.org/10.1080/10971475.2024.2384168.

10.11 Common Prosperity

Common prosperity is a socio-economic vision in China emphasising moderate wealth for all rather than allowing a small elite to dominate wealth and opportunity. It aims to reduce income inequality, expand the middle class, and recalibrate China's development model to be more inclusive, sustainable, and equitable. The term has deep roots in the Chinese Communist Party (the CCP) ideology, but was revived and re-emphasised under Xi Jinping in the 2020s as a guiding principle for the next stage of China's economic development, particularly after decades of high-speed growth that created vast regional and class disparities. This is a term previously used by Mao and Deng, though the latter also declared that the new economy would "let some get rich first".

Given the pronounced urban-rural wealth disparity and significant regional economic imbalances—particularly the marked affluence of the coastal belt compared to the western regions—President Xi Jinping's objective of reducing wealth inequality can be understood as consistent with declared socialist principles and as a measure to mitigate potential social instability arising from segments of the population largely excluded from the substantial wealth accumulation experienced in major urban centres. In fact, China's Gini index rating (indicating the level of wealth inequality within a society) is worse with regard to inequality than France, Japan and Taiwan—not an endorsement of a successful socialist economy.[26] There are challenges to achieving this goal of common prosperity, but these need to be swiftly overcome if China wishes to balance its own economy and the global trading system.

10.12 Suppressed Consumption: The Core of China's Economic Imbalance

The grand solution for China's economy is uplifting and empowering the spending capacity of the average householder to raise the consumption rate. To illustrate, China's consumption rate is under 40% as a percentage of GDP. To contrast, the US consumption rate is around 70%, the euro area around 55–60%, Japan about 53% and India approaching 60%.[27] China's structurally elevated domestic saving rate results from a decades-long development model that transfers income from households to subsidise the economy's supply side—namely, the production of goods and services. Consequently, household income growth has not kept pace with productivity growth, leaving Chinese households unable to consume a significant portion of

[26] World Bank. 2025b. Gini Index (World Bank Estimate). https://data.worldbank.org/indicator/SI.POV.GINI. Accessed 25 May 2025.

[27] Valev, Neven, Franziska Bieri, and Menna Bizuneh. 2025. China: Household consumption, percent of GDP. The Global Economy https://www.theglobaleconomy.com/china/household_consumption/. Accessed 18 May 2025.

their output. These transfers occur through both overt subsidies and predominantly through implicit and hidden mechanisms.

Examples of the latter encompass directed lending, an undervalued exchange rate, restrictive labour policies, inadequate social welfare systems, and excessive investment in transport infrastructure. Such policies inherently contribute to higher national savings. By subsidising production, China effectively exports its surplus savings and the associated domestic demand shortfall. China's pre-eminence in certain manufacturing industries is not, in itself, incongruous with free trade or comparative advantage. The critical issue for the global economy is the phenomenon of excess savings. This practice is not unique to China; other nations, including Germany and Japan, exhibit similar behaviours. The core problem is that these surplus savings signify the suppression of domestic wages and, therefore, domestic demand, as a strategy to achieve global competitiveness.[28]

10.13 Rectifying Imbalances

To rectify the economic imbalances detailed in this chapter, a series of policy interventions are recommended. Firstly, reforming the *Hukou* registration system is crucial for enhancing labour market efficiency and social equity. Secondly, the social safety net must be substantially reinforced by bolstering healthcare services and pension schemes. Thirdly, a sustainable resolution to local government indebtedness is imperative. Fourthly, restructuring SOEs should be explored as a mechanism to transfer wealth to the household sector. Fifthly, interest rate policies require recalibration to ensure fairer returns for household depositors relative to corporate borrowers. Sixthly, maintaining an appropriately valued Chinese yuan is essential for preserving domestic consumer purchasing power. Seventhly, comprehensive tax reform should aim to reduce the fiscal burden on middle and lower-income earners while increasing it on affluent segments; the VAT system should be revised to enhance household consumption capacity.

Finally, liberalising state-run labour unions to strengthen worker representation and collective bargaining power is recommended to promote wage growth and stimulate consumer demand. These policy recommendations have been proposed by both local and foreign economists and generally accepted by the Chinese government. Implementation is the key issue. These reforms can be destabilising and challenge the wealth and power of Chinese elites. Fortunately for China, in this instance, it is an authoritarian government that controls all levers of power, including finance to the provinces. Most importantly, power is overwhelmingly concentrated in the hands of the "chairman of everything", Xi Jinping. There is massive corruption within the Chinese system, as detailed by Minxin Pei,[29] and President Xi has

[28] Pettis and Klein, *supra*, n.7.

[29] Pei, *supra*, n.19.

targeted this weakness of the Leninist political system, while also eliminating any threats to his rule. This indicates that he is well positioned to tackle these reforms and resist challenges from elites who fear loss of influence and wealth. Xi can work under the banner of "common prosperity" to push through reforms and rebrand it as the "People's Economy for the 21st Century".

10.14 The Political Imperative for Economic Reform in China

There are three credible books that have evaluated "Xi Jinping Thought" and what the ideological views of the Chinese president are. Former Australian Prime Minister Kevin Rudd believes that Xi is driven by ideology and considers the West to be declining and the East rising, particularly China. However, Xi is also in favour of "Marxist Nationalism" with greater state control and central planning.[30] In French journalist Bougon's assessment, Xi manoeuvres between conflicting ideological forces in China, influenced by advisors like Wang Huning.[31] The third book by Tsang and Cheung argues that Xi's ideology is not rigid and instead is about consolidating the party's power rather than about socialism.[32] If these authors are discerning Xi's outlook correctly, it would seem that the focus is on party control, the ascendancy of China and preventing collapse.

Currently, China's economy faces severe challenges as outlined in this chapter. If they are not addressed, China may not collapse but could sink into a 1990s Japan-style stagflation era. This would mean much lower growth and a stall in China's rise to world economic pre-eminence; moreover, with high youth unemployment, there could be another Tiananmen incident due to unrest and disillusionment with the economy. This necessitates Xi to exercise his ideological flexibility and implement the suggested reforms. These proposed measures would likely result in diminished influence for established elite factions, greater public oversight or reorientation of specific state industries, and reduced discretionary power for local governments. Concurrently, the national economy would move towards greater internal balance, with households experiencing increased financial empowerment and enhanced consumption capabilities. An added advantage would be less reliance on external markets. Consequently, China's international trade patterns would likely shift towards higher import volumes and lower export volumes, aiding in the correction of global trade disparities and supporting the continuation of sustainable globalisation. If not, the world may break into mostly separate trading blocs with the US and China

---

[30] Rudd, Kevin. 2024. *On Xi Jinping: How Xi's Marxist nationalism is shaping China and the world.* New York: Oxford University Press.

[31] Bougon, François. 2018. *Inside the mind of Xi Jinping* (trans by Vanessa Lee). London: C. Hurst & Co.

[32] Tsang, Steve, and Olivia Cheung. 2024. *The political thought of Xi Jinping.* New York: Oxford University Press.

seeking autarkic-style economies and the world may be transported back to a 1930s scenario that did not end well.

10.15 India's Road to Globalisation

India's economic landscape has undergone a profound transformation since the landmark economic reforms of 1991, which marked a decisive shift from a largely closed, state-controlled economy towards greater integration with global markets. This process of globalisation has ushered in an era of strong economic growth and development, propelling India to become the world's fourth-largest economy in 2025, though still five-times smaller than China's. The liberalisation policies attracted moderate foreign direct investment (FDI), facilitating technology transfer and fostering human capital development, particularly in the information technology (IT) sector. India's prowess in services exports, notably IT and business process outsourcing, illustrates the opportunities provided by globalisation, positioning the nation as a global leader in these knowledge-intensive domains.

However, this integration has been uneven, revealing a complex interplay of opportunities and persistent challenges. While the services sector has flourished, India's manufacturing sector has struggled to achieve comparable global competitiveness and scale. This disparity raises a critical research question: why has India, despite its vast potential and economic liberalisation, failed to match China's ascendancy as a global exporter of manufactured goods? This section will delve into the multifaceted reasons behind this divergence, examining key structural impediments such as inadequate infrastructure, quality education for workers, rigid labour laws, and bureaucratic red tape. Furthermore, it will explore the underlying political and institutional factors that have hindered meaningful reform, provide a comparative perspective with China's manufacturing success, and propose actionable solutions with a realistic timeframe to propel India towards becoming a formidable manufacturing hub.

10.16 The Manufacturing Dilemma: India Versus China

India's manufacturing sector contributes approximately 15% to its GDP, a figure significantly lower than China's 27%. This modest share and the sector's struggle to generate mass employment for the vast workforce transitioning from agriculture highlight a "missing middle" in India's industrial structure, characterised by a preponderance of very small and very large firms, but a dearth of competitive medium-sized enterprises. This stands in stark contrast to China's manufacturing might, which saw its exports exceed $3.5 trillion in 2024, while India's total merchandise

Table 10.1 Comparing India and China's GDP, FDI and exports

Year	Country	GDP growth (%)	FDI inflows (Billions USD)	Merchandise exports (Billions USD)
2019	India	3.90	50.6	324.6
	China	6.00	141.2	2499.00
2020	India	−5.80	64.3	291.9
	China	2.20	149.3	2591.00
2021	India	9.70	44.7	422
	China	8.40	181	3364.00
2022	India	7.00	49.9	453.4
	China	3.00	189.1	3594.00
2023	India	7.80	28.1	437.1
	China	5.20	42.7	3380.00
2024	India	6.80	N/A	N/A
	China	5.00	N/A	N/A

Source: Compiled by the author from international organisations including the World Bank, International Monetary Fund (IMF), United Nations Conference on Trade and Development (UNCTAD), and the World Trade Organization (WTO)

exports were around $450 billion.[33] Even more statistically revealing, are the global manufacturing export figures. China's share of global exports is 30%, whereas India's is under 3%. Several critical factors explain this significant divergence (Table 10.1).

10.17 Infrastructure Deficiencies

A foundational impediment to India's manufacturing competitiveness is its persistent infrastructure deficit. While recent investments in transport and digital networks have brought improvements, substantial gaps remain, particularly in power supply reliability and logistics. Inadequate road and rail networks, coupled with overcrowded ports and airports, contribute to high logistical costs and significant delays, rendering Indian manufacturers less competitive globally. For instance, exporting from India can take approximately 17 days, compared to just 5 days from Singapore or other Southeast Asian nations, with associated shipping costs being considerably higher. These inefficiencies directly inflate production and transportation costs, hampering industrial expansion and making manufacturing uncompetitive. India is projected to require an investment of approximately $840 billion until 2036 to meet the growing demands of urbanisation and economic development, yet many projects

[33] Statista. 2025. India-China trade relations—statistics & facts. Accessed 20 June 2025. https://www.statista.com/topics/13109/india-china-trade-relations/.

face cost overruns and significant delays due to factors like poor project reports and approval bottlenecks.[34]

10.18 Human Capital and Quality Education

While India boasts a large and young population, a key challenge lies in the quality of education and skill development for its manufacturing workforce. The integration with global markets has driven demand for skilled labour, prompting the establishment of premier educational institutions like the Indian Institutes of Technology (IITs) and Indian Institutes of Management (IIMs). However, India's economic growth has disproportionately benefited a relatively small number of well-educated and skilled workers in knowledge-intensive service sectors. This has led to widening earning differences and income inequality, as the skill premium rewards those with advanced technical and managerial abilities. The educational system often fails to align its curriculum with the evolving needs of modern manufacturing, lacking sufficient focus on automation, AI, robotics, and data analytics. Despite initiatives like the "National Policy for Skill Development & Entrepreneurship", the availability of labour with the required skills for value-added manufacturing remains a significant challenge, hindering India's competitiveness.[35]

10.19 Labour Market Rigidities

India's labour laws are among the most stringent in the world, posing significant hurdles to the expansion of labour-intensive manufacturing. A multitude of central and state labour laws (44 central laws and hundreds of state laws) create a complex and often contradictory regulatory environment. These laws, particularly the Industrial Disputes Act of 1947 and its subsequent amendments, make it costly and difficult for firms with more than 100 workers to reduce their workforce, even during economic downturns. This discourages formal-sector firms from hiring new employees and expanding their operations, pushing a large proportion of the workforce into the informal sector, where job security and benefits are minimal or nonexistent. The unintended consequence is that Indian manufacturing tends to be capital- and skill-intensive, rather than labour-intensive, which is counter-intuitive for a labour-abundant economy. This rigidity severely restricts job creation in manufacturing, leading to "jobless growth" and limiting the mobility of low-skilled labour out of agriculture. Despite some labour reforms in 2020, India still requires

---

[34] Global Trade Research Initiative (GTRI). 2024. Building better: India's path to superior quality infrastructure. https://gtri.co.in/DisplayFlagshipReports.aspx?ID=43. Accessed 11 June 2025.

[35] Sharma, Shalendra D. 2018. *A political economy of the United States, China, and India.* Cambridge: Cambridge University Press.

improvements to attract foreign firms and improve its labour environment if it intends to compete with other emerging economies.[36]

10.20 Bureaucratic Hurdles and Red Tape

The regulatory environment in India, despite ongoing reforms, remains complex and burdensome. Multiple clearances required at both state and central levels, coupled with bureaucratic delays, continue to deter investment and stifle business growth. India's ranking in global "Ease of Doing Business" reports, while showing improvement, still reflects these underlying challenges. Excessive paperwork, prolonged approval processes, and a lack of performance-based accountability within the bureaucracy contribute to inefficiency and a perception of unpredictability for investors. Issues such as slow land acquisition and difficulties in contract enforcement further compound the problem, increasing operational costs for businesses.

10.21 Other Contributing Factors

Beyond these primary issues, other factors have also constrained India's manufacturing growth. A historical focus on protecting small-scale industries through reservation policies, which prohibited large firms from producing certain daily-use products, limited economies of scale and hindered technological adoption. While these policies have largely been dismantled, their legacy contributed to a fragmented manufacturing base. Furthermore, India's trade policy, characterised by higher import duties compared to its Free Trade Agreement (FTA) partners, has often resulted in widening trade deficits rather than increased exports, as foreign goods gain a price advantage in the Indian market while Indian goods face low or zero tariffs in partner countries anyway. This has undermined the potential benefits of FTAs for domestic manufacturing.

10.22 Why Reforms Lagged: Political Economy and Institutional Challenges

The persistence of these structural issues can be largely attributed to the complex political economy of India. The country's democratic framework, while fostering political empowerment for marginalised groups, has also led to a system susceptible

---

[36] Bhuta, Aishwarya. 2022. Imbalancing act: India's industrial relations code, 2020. *Indian Journal of Labour Economics*. 65(3): 821–830. https://doi.org/10.1007/s41027-022-00389-3.

to competitive populism and the influence of powerful vested interests. Reforms, particularly those related to labour laws, often face immediate and strong backlash from opposition parties, labour unions, and civil society groups. This makes it politically challenging to implement changes that might entail short-term disruptions but are necessary for long-term economic gains. India's federal structure, with both central and state governments holding jurisdiction over key policy areas, can lead to inconsistencies and implementation challenges. The lack of a unified approach to reform, coupled with bureaucratic inertia, further complicates the process of change. The allure of protectionist measures over deeper global economic integration, favoured by certain lobbies, also acts as a significant obstacle to expanding manufacturing growth and export competitiveness.[37]

10.23 China's Ascendancy in Global Manufacturing

In stark contrast to India, China's remarkable success in becoming the "world's factory" can be attributed to a deliberate and comprehensive strategy. Following its economic reforms in 1978, China systematically invested in world-class infrastructure, including expansive expressways, high-speed rail networks, and modern port facilities. These investments drastically reduced logistical costs and facilitated both domestic and international trade, creating an efficient environment for manufacturing. China also effectively leveraged its massive market size to attract FDI, which brought not only capital but also advanced technology and managerial expertise. Through joint ventures and strategic partnerships, China systematically absorbed and adapted foreign technologies, rapidly closing its technological gap with developed economies. Furthermore, the Chinese government prioritised human capital development, with significant investments in post-secondary education and vocational training to create a skilled and versatile workforce aligned with industrial needs. Its state-guided industrial policies, combined with a pragmatic approach to market liberalisation while maintaining political control, enabled the creation of large-scale, export-oriented manufacturing industries that could exploit economies of scale and integrate deeply into global value chains.[38]

[37] Mohan, Rakesh, 2022. *India transformed: 25 years of economic reforms.* New Delhi: Penguin Viking.

[38] Kuo, Kaiser. 2025. How China got rich: A deep dive into China's 40-year history of economic transformation. World Economic Forum. https://www.weforum.org/stories/2025/06/how-china-got-rich-40-year-history-of-economic-transformation/. Accessed 20 June 2025.

10.24 India's Success in the Services Industry

While manufacturing has lagged, India has carved out a unique and impressive niche in the global services industry, particularly in IT and IT-enabled services. This sector has been a primary beneficiary of globalisation, leveraging India's large pool of English-speaking, skilled professionals and the advent of high-speed internet. Software services exports reached $205.2 billion in FY24, with the United States being the largest market. Cities like Bangalore have emerged as global tech hubs, performing a wide range of IT-related activities, from advanced software production and programming to business process outsourcing and call centre operations. This success has created millions of high-paying jobs and positioned India as a global leader in IT services. However, this growth has been concentrated in knowledge-intensive sectors, primarily benefiting a relatively small number of highly educated workers, thus contributing to widening income inequality. Unlike labour-intensive manufacturing, the services sector, including tourism and hospitality, can only absorb a limited number of low-skilled workers migrating from rural areas. Despite its triumphs, the IT services sector faces challenges from increasing automation, visa restrictions in key markets, and intensified competition for skilled talent, necessitating continuous reskilling and upskilling initiatives.[39]

10.25 Progress Made in Advancing India's Economy

The Indian government has unveiled a forward-looking Union Budget for 2025, fostering a more conducive environment for foreign investment through a series of significant policy reforms. The budget is being hailed as a catalyst for attracting substantial FDI, with measures aimed at enhancing the ease of doing business, opening up key sectors, and providing tax certainty. These reforms are anticipated to provide a significant spur to the Indian economy, fostering growth, creating jobs, and bolstering infrastructure development.

India is set to launch a new "Investment Friendliness Index" for states in 2025. The main objectives of this upcoming index are to:

- Measure and compare how states and union territories perform in attracting and facilitating investment.
- Guide investors in identifying the best states for investment.
- Motivate states to improve their rankings by addressing shortcomings in their policies and business environment, fostering "competitive cooperative federalism."

[39] Alonso, Cristiano, and Margaux MacDonald. 2024. Advancing India's structural transformation and catch-up to the technology frontier in services. International Monetary Fund. https://www.imf.org/en/Publications/WP/Issues/2024/07/08/Advancing-Indias-Structural-Transformation-and-Catch-up-to-the-Technology-Frontier-551435. Accessed 20 June 2025.

10.26 Trade Agreements

The EU-India FTA: key areas of this agreement include significant tariff reductions on a wide range of goods, particularly in sectors like textiles, automotive parts, and electronics. The agreement also provides greater market access for Indian IT and business services professionals in the EU. The FTA is expected to be a game-changer for attracting European investment. The investment protection chapter will provide robust legal safeguards for EU investors, reducing perceived risks. Enhanced market access will encourage European companies to "make in India" for both the domestic market and for export back to the EU, thereby boosting manufacturing and creating jobs.

A key highlight in the UK-India Trade Deal is the United Kingdom (UK) offering substantial tariff concessions on Indian goods, including textiles and agricultural products. Focus on investment is a cornerstone of this deal, providing strong assurances to UK investors. The agreement is expected to unlock significant UK investment in India's financial services, legal and manufacturing sectors. The easier mobility for professionals will encourage UK firms to set up and expand their operations in India, leveraging the country's vast talent pool.

10.27 Proposed Solutions and Implementation Roadmap

To unlock its full manufacturing potential, India must undertake comprehensive and sustained reforms across several critical areas. Implementing such changes presents a significant challenge, potentially facing obstruction from vested interests who benefit from a protected market and from political rivalries between state and central governments. Prime Minister Modi's political strength, experience, and cachet may make India's current political environment particularly conducive to pushing through the necessary reforms. While reshoring manufacturing for products like the iPhone to the US is likely infeasible due to prohibitive labour costs, it is also important to emphasise that a direct, one-for-one substitution for China's established pre-eminence is not a realistic outcome in the near future. China's unparalleled scale, deep integration within global supply chains, and strategic investments in advanced manufacturing entrench its formidable position. The goal for India, therefore, should not be to replace China, but to position itself as a compelling global alternative through substantial domestic reforms.

A foundational element of this transformation is a comprehensive infrastructure overhaul, a long-term project estimated to take 5–10 years. This requires directing substantial public and private investment—far exceeding current allocations—towards improving physical infrastructure such as roads, railways, ports, and a reliable power supply. While initiatives like the National Infrastructure Pipeline are positive steps, they demand accelerated implementation and efficient execution. To complement this, India must enhance its logistics efficiency by developing integrated networks and dry ports to reduce transportation costs and transit times, which involves streamlining customs procedures and improving port functionality. Furthermore, robust urban infrastructure, including housing, sanitation, and transport, is essential to support industrial zones and attract the necessary talent.

Beyond physical infrastructure, the development of human capital over the next 5–15 years is equally critical. This begins with reforming educational curricula, from vocational institutes to engineering colleges, to align with the demands of modern manufacturing by incorporating subjects like automation, robotics, AI, and data analytics. Stronger partnerships between educational institutions and industries are needed to create a pipeline of skilled graduates through internships, apprenticeships, and hands-on training. For the existing workforce, large-scale and accessible reskilling programmes are essential, while a broader push to promote STEM education will secure the talent pool for future manufacturing disciplines.

These efforts must be supported by a modernised regulatory framework, achievable within a 3–5-year timeframe. A key priority is the simplification and rationalisation of India's complex labour laws into a more coherent structure. This involves introducing greater flexibility in hiring and firing practices, particularly for larger firms, while simultaneously strengthening social security nets to protect workers—a balance crucial for incentivising formal employment and business scalability. Concurrently, improving the ease of doing business is paramount. Implementing effective single-window clearance systems, digitalising government processes, and introducing performance-based accountability within the bureaucracy will reduce delays and red tape. Adopting proven strategies, such as developing industrial zones with pre-approved clearances, can further expedite the establishment of manufacturing facilities.[40]

Finally, these domestic reforms must be guided by strategic and ongoing trade and investment policies. A long-term priority should be to emulate China's success in developing end-to-end product ecosystems, fostering collaboration between major anchor firms and local component suppliers. Attracting a few large, transformative global manufacturers can act as a catalyst, upgrading domestic industries and integrating them into global value chains. Furthermore, all free trade agreements must be carefully reviewed to ensure they genuinely benefit India's exports and domestic manufacturing rather than simply increasing import deficits. Policies should be geared towards encouraging domestic value addition, thereby discouraging a "trading mentality" where goods are merely imported for final assembly.[41]

---

[40] Sharma, *supra*, n.35.

[41] Subramanian, Arvind, and Felman, Josh. 2024. *India's Path to global leadership*. New Delhi: Penguin Business.

10.28 Conclusion

Globalisation has presented India with a unique dual narrative: a soaring services sector success story juxtaposed with a struggling manufacturing landscape. While India has demonstrated its capacity to thrive in globally integrated knowledge-intensive industries, its failure to match China's manufacturing export dominance stems from persistent structural deficiencies. Inadequate infrastructure, a mismatch between education and industrial skill requirements, rigid labour laws, and a complex bureaucratic environment have collectively hindered the growth of a competitive and employment-generating manufacturing base. The political economy of India, characterised by democratic contestation and powerful vested interests, has often slowed down crucial reforms.

To bridge this manufacturing gap, India must embark on a renewed and vigorous reform agenda. This necessitates a comprehensive infrastructure overhaul, a strategic reorientation of education and skill development towards manufacturing needs, and a continuing pragmatic modernisation of labour laws that balances flexibility with worker protection. Furthermore, decisive bureaucratic reforms are essential to foster an environment conducive to industrial growth and investment. By learning from China's success in building a robust manufacturing ecosystem and leveraging current geopolitical shifts like the restructuring of US trade tariffs, India has an unprecedented (and possibly final) opportunity to substantially transform its manufacturing sector for global exports. Such concerted efforts, implemented within a clear timeframe, are not just economic imperatives but vital steps towards achieving more inclusive growth and accelerating India's position to a truly global economic power.

References

Allison, Graham, et al. 2013. *Lee Kuan Yew: The Grand Master's insights on China, the United States, and the world.* Cambridge, MA: The MIT Press.

Alonso, Cristiano, and Margaux MacDonald. 2024. *Advancing India's structural transformation and catch-up to the technology frontier in services*. International Monetary Fund. https://www.imf.org/en/Publications/WP/Issues/2024/07/08/Advancing-Indias-Structural-Transformation-and-Catch-up-to-the-Technology-Frontier-551435. Accessed 20 June 2025.

Asia Society Policy Institute's Center for China Analysis and Stanford Center on China's Economy and Institutions. 2023. *China's property sector: A roundtable summary report.* https://asiasociety.org/new-report-chinas-property-sector-roundtable-summary-report. Accessed 25 May 2025.

Australian Strategic Policy Institute. 2024. *ASPI's two-decade critical technology tracker: The rewards of long-term research investment.* https://www.aspi.org.au/report/aspis-two-decade-critical-technology-tracker-the-rewards-of-long-term-research-investment/. Accessed May 26 2025.

Bhuta, Aishwarya. 2022. Imbalancing act: India's industrial relations code, 2020. *Indian Journal of Labour Economics* 65 (3): 821–830. https://doi.org/10.1007/s41027-022-00389-3.

Bougon, François. 2018. *Inside the mind of Xi Jinping* (trans by Vanessa Lee). London: C. Hurst & Co.
Claudio-Quiroga, Gloria, Luis Alberiko Gil-Alana, and Andoni Maiza Larrarte. 2025. Persistence in China's household consumption level: implications for the new growth model. *Journal of Economic and Finance* 49:283–298. https://doi.org/10.1007/s12197-025-09709-x.
Dizikes, Peter. 2021. Q&A: David Autor on the long afterlife of the 'China Shock'. *MIT News*. https://news.mit.edu/2021/david-autor-china-shock-persists-1206. Accessed 31 May 2025.
Douglas, Jason, Jon Emont, and Samantha Pearson. 2024. China's flood of cheap goods is angering its allies, too. *The Wall Street Journal*. https://www.wsj.com/world/china/chinas-flood-of-cheap-goods-is-angering-its-allies-too-51284954. Accessed 23 May 2025.
Global Trade Research Initiative (GTRI). 2024. *Building better: India's path to superior quality infrastructure*. https://gtri.co.in/DisplayFlagshipReports.aspx?ID=43. Accessed 11 June 2025
Harvey, David. 2010. *A companion to Marx's capital*. London: Verso.
Jin, Keyu. 2023. *The new China playbook: Beyond socialism and capitalism*. New York: Viking.
Kuo, Kaiser. 2025. *How China got rich: A deep dive into China's 40-year history of economic transformation*. World Economic Forum. https://www.weforum.org/stories/2025/06/how-china-got-rich-40-year-history-of-economic-transformation/. Accessed 20 June 2025.
Leahy, Joe, Nian Liu, and Ryan McMorrow. 2025. The lessons from China's dominance in manufacturing. *Financial Times*. https://on.ft.com/43ADe7w. Accessed 29 May 2025.
Liu, Zongyuan Zoe. 2024. China's real economic crisis: Why Beijing won't give up on a failing model. *Foreign Affairs*. https://www.foreignaffairs.com/china/chinas-real-economic-crisis-zongyuan-liu. Accessed 29 May 2025.
McCormick, Myles. 2025. G7 ministers threaten more sanctions against Russia over Ukraine war. *Financial Times*. https://on.ft.com/4dAMGg6. Accessed 29 May 2025.
Mohan, Rakesh. 2022. *India transformed: 25 years of economic reforms*. New Delhi: Penguin Viking.
National Bureau of Statistics of China. 2025. *Households' income and consumption expenditure in 2024*. https://www.stats.gov.cn/english/PressRelease/202501/t20250124_1958443.html. Accessed 29 May 2025
Pei, Minxin. 2016. *China's crony capitalism: The dynamics of regime decay*. Cambridge, MA: Harvard University Press.
Pettis, Michael. 2014. *The great rebalancing: Trade, conflict, and the perilous road ahead for the world economy*. Updated Edition. Princeton, NJ: Princeton University Press.
Pettis, Michael, and Matthew C. Klein. 2020. *Trade wars are class wars: How rising inequality distorts the global economy and threatens international peace*. New Haven: Yale University Press.
Rozelle, Scott, and Natalie Hell. 2020. *Invisible China: How the urban-rural divide threatens China's rise*. Chicago: University of Chicago Press.
Rudd, Kevin. 2024. *On Xi Jinping: How Xi's Marxist nationalism is shaping China and the world*. New York: Oxford University Press.
Setser, Brad. 2024. The dangerous myth of deglobalization: Misperceptions of the global economy are driving bad policies. *Foreign Affairs*. https://www.foreignaffairs.com/china/globalization-dangerous-myth-economy-brad-setser. Accessed 20 May 2025.
Sharma, Shalendra D. 2018. *A political economy of the United States, China, and India*. Cambridge: Cambridge University Press.
Statista. 2025. *India-China trade relations—Statistics & facts*. https://www.statista.com/topics/13109/india-china-trade-relations/ Accessed 20 June 2025.
Subramanian, Arvind, and Josh Felman. 2024. *India's path to global leadership*. New Delhi: Penguin Business.
Tsang, Steve, and Olivia Cheung. 2024. *The political thought of Xi Jinping*. New York: Oxford University Press.
U.S. Bureau of Economic Analysis. 2020. *U.S. international trade in goods and services*. https://www.bea.gov/index.php/news/2021/us-international-trade-goods-and-services-december-2020. Accessed 22 May 2025.

Valev, Neven, Franziska Bieri, and Menna Bizuneh. 2025. China: Household consumption, percent of GDP. *The Global Economy*. https://www.theglobaleconomy.com/china/household_consumption/. Accessed 18 May 2025.

Wang, Zheng, Liyue Lin, Shuangshuang Tang, and Yang Xiao. 2023. Migration and migrants in Chinese cities: New trends, challenges and opportunities to theorise with urban China. *Transactions in Planning and Urban Research* 2 (4): 317–331. https://doi.org/10.1177/27541223231217431.

Wen, J. 2011. Report on the work of the government. In *Delivered at the fourth session of the eleventh national people's congress*. http://www.npc.gov.cn/npc/index.html. Accessed 20 May 2025.

World Bank. 2025a. *Exports of goods and services (current US$)—China*. https://data.worldbank.org/indicator/NE.EXP.GNFS.CD?locations=CN. Accessed 29 May 2025.

World Bank. 2025b. *Gini Index (World Bank Estimate)*. https://data.worldbank.org/indicator/SI.POV.GINI. Accessed 25 May 2025.

Yao, Yang. 2024. Top economist Yang Yao: Can Beijing save China's economy from real estate and debt? *ThinkChina*. https://www.thinkchina.sg/economy/top-economist-yang-yao-can-beijing-save-chinas-economy-real-estate-and-debt. Accessed 22 May 2025.

Yellen, Janet L. 2024. *Remarks by Secretary of the Treasury Janet L. Yellen at a press conference*. U.S. Department of the Treasury. https://home.treasury.gov/news/press-releases/jy2241. Accessed 23 May 2025.

Zhang, Xiao, and Satish Chand. 2024. An analysis of the Chinese pension system pointing to the urgent need for reform. *The Chinese Economy* 58 (2): 174–188. https://doi.org/10.1080/10971475.2024.2384168.

Chapter 11
Global Health as the Canary in the Globalisation Coal Mine

Wendy Elizabeth Bonython

Abstract Globalisation offers a mixed bag of risks and benefits for global health. Many promised benefits of globalisation—increased access to expertise, technologies and products offering solutions to global health challenges—have not equitably improved health outcomes. Institutions associated with globalisation and health have delivered uneven results, partly because of incoherence in functions and objectives. The COVID-19 pandemic demonstrated deep structural weaknesses affecting healthcare within the existing model of globalisation. Issues included breakdown of information-sharing between states, hampering surveillance and identification efforts; politicisation of governance and funding arrangements underpinning the World Health Organisation; inadequacies within the IP protection system; and re-emergence of sovereignty-based restrictions on global flows of critical resources including vaccines, pharmaceuticals, and medical equipment. COVID-19 highlighted vulnerabilities to rapid global dissemination of disease outbreaks mediated by human migration, supply chain disruption of critical resources and commodities, and under-development of domestic research, development and manufacturing capabilities. This chapter reviews COVID-19 through a public health globalisation lens. It focuses on the conflicting roles and priorities of key institutions responsible for the global response to the pandemic, considering failures and frequently disregarded successes. It identifies the impact of key post-pandemic responses including the US withdrawal from the WHO and the recent Pandemic Agreement. It concludes by considering potential futures for existing models of globalised health in an erratically de-globalising world.

W. E. Bonython (✉)
Faculty of Law, Bond University, Robina, QLD, Australia
e-mail: wbonytho@bond.edu.au

U. H. Ghori, J. Farrar (eds.), *Globalisation Disrupted*,
https://doi.org/10.1007/978-981-95-3997-0_11

11.1 Introduction

The COVID-19 pandemic was an era-defining event, a "canary in the coalmine" of global health governance. It caused immense social and economic disruption, with long-term impacts. The first pandemic of our neoliberal century, it prompted recurrent speculation that COVID-19 would bring about the end of globalisation.

Predicting that COVID-19 will cause the end of globalisation begs critical questions. These include understanding what globalisation is in order to be able to understand what its decline and ultimate end might look like. It requires understanding of the relationship between globalisation and health, including the benefits and threats to health associated with globalisation, and how institutions of globalisation—particularly the World Trade Organisation (WTO) and the World Health Organisation (WHO)—have shaped the ongoing global response to COVID-19.

Following the introduction, Sect. 11.2 of this chapter contextualises globalisation and global public health. Section 11.3 considers globalisation pandemic facilitator, and shaper of national and global responses in an era of authoritarian populism and challenges to neoliberalism. Section 11.4 reviews subsequent developments in global affairs in the aftermath of the pandemic. Section 11.5 reflects on the future of globalisation in a post-pandemic world, observing that the relationship between the pandemic and globalisation is multifaceted, both correlative and causative. The chapter concludes that globalisation's structural weaknesses pre-dated the pandemic, and that globalisation and its institutions, subject to modification and despite deglobalisation during the second Trump presidency, will survive the current wave of post-pandemic reforms.

11.2 Globalisation and Health

"Globalisation" describes "growing interdependence of the world's economies, cultures, and populations, brought about by cross-border trade in goods and services, technology, and flows of investment, people, and information".[1] Globalisation is not static.[2] Loots describes discrete periods within post-1945 globalisation, including periods of "slowbalisation" ("continued integration of the global economy via trade, financial and other flows, albeit at a significantly slower pace"); deglobalisation ("retraction from globalisation movement towards a less connected world,

[1] Kolb, Melina. 2024. What is globalization? And how has the global economy shaped the United States? Pieterson Institute of International Economics. https://www.piie.com/microsites/globalization/what-is-globalization#:~:text=Globalization%20describes%20the%20growing%20interdependence,investment%2C%20people%2C%20and%20information. Accessed 24 May 2025.

[2] Loots, Elsabe. 2022. Is the world retracting from globalization, setting it up for a fifth wave? The Conversation. www.theconversation.com/is-the-world-retracting-from-Globalization-setting-it-up-for-a-fifth-wave-186003. Accessed 24 May 2025.

characterised by powerful nation states, local solutions and border controls rather than global institutions, treaties and free movement"); "hyperglobalisation" (intense development of interconnectedness across a range of systems including trade, politics, and movement of people); and "reglobalisation" (a response to "retraction causing political, economic and social imbalances").

The emergence of global governance institutions is a feature of post-1945 globalisation. Ostensibly global in constituency, these institutions embody the international liberal or rules-based order underpinning contemporary geopolitics: a necessary response to the challenges and opportunities created by globalisation which erode national borders and governance systems.[3] Zurn comments:

> There is hardly a modern political institution which is not allegedly challenged, transformed, or undermined by globalization. Globalization is not only said to be curbing the autonomy of nation states and enforcing a convergence of national policies but also disabling democracy and with it the legitimacy of national political systems, altering the nature of sovereignty and thus ultimately transforming the fundamental structures of international politics from an anarchic to a global governance system.[4]

Liberalism under the international order is contested, potentially referring to economic, political, or other forms of liberalism.[5] Definitional debates overshadow the origins of liberalism. In 1848, Mill famously connected flourishing international trade to reduced appetite for international conflict:

> It is commerce which is rapidly rendering war obsolete, by strengthening and multiplying the personal interests which are in natural opposition to it. And it may be said without exaggeration that the great extent and rapid increase of international trade, in being the principal guarantee of the peace of the world, is the great permanent security for the uninterrupted progress of the ideas, the institutions, and the character of the human race.[6]

That vision fostered global standardisation initiatives and intellectual property (IP) agreements[7] that were forerunners of the Trade Related Aspects of Intellectual Property (TRIPS) and TRIPS-plus agreements discussed later in this chapter. They were agnostic about human rights (other than property) and health. Statesmen after two world wars sought to promote that cooperation and trade between states. Clause 4 of the 1941 Atlantic Charter explicitly referred to ensuring "the enjoyment by all

---

[3] Slobodian, Quinn. 2018. *Globalists: The end of empire and the birth of neoliberalism*. Cambridge, MA: Harvard University Press.

[4] Michael, Zurn. 2012. Globalization and global governance. In *Handbook of International Relations*, eds. Walter Carlsnaes, Thomas Risse, and Beth Simmons, 401–425. London: Sage Publications.

[5] See for example Ikenberry, G. John. 2020. *A world safe for democracy: Liberal internationalism and the crises of global order*. New Haven: Yale University Press. Mirowski, Philip. 2017. *Never let a serious crisis go to waste: How neoliberalism survived the financial meltdown*. London: Verso.

[6] Mill, John Stuart. 1848. *Principles of political economy*. London: Parker. See also Palen, Marc-William. 2024. *Pax economica: Left-wing visions of a free trade world*. Princeton: Princeton University Press.

[7] Sell, Susan and Christopher May. 2001. Moments in law: contestation and settlement in the history of intellectual property. *Review of international political economy* 8: 467–500. https://doi.org/10.1080/09692290110055849.

states, great or small, victor or vanquished, of access, on equal terms, to the trade and to the raw materials of the world which are needed for their economic prosperity". Clause 5 addressed the need "to bring about the fullest collaboration between all nations in the economic field with the object of securing, for all, improved labour standards, economic advancement, and social security".[8]

Ensuring equal access on equal terms for all states was considered to require robust global governance frameworks and institutions to uphold an agreed system of rules governing trade and transnational interactions. Barnett et al observed:

> Global governance began in the mid-nineteenth century and accelerated after the First World War. But it came of age in the post-Second World War era. In response to the lessons learned from the collapse of international order between the wars, and the need to rebuild after the devastation wrought by the Second World War, states, with the USA in the lead, set out to create a new and comprehensive set of international organizations to tackle a growing list of shared global challenges.[9]

Global governance institutions emerging alongside the United Nations in the aftermath or 1945 included the International Monetary Fund and the International Bank for Reconstruction & Development, now part of the World Bank. [10] Although an International Trade Organisation (ITO) was initially envisaged, trade liberalisation was instead pursued via the 1947 General Agreement on Tariffs & Trade (GATT) promoting liberalisation of trade in goods between member states but biased towards the global North as a generator of health-related technologies and consumer of commodities from the South.

It was not until 1995 that the World Trade Organisation was established,[11] supplementing the "provisional" GATT arrangements by expanding global governance of trade (and protecting North interests) to include services and IP. The WTO is a rule making body (agreements governing trade are negotiated by member states) and a dispute resolution forum. One of the most significant agreements overseen by the WTO is the TRIPS agreement,[12] outlining minimum standards of IP protection and reinforced by controversial Free Trade Agreements negatively characterised as TRIPS-plus.[13] TRIPS- and therefore the WTO—is fundamental to globalisation of

---

[8] Declaration of Principles issued by the President of the United States and the Prime Minister of the United Kingdom. 1941. https://www.nato.int/cps/en/natohq/official_texts_16912.htm. Accessed 26 May 2025.

[9] Barnett, Michael, Jon Pevehouse, and Kal Raustiala. 2021. Introduction: The modes of global governance. In *Global Governance in a World of Change.* eds. Michael Barnett, Jon Pevehouse, and Kal Raustiala, 1–47. Cambridge: Cambridge University Press.

[10] United Nations Monetary and Financial Conference. Articles of Agreement of the International Monetary Fund. Adopted at the United Nations Monetary and Financial Conference. 1944. https://www.imf.org/external/pubs/ft/aa/. Accessed 26 May 2025.

[11] Marrakesh Agreement Establishing the World Trade Organization, 1994. https://www.wto.org/english/docs_e/legal_e/marag_e.htm. Accessed 27 May 2025.

[12] Matthews, Duncan. 2003. *Globalising intellectual property rights: The TRIPS agreement.* London: Routledge.

[13] Sell, Susan. 2007. TRIPS-plus free trade agreements and access to medicines. *Liverpool law review* 28: 41–75. Ruse-Khan, Henning Grosse. 2018. *From TRIPS to FTAs and back:*

health care, as it governs the IP arising from pharmaceuticals—an historical source of trade barriers inhibiting access to essential medicines in many of the world's less and least developed nations, where indigenous pharmaceutical manufacturing capacity is immature or non-existent.

Despite early framing of globalisation, confining it to trade and economics and security, globalisation and consequently global governance affects a far broader range of activities, notably including health. Created in 1948, the WHO was the first UN specialised agency to have unanimous member state support.[14] The WHO's objective is "attainment by all peoples of the highest possible level of health",[15] defined as "a state of complete physical, mental, and social well-being and not merely the absence of disease or infirmity".[16]

The WHO's remit is broad, encompassing all aspects of public health. Its legitimacy depends on acceptance by member states.[17] Key WHO functions include its role in surveillance and reporting of outbreaks of infectious disease; coordination of regional and global responses to disease outbreaks; and promotion of access to essential medicines, under its role in advocating for universal health coverage, ensuring access to a "full range of quality health services" for all, without causing financial hardship.[18] The WHO's activities are directly impacted by globalisation. It is both a product of globalisation, and susceptible to its currents. The WHO's definition of globalisation—"increased interconnectedness and interdependence of peoples and countries"—emphasises both liberalisation of border restrictions, and institutions and policies supporting that liberalisation.

Health benefits expectations underpinning globalisation, i.e., a globalised world will promote economic growth raising the economic status and security of all states, including the least developed nations, (through for example trickle down investment in health initiatives leading to better population health outcomes), have not necessarily materialised. Labonte notes:

> one of the more contentious positive health claims made for globalization (is) that of the contribution of liberalized markets to economic growth. This argument holds that trade and investment liberalization improves growth, which generates wealth that reduces poverty. Poverty reduction, in turn, improves health (poverty being the single greatest risk condition for disease), creating more productive and skilled workers, which spur the economy to even

Re-conceptualising the role of a multilateral IP framework in a TRIPS-plus world. The Hague: T.M.C. Asser Press.

[14] Shimkin, Michael B. 1946. The World Health Organization. *Science* 104: 281–283.

[15] Constitution of the World Health Organization. 1946. WHO Interim Commission. https://apps.who.int/gb/bd/PDF/bd47/EN/constitution-en.pdf?ua=1 Accessed 26 May 2025.

[16] Preamble to the WHO Constitution. 1946. WHO Interim Commission. https://apps.who.int/gb/bd/PDF/bd47/EN/constitution-en.pdf?ua=1. Accessed 26 May 2025.

[17] Gostin, Lawrence, Devi Sridhar, and Daniel Hougendobler. 2015. The normative authority of the World Health Organization. *Public Health* 129: 854–863.

[18] World Health Organisation. Universal health coverage (UHC)—fact sheet. 2025b. https://www.who.int/news-room/fact-sheets/detail/universal-health-coverage-(uhc). Accessed 26 May 2025.

> greater growth and more trickle-down health. It is by interrogating the links in this 'virtuous circle,' however, that globalization's health risks begin to emerge.[19]

Positive health benefits of globalisation may include improvements in child and maternal health outcomes, as well as greater recognition of human rights, which can translate into better overall health. For instance, progress in addressing gender discrimination has been significant for women's health issues, while tackling cultural and racial discrimination has helped reduce barriers to universal healthcare access. Moreover, heightened attention to human rights in specific contexts—for example, the impact of poor working conditions on the health of low-paid workers in outsourced manufacturing—has drawn global scrutiny. This is especially salient given the tendency of wealthier nations to offshore low-value and hazardous production to the Global South.

An additional health benefit attributed to globalisation is increased awareness of the indirect effect of other social factors on health—the social determinants of health—and publication and investment in those factors. In practice the diffusion to communities most in need of the health benefits attributable to globalisation has been uneven. Pang and Guindon observe:

> The links between globalization and health are complex and globalization is a multifaceted phenomenon that can affect health in myriad ways. Its consequences can be either direct, at the level of whole populations, individuals and healthcare delivery systems, or indirect, through the economy and other factors such as education, sanitation and water supply.[20]

From the perspective of global health diffusion of knowledge, people and goods as a direct consequence of globalisation has had mixed outcomes. Knowledge and information-sharing featured prominently (both negatively and positively) during the initial phases of the COVID-19 pandemic, when the WHO's disease outbreak surveillance system identified and responded to the emerging COVID-19 outbreak,[21] only for responses to the outbreak to be hampered by poor transfer of knowledge and technologies regarding vaccine development and production.[22] Importantly, other globalisation governance entities such as the WTO are arguably directly responsible for the obstructed diffusion of technology, via the patent system (discussed in more detail in Sect. 11.3 in the context of COVID-19 vaccine technology)

[19] Labonté, Ronald. 2015. Globalization and health. In International encyclopedia of the social & behavioral sciences, ed. James D. Wright, 198–205. Amsterdam: Elsevier.

[20] Pang, Tikki, and Emmanuel Guindon. 2004. Globalization and risks to health. *EMBO Reports* 5: s11–s16.

[21] Independent Panel for Pandemic Preparedness and Response. 2021. COVID-19: make it the last pandemic. https://theindependentpanel.org/. Accessed 26 May 2025.

[22] Dagovetz, Michael, et al. 2025. Global COVID-19 vaccination challenges: Inequity of access and vaccine hesitancy. *Journal of Medicine, Surgery, and Public Health*. https://doi.org/10.1016/j.glmedi.2025.100197. Wouters, OJ, et al. 2021. Challenges in ensuring global access to COVID-19 vaccines: production, affordability, allocation, and deployment. *Lancet* 397:1023–1034. Kalha, Komal. 2021. Why we must remove barriers to trade to achieve vaccine equity. International Federation of Pharmaceutical Manufacturers and Associations. https://www.ifpma.org/insights/why-we-must-remove-barriers-to-trade-to-achieve-vaccine-equity-step-3/. Accessed 26 May 2025.

broadly perceived as hampering access to essential medicines by the poorest countries.

Movement of goods via a liberalised trade system has had major impacts on the distribution of the global non-communicable disease burden. Liberalised movement of people, however, has arguably had the most significant effect on health in recent times. Increased transnational health workforce mobility has potentially distortive effects on access to healthcare for people in less developed or insecure countries where trained healthcare providers may be inclined to seek better remunerated or more secure work in the North.

However, globalisation's emphasis on increasingly liberalised and rapid movement of people and goods—including animals—means diseases—including novel communicable diseases—spread more quickly between and within nations, increasing risks of global pandemics. "One Health" is a formal interdisciplinary framework examining the relationships between humans, animals, and the environment, and how interactions between them– many of which relate to globalisation, including climate change and urbanisation– lead to outbreaks of pandemic potential disease.

WHO's role coordinating the global public health aspects of the One Health response to disease risk posed by the human-animal-environment interface directly informs and supports WHO's work in the Health Emergencies Programme, which

> works with all countries and partners to ensure the world is better prepared for all-hazards health emergencies that threaten global health security. We work around the world to research, prevent and manage epidemic and pandemic-prone diseases; to strengthen and expand systems to rapidly detect, investigate and assess potential threats to public health; and to respond immediately and systematically to manage acute emergencies. In some conflict affected and humanitarian settings, WHO staff and operational partners even act as health-care provider of last resort.[23]

In responding to health emergencies, the WHO is governed by the International Health Regulations (IHRs), legally binding international law agreed to by 196 member states which outlines member state obligations in the event of an outbreak of disease or other public health risk posing significant risk to public health. The IHRs, along with guaranteeing rights to affected individuals, contain criteria for declaration by the WHO of a Public Health Emergency of International Concern (PHEIC). That declaration enables the WHO to exercise additional powers to respond to that disease outbreak.[24] Declaration is a critical threshold in triggering a global response to an emerging or deep-seated global health crisis.

[23] WHO. 2025a. WHO's Health Emergencies Programme. https://www.who.int/our-work/health-emergencies#:~:text=WHO's%20Health%20Emergencies%20Programme%20has,that%20threaten%20global%20health%20security. Accessed 26 May 2025.

[24] Note that WHO is dependent on cooperation: its powers do not mandate "on the ground" intervention in states, analogous to controversies about humanitarian military intervention discussed in works such as Ayoob, Mohammad. 2002. Humanitarian intervention and state sovereignty. *The international Journal of Human Rights* 6: 81–102.

The consequences of globalisation for health go beyond the increased movement of people/goods facilitating the increased spread of infectious disease or opportunities for global assistance by an ostensibly apolitical UN agency.[25]

In a 2008 speech on "Globalization and Health", the WHO Director-General described the uneven and unfair distribution of the burden of negative impacts associated with globalisation, noting the "bitter irony" of rising healthcare costs forcing an additional 100 million people into poverty.[26] He observed the "health sector had no say" when policies leading to globalisation's negative health consequences were designed and implemented, noting health's powerlessness to influence global economic decisions, despite remaining "at the mercy of the global economy, a sector where budgets can be cut when the money gets tight". Many of his criticisms hold true. Structural reform to the global economy to prioritise health as "the foundation of economic productivity and prosperity" in the face of globalisation remains elusive. Health care remains unaffordable for many in Trump's America and elsewhere.

11.3 Globalisation in a Global Health Crisis: COVID-19

The first reports of the novel illness now identified as COVID-19 emerged from Wuhan (PRC) in November 2019. Three separate disease surveillance mechanisms detected COVID-19 by 31 December 2019, demonstrating that the WHO's surveillance system worked.[27] The subsequent response under the IHRs, however, was less effective.

The IHRs seek to manage disease outbreaks by limiting the threat to international public health, while avoiding unnecessary interference with global movement of people and goods.[28] The IHRs require the participation of each State Party in national and transnational disease surveillance networks linking local health workers and government decision-makers to the WHO,[29] a structure facilitating rapid

[25] It is axiomatic that institutions develop their own agendas and are susceptible to capture by some stakeholders rather than being substantively neutral, highlighted in Davis, Christina. 2023. *Discriminatory clubs: The geopolitics of international organizations.* Princeton: Princeton University Press. Siddiqi, Javed. 1995. *World health and world politics: The World Health Organization and the UN system.* Columbia, SC: University of South Carolina Press. Melillo, Margherita. 2022. The uneasy coexistence of expertise and politics in the World Health Organization. *International Organizations Law Review* 19: 301–331.

[26] Sachs, J. Speech by the Director-General on Globalization and Health. 2008. https://www.who.int/director-general/speeches/detail/globalization-and-health. Accessed 27 May 2025.

[27] Independent Panel for Pandemic Preparedness and Response, *supra,* n. 21. See also Avant, Deborah, Martha Finnemore, and Susan Sell. 2010. Who governs the globe. In *Who governs the globe*, eds. Deborah Avant, Martha Finnemore, and Susan Sell, 1–32. Cambridge: Cambridge University Press.

[28] World Health Organisation. 2016. International Health Regulations (2005). https://iris.who.int/handle/10665/246107. Accessed 27 May 2025.

[29] Ibid.

communication regarding localised outbreaks of disease and recommendations for response between WHO and local authorities.

Additionally, each State Party is required to implement disease surveillance capabilities at a local level to minimum capability standards.[30] Reporting thresholds and mandating notification of disease outbreaks to the WHO via the surveillance networks are also set out in the IHRs, via a decision-making framework. That framework separates disease outbreaks detected by local and national surveillance systems into three streams.

The first stream triggers immediate WHO notification, applying to any outbreak of specified diseases including smallpox, some polio variants, novel influenza subtypes affecting humans, and severe acute respiratory syndrome. Under the second stream, outbreaks of other specified diseases including cholera and pneumonic plague; or diseases known to be of particular national or regional concern, are assessed against sequential criteria considering the public health impacts of the outbreak; whether it was expected; whether it poses a risk of transnational spread; and whether it will potentially disrupt international traffic and trade, to determine whether it meets the WHO notification threshold.

Characterisation of diseases within these two streams provides insight into the expected future sources of pandemic and epidemic disease. Prior to the emergence of COVID-19, much pandemic planning anticipated that the next "big" disease outbreak would be a novel influenza subtype; or, alternatively as the most recent prior widespread disease outbreak, a re-emergence of SARS, both of which fall within category 1. Conversely, the Ebola outbreaks in Africa, declared to be PHEICs in 2014 and 2019, respectively fall within category two.

COVID-19, as a novel disease, fell within the third stream of the WHO notification decision-making framework, as did the earlier Zika outbreak first identified in Brazil, along with the two Mpox PHEIC declarations made since COVID-19. This operates as a catchall for "any event of public health concern, including those of unknown causes or sources and those involving other events or diseases" than those identified under the other two streams, intentionally capturing outbreaks of novel disease, and thereby avoiding the potential for gaps and delays in notification and outbreak response arising from unfamiliarity with the causative agent, or uncertainty about its source or progression.

Once outbreaks are determined to be events of public health concern under the framework, the same factors identified above for the second stream, public health impact, unexpectedness of the outbreak, risk of international spread and impact on international travel and trade, are considered. Based on that consideration, notification to the WHO will either be required, or not, in which case the state member will continue to monitor the outbreak locally.

After the WHO is notified of the outbreak, it commences collecting and verifying information from both the notifying state and other states that may be affected. Based on that evidence, an expert body—the Emergency Committee—can advise

[30] Ibid.

the Director-General to declare that the outbreak constitutes a public health emergency of international concern (PHEIC),[31] empowering WHO to recommend temporary measures for national implementation to control any diffusion. Measures include controls on the movement of "persons, baggage, cargo, containers, conveyances, goods and/or postal parcels to prevent or reduce the international spread of disease and avoid unnecessary interference with international traffic."[32]

Following receipt of the notification of the outbreak via the various channels, WHO communicated an official alert to all countries, while pursuing consultation and verification requirements set out under the IHRs. At its initial meeting in mid-January, the Emergency Committee charged with advising the Director-General recommended delaying declaration of the outbreak as a PHEIC. By their subsequent meeting in late January, Wuhan was in lockdown, and the first international cases had been identified, leading the Committee to advise declaration of a PHEIC. At the time of the declaration on 30 January, 98 cases in 18 countries outside China had been confirmed; however, travel restrictions were not recommended as part of the initial PHEIC declaration.[33]

At this point, unfortunately, the international community's response to COVID-19 stalled, as nations failed to appreciate the significance of the PHEIC declaration. As noted by the Independent Panel's report:

> The IHR (2005) do not use or define the term "pandemic"...As COVID-19 spread during February 2020, and there was an apparent lack of understanding that declaring a PHEIC was to sound the loudest possible alarm, there was an increasing clamour for WHO to describe the situation as a pandemic. Eventually, stating that it was alarmed by the extent of both the spread of the disease and the level of inaction in response, WHO went on to characterize COVID-19 as a global pandemic on 11 March 2020, when there were a reported 118 000 cases in 114 countries.[34]

Finding that "early responses lacked efficiency and effectiveness", the Independent Panel observed:

> The declaration of a PHEIC by the WHO Director-General on 30 January 2020 was not followed by forceful and immediate emergency responses in most countries, despite the mounting evidence that a highly contagious new pathogen was spreading around the world. For a strikingly large number of countries, it was not until March 2020, after COVID-19 was characterized as a "pandemic", and when they had already seen widespread cases locally and/or reports of growing transmission elsewhere in the world, and/or their hospitals were beginning to fill with desperately ill patients, that concerted government action was finally taken.[35]

---

[31] Ibid.

[32] Ibid.

[33] Independent Panel for Pandemic Preparedness and Response, *supra*, n.21.

[34] Ibid.

[35] Ibid.

That "concerted government action" included lock downs, travel restrictions, mask mandates, and contact tracing.[36]

By the time the WHO Director-General declared the end of the PHEIC in May 2023,[37] over 765 million cases had been confirmed worldwide, with more than 6.9 million associated deaths.[38] In his first term, President Trump denounced China's perceived lack of cooperation with containment and information-sharing efforts, and the WHO's perceived failure to hold China accountable. These criticisms led to an announcement that the US would withdraw from the WHO.[39] President Trump's first term ended before the requisite 1-year notification period for withdrawal elapsed.[40] President Biden subsequently withdrew the notification of withdrawal.[41] On the first day of his second term in office, President Trump reinstated it, starting the clock on another 12 month notification period of intention to withdraw.[42]

From a global health perspective there are several observations to be made about this sequence of events. Firstly, the US was historically one of the architects of the global governance system which emerged from the rubble of WW2, including active promotion of the WHO. Secondly, the US has traditionally been a major funder of work by the WHO.[43] Alongside the Executive Order withdrawing from the WHO, Trump has dismantled critical foreign aid programs operating via USAID, many

---

[36] Ghebreyesus, Tedros Adhanom. 2020. Director-General's opening remarks at the media briefing. https://www.who.int/director-general/speeches/detail/who-director-general-s-opening-remarks-at-the-media-briefing-on-COVID-19%2D%2D-11-march-2020. Accessed 26 May 2025.

[37] Ghebreyesus, Tedros Adhanom. 2023. Director-General's opening remarks at the media briefing. https://www.who.int/director-general/speeches/detail/who-director-general-s-opening-remarks-at-the-media-briefing%2D%2D-5-may-2023. Accessed 26 May 2025.

[38] World Health Organisation. 2023. WHO coronavirus (COVID-19) dashboard. https://COVID19.who.int/ Accessed 6 May 2025.

[39] McNeil Jr., Donald G., and Andrew Jacobs. 2020. Trump says US is leaving WHO, but experts aren't so sure. *The New York Times*. https://www.nytimes.com/2020/05/29/health/virus-who.html Accessed 24 May 2025. Rauhala, Emily, Karoun Demirjian, and Toluse Olorunnipa, 2020. Trump administration sends letter withdrawing US from World Health Organization over coronavirus response. *The Washington Post*. https://www.washingtonpost.com/world/trump-united-states-withdrawal-world-health-organization-coronavirus/2020/07/07/ae0a25e4-b550-11ea-9a1d-d3db1cbe07ce_story.html Accessed 24 May 2025.

[40] Gostin, Lawrence et al. 2020. US withdrawal from WHO is unlawful and threatens global and IS health and security. *The Lancet* 396:293–295.

[41] Ravelo, Jenny Lei. 2021. On his first day in office, Biden retracts US withdrawal from WHO. Devex. https://www.devex.com/news/on-his-first-day-in-office-biden-retracts-us-withdrawal-from-who-98961. Accessed 24 May 2025.

[42] The White House. 2025. Presidential Actions: Withdrawing the United States from the World Health Organization. https://www.whitehouse.gov/presidential-actions/2025./01/withdrawing-the-united-states-from-the-worldhealth-organization/?utm_source=wh_social_share_button. Accessed 26 May 2025. Yarney, Gavin and Boghuma Titanji. 2025. Withdrawal of the United States from the WHO- How President Trump is weakening public health. *The New England Journal of Medicine* 392:1457–1460.

[43] Reddy, Srikanth, Sumaira Mazhar, and Raphael Lencucha, 2018. The financial sustainability of the World Health Organization and the political economy of global health governance: a review of funding proposals. *Globalization and Health* 14: 1–11.

directly partnered with or alongside WHO initiatives, creating a major hole in global development and public health capability.

Thirdly, US withdrawal from WHO can, in many respects, be construed as another manifestation of long-simmering frustrations between China and the US arising from concerns about China's expanding military capability, increasing regional influence, and increasingly sophisticated technological and manufacturing capacity, including deep concerns about IP infringement. It is interesting, if speculative, to wonder whether the US's reaction would have differed if COVID-19 had emerged anywhere but China.

Fourthly, the framing of the withdrawal—complete with the US calls for a parallel institution headed by an American which privileges US perspectives in decision-making[44] reflects the increasingly "Make America Great Again" nationalist sentiment prevalent throughout the US politics. That jars with principles of cooperation, equality and solidarity foundational for global governance institutions, aspirations whose support has intensified, rather than diminished, with the post-pandemic amendments to the IHRs and the Pandemic Agreement, discussed in Sect. 11.4. Additionally, creation of a WHO alternative is likely to result in duplication of effort, and suboptimal investment of already scarce global health resources. The WHO is recurrently criticised for its expensive cumbersome bureaucratic framework, unlikely to be improved by creation of another major governance institution in an already crowded global health space.

Fifthly, are the US criticisms justified? How have the relevant institutions—specifically the WHO—responded to that criticism? In the next section of this chapter, the functions of the IHRs and the WHO are unpacked, along with criticism of the WTO and TRIPS once vaccine access became a significant source of global discontent.

Despite initial declarations of transnational solidarity in the early stages of COVID-19, including through vaccine research funding mechanisms such as COVAX and the ACT Accelerator, trust between states, and between states and WHO, was uneven. WHO's Director-General observed its massively disruptive effect on economic activity and movement of people, and reflected that COVID-19

> exposed political fault lines, within and between nations. It has eroded trust between people, governments and institutions, fuelled by a torrent of mis- and disinformation.[45]

Two salient issues are related to the COVID-19's origins and the emergence of vaccine nationalism. Conflicting narratives about COVID-19's origins have emerged in scientific literature and political discourse. Initially, thought to have originated in

[44] Sokunbi, Taiwo, Abbas Umar, and Uko Eyo. 2025. Implications of U.S. withdrawal from the World Health Organization on health financing in Africa. *Health Policy*. https://doi.org/10.1016/j.hpopen.2025.100142.

[45] Buse, Kent et al. 2025. President Trump wants an alternative to the World Health Organization: how should we respond? *BMJ*. https://doi.org/10.1136/bmj.r188.

the seafood market from a natural zoonotic (species-jumping) event,[46] an alternative narrative postulates that COVID-19's origins were anthropogenic. This theory proposes that breached laboratory safety protocols at Wuhan Institute of Virology inadvertently released a genetically modified coronavirus strain created to better understand viral pandemics. The controversy featured revelations that some research had previously received funding from the US National Institutes of Health.

As this counter narrative gained traction, countries demanded that China provide additional assistance to investigators seeking to uncover the outbreak source, claiming that China was uncooperative or seeking to obfuscate the pandemic's origin. Despite findings by a US Congressional Subcommittee that the virus was likely the result of a "lab leak" from the Wuhan Institute,[47] supplemented by a "low confidence" CIA assessment that a lab leak was a 'more likely' source than the natural zoonotic event alternative,[48] scientific and international communities remain largely uncommitted to adopting this theory as the "official" origin narrative.[49] Claims of a Chinese cover-up did little to promote trust during the pandemic; criticisms of the WHO's approach to engaging with China were used to justify US withdrawal from the WHO in both of President Trump's terms as President.

Alongside distrust over COVID-19's origins and the WHO's response, tensions over access to medicines and equipment required to treat the sick, and protect health workers, emerged quickly. States were accused of stockpiling equipment and medications (sometimes in anticipation of an expected future surge in patient numbers), thus depriving countries in serious need. The accusations were salient as globalisation meant much of the world was wholly dependent on research and manufacturing in a handful of nations such as the UK and the US.

Despite efforts to establish collaborative frameworks to accelerate and facilitate the "development, production, and equitable access to COVID-19 tests, treatments, and vaccines" in the early stages of the pandemic, these initiatives faltered once vaccines became available. By mid-2020 the first COVID-19 vaccines to receive emergency authorisation for use were rolling out. These were rapidly overtaken by development of the Oxford-AstraZeneca adenovector vaccine, and subsequent emergence of the more-effective mRNA vaccines including those developed by Pfizer and Moderna. Supplies were unevenly distributed and by 2021, limitations of the COVAX scheme were evident. In January 2021 WHO observed:

---

[46] Choo, Siew Woh et al. 2020. Are pangolins scapegoats of the COVID-19 outbreak-CoV transmission and pathology evidence? *Conservation Letters* 13: 1–12. https://doi.org/10.1111/conl.12754. Hassanin, Alexandre, Philippe Grandcolas, and Géraldine Veron: 2021. Covid-19: natural or anthropic origin? *Mammalia* 85: 1–7.

[47] U.S. House of Representatives. 2024. After Action Review of the Covid-19 pandemic: The lessons learned and a path forward. https://oversight.house.gov/wp-content/uploads/2024/12/2024.12.04-SSCP-FINAL-REPORT-ANS.pdf. Accessed 28 May 2025.

[48] CIA now backs lab leak theory to explain origins of Covid-19. 2025. The Guardian. https://www.theguardian.com/society/2025./jan/26/cia-now-backs-lab-leak-theory-to-explain-origins-of-covid-19. Accessed 24 May 2025.

[49] Jin-Hong, Yoo. 2025. On the controversies surrounding the *lab-leak* theory of COVID-19. *Journal of Korean Medical Science* 40. https://doi.org/10.3346/jkms.2025.40.e153.

> More than 39 million doses of vaccine have now been administered in at least 49 higher-income countries. Just 25 doses have been given in one lowest-income country. Not 25 million; not 25 thousand; just 25.[50]

The mechanisms ultimately failed to meet the target of vaccinating 40% of the population in all countries by the end of 2021. Meanwhile other countries (principally wealthier countries with domestic vaccine manufacturing capabilities) stockpiled vaccines, using powers under bilateral and contractual relationships with vaccine manufacturers to sequester vaccine output.

That vaccine sovereignty or vaccine nationalism led to India and South Africa petitioning the WTO in October 2020 for grant of a temporary waiver of IP protections contained in TRIPS for COVID-19 vaccines and related equipment and technologies. TRIPS establishes minimum standards for IP protection in all member states,[51] including periods during which IP rights holders can exclusively determine how and if the IP will be used. Despite explicit recognition of both a desire to prevent IP protections becoming a barrier to trade, and recognition that IP involves private rather than community rights,[52] there is widespread perception that TRIPS privileges the North by prioritising those rights above other considerations, notwithstanding Article 7 stating that IP protections should be "to the mutual advantage of producers and users of technological knowledge and in a manner conducive to social and economic welfare, and to a balance of rights and obligations".[53]

TRIPS permits compulsory licensing, whereby IP holders may be forced to grant others licenses to use their property, in return for some level of payment. Uncertainty about the scope of the compulsory licensing provisions and wariness regarding retaliation deters many states from relying on them. The circumstances under which compulsory license powers can be exercised were clarified under the 2007 Doha Declaration, which confirmed, via insertion of Article 31*bis*, that an exporting member state (which might not have developed the pharmaceutical) is permitted to issue a compulsory licence enabling the production of pharmaceuticals and their export to other member states, in situations of "national emergency or other circumstances of extreme urgency", such as "public health crises, including those related to HIV/AIDS, tuberculosis, malaria and other epidemics", where the importing member state lacks endogenous manufacturing capacity.[54]

In contrast to the compulsory license arrangements described above, India and South Africa sought a waiver of TRIPS protections entirely. Under the waiver, no IP protection would be available to developers of COVID-19 vaccines and related technologies until the COVID-19 pandemic was brought under control. The waiver

---

[50] Ghebreyesus, Tedros Adhanom. 2021. WHO Director-General's opening remarks at 148th session of the Executive Board. https://www.who.int/director-general/speeches/detail/who-director-general-s-opening-remarks-at-148th-session-of-the-executive-board. Accessed 25 May 2025.

[51] Agreement on Trade-Related Aspects of Intellectual Property Rights (TRIPS). 1994. https://www.wto.org/english/docs_e/legal_e/27-trips_01_e.htm Accessed 28 May 2025.

[52] Ibid.

[53] Ibid.

[54] Ibid.

proposal relied on provisions of Article XI (3) of the Marrakesh Agreement which established the WTO[55]:

> In exceptional circumstances, the Ministerial Conference may decide to waive an obligation imposed on a Member by this Agreement or any of the Multilateral Trade Agreements, provided that any such decision shall be taken by three fourths of the Members unless otherwise provided for in this paragraph. Subsection 4 of Article XI requires that the Ministerial Conference, in granting the waiver, must both outline the 'exceptional circumstances' grant of the waiver relies on, as well as set an expiration period, at which point the waiver either lapses, or can be extended provided the exceptional circumstances continue to prevail.

Waivers provide a more comprehensive override of IP protection because compulsory licenses require remuneration of the IP holder and secondly require specific identification of the importing markets. A waiver, in contrast, can be interpreted as declaring that no IP protections or restrictions apply, including no restrictions on who can use the IP, or where products made using the IP can be exported.

The waiver proposal split the WTO. It was generally opposed by countries with endogenous pharmaceutical manufacturing capabilities whilst being supported by countries with limited access to vaccines under global distribution networks; or countries with endogenous manufacturing capacity but lacking the IP which would enable them to produce vaccines for domestic use, and export to other countries in need.

Criticisms of the waiver included that IP was not the only barrier to access, and that IP protection was necessary to encourage investment in pharmaceutical research and development. Other access barriers include logistics and export restrictions, and national regulatory processes.

In 2022, a much narrower waiver restricted to COVID-19 vaccines was granted, by which time demand for vaccines had dropped significantly, and no country formally registered its intention to use the COVID-19 TRIPS waiver. Instead, it became apparent that the main challenges associated with vaccinations related to equitable and efficient distribution, rather than insufficient production, which had been managed in the interim through ordinary voluntary IP licensing arrangements established in national and regional systems and through TRIPS.

11.4 What Next for Globalisation and Health?

The pandemic identified structural weaknesses within the international community, including an increasing preference by many states for nationalist approaches inconsistent with the foundational solidarity aspirations espoused in globalisation. Mutual reliance by nations for trade and other activities may be insufficient to keep the international order from collapsing into conflict again, as it did in World Wars I and II. Since the end of the pandemic, we have for example seen a much more strident

[55] Marrakesh Agreement Establishing the World Trade Organization, *supra*, n. 11.

approach to national exceptionalism in the US, including through imposition of extraordinary tariffs, withdrawal from global institutions including the WHO, and cancellation of most US foreign aid. Although evident in President Trump's first term (which, along with BREXIT, predated the outbreak of COVID-19) that exceptionalism in 2025 is reshaping both global trust and the international order.

It is likely that the WHO and Trump's other targets such as UNESCO will survive, albeit perhaps after a significant period of reform, driven at least in part by addressing the funding shortfalls. Eroded perceptions of legitimacy will take longer to recover. Responding to criticisms identified in the initial Independent Panel report and elsewhere, in 2023 the World Health Assembly agreed to update the IHRs.[56] One overarching change to the IHRs was a reframing of the Regulations towards the principles of equity and solidarity, introduced through amendment to Article 3(1) and echoed through amendment of Articles 13, which now provides for *equitable access* to relevant health products; and Article 44, which now requires financing support to *equitably address* the needs of developing countries. That aspiration is not enforceable.

Other dominant changes relate to inclusion of greater detail, including explicit recognition of a pandemic disease outbreak, within the PHEIC framework. The amended Article 1 now includes defines a "pandemic emergency" as something requiring

> rapid, equitable and enhanced coordinated international action, with whole- of-government and whole-of-society approaches.[57]

Article 12(4)bis also requires that a PHEIC must be accompanied by a determination whether the PHEIC additionally constitutes a pandemic emergency. In making recommendations in response to a declaration, the WHO must now consider impacts on international movement of people (including health workers and people caught in humanitarian crises) and food and health supply chains. "Relevant health products" is now defined in Article 1: "it encompasses medicines and vaccines, diagnostic tests and personal protective equipment." Other amendments extend the core surveillance and reporting capabilities under the IHRs to include preparedness and prevention, alongside strengthening governance, reporting and financing for capacity building.

Despite superficially appearing to enhance regional approaches to surveillance, cooperation and capacity-building, as well as post-emergent information-sharing, it seems unlikely that the reformed the IHRs will translate into better regional public health cooperation. The IHRs remain expressly deferential to the ideas of borders, nations, and states, and view responses to emerging threats from the perspective of

---

[56] Berman, Ayelet and Kriti Sharma. 2024. The new amendments to the international health regulations. Centre for International Law. https://cil.nus.edu.sg/wp-content/uploads/2024/06/The-New-IHR-Amendments-2024_27.06.2024-FINAL.pdf 3-5. Accessed 24 May 2025.

[57] World Health Assembly. 2024. International Health Regulations (2005). https://apps.who.int/gb/ebwha/pdf_files/WHA77/A77_ACONF14-en.pdf. Accessed 24 May 2025. As a definitional change the amendment does not compel action by member states.

the roles and responsibilities of state actors. It is not, therefore, clear how effective the reformed the IHRs will be in the event of a withdrawal of cooperation with the WHO by a state hosting a disease outbreak; nor how effectively the WHO will be able to share information about disease outbreaks with regional partners, in the event a rogue regional member refuses to comply with their surveillance and reporting obligations under the IHRs. Regional cooperation in public health emergency surveillance, prevention, and responses, therefore, remains likely to depend on consensus in at least some regions, and therefore aspirational: just as some regions were highly cooperative at least some of the time during COVID-19, others were hampered by poor information flows and limited sharing of resources, a trend that seems likely to continue or worsen in the face of increasing geopolitical instability.

The IHR amendments do not specifically address technology transfer, underlying the IP disputes surrounding COVID-19 vaccines, or issues around sharing of pathogen sequence data. Both issues were originally featured in discussions regarding the amendments; they were dropped from the final versions.[58]

Further reforms to pandemic responses include adoption on 20 May 2025 by the World Health Assembly (WHA) of the Pandemic Agreement—a proposed global treaty. Consistent with withdrawal from WHO, the US was a notable absence from the 2025 WHA. Of those states in attendance, none opposed the adoption.

The Agreement's Preamble expressly references many issues that emerged during the COVID-19 pandemic, including inequitable access to COVID-related health products; barriers to access through uneven distribution of manufacturing capability, IP and distribution networks; and the need to strengthen surveillance and response coordination.[59]

Key provisions of the Agreement include incorporation of One Health (expressly recognising the interdependence of human, domestic and wild animal health, and the environment more broadly) into pandemic responses.[60] Article 2 expressly preserves state sovereignty while acknowledging the importance of human rights and humanitarian law and embedding the principles of solidarity and equity. Articles 9 and 10 expressly address knowledge sharing and capacity building, and relevant health product production, in geographically diverse contexts.

Articles 11, 12, 13, 14, and 18, addressing technology transfer, pathogen access, logistics, and funding, are yet to be finalised. The most controversial aspects of the Agreement, they will require significant negotiation regarding their implementation prior to ratification of the treaty, and will ultimately determine which states accede, and which do not. An Intergovernmental Working Group will need to negotiate a Pathogen Access and Benefit Sharing Scheme, outlined in Article 12 before the Agreement is opened for signature. Much work setting up the Coordinating Financial Mechanism for pandemic prevention, preparedness and response, under

---

[58] Berman and Sharma, *supra*, n. 56.

[59] World Health Assembly. 2025. Pandemic Agreement. https://apps.who.int/gb/ebwha/pdf_files/WHA78/A78_R1-en.pdf. Accessed 26 May 2025.

[60] Ibid.

Article 18, remains to be done, along with establishment of the Global Supply Chain and Logistics Network (GSCL). Notwithstanding these challenges, the Pandemic Agreement demonstrates willingness by some of the international community to engage constructively with each other and global governance issues to address common threats in an increasingly fractured world.

In isolation, the Agreement cannot solve imbalances between TRIPS, the WTO, health and human rights amply demonstrated during COVID-19. Notwithstanding the theoretical potential of the compulsory licensing provisions, they played no significant role in facilitating access to vaccines and other technologies. Why they were not used requires careful consideration, revealing either structural defects or (more likely) highlighting distribution, rather than manufacturing capacity, was the core deficit. Similar observations may be made about the TRIPS waiver, noting that by the time the waiver was granted, it was too late. If waiver or compulsory licensing are to be of substantive benefit, COVID-19 reveals the need to expedite bureaucratic processes and minimise procedural delays imposed by obstructionist member states. A better approach might be to further refine compulsory licensing mechanisms. Operational mechanisms that provide rapid access to IP in circumstances where some protection remains are more attractive to rights holders than a waiver model where potentially all IP protection ceases.

In May 2022 the Independent Panel reported on the loss of life due to COVID-19:

> These losses were preventable but not prevented. The inequitable market- based system that existed before SARS-CoV-2 led to inevitable, deadly gaps in access in low- and middle-income countries. Too many countries delayed implementing or politicised measures that protect people from infection and disease. … the objections of a handful of influential countries have led to failure during a pandemic. Without a change of approach to consider pandemic tools as global public goods, we will see a repeat of these drawn-out processes when a new pandemic threat emerges.

Three years later, some progress on these fronts has occurred. Whether it proves sufficient to address these issues when—rather than if—the next pandemic emerges, only time will tell. Overarching tensions and objective incoherence between states and institutions persists; suspicion among the international community increases; and financial pressures on institutions and lower income countries are intensifying with the US withdrawal of membership or financial contributions from global institutions, notwithstanding some easing of the economic downturn prompted by COVID-19.

Adding to the complexity at the intersection of trade, health and globalisation is the looming threat of the White House to restructure the global pharmaceutical market as part of its next wave of tariff impositions. Trump has claimed that countries with universal health coverage schemes that subsidise pharmaceuticals through governments negotiating drug prices directly with manufacturers has led to those same manufacturers charging US patients more as a means of offsetting the losses flowing from the government bulk payments. Implications of current erratic US policy may reshape the target markets and product profiles of non-US manufacturers, potentially causing relocation to the US to avoid tariffs. Regardless of the ultimate impacts of "America First", short-term disruption of pharmaceutical manufacturing and production, leading to disrupted supply of essential medicines, seems inevitable. At a time when global supply chains are already struggling (and may not have fully recovered from the impacts of COVID-19) this is unlikely to inspire confidence in global governance institutions.

11.5 Conclusion

Claims that COVID-19 brought about the end of globalisation lack credibility. Globalisation is better conceptualised as a dynamic system of expansion of relationships of interdependence in the context of liberalisation of trade, economic relationships and movement of people, punctuated by periods of retraction, rather than complete breakpoints. At no point, did flows cease entirely.

The pandemic highlighted increasing tensions between China and the West (particularly the US) that already existed due to deterioration in IP and other trade matters predating COVID-19. Perceptions of Chinese non-cooperation with global efforts to understand the source of the COVID-19 outbreak reflected existing tensions within geopolitical relationships, they did not initiate them. COVID-19 did not uniquely "cause" the change in globalisation's form since the pandemic.

The more nuanced question of whether COVID-19 perhaps highlighted a need for reform of global governance institutions responsible for supporting globalisation, warrants a more sophisticated response. Although some major players have abandoned globalisation norms, retreating from liberal trade policies and withdrawing from global entities, that retreat is not universal. Other countries seem to be solidifying their relationships, and seeking new and alternate allies, and new export markets. International diplomacy still remains the preferred option in much of the world for resolving the territorial disputes currently raging between Russia and Ukraine, Israel and Palestine, and India and Pakistan. A post-pandemic migration surge has taken many nations by surprise; and, after a period of global financial downturn, many countries that experienced inflationary pressures after the pandemic are returning to a more normal economic status, albeit one that continues to show weak global growth.[61]

We may well be experiencing a "post-slowbalisation" period of erratic retraction: "super-slowbalisation" in global relationships in the aftermath of COVID-19, against a backdrop of increasing mistrust of other states and global institutions driving, for some states, a retreat towards self-interested nationalism. COVID-19 as a globalisation canary highlighted harms attributable to disregard of interdependence and undue privileging of North IP interests. As with past eras of retreat from globalisation, current deglobalisation shall end. The question that can only be answered by time is when will it end, and why?

---

[61] Zipp, Samuel. 2023. The derangements of sovereignty: Trumpism and the dilemmas of interdependence. In *Chaos reconsidered: The liberal order and the future of international politics*, eds. Robert Jervis et al, 104-115. New York: Columbia University Press.

References

Agreement on Trade-Related Aspects of Intellectual Property Rights (TRIPS). 1994. https://www.wto.org/english/docs_e/legal_e/27-trips_01_e.htm. Accessed 28 May 2025.

Avant, Deborah, Martha Finnemore, and Susan Sell. 2010. Who governs the globe. In *Who governs the globe*, ed. Deborah Avant, Martha Finnemore, and Susan Sell, 1–32. Cambridge: Cambridge University Press.

Ayoob, Mohammad. 2002. Humanitarian intervention and state sovereignty. *The International Journal of Human Rights* 6:81–102.

Barnett, Michael, Jon Pevehouse, and Kal Raustiala. 2021. Introduction: The modes of global governance. In *Global governance in a world of change*, ed. Michael Barnett, Jon Pevehouse, and Kal Raustiala, 1–47. Cambridge: Cambridge University Press.

Berman, Ayelet, and Kriti Sharma. 2024. *The new amendments to the international health regulations*. Centre for International Law. https://cil.nus.edu.sg/wp-content/uploads/2024/06/The-New-IHR-Amendments-2024_27.06.2024-FINAL.pdf 3-5. Accessed 24 May 2025.

Buse, Kent, et al. 2025. President Trump wants an alternative to the World Health Organization: How should we respond? *BMJ*. https://doi.org/10.1136/bmj.r188.

Choo, Siew Woh, et al. 2020. Are pangolins scapegoats of the COVID-19 outbreak-CoV transmission and pathology evidence? *Conservation Letters* 13:1–12. https://doi.org/10.1111/conl.12754.

CIA now backs lab leak theory to explain origins of Covid-19. 2025. *The Guardian*. https://www.theguardian.com/society/2025/jan/26/cia-now-backs-lab-leak-theory-to-explain-origins-of-covid-19. Accessed 24 May 2025.

Constitution of the World Health Organization. 1946. *WHO Interim Commission*. https://apps.who.int/gb/bd/PDF/bd47/EN/constitution-en.pdf?ua=1. Accessed 26 May 2025.

Dagovetz, Michael, et al. 2025. Global COVID-19 vaccination challenges: Inequity of access and vaccine hesitancy. *Journal of Medicine, Surgery, and Public Health*. https://doi.org/10.1016/j.glmedi.2025.100197.

Davis, Christina. 2023. *Discriminatory clubs: The geopolitics of international organizations*. Princeton: Princeton University Press.

Declaration of Principles issued by the President of the United States and the Prime Minister of the United Kingdom. 1941. https://www.nato.int/cps/en/natohq/official_texts_16912.htm. Accessed 26 May 2025.

Ghebreyesus, Tedros Adhanom. 2020. *Director-General's opening remarks at the media briefing*. https://www.who.int/director-general/speeches/detail/who-director-general-s-opening-remarks-at-the-media-briefing-on-COVID-19%2D%2D-11-march-2020. Accessed 26 May 2025.

Ghebreyesus, Tedros Adhanom. 2021. *WHO Director-General's opening remarks at 148th session of the Executive Board*. https://www.who.int/director-general/speeches/detail/who-director-general-s-opening-remarks-at-148th-session-of-the-executive-board. Accessed 25 May 2025.

Ghebreyesus, Tedros Adhanom. 2023. *Director-General's opening remarks at the media briefing*. https://www.who.int/director-general/speeches/detail/who-director-general-s-opening-remarks-at-the-media-briefing%2D%2D-5-may-2023. Accessed 26 May 2025.

Gostin, Lawrence, Devi Sridhar, and Daniel Hougendobler. 2015. The normative authority of the World Health Organization. *Public Health* 129:854–863.

Gostin, Lawrence, et al. 2020. US withdrawal from WHO is unlawful and threatens global and IS health and security. *The Lancet* 396:293–295.

Hassanin, Alexandre, Philippe Grandcolas, and Géraldine Veron. 2021. Covid-19: Natural or anthropic origin? *Mammalia* 85:1–7.

Ikenberry, G. John. 2020. *A world safe for democracy: Liberal internationalism and the crises of global order*. New Haven: Yale University Press.

Independent Panel for Pandemic Preparedness and Response. 2021. *COVID-19: make it the last pandemic*. https://theindependentpanel.org/. Accessed 26 May 2025.

Jin-Hong, Yoo. 2025. On the controversies surrounding the *lab-leak* theory of COVID-19. *Journal of Korean Medical Science* 40. https://doi.org/10.3346/jkms.2025.40.e153.

Kalha, Komal. 2021. *Why we must remove barriers to trade to achieve vaccine equity*. International Federation of Pharmaceutical Manufacturers and Associations. https://www.ifpma.org/insights/why-we-must-remove-barriers-to-trade-to-achieve-vaccine-equity-step-3/.

Kolb, Melina. 2024. *What is globalization? And how has the global economy shaped the United States?* Peterson Institute of International Economics. https://www.piie.com/microsites/globalization/what-is-globalization#:~:text=Globalization%20describes%20the%20growing%20interdependence,investment%2C%20people%2C%20and%20information. Accessed 24 May 2025.

Labonté, Ronald. 2015. Globalization and health. In *International encyclopedia of the social & behavioral sciences*, ed. James D. Wright, 198–205. Amsterdam: Elsevier.

Loots, Elsabe. 2022. Is the world retracting from globalization, setting it up for a fifth wave? *The Conversation*. www.theconversation.com/is-the-world-retracting-from-Globalization-setting-it-up-for-a-fifth-wave-186003. Accessed 24 May 2025.

Marrakesh Agreement Establishing the World Trade Organization. 1994. https://www.wto.org/english/docs_e/legal_e/marag_e.htm. Accessed 27 May 2025,

Matthews, Duncan. 2003. *Globalising intellectual property rights: The TRIPS agreement*. London: Routledge.

McNeil, Donald G., Jr., and Andrew Jacobs. 2020. Trump says US is leaving WHO, but experts aren't so sure. *The New York Times*. https://www.nytimes.com/2020/05/29/health/virus-who.html. Accessed 24 May 2025.

Melillo, Margherita. 2022. The uneasy coexistence of expertise and politics in the World Health Organization. *International Organizations Law Review* 19:301–331.

Michael, Zurn. 2012. Globalization and global governance. In *Handbook of international relations*, ed. Walter Carlsnaes, Thomas Risse, and Beth Simmons, 401–425. London: Sage Publications.

Mill, John Stuart. 1848. *Principles of political economy*. London: Parker. See also Palen, Marc-William. 2024. *Pax economica: Left-wing visions of a free trade world.* Princeton: Princeton University Press.

Mirowski, Philip. 2017. *Never let a serious crisis go to waste: How neoliberalism survived the financial meltdown*. London: Verso.

Pang, Tikki, and Emmanuel Guindon. 2004. Globalization and risks to health. *EMBO Reports* 5:s11–s16.

Preamble to the WHO Constitution. 1946. *WHO Interim Commission*. https://apps.who.int/gb/bd/PDF/bd47/EN/constitution-en.pdf?ua=1. Accessed 26 May 2025.

Rauhala, Emily, Karoun Demirjian, and Toluse Olorunnipa. 2020. Trump administration sends letter withdrawing US from World Health Organization over coronavirus response. *The Washington Post*. https://www.washingtonpost.com/world/trump-united-states-withdrawal-world-health-organization-coronavirus/2020/07/07/ae0a25e4-b550-11ea-9a1d-d3db1cbe07ce_story.html. Accessed 24 May 2025.

Ravelo, Jenny Lei. 2021. On his first day in office, Biden retracts US withdrawal from WHO. *Devex*. https://www.devex.com/news/on-his-first-day-in-office-biden-retracts-us-withdrawal-from-who-98961. Accessed 24 May 2025.

Reddy, Srikanth, Sumaira Mazhar, and Raphael Lencucha. 2018. The financial sustainability of the World Health Organization and the political economy of global health governance: A review of funding proposals. *Globalization and Health* 14:1–11.

Ruse-Khan, Henning Grosse. 2018. *From TRIPS to FTAs and back: Re-conceptualising the role of a multilateral IP framework in a TRIPS-plus world.* The Hague: T.M.C. Asser Press.

Sachs, J. 2008. *Speech by the Director-General on Globalization and Health*. https://www.who.int/director-general/speeches/detail/globalization-and-health. Accessed 27 May 2025.

Sell, Susan. 2007. TRIPS-plus free trade agreements and access to medicines. *Liverpool Law Review* 28:41–75.

Sell, Susan, and Christopher May. 2001. Moments in law: Contestation and settlement in the history of intellectual property. *Review of International Political Economy* 8:467–500. https://doi.org/10.1080/09692290110055849.

Shimkin, Michael B. 1946. The World Health Organization. *Science* 104:281–283.

Siddiqi, Javed. 1995. *World health and world politics: The World Health Organization and the UN system*. Columbia, SC: University of South Carolina Press.

Slobodian, Quinn. 2018. *Globalists: The end of empire and the birth of neoliberalism*. Cambridge, MA: Harvard University Press.

Sokunbi, Taiwo, Abbas Umar, and Uko Eyo. 2025. Implications of U.S. withdrawal from the World Health Organization on health financing in Africa. *Health Policy*. https://doi.org/10.1016/j.hpopen.2025.100142.

The White House. 2025. *Presidential actions: Withdrawing the United States from the World Health Organization*. https://www.whitehouse.gov/presidential-actions/2025/01/withdrawing-the-united-states-from-the-worldhealth-organization/?utm_source=wh_social_share_button. Accessed 26 May 2025.

U.S. House of Representatives. 2024. *After Action Review of the Covid-19 pandemic: The lessons learned and a path forward*. https://oversight.house.gov/wp-content/uploads/2024/12/2024.12.04-SSCP-FINAL-REPORT-ANS.pdf. Accessed 28 May 2025.

United Nations Monetary and Financial Conference. 1944. *Articles of Agreement of the International Monetary Fund*. Adopted at the United Nations Monetary and Financial Conference. https://www.imf.org/external/pubs/ft/aa/. Accessed 26 May 2025.

World Health Assembly. 2024. *International Health Regulations (2005)*. https://apps.who.int/gb/ebwha/pdf_files/WHA77/A77_ACONF14-en.pdf. Accessed 24 May 2025. As a definitional change the amendment does not compel action by member states.

World Health Assembly. 2025. *Pandemic Agreement*. https://apps.who.int/gb/ebwha/pdf_files/WHA78/A78_R1-en.pdf. Accessed 26 May 2025.

World Health Organisation. 2016. *International Health Regulations (2005)*. https://iris.who.int/handle/10665/246107. Accessed 27 May 2025.

World Health Organisation. 2023. *WHO coronavirus (COVID-19) dashboard*. https://COVID19.who.int/. Accessed 6 May 2023.

World Health Organisation. 2025a. *WHO's Health Emergencies Programme*. https://www.who.int/our-work/health-emergencies#:~:text=WHO's%20Health%20Emergencies%20Programme%20has,that%20threaten%20global%20health%20security. Accessed 26 May 2025.

World Health Organisation. 2025b. *Universal health coverage (UHC)—fact sheet*. https://www.who.int/news-room/fact-sheets/detail/universal-health-coverage-(uhc). Accessed 26 May 2025.

Wouters, O. J., et al. 2021. Challenges in ensuring global access to COVID-19 vaccines: Production, affordability, allocation, and deployment. *Lancet* 397:1023–1034.

Yarney, Gavin, and Boghuma Titanji. 2025. Withdrawal of the United States from the WHO—How President Trump is weakening public health. *The New England Journal of Medicine* 392:1457–1460.

Zipp, Samuel. 2023. The derangements of sovereignty: Trumpism and the dilemmas of interdependence. In *Chaos reconsidered: The liberal order and the future of international politics*, ed. Robert Jervis et al., 104–115. New York: Columbia University Press.

Chapter 12
Conclusion: Globalisation Disrupted or Re-made?

Umair Hafeez Ghori and John Farrar

Abstract The conclusion summarises the book's diverse themes. We argue that disruption in globalisation is best understood as "re-made" or "re-globalisation" rather than "de-globalisation" or a permanent fracture. We briefly discuss the drivers of change: from increasing geo-economic rivalry to the US's gradual retreat from global leadership. We refer to China's commercial primacy, pandemic-induced supply-chain fragility, institutional paralysis at the WTO, and discuss how middle powers, mega-regionals, and plurilateral initiatives (MPIA, RCEP, CPTPP) are re-making global governance. While de-globalising tendencies create overlapping spheres of influence and strategic decoupling, enduring factor endowments and commercial incentives keep states economically entangled. The chapter concludes that the "Re-made" global future will be pluralistic with multiple contested spheres of power and influence. The "Re-made" globalisation will be contingent on whether emergent institutions can reconcile legitimacy, openness, and resilience.

12.1 The Disruption and Its Nature

This book has focused on the disruption of globalisation and the rule-based order. The disruption has undermined the US hegemony and led to questions about the continuing role of the US dollar in international trade.

As we have discussed in Chap. 1, the question is whether these causes are cyclical or structural and what could replace the rule-based order based on USA hegemony. Several factors have been outlined in this book contributing to the disruption: the role of the US in leading the West during the second Trump presidency,

U. H. Ghori (✉)
Faculty of Law, Bond University, Gold Coast, QLD, Australia
e-mail: ughori@bond.edu.au

J. Farrar
Faculty of Law, Bond University, Robina, QLD, Australia
e-mail: jfarrar@bond.edu.au

U. H. Ghori, J. Farrar (eds.), *Globalisation Disrupted*,
https://doi.org/10.1007/978-981-95-3997-0_12

continued threats to financial stability and the institutional framework which supports it, rising competitiveness of China and other Asian economies, the role of the middle powers and their willingness to continue engagement regionally and globally, without the US.

12.2 The Re- or De- of Globalisation

Two overlapping narratives deserve discussion within the context of diverse thoughts on globalisation. Firstly, the "Re-" argument (referred to in this book as "re-globalisation" or "re-made globalisation") stems from the observation that a wholesale disengagement between nations has not occurred, and therefore, the rules-based system continues to survive.

An important question for the future is not only the survival of the rule-based system but also the role of international institutions in the future (ranging from global health to maintenance of peace, from dispute resolution to an increasingly digital world). The themes of Re-globalisation are reflected in chapters by Bröhmer on the EU, Farrar's contribution on BREXIT, Boulle on BRICS, Draper and Grey on Australia, Bonython on global health, and by Delios and Ferguson on the BRI.

The disruption presents both opportunities and challenges. In September 2024, the UN in the Summit of the Future produced a Pact for the Future, Global Digital Compact and Declaration on Future Generations.[1] This was an ambitious document and a valuable opportunity to mitigate the vagaries of adjustment to the disruptions in globalisation. The proposals sought to transform the model of global governance and called for a reform of international financial architecture.

The vast majority of members voted to support it. Only Belarus, Iran, Nicaragua, North Korea, Russia, Sudan, and Syria voted against it. So far, nothing is coming out of it by way of practical reforms and there has been little public debate. The US, a major donor, has supported the Pact but, at the same time, has withdrawn support for a number of UN initiatives. Continued funding by the US and involvement in the UN is under greater scrutiny, resulting in steep cuts in the UN spending, staff and programmes.

There are now two schools of thought: One is to continue to engage in discussion of reform and rationalisation. The other is that the disruption will never end and, therefore, must be managed. Given the integrative role of the US in the past, the recent policy direction adopted by Trumpian Washington is quite unfortunate. It does, however, illustrate how recent developments have eroded existing power structures.

[1] UN Sustainable Development Group (UN SDG). 2024. Pact of the Future, Global Digital Compact and Declaration on Future Generations. https://unsdg.un.org/resources/pact-future-global-digital-compact-and-declaration-future-generations#:~:text=At%20the%20Summit%20of%20the%20Future%20on%2022,Global%20Digital%20Compact%20and%20Declaration%20on%20Future%20Generations. Accessed 14 August 2025.

Beyond public international law, the fields of international trade and investment laws show new trends in selective reintegration: new trade initiatives like the digital trade agreements, RCEP, and CPTPP have brought together Western and Eastern nations in large mega-regionals, without the US. The continued proliferation and renewals of BITs/FTAs represent recombination of the globalisation trends, and not its abandonment despite the efforts by anti-globalists such as President Trump to strike "deals".

Additionally, after the crippling of the WTO Dispute Settlement System and the Appellate Body, the gradual expansion of the MPIA in April 2020 by the EU and a group of like-minded developing countries and middle powers show that, even without the US leadership, there are still strong advocates of globalism holding the line. These nations still believe in maintaining a rules-based international dispute settlement mechanism, albeit with adjustments.[2] It is rather interesting to note that the UK joined the EU-led MPIA in June 2025 underscoring that the UK still sees value in the stability that EU brings to international trade.

The willingness of middle powers and regional groups like ASEAN and the EU to continue to engage in mega-regionals, the reshaping of trade and investment rules, and the adoption of MPIA shows a glimpse of a world without US leadership. It is a very real possibility, and the EU, and other middle powers, are already preparing for this contingency in the realms of trade and investment (and perhaps even international security).

In contrast to the "Re-" argument, the "De-" argument, or "de-globalisation" is about reversal of existing trends and drastic erosion of the post-1945 global economic order and the supply chains it created. The "de-globalisation" themes show an emergence and solidification of competing rules, overlapping spheres of influence and diminishing trust in the role of multilateral institutions that balance the "open" world market. The systematic crippling of the WTO dispute settlement system is a clear example of "de-globalisation" leading to the emergence of new solutions such as the MPIA.[3] "De-globalisation" and the emergence of new realigned trends are themes captured in Ghori's chapter on rare earths and tech-decoupling, Hiscock's chapter on WTO, and Farrar and Parson's joint contribution on financial stability.

---

[2] European Commission. 2025. Multilateral Trading Order Strengthened as UK joins Interim Appeals System. Trade and Economic Security. https://policy.trade.ec.europa.eu/news/multilateral-trading-order-strengthened-uk-joins-interim-appeals-system-2025-06-26_en. Accessed 14 August 2025.

[3] WTO Plurilaterals. 2025. Multi-Party Interim Appeal Arbitration Arrangement (MPIA). Geneva Trade Platform. https://wtoplurilaterals.info/plural_initiative/the-mpia/. Accessed 11 August 2025; See also Rockwell, Keith M. 2025. The deep roots of the WTO's deadlock over dispute settlement. Hinrich Foundation. https://www.hinrichfoundation.com/research/wp/wto/deadlock-over-dispute-settlement-has-deep-roots/?utm_campaign=wp-rockwell-wto-dispute-settlement&utm_medium=email&_hsenc=p2ANqtz%2D%2DMQ3ypwgKnODVmpwHVraNzW7m-GuvTArB8jr7mam1Ulk3_x9DW7KJqtUfQV2x8mrG5OoDTJnnQGupSH92A2F9jj-vzV8A&_hsmi=375507549&utm_content=20250812-weekly-research-&utm_source=hinrich-thought-leadership. Accessed 13 August 2025.

We, however, do not view the tension between the "Re- or De-" argument as mutually exclusive. Rather, we think that disruption in the globalisation is actually best described as "Re-globalisation". The integration between nations will continue to persist rather than recede. Only the form and its vehicles will shift to more pluralistic instead of hegemonic.

In that sense globalisation is certainly not dead. It cannot be. It is simply being "Re-made."

12.3 Concluding Thoughts: Competing Futures in a Multipolar World

Our view is reinforced when we observe trade and investment becoming routed through smaller groups and coalescing of like-minded states. Additionally, mega-regionals and sector-specific plurilateral agreements show a hybrid spectrum instead of a binary "Re- or De-" characterisation. Within this hybrid spectrum, trade in goods and services, control of data, flow of capital, and the movement of people are all sliding in different directions under various compulsions. The question is not "Can globalisation survive the disruption?" Instead, the question is what kind of globalisation emerges from the disruption? Whatever model emerges must carry enough legitimacy, coherence, and openness to be sustainable in an ever-divergent world.

The disruption we speak of can hinder the Re-making process which may be hijacked by actors pursuing narrow, rather self-serving, geopolitical advantages. The chapters in this book query whether we are merely witnessing the regular cycles of ebb and flow of integration and disintegration or if the Re-making represents a deeper structural change. The disruption of post-1945 structuring of globalisation, and the consequent impact on the rule-based order by the GFC, and later by the inward-looking presidencies of Donald Trump have undermined the US hegemony and led to questions about the continuing role of the US dollar in international trade.

As we have discussed in Chap. 1 the question is whether the causes of the disruption are cyclical or structural and what could replace the rule-based order based on US hegemony. The answer to this query comes in the chapters that follow.

Chapter 2 discussed Brexit and its causes and consequences for the future of the UK and the EU. Both are closely linked with globalisation and populist dissatisfaction with the results of it. Whether another referendum would come up with the same result is questionable. We further note that even after Brexit, the UK is still compelled to deal with its European partners even where it finds itself navigating a complicated relationship with Trumpian America. The UK's joining the EU-led MPIA as an alternative dispute resolution mechanism under the WTO clearly shows that it has not pulled its eggs out of the globalist basket.

As a logical extension to the discussion on Brexit, Chap. 3 dealt with the EU, its reaction to Brexit, and the larger US tariff policy. It also discusses the internal weaknesses of the union. Chapter 3 drew on French President Macron's speeches and points to weakness in the EUs responses to international crises. It describes the difficulties of a common foreign, security policy, and the vulnerabilities within the European Parliament. The decisions of the European Courts seem to always attract lively and interesting debate by the EU Member states.

Chapter 4 dealt with the concept of financial stability and its meaning in a disrupted world. This necessarily involves discussion of the present state of the rules-based system and the role of the USD in it. Chapter 4 summarised the political and economic history since 1945 when the US emerged as the dominant global power with its economic infrastructure intact while the rest of the West was in shambles. At that time, the USD was the currency of choice which it remained until present times.

Since then, there has been some reliance on a war economy which has been due to various conflicts with unclear and unsatisfactory outcomes. The collapse of the USSR in 1990 left the US as the sole global power and this coincided with the development of modern globalisation. At the same time, the size of the US public debt continued to rise. The two Trump Presidencies led the rest of the West to question how long the present situation can continue.

Next follows a Chap. 5 on BRICS which is an important counterpoint to a concentration on the West. The West and BRICS place some reliance on the WTO and have a vested interest in its future. BRICS may well be the "new management" that may define the pluralistic direction of a "Re-made" and "Re-globalised" world. But the BRICS as an institutional alternative, and a club of non-Western middle powers, presents a threat to the US hegemony. An important member of BRICS is China which is strategic competition with the US. It includes Russia, clearly an antagonist to the US, and India, a developing country with ambitions and a protectionist trade policy that is prompting President Trump's ire.

Beyond BRICS, comes the role of middle powers such as Australia, who may not be members of BRICS but occupy a crucial "fence sitter" position? Chapter 6 discussed the role of Australia. An important theme therein is the nature and role of supply chains in international trade and what will be the effect of the tariff moves by the Trump regime.

Chapter 7 discussed the resilience of the WTO despite its uncertain future. While its institutional weaknesses have been exposed after the crippling of the WTO dispute settlement system, innovations such as the MPIA and the debates on reform have kept this important institution in the ring and on its feet.

Chapter 8 covered China and its ambitious BRI: truly touted as a game changer in globalisation. China benefited substantially from technology transfer after it joined the WTO and steadily built up its dominance in international trade. Now it is using that foundation for an increased role in international affairs. An important aspect of China's growing influence is technology development and its increasing rivalry with the US. Both China and the US are now caught in a Thucydides Trap, eerily similar to an expansionist Athens versus a stagnating hegemon, Sparta, on the cusp of losing its power.

Chapter 9 examined the selective relaxation of US semiconductor export controls against China in exchange for resumption of heavy rare earths exports. This chapter highlights the irreversible trajectory of US–China technological decoupling despite temporary trade concessions. Chapter 9 argues that temporary concessions mask a long-term US intent to impede China's access to advanced technologies as a matter of national security. The chapter envisions emergence of separate supply chains each with its own eco-systems, suppliers, and end-users. Chapter 9 also summarises three possible scenarios of decoupling between the US and China within the context of the evolving global order.

China and India's paradoxical relationship is explored in Chap. 10. Both feature as active members of BRICS but increasingly rival each other in security, trade and investments. China dominates in goods while India excels in services. The clash of competing economic models and remaking of their internal political economies is debated by Lupton in Chap. 10.

Chapter 11 discusses the fallout of the greatest disruptive event in contemporary history since Second World War: the COVID19 pandemic. The lockdowns and restrictions in the wake of the pandemic caused serious disruption of globalisation, and the world has never truly recovered even after lockdowns have been lifted. The disruption in global supply chains exposed weaknesses in international cooperation along with the ineffectual role of the WHO. The US withdrawal further damaged the global health system and threw a big question mark on the integrity of market-based model as a reliable source of maintaining public health.

What this book has shown is that the US hegemony is giving way to a multipolar world where China is a rising power. What this entails for international structures is the important question which requires further debate. Globalisation has been challenged and there is a need for a re-globalisation which addresses a broader range of issues and is more inclusive rather than exclusive. Otherwise, the world will continue to see further fragmentation and increasing disorder.

References

European Commission. 2025. *Multilateral Trading Order Strengthened as UK joins Interim Appeals System*. Trade and Economic Security. https://policy.trade.ec.europa.eu/news/multilateral-trading-order-strengthened-uk-joins-interim-appeals-system-2025-06-26_en. Accessed 14 August 2025.

Rockwell, Keith M. 2025. *The Deep Roots of the WTO's Deadlock over Dispute Settlement*. Hinrich Foundation. https://www.hinrichfoundation.com/research/wp/wto/deadlock-over-dispute-settlement-has-deep-roots/?utm_campaign=wp-rockwell-wto-dispute-settlement&utm_medium=email&_hsenc=p2ANqtz%2D%2DMQ3ypwgKnODVmpwHVraNzW7m-GuvTArB8jr7mam1Ulk3_x9DW7KJqtUfQV2x8mrG5OoDTJnnQGup-SH92A2F9jjvzV8A&_hsmi=375507549&utm_content=20250812-weekly-research-&utm_source=hinrich-thought-leadership. Accessed 13 August 2025.

UN Sustainable Development Group (UN SDG). 2024. *Pact of the Future, Global Digital Compact and Declaration on Future Generations*. https://unsdg.un.org/resources/pact-future-global-digital-compact-and-declaration-future-generations#:~:text=At%20the%20

Summit%20of%20the%20Future%20on%2022,Global%20Digital%20Compact%20and%20Declaration%20on%20Future%20Generations. Accessed 14 August 2025.

WTO Plurilaterals. 2025. *Multi-Party Interim Appeal Arbitration Arrangement (MPIA)*. Geneva Trade Platform. https://wtoplurilaterals.info/plural_initiative/the-mpia/. Accessed 11 August 2025.

MIX
Papier aus verantwortungsvollen Quellen
Paper from responsible sources
FSC® C105338

If you have any concerns about our products,
you can contact us on
ProductSafety@springernature.com

In case Publisher is established outside the EU,
the EU authorized representative is:
Springer Nature Customer Service Center GmbH
Europaplatz 3, 69115 Heidelberg, Germany

Printed by Libri Plureos GmbH
in Hamburg, Germany